A TREASURY OF
"Tradition"

A TREASURY OF

"*TRADITION*"

EDITED BY

Norman Lamm

and

Walter S. Wurzburger

SPONSORED BY

Rabbinical Council of America

HEBREW PUBLISHING COMPANY

New York

PREFACE

Launched as a semi-annual journal, *Tradition* has, in the first six years of its existence, emerged as such a significant platform that it has become necessary to issue it as a quarterly.

Many of the articles that have helped *Tradition* earn its reputation represent notable contributions to Jewish thought. They should not be relegated to the obscurity of the back numbers of a pioneering journal.

In compiling this volume—intended as a representative sample of the outstanding contributions that appeared during the years when *Tradition* was still a semi-annual—the editors were plagued by an embarrassment of riches. Limitations of space dictated the omission of much material that had lost none of its relevance with the passage of time and which should have been included in this collection.

Together with their apologies for their sins of omission, the editors wish to record their gratitude to all those contributors who granted permission to have their essays reprinted here. They also appreciate the advice and counsel which the members of *Tradition's* editorial board rendered in the preparation of this volume. The editors are especially indebted to Rabbi Israel Miller, President of the Rabbinical Council of America, for initiating and encouraging the publication of this anthology and to Rabbi Israel Klavan, Executive Vice-President of the Rabbinical Council, for his invaluable guidance and support.

A special word of thanks must be expressed to Dr. Samuel Belkin, distinguished president of Yeshiva University and a revered leader of American Orthodox Judaism, for the co-operation extended to *Tradition* from its very inception.

It is our fervent hope that this book may not only serve as a permanent record of creative religious thinking but also help link a generation in search of authentic values to the *masorah*—the ever new and relevant tradition which serves as Israel's guide to its historic destiny.

THE EDITORS

CONTENTS

CONTENTS

FOREWORD

"Tradition is a fence that safeguards the Torah," says Rabbi Akiva in *Pirkei Avot*. In a real sense, the publication of TRADITION by the Rabbinical Council of America has helped keep the Torah inviolate in the face of its detractors. The method of this defense has been to open the world of Orthodox religious thought to the intellectually sophisticated members of our contemporary space generation. It has helped them to understand, in terms relevant to the condition of modern men, the timeless values implicit in both the theoretical teachings and behavior patterns of the Jewish tradition.

This anthology is testimony to the success of our venture—a success which we consider to have exceeded our original expectations. We trust that it marks the first of many such efforts to retain, in permanent book form, stimulating and thought provoking articles from TRADITION which have lasting value.

The Rabbinical Council of America is most grateful to its devoted members Rabbi Norman Lamm, the talented pioneer Editor of TRADITION, and his equally brilliant successor Rabbi Walter Wurzburger, for their voluntary labor of love in editing both the journal and this anthology. Our heartfelt thanks to the editorial staff of TRADITION, to the gifted contributors whose articles were chosen for inclusion in this volume, and to our Executive Vice-President, Rabbi Israel Klavan, who arranged for its publication. Our gratitude too to Yeshiva University and Mr. and Mrs. Gustav Stern, whose generous aid helps make possible TRADITION's publication.

Rabbi Israel Miller
President

A TREASURY OF

"Tradition"

NORMAN LAMM

*

The Need for Tradition

"T RADITION" is perhaps one of the most misunderstood and maligned words in our contemporary vocabulary. It has been misconstrued by some as the very antithesis of "progress" and as a synonym for the tyranny that a rigid past blindly imposes upon the present. For others the word evokes different associations. Tradition becomes for them the object of sentimental adoration, the kind of nostalgic affection which renders it ineffective and inconsequential, like the love for an old and naive grandmother—possessing great charm, but exercising little power or influence.

What then do we mean by "tradition," and why have we decided to publish a journal by that name in an age when man has cast off the shackles of gravity and is on the verge of the conquest of the heavens themselves, an age which seems to have broken completely with the past which nurtured it?

By "tradition" we mean neither a slavish adherence to old formulas, nor a romantic veneration of "the good old days" which strips the past of all meaningfulness for the present. In our conception of "tradition" we do not concentrate exclusively on the past at all. The word itself comes from the Latin *tradere* which means to hand down, to transmit, to bequeath. Similarly, its Hebrew equivalent *masorah* derives from the root מסר which means "to give over." The focus of Tradition is, then, the future and not the past. "Tradition" is thus a commitment by the past to the future, the promise of roots, the precondition of a healthy continuity of that which is worthy of being preserved, the affirmation that the human predicament in general, and the Jewish situation in particular, are not frighteningly new, but that they grow out of a soil which we can know and analyze and use to great benefit.

What, exactly, does this "tradition" consist of, this "tradition"

we want to "give over" to our readers, to our future? It is the
cumulative historical experience and wisdom of the people of
Israel and the totality of its divinely revealed insights and moral
injunctions and ethical imperatives and religious instruction—in
a word, its *Torah* and *mitzvot*.

משה קבל תורה מסיני ומסרה ליהושע (אבות א, א)

"Moses received the Torah at Sinai and gave it over—*u-mesarah*
—to Joshua." That *masorah*, that Tradition—of the Sinaitic revelation, both written and oral, in all its ramifications—is the one
we espouse and want to "give over." This Sinaitic Tradition,
divinely ordained, from its very inception constituted an unyielding challenge to the unredeemed pagan world which sought to
choke it in its infancy. The *masorah* then was given over to
Joshua, thence to the Elders, and thus down through the ages—
and again and again the Word of God, expressed in the Tradition
of *Torah* and *mitzvot*, challenged the idolatry of sundry societies,
each of which was smugly certain that it and it alone embodied
the absolutes and ultimates of life to which all else must be sub-
servient.

That Tradition has not been without its detractors even within
the camp of Israel. For the *masorah* constitutes a burden upon the
Jew: it obligates him to a discipline of personal holiness called
halakhah; it informs him of the fact that God and not he is the
center of the universe; it makes him, as its bearer, the target of
the forces of rebellion from within and of anti-Semitism—really
anti-Sinaiism—from without; it imposes upon him the responsibility to transmit—מסר—this Tradition to others. The Tradition
was attacked at every stage of its development. The pagan world
thought its concept of God absurd and the Sabbath the invention
of lazy people. The early Christians attacked it as legalistic and
devoid of love. The Sadducees accused it of inventing elaborate
fictions and of subverting the very Torah it sought to perpetuate.
The Karaites repeated the charge in new forms throughout the
Middle Ages. And in modern times too, the Sadducee-Karaite
heresy, in various garbs, has kept up a sustained attack on Orthodox Judaism, as the authentic Tradition is now known.

The modern era generated a host of new ideologies which increased the confusions of those who sought a viable philosophy of life in a world of profound technological and social revolution. With every major scientific achievement and technological "breakthrough," modern man's self-estimation changed. This change in self-estimation, in man's view of man and his place in the universe, took on a paradoxical form. On the one hand, modern man was constantly amazed at his own genius and power. He marveled at his newly acquired strength, sneered at the primitive mentality of his predecessors, and arrogantly began to think of himself as a god. And concomitant with this self-apotheosis, came an equal and opposite reaction: a feeling of desperation, a sense of being lost and without moorings, a terrible cosmic loneliness. The "existential crisis" was deepened as a result of the self-deification; for the more man created, the more he was at the mercy of his creations; the more he *did* the less he *was*; the more he considered himself a god, the greater became the distance between himself and God.

Jews were affected by this modern crisis perhaps more than all others. A sensitive, marginal, minority group, they possessed, in addition, a traditionally high valuation of freedom and of intellect. The Emancipation gave them the freedom they so long cherished and which was so long denied to them. The new ideological currents were made to sound intellectually appealing, and the advances in the sciences and the arts were, after all, matters of the mind in which Jews were participants and often leaders. And so Jews threw themselves with abandon into the preoccupations of the modern world, and they felt beholden to this world and adopted, along with all else, its neurotic, paradoxical view of man.

Tradition—*the* Tradition—was therefore largely abandoned. It was looked upon as hopelessly irrelevant. But this disfavor into which the Tradition fell was not only or even primarily the result of an ideological incompatibility with modern western civilization. There were simpler and more embarrassing reasons for the ebb of *Torah* and *mitzvot*. The great migrations of the Jews created agonizing cleavages between the generations. Old fashioned mannerisms, dated dress, social and linguistic maladjustment of the parents, made the children think that the Tradition too was incapable of efficacy in the culture of today. Religious education

—the "giving over" of the great body of Jewish wisdom—was sorely neglected, especially in America. And so those who spoke in the name of the Tradition, those who sought to transmit and communicate its holy contents to the new, modern Jew, were simply not understood. The difficulty lay mostly in *communication*. Yiddish instead of English, the foreign accent, European mannerisms, the lack of education, the abrupt cultural discontinuity, and the inability and apparent unwillingness to re-express valid truths in a contemporary idiom—these were problems of communication, not of basic philosophy. And it was this lack of communication which left so many Jews ignorant of the light that the Tradition could shed on the basic problems of the modern world. Thus, Orthodoxy was not tried and found wanting but— to paraphrase a famous writer—it was not tried in the first place by great numbers of people as a working philosophy in the context of modern life.

What was supposed to take the place of Orthodoxy, of the Tradition? Assimilation in its full, blatant form was ruled out as a mass-movement for Jews. First, the gentile world was not ready to accept them. Second, even Jews who had cut themselves off from loyalty to the main body of the Tradition were reluctant to commit collective spiritual suicide. The course that was chosen, then, was to assimilate not Jews but Judaism. Torah was to be rewritten in the universalist accents of a high-sounding liberal humanism; God was to be remade in the image of man; and the Tradition was to be reshaped to conform to contemporary standards of taste. Those who refused to participate in this devious form of assimilation, or "Americanization" or "acculturation" as it was now euphemistically called, were branded as "orthodox" and cavalierly dismissed as religious relics, as fossils of a vanishing faith—as if the Tradition were not a stubborn and imperishable historical fact, as if the Word of God could die by human decree or change by majority vote.

More recently, however, there have been decided changes on the world scene that have caused, particularly in America, a perceptible reorientation vis-a-vis Orthodoxy in the total Jewish community. The horrors of the Hitler era have profoundly shaken man's confidence in the beneficent use of the power he had gotten. The creation of the State of Israel has done more than give all Jews a collective pride in their people. It has also given them a sense of rootedness in the long history which gave birth to the little bit of Middle Eastern geography. The old academies of Jewish learning which grew up slowly in lower Manhattan and Brooklyn and Chicago came into their own, until today we have schools such as Yeshiva University which are unique phenomena in Jewish history. In these schools Orthodoxy is taught and learned and lived in the idiom of Western culture and in native American accents. The newly established network of *yeshivot ketanot* or Day Schools is feeding a steady stream of students into the schools of higher Jewish learning, while at the same time exerting a powerful influence in the local communities in which such schools exist. The Rabbinical Council of America, the sponsor of this journal, represents a new type of Orthodox rabbi. He is not only English speaking, but thoroughly conversant with the secular culture of the day. At the same time, he is, of course, an expositor of the Torah and the Talmud, the basic stuff of the Tradition. Here then is American Orthodoxy, with dignity, with intellectual honesty, with absolute faith in the Divine origin of the Tradition it represents. Most important, it is an Orthodoxy which has opened the channels of communication with the contemporary generation, so that the Tradition in all its fulness and beauty and holiness can now be presented to those Jews who sincerely are groping for direction and meaningfulness, for a way to live their lives in the framework of the authentic Jewish tradition.

This is the function of TRADITION—to interpret the Tradition, the Word of God, the heritage of *Torah* and *mitzvot*, in a manner and form that the modern, educated, thinking Jew can understand. The modern Jew has, by and large, given up his pat, dogmatic answers of doctrinaire liberalism and meliorism, and has now turned for direction to the classical sources of Jewish life. Now that the channels of communication between him and the Tradition are open, all that remains is—to teach, to interpret, to explain. This and this alone is our purpose, our only reason for existing. We make no pretenses of being "non-partisan," for in truth we doubt the wisdom of neutrality on the great questions

of the day. TRADITION is a "Journal of Orthodox Jewish Thought."
In these pages responsible thinkers will explicate our faith, teach
its principles, and demonstrate its relevance to the concerns of
contemporary men.

We hope at first to publish TRADITION semi-annually. Later,
we shall perhaps begin to publish quarterly. Yet even this first
issue could never have seen the light of day if not for the encouragement and constant help of my colleagues on the Editorial
Committee, the personal interest taken in our work by Rabbi
Solomon Sharfman, President of the Rabbinical Council of
America, and the warm cooperation of Orthodoxy's distinguished
leader, Dr. Samuel Belkin, President of Yeshiva University.

Defining מסר, the root of *masorah* or "tradition," Rabbi David
Kimchi, the great medieval linguist, writes: ענינו הנתינה בכל לב
—"it means to give with the whole heart." We of the Editorial
Committee give to our readers this first fruit of our labors, and
we give it with our whole heart; and with our whole heart do we
pray that TRADITION will succeed in its sacred task of reinterpret-
ing to our fellow Jews the divinely given Tradition.

RELIGIOUS EXPERIENCE AND THE HALAKHAH

EMANUEL RACKMAN

*

The Dialectic of the Halakhah

PHILOSOPHERS of Judaism find it impossible to interpret their subject without considering its many antinomies. In Judaism, God is immanent as well as transcendent. The prophets articulate lofty ideals of universalism at the same time that they emphasize the particularistic character of the chosen people. Law is of primary importance while the message of freedom is grafted on almost every precept. Other-worldliness and this-worldliness commingle in virtually all the concepts. And the most visionary of hopes co-exist with an unmistakable pragmatism, even with a hardened realism.

Judaism's antinomies are important for an understanding of not only its theology and ethics, but also its Halakhah. Indeed, the data of Jewish theology and ethics are usually derived from the Law which fixes the essential character of all of Judaism. Unfortunately, however, many who are presently called upon to resolve questions of Jewish law are often oblivious to the antinomies which are implicit in their subject. Altogether too frequently they seize upon one or another of two or more possible antithetical values or interests between which the Halakhah veers, and they assume that there must be an exclusive commitment to that single norm. The dialectic of the Talmud, however, reveals quite the contrary. Implicit in almost every discussion is a balancing of the conflicting values and interests which the Law seeks to advance. And if the Halakhah is to be viable and at the same time conserve its method and its spirit, we must reckon with the opposing values where such antinomies exist. And equilibrium among them must be achieved by us as objective halakhic experts rather than as extremists propounding only one of the antithetic values.

The very process of halakhic development involves the quest for such equilibrium. On the one hand, there are the authorities:

revealed texts, revealed norms, and the dicta of sages whose pre-
scriptions are almost as sacred as the revealed data (because
what the sages of each generation ordain becomes part of the
tradition which the revealed texts enjoin us to obey). On the
other hand, the Law's doctors are themselves partners in the development of the Law. Indeed God abdicated in their favor when
He bequeathed the Law to them. He thereby restrained Himself
from any further revelations. The Talmud tells us that Rabbis
are not to rely upon heavenly voices or miracles. They are to act
as sovereigns in the sphere of halakhic creativity allocated to them.
Can one conceive a more difficult equilibrium than this—sub-
servience to mountains of authority coupled with a well-nigh
arrogant usurpation of legislative and judicial power over the
divine legacy? Yet both poles play their necessary roles in halakhic
development.

If not for Halakhah's theocentric character, it would be no
different from other legal systems that are rooted only in history
and economics. Because its students are committed to the divine
origin of the Law, their creative achievement in the Law is ever
oriented to the fulfillment of God's Will. In order that we never
lose sight of this commitment, the Law includes mandates that
are also supra-rational—inexplicable in terms of human values
and interests. Thus Dr. Samuel Belkin, president of Yeshiva
University, maintains that even the supra-rational commandments
of the Torah have a purpose although we may not fathom their
reason.[1] These mandates are to be obeyed solely because God
decreed them. Such mandates are to be found in every branch of
the Law. Obedience to them is of the essence of one's religious
experience—one obeys not because one understands but rather
because one believes. As children sometimes obey parents not
because they comprehend but because they trust, so are we to
obey God. It was to conserve this attitude that our Sages hesitated
to make too explicit their own analysis of the Law in terms of
human values and interests. Such analyses might prompt students
to embrace a completely humanistic approach to the Law which
would thus lose its theocentric character altogether. In a general
way they did explore the rationale of most of the *mitzvot*, but

in the articulation of specific rules they did not presume that they completely fathomed the teleology of all the revealed texts.

Yet God gave the Law to the Jewish people who alone were responsible for its development. As humans they crave to understand what they are commanded to perform. Moreover, their needs are not the same in every age or clime. The Torah itself takes note of these factors. It appeals to man to comprehend the justice-content of the Law. It also bids him to live by the Law, and not perish because of it. Moses' successors were vested with authority not only to interpret the Law but to constitute themselves as authorities in every generation. The Rabbis often undertook not only to rationalize the presumptively supra-rational, but also to suspend, even overrule, the revealed words of God.

The late Justice Benjamin Cardozo once essayed to describe what it is that a judge does when he engages in the judicial process creatively. The conclusion is inescapable that one can acquire that art only after years of pre-occupation with the law, its history, its ideals, its methodology, its philosophy. So is it with Torah —until one has studied long and much from earlier masters, one does not learn how to balance one's commitment to authority with one's obligation to be the master instead of the obedient servant. Both imitation and originality play their part in the process. Modesty coupled with respect for forbears commingles with self-reliance.

The need to achieve equilibrium among values is even more apparent when one is dealing with the rules of law themselves. Particularly in the area of personal status do we find the dialectic of the Talmud balancing opposing interests and veering between antithetical values. In this paper we shall attempt to demonstrate that the Jewish law of personal status represents, in part, the achievement of an equilibrium between conflicting interests.

True, many of the norms remain supra-rational. Without such theocentric roots, the Law would become altogether positive in character. But there are many areas for rabbinic creativity and in these areas rabbis must be mindful of ends.

THE LAW OF SLAVERY

Without reference to the existence of conflicting values in the
Jewish law of personal status, one might accuse the Halakhah
of discrimination against the non-Jew in general and the non-
Jewish slave in particular. The provisions applicable to Jewish
slaves were in fact more liberal than those applicable to non-
Jewish slaves. However, an analysis of the different interests which
the Law sought to conserve will more than justify the less favored
status accorded non-Jewish slaves. For the Rabbis sought to balance their love of freedom with their firm insistence on high
moral standards for the Jewish people. In the case of Jewish
slaves, the love of freedom was the dominant interest; in the case
of non-Jewish slaves that value yielded to the concern for sexual
morality.

Jewish Slaves

It is incontrovertible that the elimination of Jewish slavery
was a goal of the Halakhah. Those who heard on Mount Sinai
that all Jews were God's servants were not to become indentured
to co-religionists who shared with them a common bondage to
the same Master. Therefore, the circumstances under which the
Written and Oral Law tolerated Jewish slavery were very limited.
A Jew could be sold by the court only if he had stolen and was
so destitute that he could not atone for his crime by the payment
of money.[2] However, to punish such a sinner with slavery meant
that the plight of his family would be even further aggravated.
For that reason the master was required to support the slave's entire family.[3] The Halakhah was, nonetheless, concerned that wife
and children have the benefit of a free head of the household.
It therefore ordained that the slave be permitted to redeem himself from his bondage whenever he acquired funds for that purpose. His wife was allowed to engage in gainful employment in
order that he might accumulate such funds. None of her earnings
belonged to her husband's master, even though the master remained responsible for her and her children's maintenance.[4] The
amount the slave was to pay the master for his freedom was pro-
portionate to the still unexpired portion of his six-year term of

slavery. If the slave had no wife and children of his own prior to his enslavement, the master was not permitted to give him a non-Jewish slave as a mate, lest he become so attached to her that he choose to remain a slave and never wed and raise a family of Jewish freemen.[5] The Law sought not only to advance the ideal of freedom but also to conserve the many values of Jewish family life. Even in those isolated instances where the master was permitted to cause the Jewish male slave to mate with a non-Jewish female slave—the only instance justifying the contention that the master owned the very body of the slave—the moral standards of a monogamous relationship were applicable and promiscuous relationships were prohibited.[6] The institution of slavery was never to place in jeopardy the lofty moral ideals of the Law. That is also why no compromise whatever was permitted in connection with the Jewish female slave. She was automatically emancipated at puberty unless she had theretofore wed her master or his son.

Non-Jewish Slaves

In the case of Jewish slaves, the ideals of freedom and family morality are seldom in conflict. However, the Law pertaining to non-Jewish slaves can only be understood in the light of the conflict that prevailed between these values. The Halakhah rarely permitted even a non-Jew to be enslaved without giving him sufficient status as a Jew to insure the protection of his life and limb and his partial participation in the religious life of family and community. As such, he had a higher status than even a free Gentile. If the non-Jew did not want to be subject to the Law, his master was required to sell him to a non-Jew.[7] If he was bought originally from a non-Jew with the express proviso that he not be converted to Judaism, then he had to acquiesce at least to the observance of the seven Noahide laws.[8] It seems, however, that non-Jewish slaves preferred Jewish owners. As a consequence of their becoming members of a Jewish household, pursuant to the performance of the appropriate rituals, they could not be harmed with impunity. There was no difference whatever in the law of homicide, whether wilful or accidental, between one who killed a Jewish freeman and one who killed a non-Jewish slave.[9] Torts committed against the non-Jewish slave were actionable. Though the recovery was the master's, the injuring of slaves was deterred by the very fact that the tort was actionable. The master himself did not escape with impunity for his own torts against his non-Jewish slave. Emancipation of the slave might be the consequence of the master's tort. Under certain circumstances the master would even pay the death penalty for killing his slave,[10] though the Law also sought to protect his disciplinary authority. If a master refused to feed his non-Jewish slave (presumably as a disciplinary measure), the community performed this obligation for the slave as it performed it for the poor generally. The Rabbis even penalized a Jewish master who sold his slave to a non-Jew who would not respect the non-Jewish slave's right to observe Sabbaths and festivals.[11] The master was compelled to repurchase the slave, though the cost of the repurchase might be ten times the amount of the original sale. Moreover, the master could not sell a non-Jewish slave even to a Jew who resided outside the Holy Land.

Nonetheless, the Law frowned upon the emancipation of the non-Jewish slave. Such emancipation would give the non-Jewish slave the status of a full-fledged Jew and the Law did not encourage this way of increasing the Jewish population. The Law abhorred the less stringent sexual code prevailing among non-Jews. Many authorities even observed that the non-Jewish slave might prefer slavery, with its license for promiscuity, to freedom as a Jew with its stern limitations on sexual relationships.[12] Not having been reared in a milieu which stressed the high moral standards of the Law, the non-Jewish slave was not to be catapulted into a free society which would make him unhappy or which he would corrupt. Nonetheless, our Sages ruled that if by emancipation a moral purpose was achieved or a *mitzvah* fulfilled, one may violate the injunction against freeing a non-Jewish slave. For example, the Law urges that a promiscuous non-Jewish female slave be freed in the hope that she marry and establish a monogamous relationship with a husband, infidelity to whom would be less probable because of the threat of the death penalty.[13]

Rules applicable to non-Jewish slaves thus involve a delicate balancing of the values of freedom and family purity. In the case of Jewish slaves the two values usually yield the same result, or at least are seldom in conflict with each other.

Employer-Employee Relationships

While an analysis of the master-slave relationship may be altogether academic, the relationship of employer and employee has contemporary significance. Jewish law was always aware of the danger that the wage earner might sink to the low status of a slave. It does not matter that he freely contracted to work—a man might also freely contract to be a slave! Therefore, the values which the Law seeks to conserve in the rules governing the employer-employee relationship are essentially those of master-slave relationship—freedom and morality. However, an added value was considered—the sanctity of the pledged word. Jewish labor law developed as a delicate balancing of all these values.

If a man sold himself as a slave for a fixed term, the Law might tolerate the voluntary forfeiture of his freedom. Many people are too immature to cherish freedom; they prefer security. Others might choose slavery in order to obtain bulk sums at the time of sale. The Halakhah, therefore, did not outlaw the transaction. However, the man who voluntarily sold himself into slavery could not expect thereby to enjoy the looser standard of sexual morality; he was not permitted to mate with non-Jewish female slaves. He could not choose a form of family life less holy than a freeman. Moreover, if he sought escape from other moral and religious standards by becoming indentured to Gentiles, his family was compelled to redeem him.[14]

More common than voluntary servitude was the long-term wage contract. Here the conflicting values are freedom and the sanctity of the pledged word. To protect the first value, the contract could not extend beyond the three-year period; otherwise the employer-employee relationship might approach the master-slave relationship. In addition, the employee was permitted to quit at any time, even before the expiration of the three year term. The employer was bound for the full period.

However, favoring the employee so that he could quit at any time hardly induces respect for the pledged word of a party to a contract. For that reason, if as a result of the breach of promise

the employer suffered an irreparable loss, the employer's promise
to increase the wage because of the threat of a walk-out is unen-
forceable.[15] Thus the employee's freedom did not become license
to do harm.

These simple principles are also applicable to organizations of
laborers. The law recognizes the right of workers to organize and
bargain with employers. The majority in the group may bind the
minority. The individual worker may leave the group, but if he
accepts employment it has to be on terms fixed by his colleagues.[16]
The duly constituted municipal authorities may exercise some
power over the decisions of the unions to insure the fairness of
their regulations.[17] But in the final analysis the Law seeks to safeguard the freedom of the individual laborers and the groups they
constitute even as it strives to make them fulfill their commitments to each other and to their employers where there is in-
jurious reliance upon their pledged word.

THE LEGITIMACY OF CHILDREN

The Law was also concerned with antithetical values in the
question of legitimacy. On the one hand, the level of morality
was to be maintained. Since courts can hardly deal with anything
but overt acts, and since most sinful sexual relationships are consummated in secret, these would normally lie beyond the reach
of the Law's sanctions. For that reason the Law had to employ
a different kind of deterrent—the fear lest the illicit intercourse
yield a bastard. On the other hand, this might require the abuse
of the innocent, and in justice, paraphrasing a biblical and talmudical dictum, it is inevitably asked: "Shall one enjoy the sin
and another pay the penalty?"

Here again we have a conflict in values. To promote sexual
morality, the Law induces the dread that the sinner will bear
the burden of an illegitimate child. The same Law, however,
eloquently ordains that no one shall be punished for another's
sin. Talmudic texts and commentaries give abundant evidence
of the delicate balancing of the interests involved here. The social stigma and ostracism, the consequence of illegitimacy, was
magnified to the horror and chagrin of all sensitive souls, while

at the same time the Law made it virtually impossible to prove that any one was a bastard and frowned upon the publicizing of such rare instances as were conclusively established.[18]

In an interesting set of hypothetical cases the Talmud informs us by inference that the stigma attached to illegitimacy was so great that the mothers of illegitimate infants would rather murder than abandon them.[19] If one came upon a foundling whose mother took precautions to insure the child's survival, though she was then and there abandoning it, the foundling was presumed to be legitimate, for if the child was illegitimate the mother would rather have sought its death. So successfully did the Law induce the dread of illegitimacy!

Yet how could illegitimacy be proved? Children born out of wedlock were legitimate. Moreover, children born of certain unlawful marriages were legitimate. Only such children were bastards who were products of incestuous or adulterous relationships in which no lawful marriage could ever be consummated between the parties, such as a child born of cohabitation between mother and son. But how could one prove that a child was born of an adulterous relationship when every husband was presumed to be the father of all children that his wife bore? Even if the husband was away for years, who could tell but that he came on a magic carpet in the dead of night to cohabit with his wife and impregnate her? [20] Or who knows but that the wife conceived artificially? Even the mother's admission that the child was illegitimate had no probative value. She was incompetent to testify. Her husband's testimony was also unacceptable for he was conclusively presumed to be the father. If he sought to deny paternity of his wife's child, his testimony would place his wife in jeopardy as an adulteress, and he was therefore incompetent to testify. A natural father might testify that a person whom he knows to be his son is illegitimate. But who would be so foolish as to volunteer such information! And who could ever be sure that a particular child was his! That the community may have doubts is not sufficient basis for the attachment of an adverse status to the child. The Law made this clear: only they whose illegitimacy is certain are bastards, not they whose illegitimacy is doubtful.

The ancients were no less sensitive than moderns to the ethical problem involved in penalizing children for the sins of their parents. In one talmudic text a method is indicated for the termination of a marriage by annulment instead of divorce, and as a result acts of adultery theretofore committed by the wife are no longer punishable. Since the annulment is retroactive, it follows that the woman was not wedded when she cohabited with men other than the one whom she once regarded as her husband and who now, as a consequence of the annulment, was nothing more than one of her many sex partners. The Rabbis, however, asked about the status of the children that she bore during the period of the marriage before its annulment. The retroactive annulment would make all of them legitimate since there was no adultery whatsoever. Would not this be a way of subverting the biblical directives on bastardy? The Rabbis answered: "Would that we had equally effective ways of removing all illegitimacies!" [21] And they did expound other ways.

True, they never completely declined to use the stigma of illegitimacy as a deterrent for illicit intercourse. The only effective deterrent had to involve the suffering of the guiltless. Yet the Law also reduces the incidence of such suffering to a minimum. It encouraged a minimum of notoriety when a judgment of illegitimacy was inescapable. The Rabbis would communicate the information to each other clandestinely once in seven years.[22] Even when the Messiah comes and reveals unto each and every Jew the name of the tribe whence he descends, he will nonetheless withhold all information about legitimacy and illegitimacy. If a bastard—concealing his identity—had managed to marry into a family of lofty status, and by imputation had acquired the same status for himself, the Messiah will not betray him! [23]

It is typical of the Law's method that it first creates the badge of illegitimacy, and then mitigates the evil consequences. The Law has to do both in pursuit of the interests it seeks to fulfill. Again we see how halakhic creativity involves a continuous oscillation between conflicting values.

A similar dialectic can be found in innumerable folios of the Talmud dealing with virginity. To impress girls with the importance of pre-marital chastity, the Law makes much of the maidenhead. Special ceremonies marked the marriage of the virgin. The

amount specified for her benefit in the Ketubah (marriage contract) was double the amount indicated for a widow or divorcee.
Only a virgin was eligible for marriage to the High Priest. And
the Law did not indulge the girl to pretend to be that which
she was not. The husband could complain to the court that he
had been deceived. In fact, the wedding date was fixed on the
eve of a day when the court would be in session in order that
the husband might make diligent application for the annulment
of the marriage for fraud, or at least the reduction of the benefits
due his wife because she was not a virgin.[24] On the basis of such
texts alone, one might even be tempted to say that the Law was
overestimating the value of virginity per se. This, however, is not
the case. The Rabbis were concerned rather with the importance
of sanctions that would encourage chastity. As in the case of
bastardy, they simply wanted a threat that would deter. Yet, if
a husband did come complaining, it was almost impossible for
him to prevail. Virtually any facts the wife offered in justification were believed. She might even claim that she was raped
after her betrothal (kiddushin) and she would lose naught unless she were married to a priest. She might claim accidental
loss of virginity, in which case the marriage was not affected
even though the amount indicated in her Ketubah might be reduced (some rabbis maintained that even this loss would not
be sustained). In communities where between betrothal and the
consummation of the marriage—the interval was usually a year
—the bride and groom were permitted to see each other without
benefit of chaperone, she could attribute the loss of virginity to
her premarital intimacy with her husband. Rare indeed were the
circumstances where the husband's complaint was of any avail.
The Rabbis gave the husband cause for even greater distress.
If he did complain, they cross-examined him as to how he had
become such an expert that he was able to distinguish between
a virgin and a non-virgin. According to one view they could flog
him for having been so promiscuous as to become an expert!
In the same passage the Talmud tells us of rabbis before whom
husbands came complaining and who in each case managed to
restore the confidence of the husband in his wife's chastity by
convincing him that he had erred. The net result of the dialectic

is that the Law accentuated the importance of chastity by creating the threat of embarrassment, but the husband could hardly ever prevail against his wife. The Law promoted the value of chastity but did not forfeit any of its dedication to the dignity of women.

In this connection an appeal must be made to Israel's halakhic authorities not to become obsessed with devotion to one value at the cost of another. When they ponder, for example, the status of Karaites whose family law for centuries has deviated considerably from the standards prevailing in the rest of the Jewish world, or when they deal with Jews returning from lands of exile where frequently, without fault on their part, there was little observance of the requirements of Jewish law, and as a result, the halakhic authorities must reckon with the legitimacy or illegitimacy of many persons born to these families, then the total law and all the values it sought to conserve should be considered. If the rabbis seek to achieve an equilibrium of interests, a more moderate approach will make a great contribution to their people and the law.

THE LAW OF DIVORCE

Interestingly enough, the values of freedom and morality suggested in connection with the law of slavery, also play an important role in the Jewish law of divorce. To expand the freedom of the parties to the marriage contract requires the broadening of the area in which their consent is the ultimate consideration. Furthermore, to expand freedom one normally dispenses with formalities. The cause of morality, on the other hand, is best served by formal procedures and by limiting the freedom of the parties to do whatever pleases them. The cause of morality also requires that divorces have some finality about them. Let us see how these values affect the legal rules and make the Jewish law of divorce more intelligible to moderns.

The Roles of Husband and Wife

The marital status is initiated when the groom performs a symbolic act of acquisition with the consent of the bride or her father. Similarly, to dissolve the relationship the Torah demands that he initiate the action. The husband must cause the bill of divorce to be written. Critics of the Law question this focus of attention upon the male. However, it is not difficult to accept the logic of the Halakhah which requires that he who created the state of *kiddushin* should be the one to undo it.

The husband's active role in creating the marriage bond is derived from a premise that is present in all of Judaism—including the Kabbalah—that the male is regarded as the active principle in the universe and the female as the passive principle. In nature it is the male who actualizes the reproductive potential of the female. In wooing, too, Judaism regarded the male as the proposer.

Yet the consent of the female is considered most important. Without it the marriage may not be consummated. The Law magnifies the role of the wife's consent in sexual relations too. Ultimately, her consent to a divorce became one of the Law's requirements. The need for her consent was slower in coming only because the Law was more preoccupied with her protection against hate and abandonment, and assumed that it served no purpose to keep her wedded to a man who did not respect her. The Ketubah was created to discourage divorce. It obliged the husband to make adequate provision for his wife's maintenance throughout the marriage and substantial payments in the event of divorce or widowhood. This obligation reduced the incidence of divorce and shielded the wife against desertion by her mate. Subsequently, the consent of the wife became a legal prerequisite to its validity. In this way the Law virtually equalized the roles of the spouses in both marriage and divorce, although it was still the male who was to perform the necessary acts.

The substitution of a rabbinic tribunal for the husband as the initiating agent has been proposed as a solution to the present problems of the Jewish law of divorce. But it is not a solution that conforms to the spirit of the Halakahah and the Jewish principle that only husband and wife shall create or dissolve the marital status. As long as the Law does not transfer the solemnization of the marriage—or most other religious acts—to a rabbinic tribunal, it does not transfer the power to divorce from the husband to a rabbinic tribunal. The emphasis, therefore, on the role of the spouses as individuals in the creation and termination of the marital status is an instance of the Law's concern for personal freedom.

Formality and Finality

Still other values remain to be reckoned with. First, the formal character of the act of divorce might be an added deterrent to hasty divorce action by the husband. Second, who knows better than moderns how farcical divorce proceedings can be when only the spouses' consents are required, and how adverse are the effects of such proceedings on the moral standards of the community! Formality and finality promote these standards.

When a divorce is consummated, a sacred bond is being dissolved. Many grave consequences flow from it: the eligibility of the wife for another marriage, and her release from all the prohibitions against adultery. Jewish law, which generally dispenses with formalities in connection with most of its civil law, is, therefore, meticulously formal with regard to the bill of divorce. In addition, the divorce must be one of complete finality, or else it is totally invalid. Remarriage is permitted without exception, otherwise the divorce is meaningless. The legal status flowing from modern decrees of separation is not countenanced. Through marriage, the cause of family morality is to be advanced; divorce must not be allowed to place it in jeopardy. Separation agreements or decrees in modern times imply sexual continence; human nature being what it is, adulterous and extramarital cohabitation often ensues. Jewish law cannot permit such conditions. A husband (other than a *Kohen*) who had divorced his wife may remarry her on one condition. If the wife had married someone else after her divorce, and her second marriage was terminated by her widowhood or divorce, she may not marry her first husband. This is a significant deterrent to hasty divorces and also to the lawful exchange of wives by husbands who would make a mockery of the marital relationship. Divorces are thus given the effect of finality. For this reason cohabitation between a man and a woman after their divorce might invalidate the divorce. The Law glorifies friendship, but does not favor the "friendship" of divorced couples of which modern society has a notorious incidence.

Because divorce is so final, and in the case of *Kohanim* absolutely irrevocable, the Law seeks to impress the spouses with the awesome character of the step they are taking. Anything less than a meticulously formal procedure would cause people to underestimate the sanctity of marriage, mentioned in the husband's recitation of an ancient wedding formula, "Behold thou art consecrated unto me." The dissolution of an act of consecration requires the services of a scribe who will prepare a personalized instrument at the husband's request. The Rabbis added the requirement that the instrument include an exact rendition of the attendant circumstances of time and place. Interestingly enough, since the divorce severed all bonds between the spouses, the bill of divorce must be a detached piece of parchment, an object whose very detachment from mother earth symbolizes the rendering asunder of two individuals.

Reformers in Judaism have made of divorce a matter of purely secular concern. The Rabbis would not tolerate a condition born of a solemn act of consecration to come to an end without the Law's involvement. Even animals once consecrated to Temple use cannot pass to another status without a form of redemption; without some formal act, even their death does not release them from their erstwhile holiness. How could the Law be less attentive to marital relationships! Talmudic authorities may have debated the validity of divorce granted by non-Jewish courts.[25] However, the weight of authority and practice supported the position that divorce, like marriage, must follow a Torah pattern.[26] Tradition prescribes how the divorce shall be written, attested, and delivered. The slightest variation might invalidate it.

The Conflict of Values

The formality and finality of the divorce are means used by the Law to insure a high regard for the sanctity of the marital relationship. Occasionally these means came into conflict with the ideal of consent which, philosophically speaking, is a badge of human freedom. Strict formal requirements in any branch of jurisprudence are usually the greatest hindrance to the fulfillment of the consent (or will) of a person. The Law has to veer between these values in many a situation.

If consent is all important, then conditions ought to be permitted. Obviously conditions detract from finality. Conditions may or may not be fulfilled, and the divorce may or may not become effective.

The Law, however, does permit the stipulation of conditions. The conditions most often suggested in the Talmud are those benefiting the wife—conditions that would prevent her from becoming a "grass widow" or spare her the burden of the levirate law. In her interest the Law's concern for finality is compromised and the area of consent is expanded. However, the Talmud suggests that often conditions tend to make the wife even more the prisoner of her marital bonds. If, for example, a husband should grant a divorce conditional upon his not returning home by a certain date, and he should be prevented from returning by unavoidable accident or duress, the condition ought not to be regarded as fulfilled. If so, no such conditional divorce would ever in fact emancipate a pious woman. She would always fear that non-fulfillment of the condition was due to duress or unavoidable accident. For that reason the Rabbis rule that duress or unavoidable accident does not affect the divorce. The Law makes the value of the divorce's finality more important than the value of consent. The husband is presumed *ab initio* to waive his right ever to claim duress or unavoidable accident.

For similar reasons, the Law sometimes compromises its concern for the rigidly formal character of the divorce and its manner of execution. In the event of an emergency the Law relaxes the strict requirements circumscribing the husband's designation of an agent to give his wife the writ. If the husband was en route to captivity and wanted to release his wife from the marriage bond, or if the husband was dying and wanted to release his wife from the ties of the levirate law, his authorization of the divorce could be most informal. In such a case the Sages expanded the area of consent and made it the overriding factor. Form was sacrificed.

Yet in other situations they did the very opposite. They re-

stricted the power of the husband to revoke the agency he had
created to give his wife a divorce. Their most revolutionary
achievement was their use of force against the husband, compelling him to say that he consents to the execution of a divorce
to his wife in such cases when they felt that the marriage ought
to be terminated. The wife can precipitate such action in many
instances. Sometimes she might forfeit her Ketubah, but she nonetheless obtains her freedom. Here actual consent was ignored altogether and all the emphasis was placed on form.

How did the Rabbis rationalize their performance? They were
loath to tamper with biblical requirements. But they presume
that every marriage is consummated with the understanding that
it is subject to rabbinic authority and that their will is the will
of the spouses forever. The consent on which they rely is an imputed consent—indeed, imputed from the date of the marriage.

The conflict between the values of finality and consent is most
evident in the later development of the Law's attitude toward
conditional divorces. It has already been observed that to permit
conditions in the granting of divorces is to magnify the area of
consent and to diminish the element of finality. It is interesting
that when the wife's consent to the divorce was not a prerequisite
for its validity and there were few restrictions on the husband,
the Law permitted the use of conditions in the hope that fewer
divorces would become final. But when the wife's consent to
the divorce became a prerequisite for its execution and delivery,
(about 1000 C.E.), the granting of conditional divorces was generally outlawed. The communities could well afford to be more
concerned about finality than consent, particularly since the special circumstances in which the use of conditions might be helpful
to the wife could be handled differently. Yet until today some
forms of conditional divorce are in use, as in the case of soldiers
going off to battle who, following the precedent of King David's
soldiers, divorce their wives conditionally or absolutely pending
their return by a fixed date.

It thus appears that the Law's dialectic with regard to divorce
veers between concern for the sanctity of the marital relationship
and concern for the freedom of the parties.

The Present

It is with regard to divorce law that there is presently the greatest need for halakhic creativity. Those who clamor for change make it appear that the Halakhah is unfair to women. Those who resist change rest their case on numerous maxims which make one dread any tampering with the sanctity of the marital status. Neither group does justice to the Halakhah. The former ignore the overwhelming evidence to be found in thousands of talmudic folios which deal with the obligations of a husband to a wife. The latter freeze the Halakhah against further development by ignoring the dialectic which is the very essence of the halakhic process.

True, the talmudic dialectic is not necessarily a quest for a reconciliation of opposites in a new synthesis. More often, it seeks the retention of the antithetical values and their fulfillment in the legal order. Thus, tradition continues to live on, but the future is not altogether determined by the past. The dialectic confirms the role of history while allowing for progress. However, he who takes one polar view or another all the time seldom equivocates. If the Israeli rabbinate were to follow this course in matters of personal status it would rapidly forfeit its exclusive jurisdiction in this area. Fortunately, it appreciates its grave responsibility. However, in its fear of, or respect for, the extremists it often fails to take the steps which it knows are required by the halakhic process and consonant with its goals. Perhaps a candid articulation of the process and its goals would not only enhance the general appreciation of the Law and contribute to its development, but also relegate the extremists to peripheral status in the traditionalist Jewish community, where they can then serve in the role of vigilantes as in any social system. Certainly something must be done to prevent a recurrence of the late Chief Rabbi Herzog's sad confession that he had devised halakhic means of promoting the equality of men and women in rights of inheritance but was prevented from implementing his decision by extremist colleagues in Israel.[27] The result was that the people of Israel ultimately had to ignore their halakhic experts and legislate, through their popularly elected Knesset, a law not based on Halakhah but in fact closer to halakhic axiology than that of the position of the Chief Rabbi's controversialists. It is important that the Knesset shall not be forced by rabbinic intransigence to act in matters of family law. The *Kulturkampf* in Israel would then be on in earnest and a hopeless schism would inevitably follow. The Israeli rabbinate can avert such a tragedy. It can further develop the talmudic dialectic and not freeze the law in one or another pole of the antinomies.

NOTES

1 S. Belkin, *The Philosophy of Purpose* (New York: Yeshiva University, 1958).

2 *Kiddushin* 18a.

3 *Ibid.*, 22a.

4 Maimonides, *Hil. Avadim* 3:2. Nachmanides disagrees; see comment of *Mishneh le'Melekh, ad loc.*

5 *Kiddushin* 20a.

6 Maimonides, *Hil. Avadim* 3:5.

7 *Yevamot* 48b.

8 Maimonides, *Hil. Milah* 1:6.

9 *Makkot* 8b.

10 Exodus 21:20.

11 *Gittin* 43b.

12 *Ibid.*, 13a.

13 Maimonides, *Hil. Avadim* 9:6.

14 *Ibid.* 2:7

15 *B. Metzia* 75b.

16 *B. Batra* 8b and 9a.

17 See M. Findling, *Techukat ha-Avodah* (Jerusalem: Schreiber, 1945), pp. 19–20.

18 *Kiddushin* 71a.

19 *Ibid.* 73a, b.

20 Comments of Tosafot and Asheri on *Kiddushin* 73a, and text cited by them from Jerusalem Talmud.

21 *Shitah Mekubetzet, Ketubot* 3a.

22 *Kiddushin* 71a. The medieval rabbis were more vigilant.

23 *Ibid.* 71a, and Maimonides, *Hil. Melakhim* 12:3.

24 *Ketubot* 2a.

25 *Gittin* 10b.

26 See I. Porat, *Mevo ha-Talmud* (Cleveland: 1941), pp. 60–62.

27 See I. Herzog, "Hatzaat Tekanot bi-Yerushot," *Talpioth* (Nisan 5713), pp. 36–37.

ALEXANDER CARLEBACH

*

Autonomy, Heteronomy, and Theonomy

THE OVERWHELMING stress on Torah as Law, as a normative
system of duties imposed on the Jew, has tended to result in
an overemphasis on the heteronomous character of Judaism.* It is
the purpose of this essay to examine this fundamental and perennial problem of religion: autonomy versus heteronomy.

It will be necessary to define the essence and extent of the
problem and to recognize its position in relation to cognate
themes of religious philosophy. To the Jew who has accepted
Torah as the sum total of divine revelation and who believes in
such revelation as both possible and necessary and, moreover,
as a historical fact, the question of autonomy is first of all one
of *motivation*. Do we perform our duties as men and Jews solely
in blind submission to the will of God, or because and only insofar as our own human mind and instinct, our thinking and
feeling approve of and harmonize with the demands of Torah
and Him Who gave it? The word "blind" in the first half of the
alternative and the phrase "and only insofar as" in the second
indicate that we have stated the two extreme antitheses between
which intermediate and compromising positions can and should
be found. The first position is, indeed, an extreme of heteronomy
pure and simple—no less heteronomous in character because it
can be named theonomy in view of its origin. From the point
of view of him who performs the command, this "blind" obedience is indeed the *Kadawer-* (cadaver) or *Hunde-gehorsam*
(canine obedience) of which Geiger wrote and which expression

* I made this criticism in a recent article in the *Jewish Review* of London,
Vol. XIV, no. 412, pp. 6–7, in which I evaluated Dr. I. Grunfeld's English
translation of Samson Raphael Hirsch's *Horeb*, the nineteenth century work
by the father of modern Orthodoxy.

so much incensed Samson Raphael Hirsch [1] and which is perhaps not as blasphemous as Hirsch thought. Once the obedience springs "from the ardent desire of the Jew to understand to obey God's declared will and to make it his own" (Dr. Grunfeld's words in answer to Geiger), one can no longer speak of a purely heteronomous motive. On the other extreme, to fulfill Torah and *Mitzvot* only because and inasmuch as they are approved by our own reason and conscience constitutes a radical rationalism and humanism which is bound to endanger our *a priori* faith in the general validity and binding force of revealed religion, of Torah in particular.

TA'AMEI HA-MITZVOT

Somewhere between these two polar positions of exclusive heteronomy or autonomy must be sought others, intermediate ones, which will try, in different ways and by various degrees, to compromise between them and to harmonize the motives of religious and moral conduct. The need to do so has been the main incentive for the search for *ta'amei ha-mitzvot*, the reasons of the commandments of the Torah. This in turn is only an aspect, though an important one, of the general problem posed by the duality of revelation and reason which has been the dominating theme of Jewish religious philosophy from Saadia onward. In its most acute form it puts before reason the necessity to justify why divine revelation was and is necessary in addition to what man's own thinking, methodically or by intuition, may reveal to himself. It is across this bridge of rationalization that the voice of God speaking to man and the inner voice of man's reason and conscience are able to meet; reason, in the widest sense of the word, thus becomes the common denominator of autonomous and heteronomous morality. In a way, revelation is at a disadvantage here, as the reasonableness of our own autonomous moral demands appears to be self-evident and somehow inherent in and synonymous with the attitude and actions required, which is not always the case with the contents of revelation coming, as it were, from the outside. Reason is thus apt to sit in judgment over what has been revealed to us. This disadvantage finds some compensation in that revelation speaks with greater authority and objectivity than that enjoyed by the more subjective and fallible judgments of man. It is, in fact, through this clash of objective authority and autonomous though subjective freedom on the battlefields of reason that the fate of our ethico-religious existence is decided.

While the search for *ta'amei ha-mitzvot* may produce agreement and consonance of moral motivation over a wide area of our Torah-given duties, there remain important sections that resist rationalization, failing to satisfy either our logic and reason or our moral judgment, or are even felt to be antagonistic to them. This, in turn, has resulted in the division and classification of commandments according to the extent of their conformity to the standards of autonomous reason and morality. While it is, of course, possible and perhaps even desirable that our reason and conscience should submit to what is recognized as the command of an over-riding authority and wisdom, there is surely a limit both to the extent and the universality to which such submission can be accepted as possible or legitimate, taking into account the very premises and fundamentals of Torah revelation, let alone those of a purely humanistic, inner-worldly orientation. What we consider possible in this respect, not merely for a particular individual or group, but as generally valid, must have a strong bearing on what is, philosophically and religiously, legitimate and admissible.

TWO SOURCES

The dichotomy between autonomy and heteronomy in the field of Torah life and observance gains particular sharpness where it reveals not merely a diversity in motivation but a difference in value judgment expressing itself either in indifference or in antagonism. We are not thinking here, I repeat, of an extreme philosophical position (such as adopted by Kant) which recognizes the human conscience and its categorical imperative as the only possible source of moral ideas and rules of conduct and which denies both the possibility and the need for a heteronomous revelation. But even for those who accept a duality of sources for human and Jewish religious morality—and they are the vast majority of Jewish teachers and thinkers across the ages—and who conceive of a Torah-inspired life as one where divine revelation embodied in a historical tradition plays a decisive role alongside human reason, feeling, and conscience, the failure of communication or a conflict between these two sources remains an ever present possibility, whether in the realm of thought and theory, or in that of practical performance, generally or in a particular historical or personal situation. This possibility must not be confused with the obvious and unavoidable tension which needs exist between the moral and religious demands of a normative system of law and the weakness of the flesh and of nerve which too often leave the former unfulfilled. This, in turn, cannot entirely be separated from the material conditions of life which themselves are interwoven with the intellectual climate prevailing at any given moment of history. It cannot be denied that such temporal circumstances have a bearing on the ability and/or willingness of the individual Jew or an entire group of Jews to live up to the eternal standards of Torah life. All the same, the problem has to be viewed on its highest and most general level and with the utmost seriousness as one of the sparking points of religion in general and of Torah Judaism in particular, before it can be viewed against the backdrop of a particular civilization, of the human and Jewish condition at a given point of its progress in history.

In attempting in what follows to sketch our problem as it presented itself and the treatment it received in the main periods of Jewish history, it will become only too evident that one is dealing not only with a crucial question confronting the modern Jew but with a hardy perennial which has to varying degrees exercised Jewish religious thought and thinkers at almost every stage and age.

THEONOMY IN THE BIBLE

What about the Bible? Here, in this primary source book of divine revelation, we may hope to find, though not in the form of ordered and systematic thought, the raw material for the con-

struction of an integrated religious and philosophical view. Not
that the Bible proclaims its message in a religio-historical vacuum,
for many an idea and institution in the Torah must be understood against the background of the civilization of contemporary
antiquity. However, the idea of absolute obedience and service
to the voice of God is certainly paramount in the Pentateuch
and in large areas of the prophetic, historical, and wisdom
books.

The exhortation, "And now, if you will harken unto my voice"
(Exod. 19:5), is an integral part of the programmatic preface to
the revelation on Sinai and this is echoed and re-echoed, particularly in Deuteronomy. Already of Abraham it was said, "because
he hearkened unto My voice" (Gen. 26:5), and he is generally
taken as the exemplar of blind and unconditional obedience to
the voice and will of God as shown in the story of the *Akedah*
(the sacrificial binding of Isaac). But in spite of the strong heteronomous note, the autonomous one is heard often and unmistak-
ably. That man, created in the image of God (and therefore
endowed by Him with a share of His own spirituality), possessed
ab initio and *a priori* moral sense and freedom can be seen from
many of the stories and statutes of the Bible, both before and
after Sinai. "The Seven Noachide Laws" are not all explicit and
though they were found hermeneutically in Genesis 2:16—here,
as elsewhere, "a verse cannot depart from its literal meaning."
Cain and Lemech, the generations of the Flood and the Disper-
sion, Sodom and Gomorrah and many others, individuals or people, are assumed in the Bible to have a sense of right and wrong,
even of the proper and acceptable way to worship God, without
having been vouchsafed an explicit supernatural revelation as was
given to Israel on Sinai.

In fact, throughout the Bible basic ethical concepts such as
charity, justice, law, purity and impurity, sanctity, abomination,
violence and others are assumed to be known and accepted in
their ethico-religious connotations. The laws of God are recognizable both by Israel and the nations as righteous statutes and
laws (*chukim u'mishpatim tzadikim*), and the Torah is recognized
as neither too difficult (intellectually) nor too far (strange) for

Israel; it is "in your mouth and in your heart to do it" (Deut. 30:24). And even if "in your mouth" refers, as S. R. Hirsch and D. Hoffmann explain, to the "from mouth-to-mouth" tradition, "in your heart" can only mean that the word of the Torah must find an instantaneous echo and understanding. Where the fear of God is mentioned as the awareness of a general morality, it is not so much the idea that this morality stems from God but that He is its guarantor and will punish those who violate it. Moreover, one cannot say that the Pentateuch contains rules for all possible conditions and problems and that in it all religion and all morality are exhaustively expressed. If that were so, there would have been no need at all for prophetic and other biblical utterances or indeed for the Oral Torah of our sages, all of which is comprised under the term of *Kabbalah* (Tradition).

In the prophetic books, too, the ideas of heteronomy and autonomy find equal expression, the former as in Samuel's words,

Hath the Lord as great delight in burnt-offerings and sacrifices,
As in harkening to the voice of the Lord?
Behold, to obey is better than sacrifice,
And to harken, than the fat of rams.[2]

Even here the idea of mere obedience is softened by the protest against sacrifices as a possible "bribe" for God. Nor was Saul's disobedience prompted by "humanitarian" considerations, though a passage in *Yoma* 22b imputes these to him. But Micah, in a very similar appreciation of the relative value of sacrifices, whether human or animal, addressing himself to man (not to Israel!) makes his classic proclamation of prophetic morality on what God requires from man: justice, loving-kindness, and modesty. The same train of thought, appealing in the name of God to that innate feeling of right, of kindness and decency in man, as opposed to mere formal, outward, mechanically performed religious acts, can be found in many prophetic passages such as in the 58th chapter of Isaiah, the Yom Kippur *Haftarah*. It would be tempting and worthwhile to examine each book of the Bible from the angle of autonomy versus heteronomy, but what has been said must suffice.

TALMUD AND MIDRASH

Turning now to the sages of the Talmud and Midrash, we hope to find with them even more guidance and enlightenment on the problem before us. They were no more systematic philosophers than those who conveyed to us the revelation contained in the Bible, though according to their own particular method and style they treated theological and philosophical questions in a more reflective and dialectic way than the Bible with its greater immediacy and spontaneity. This is due, in no small measure, to the fact that the rabbis were active in a historical setting in which the challenge of foreign ideas and civilizations on Jews and Judaism was more pressing than ever before. Hellenism, Roman institutions, emerging Christianity and other syncretistic oriental faiths and cults, not to mention the internal struggles caused by the Sadducees, the Essenes and other splinter sects, forced the rabbis to formulate Torah views and attitudes and place them before their hearers and disciples. Inevitably the cut and thrust of these grand debates, the confrontation, in particular, with triumphant Hellenic and Hellenistic civilization, exercised a deep influence on these teachers, helped them to clarify their own Torah-based ideas, to reject what ran counter to them and adopt or adapt what appeared true and useful. This applies in particular to the humanistic elements in Hellenism which made man and his reason the measure of all things. This idea dominated the mind of men in the Hellenistic era and penetrated into the Jewish domain as well. The rabbis, therefore, had to deal with this religious challenge. Their freedom of thought and expression was all the greater as every individual teacher was making *his* contribution in accordance with his own character and temperament, his training and experience, and at the same time he was aware of all those others who worked towards the same end. Thus, over the generations, they produced in the dialectic system of *Aggadah* a kaleidoscopic wealth of views which left no aspect of any possible problem outside their intellectual or religious probe.

Before we examine some of the halakhic or aggadic statements that seem to bear on the problem of theonomy, we ought to recognize to what extent the very activity and method of the sages of Talmud or Midrash sheds light on the problem mentioned. Leaving aside those traditions which, as Oral Torah in the narrow sense of the word, have been preserved for us in this literature, the teachings and interpretations resulting from the inexorable intellectual debate to which the rabbis submitted every detail of Torah show that the sovereignty of men's logic was the unspoken but unquestioned *a priori* assumption of all their work. The fact that the traditional hermeneutical rules are considered *Halakhah le-Mosheh mi-Sinai* (Halakhah given to Moses on Sinai)—not all of them being purely logical rules—makes them no less an inherent, autonomous function of the human mind. In other words: Oral Torah, in the wider sense, is the product of the clash and interaction of the written Torah, as well as the rest of Scripture and other traditional material, with the logical mind and the moral sense of our sages. This is perhaps less obvious than it sounds. Is it really self-evident that Torah and *Mitzvot* must be subject to the Law of Contradiction? I submit that it is not, unless, of course, one sees in God-given human reason the arbiter of revelation. And what is true of intellect and logic is true of moral sense and intuitive feeling as well. What is it that entitles the rabbis to raise moral objections to stories and actions described in the Bible, to aspects of its legislation, unless they assumed their right and duty to listen to the voice of their minds and hearts? When they ask, "If a man has sinned, wherein has the animal sinned" (*Yoma* 22b; *Sanhedrin* 54a) or, "How may one do business with one's neighbor's cow?" (*Bava Metzia* 35b) or when they state, for example, "A sinner should not have any profit" (*Ketuvot* 11a), they assume the validity of certain unstated and yet self-evident moral principles to which Torah law and teaching is expected to conform. The rabbis, of course, never doubt that they do conform and they regard it their duty to prove it, despite any *prima facie* difficulties. Suffice it to say that here we have before us the basic, essential mechanism of the Oral Torah and incidentally the justification of autonomous reason, both logical and moral, as being in partnership with the Giver of the Torah in the full revelation, deployment and continuous potency of the Sinaitic message.

There is, of course, no shortage of rabbinic statements asserting the heteronomous, theonomous character of Torah and *mitzvot*. Man and the Jew in particular stand to God in the relation of either son or servant, implying obedience to His will either out of reverent fear or love, or both. In either case, what man does for these motives is determined solely by being the will and command of God. (We may leave aside for the moment the question whether the ability of man to love and fear God is not in itself the beginning of his autonomy.) Terms as fundamental and ubiquitous as acceptance of the yoke of Heaven (or of *mitzvot*, or of Torah) show a prevalence of the idea of heteronomy, of obedience to God, the Law-giver, as the dominant religious motive of our conduct. Its most general formulation as a deliberate submission, not to say abdication, of one's own will and reason is found in the midrashic elaboration of Israel's declaration at Sinai: "We shall do and we shall listen;" [3] on the other hand, God was said to have threatened to bury them under the mountain [if they did not accept the Torah]. Perhaps too much should not be made of these homilies; the early act of more or less free acceptance of the Torah is periodically renewed, as stated in the Bible and described by our sages in the words, "they confirmed what they had already accepted." [4] This is quite apart from the rabbis' insistence on the need for a daily renewal by the individual of his submission to the divine yoke.

TWO CATEGORIES OF MITZVOT

In any event, the idea of theonomy in these terms or statements is perhaps less explicit than in the much quoted passage of Rabbi Elazar ben Azaryah: [5] "How do we know that we should not say, 'I have no desire to eat swine's flesh' or 'I have no desire to commit a forbidden sexual act'; on the contrary we should say, 'I have a desire for these forbidden things, but what can I do when my Father in Heaven decreed that they are forbidden to me.'"
Maimonides quotes this statement in his Introduction to *Avot* (Chaper 6), but both the examples cited by Rabbi Elazar and by Maimonides are restricted to a particular type of *mitzvah*. Maimonides [6] identifies them as those commandments of tradition [7]

which cannot be explained rationally, as opposed to those commandments which can be derived by reason. These categories were introduced into Jewish philosophy by Saadia, and were anteceded by the division of *mitzvot* into those which, if they had not been written in the Bible, should by right have been written, and those to which the Satan objects.[8] The latter are, of course, those which Hirsch [9] has grouped together as statutes (*chukkim*), and although he refuses to regard them as either irrational (Rashi) or esoteric (Maimonides), they are largely those which though capable of rationalization are not postulated by reason. It is difficult to understand why Rabbi Elazar ben Azaryah included illict sexual relations in this category; they are, in fact, included among the "rational" ordinances in *Yoma* and *Sifra*. Yet, only to this limited group of *Mitzvot* are applied the apodictic declarations: "I am the Lord Who have decreed (the *chukkim*) and therefore you are not permitted to criticize, to change, or to transgress." In any event, the emphasis on heteronomy in the passage quoted is a limited and not a general one.

METZUVEH VE'OSEH

Another much quoted passage emphasizing the heteronomous nature of the *mitzvot* is Rabbi Chanina's statement [10] that "he who fulfills a commandment because he is commanded to do so is greater than he who fulfills it although he is not commanded to do so" which appears to have been accepted as authoritative.[11] Here we find no restriction as to the type of *mitzvah*; but on the other hand, no scriptural proof is adduced by or for Rabbi Chanina. The word "greater" is explained in the Gemara as referring to the reward to be expected and not to the intrinsic religious value of the act, though the two are very much connected. Tosafot justifies the greater reward by saying that to conform to a command involves painstaking care and trouble not present with one who performs voluntarily.* This, of course, is far removed from the ideological pathos with which Hirsch and his disciples pro-

---

* Nor does Rabbi Chanina deny his due reward to the latter, a side of the medal which has often been stressed by, among others, Maimonides (*Guide to the Perplexed*, III, 17).

pound the idea of heteronomy. One would have to reconcile or rather dialectically confront Rabbi Chanina's bold assertion with other rabbinic statements which extol the virtue of those who act without being commanded.[12] Perhaps what he wishes to state is a maxim of religious pedagogy, stressing the value of obedience to the will of God, rather than a theological principle. Let us note that such a staunch defender of autonomy as Moritz Lazarus [13] found it perfectly possible to harmonize autonomous religious ethics with the normative tendency (*Gesetzlichkeit*) which is expressed in Rabbi Chanina's dictum.†

BALANCING OF FORCES

It would appear from the foregoing that our sages, or rather those among them who pronounced on our problem and on those akin to it, adopted a dialectic method not so much to arrive at the truth as to assure the full, continued, and correct observance of *Mitzvot* and to defend the Torah against critics and adversaries from both outside and inside. It was this primarily educational but also apologetic task which was their main object and concern. That the whole Torah and all *mitzvot were* "all given by the one shepherd from the mouth of the Lord of all works" was as axiomatic with them as that absolute obedience was demanded. They were equally convinced that God requires nothing from man but

† In *Berakhot* 33b (cf. *Yerushalmi, ad loc.*) the Mishnah says, "If one says, 'May Thy mercies extend to a bird's nest,' we silence him." The Gemara explains this reproof of an apparently innocent expression with the criticism, "He presents the decrees of God as deriving from mercy whereas they are but decrees"—certainly a heteronomous attitude. It should be noted, however, that this is only one of several explanations given in the Babylonian and Palestinian Talmud. The reason of mercy, rejected in the Gemara quoted, is in fact adopted by the Midrash (*Vayikra Rabba* XXVII), by one of the *Targumim*, and also by Rashbam. I refer the reader to the excellent discussion of this passage by Joseph Wohlgemuth in *Das jüdische Religionsgesetz in jüd. Beleuchtung*, II, p. 31–32 and his suggestion that instead of decree one should read *din* (law), thus giving the statement a very different and more plausible meaning. On the basis of the present reading, however, the law regarding the sending away of the mother bird would have to be ranged with the group of statutes mentioned before (cf. Rashi, *ad loc.*) and the idea expressed in the Gemara would lose its general character.

what is reasonable and morally right and useful, even if occasionally this was not apparent. By stressing or elucidating the "morality" and rationality of *mitzvot* they appealed to the human heart
and mind whose approval would reinforce obedience and conformity to the will of God. Where there was difficulty, they would
fall back as a last resort upon heteronomy (theonomy) as the
inescapable normative appeal and motive for performance. From
their understanding of Scripture as much as from their rational or
instinctive experience they had a high opinion of the place of man
in the God-given order of things in which he was "but little less
than the angels" by virtue of his spirit, his consciousness, his
intellectual and moral freedom and potentialities. Greater even
than the Angels of Service, he was capable of becoming God's
partner in the work of creation and *was*, in fact, his partner in
achieving the purpose of that creation. When man merges his
will with that of his Creator (*Avot* 2:4), the problem of heteronomy is effectively solved. But before this happens, the balancing
of the two motive forces, which do not always pull in the same
direction, is as difficult as it is necessary. Rationalists, both inside
and outside the talmudic world, fear that over-emphasis on heteronomy is not only intrinsically wrong but tactically dangerous as
it might lead to a revolutionary explosion of the human mind.
But there are others who fear that by encouraging the human
mind to assert its autonomy, it will set itself up as a supreme
authority with dire consequences for belief and observance.

This danger became manifest, even within the talmudic period,
for those sections of Jewry who lived in the Hellenistic diaspora
and were therefore much more exposed to the influence of Greek
and Hellenistic thought and civilization. They are best typified by
Philo and Josephus. Hellenists believed in the existence of an
autonomous natural law * before whose tribunal all legislation
had to justify itself. And Jewish-Hellenistic writers set their whole
pride and employed their considerable gifts in proving that in
fact our Torah fulfilled all moral and utilitarian demands of the
jus naturale. They addressed themselves not only to their fellow

---

* The distinction between man-made state laws and a natural, universal
one is already made by Aristotle and by others before him.

Jewish Hellenists, who were very much in need of encouragement
in whatever observance was still theirs but also apologetically and
as religious propaganda to a large Gentile public which, as we
know, were interested in and attached to Jewish faith and practice.
Inevitably the question of the divine origin and authority of Torah
and *Mitzvot* became less important than their intrinsic value and
philosophical and moral character in the eyes of Greek science.
It also led to greater value being attached, at least by the intelligentsia, to obviously ethical laws in preference to purely religious
and ceremonial observances. On the other hand, it was just those
which gave Judaism its characteristic distinction from other religions and it was they which appealed to the Gentile imagination.
While to us today Hellenistic Judaism seems shadowy and diluted
compared with its talmudic and medieval counterparts, one must
give their due to those who wrestled hard with the problems of
keeping Jews loyal to their heritage in a spiritually hostile environment and under adverse conditions. We may have much to learn
from an episode and experience in Jewish history, the setting of
which has so many parallels with our own.

FROM SAADIA TO ABRAVANEL

Jewish philosophy in the Middle Ages is even for us moderns
a most important laboratory of ideas. Philosophers from Saadia
to Abravanel are distinguished from Philo and other Hellenists
in that the former were firmly rooted in the entirety of rabbinic
tradition and, on the other hand, were of much greater stature
as philosophers and scientists. While Judaism in the age of Hellenism faced the challenge of an all-pervading popular culture, the
medieval philosophers dealt chiefly with an intellectual and academic problem: the relationship between reason and revelation.
The Middle Ages differed from antiquity in that the demand for
a deep, self-searching philosophical examination was addressed by
Greco-Arabic philosophy to a Jewish-Islamic-Christian world which
was deeply rooted in their respective and, in important points,
identical religious attitudes. The idea of God as the Creator, the
Law-giver and Redeemer of the universe and mankind was common ground, and so was an *a priori* acceptance of theonomy—

heteronomy as the mainstay of religion. For Jewish philosophy this meant the absolute validity of the received talmudic tradition and the unquestionable legitimacy of the claim of Torah and *Mitzvot* to obedience.

The philosopher-sages of Judaism over a period of more than 600 years had to deal to a much greater extent than it ever was incumbent upon the sages of Talmud and Midrash, with the confrontation of tradition with the philosophy and science of the various schools—Kalam, Neo-Platonic, Aristotelian—which dominated the thinking of the Middle Ages. The legitimacy and indeed religious importance of this confrontation was recognized by the great majority of writers. Even the minority, which denied this legitimacy, freely used both the method and terminology of philosophical inquiry. In the name of autonomous human reason, which was the progenitor of all philosophy and science, one studied not only the basic theological and metaphysical questions such as God and His attributes, the meaning of existence, body and soul, immortality, and, in particular, the place of revelation in the order of things, but also, and as a logical consequence, the reasons of individual or groups of *mitzvot*. Reason is not, here as elsewhere, limited to intellectual processes, but includes and occasionally is conceived as the moral sense of man, as in Kant's Practical Reason. It is evident that the problem of autonomy as opposed to the heteronomy of revealed religion is implicit, if rarely explicit, in the philosophical labors of the Middle Ages. An occasional voice can even be heard as early as the 11th century, if not from rabbinic at least from Karaite Judaism, which makes use of "the whole arsenal of arguments which at [the] beginning of modern times have been advanced on behalf of the idea of an autonomous morality." [14] Reason, on the other hand, has to justify itself, its rights and functions, alongside revelation as its competitor as a source of knowledge and a guide in human conduct; and perhaps its greatest justification from the point of view of Torah lies in its being the chief instrument of investigation and interpretation of the meaning of Torah. But it is reason, too, that has to justify the need for revelation alongside or over and above what reason knows unaided. There could, of course, be no guarantee that reason would confine itself to exposition and justification. What

if, like another "Sorcerer's Apprentice," the human mind would
strike out on its own, as it were, and become the critic and rival of
revelation instead of its faithful supporter and companion. Saadia,
in fact, confines reason to this latter role and he was followed in
this in modern times by S. R. Hirsch.

In this process of examination the medieval philosophers naturally arrived at a division of *mitzvot* which we mentioned previously as having occurred already to the sages of the Talmud. This
twofold division into those of Reason and those of Revelation
(Tradition and Obedience), which from Saadia onwards we find
in varying forms and contents with most of the philosophers, may
not be identical in strictly philosophical terms with that of the
Talmud and Midrash, but the connection cannot be denied. But
to distinguish these two categories at once raises the question of
their relative roles and importance. While the more rationalist
were inclined to put the value of rational commandments above
that of traditional ones, Judah Halevi, for instance, reverses this
order. Both sides realize the danger which such a differentiation
means to observance, and they try to counter this by laying great
stress on observance of *mitzvot*, whether their reasons are known
or acceptable to reason, or not. On the other hand, when early
teachers of Mussar such as Bachyah ibn Pakudah emphasized the
duties of the heart as truly important in contradistinction to mere
legalism and formal religiosity, then this was only another variant
of the division and the dialectic of which we have spoken. Inquiring into the meaning and purpose of individual *mitzvot* or Torah
institutions sometimes involved advancing historical reasons (e.g.,
Maimonides' explanation of the sacrifices) which seemed to run
counter to their eternal validity. Here, too, philosophers tried to
guard against danger by stressing the unchangeable authority of
Torah. But here again such differentiations among *Mitzvot* as to
their relative importance and even their continued or time-bound
validity had already been made by our sages in the Talmud and
Midrash; and they, too, had thought it wise to warn the religious
Jew not to allow such distinctions to influence his conduct.

Once more we have seen how in a vital period of Jewish continuity *and* creativity, a fine but essential balance was kept between Reason and Revelation, between the voice from on high

and that from inside. Sure enough, in every generation there existed alongside the spokesmen of a philosophical and scientifically based Judaism those rabbinic leaders who saw no need for philosophy to underpin a self-evident, self-supporting faith and way of life; who were content to look inward and let the great world go by, seeing only the dangers of heresy and religious estrangement lurking in the domain of rational inquiry. It would be facile to divide the medieval world into philosophers and halakhists. Most of the former were great expounders of Halakhah as well, and many purely rabbinical luminaries in those centuries had a good general education and were not hostile to philosophy and science. The frontiers often ran right through one personality as in Rambam-Maimonides. These men were perhaps less monolithic than we imagine, being only too well aware of the challenges and the dangers in them. They were above all deeply religious men, attached with every fibre of their being to the God and Torah of Israel. They could afford the courage and intellectual honesty required to walk the tightrope that swung between their intuitive, inborn, and often mystical union with Torah and *mitzvot* and the inescapable demands of their intellect.

One cannot be sure to what extent the philosophical discussion of the Middle Ages—say from Saadia to Maimonides—affected Jewish communities beyond the intellectual elite. The explosion and controversies of the post-Maimonidean age show, in any event, that philosophical ideas had—in one shape or another—percolated to broader strata of the population with often undesirable effects on belief and practice. The opposition, whether violent or moderate, to philosophical inquiry now began to dominate Jewish life in Europe, with the almost exclusive emphasis on Halakhah being reinforced by a growing interest in Kabbalah. But even to the end of the 13th century and the Expulsion, philosophical studies continued in Spain and southern France. The many important works written in this period—Levi ben Gershon, Crescas, Duran, Albo, Abravanel—presuppose a public interested in theological problems. Philosophy and science were blamed for the weakness and lack of *mesirat nefesh* (readiness to face martyrdom) shown by large sections of Spanish Jewry during the persecutions of 1391–1492. However that may be, it is equally true that some of the finest spirits and men of high education preferred exile to apostacy. The late flowering of Jewish thought in Italy after the Expulsion was largely due to Spanish emigrants. Little new, however, was added to the discussion of the problem of theonomy by the thinkers coming after Maimonides. And in the communities of northern Europe the problem did not exist. Jews were content and happy to perform the will of their Creator—with no questions asked.

MENDELSSOHN

The Renaissance, the age of humanism and Reformation which had conquered Europe and was followed in the 17th and 18th centuries by a revolutionary upsurge of the human mind and scientific discovery, made hardly any impression on the introverted life of the Jewish communities. Only as the 18th century advanced did intellectual and social cracks begin to appear in the armor, and "modern times" began to catch up with Jewry. The outstanding symbol of this development is Moses Mendelssohn, the man who unlocked the gates of European culture for himself and his people. It is, therefore, not without irony that it should be he, the Socrates of his time, who has been so much maligned by those in the Orthodox camp (who probably never read a line of his), who most strongly asserts the heteronomous character of Judaism by defining it as revealed *legislation* and *not* as a system of ideas and beliefs. In this distinction he was no doubt influenced by Spinoza who, in his *Tractatus*, had described the laws of the Torah as the state law of a no longer existing Jewish state and therefore no longer in force. Mendelssohn maintains the exclusive legal and practical character of Torah but insists on its timeless validity. The Torah, which merely tells us what to do or what not to do and not what to think or to believe, gives the philosopher absolute freedom in the realm of thought and inquiry. The eternal verities need no revelation except that which has its source in the human mind.

This was a doubtful gain for the principle of theonomy without any guarantee that the human mind will not use its freedom to question the assumptions and legitimacy of the divinely revealed legislation. Mendelssohn, in all his sincere loyalty to Torah and *mitzvot*, is the model not of the Orthodox but of the "orthoprax" Jew who tries to keep his intellect and his religious observance in two watertight, non-intercommunicating departments. It is, of course, not true that the Torah does not require beliefs from us, that it has no dogmas. Mendelssohn himself has not been absolutely consistent in his assertion. But his ideology, which embodied much of the teachings of the medieval philosophers, suited his particular position, straddling European philosophy and Halakhah-controlled Jewish life. His was indeed a philosophy of transition leading to, but stopping at, the threshold of a new age.

KANT

The man whose philosophy heralded a true revolution in modern thought in general and in views of religion and revelation in particular was Immanuel Kant. After him, things would never be the same. His teachings, for better or worse, dominated Jewish thinking throughout the 19th century and beyond. Never before had the autonomy of ethics and anything that deserved the name of religion been asserted with such vigor and clarity. Not only were they autonomous, exclusive of external revelation, which was denied both as a fact and as a possibilty, but religion was limited to and identified with ethical conduct as dictated by human conscience alone, thus depriving the greater part of *mitzvot*, all that dealt with man's relations to God, of any meaning and value. The one-sided, over-rationalistic nature of Kant's Practical Reason and morality as a substitute for living religion was soon enough recognized, particularly by the Schleiermacher school and the romantic movement which sought to re-instate religious feeling, as the sole basis of religion. But this was of small value to the believers in historical revelations and religious systems based on them. This is not the place to describe the deep religious inspiration that is one of the mainsprings of the Kantian system of religion and ethics and its undiminished religious value and potency for those who cannot conceive of religion without a full commitment of man's rational faculties and his inborn conscience and sense of duty. All the more blatant is Kant's failure to give due recognition not only to the intuitive, affective and imaginative areas of the human psyche but to the role played by the historical religions and—by implication—by the acts of revelation and processes of tradition on which they are founded.

Quite apart from the overriding importance of Kant for the history of philosophy and for the philosophy of religion and our problem of autonomy versus heteronomy in particular, his influence on Jewish thinkers during the last century and a half has been decisive even where these went critically beyond their master's teachings. Essentially, the ideology of the Reform movement, with its rejection of ceremonial in favor of ethical religion, is based on Kant. The leaders of Reform, Geiger in particular, realized that this new conception of religion was diametrically opposed to what Judaism had meant in the past. They only lacked the philosophical consistency and clarity, and perhaps the courage (something which should not be held against them) to do away entirely, as a matter of principle and not of expediency, with Torah and *mitzvot*. There were others, however, who presented a Judaism in which Kant was forcibly joined with the traditional concept of Jewish religion and ethics. Such was the achievement of Moritz Lazarus, and, above all, of Hermann Cohen. While the latter, in his published writings, would not go beyond the essentially Kantian concept of the Religion of Reason identified by him with Judaism, in his old age and in his lectures to students of the *Berlin Hochschule für die Wissenschaft des Judentums*, he felt constrained to admit that certain basic concepts of the Torah could not be explained and rationalized and were "wonders and miracles." Shades of Nachmanides!

S. R. HIRSCH

Even S. R. Hirsch and S. D. Luzatto, who in the 19th century were the champions of heteronomy against the Kantian maelstrom of autonomy, would not go so far as to deny the existence of an inner autonomous revelation which was complementary to the theonomous one. Hirsch saw no need to differentiate between moral and purely religious duties. The philosophical fusion of all *mitzvot*, of the entire Torah, into a harmonious ethico-religious system is his great achievement. That some essential ingredients of Jewish reality escaped him and found no place in his monumental structure need not concern us here. His overemphasis on heteronomy, his constant appeal to the obedience of the *homo Judaeus* to the will of God, is more apparent than real, more declamatory than systematically dominant. He often enough gave due weight to the voice of God that speaks *out* of man even if in general he stresses that voice that speaks *to* him. We have already pointed out, in our discussion of Saadia, whom Hirsch follows in this respect, how precarious the somewhat artificial restrictions are which they impose on the human mind in its relation to revelation and tradition. But one must pay tribute to the courage of Hirsch for proclaiming a new religious humanism, the human element in the Jew and his Torah, as well as the universalist concern and validity of our Torah. Hirsch, not unlike Mendelssohn before him, had to fight a battle on two fronts: against the radicalism of Reform and assimilation and the obscurantism and ossification of the surviving past. He was no less a son of the 19th century, the ideals of which he shared, than a sincere and enthusiastic exponent of an integral traditional Judaism. He was much more successful than Mendelssohn in harmonizing these two tendencies, whatever limitations his historical position inevitably imposed on his system and ideology.

The weak spot in that system is its lack of historical thinking. The facts of revelation are strictly confined in time and place, and three and a half thousand years of Jewish history have no part to play in that revelation. Here lies the cause of the violent controversy between Hirsch on the one hand and Zechariah Frankel and the school of Positive-Historical Judaism on the other.* For the latter history mattered. In those millenia Sinaitic Revelation had its chance fully to deploy and develop, particularly in the Oral Law and Tradition contained in rabbinic literature. For Frankel

---

* For a critique of the underlying assumptions of the positive-historical position, see Walter S. Wurzburger's "The Oral Law and the Conservative Dilemma" in the Fall 1960 issue of TRADITION, pp. 82–88. The same article also shows how the Orthodox position can incorporate an awareness of historic processes.—Ed.

and his school this process of evolution continues and cannot be limited artificially. Hirsch, in his staunch belief in a once-and-for-all revelation, and in spite of what is called his "humanism," could only suspect heresy in the historical approach, an encroachment of the human element on what must be conceived as exclusively divine. But history should not be denied its meaning and value for the unfolding of truth and Torah, as a school in which the Jewish people—and humanity—learn to bring the potentialities of Sinai into more and more actuality. The yoke of the Kingdom of Heaven and that of *mitzvot*, and this is what theonomy—heteronomy means, is so much easier to accept and so much lighter to bear as the partnership of man with the Giver of Torah becomes evident.* This dynamic view of Torah, though it has been adumbrated in the Aggadah, is no doubt the most fruitful contribution which the 19th century has made to the solution of the problem of religious heteronomy, breaking to a large extent the vicious circle of the either-or which had made the issue so intractable. It shall not be denied that the historical evolutionary approach has its dogmatic difficulties and indeed dangers. But so had earlier attempts to find a compromise between autonomy and heteronomy.

FRANZ ROSENZWEIG

Before we sum up, a few sentences ought to be devoted to that great Jewish thinker and *Baal Teshuvah*, Franz Rosenzweig. This mind and soul of a giant was not only heir to the fullness of philosophical tradition, both Jewish and general, but also an outstanding example of the perplexities which beset the Jew in the 20th century. This pupil of Hermann Cohen and the neo-Kantian school had undergone that great transformation which set him on the road of return to the God of Abraham, Isaac and Jacob and away from the God of philosophers. Jewishness was for him not

---

* Man's creative role in the halakhic process is described in "Ish ha-Halakhah," the classic study by Rabbi Joseph B. Soloveitchik, *Talpioth*, 1944, pp. 651–735. Cf. also Rabbi Emanuel Rackman's "Israel and God, Reflections on their Encounter," *Judaism*, 1962, pp. 233–241 and "Truth and Wisdom: An Orthodox Approach," *Judaism*, 1961, pp. 148–50.—Ed.

ideology and thought processes but experiences, renewed and growing experiences. The European, the philosopher, and the poet in him demanded freedom of thought and action; the enthusiastic Jew, submission to God's Torah and His all-embracing, ubiquitous *Mitzvot*. For him, the acceptance of the yoke of *mitzvot* was a deadly serious matter, confronting him ever afresh with the need for a decision whether to keep this or that *mitzvah* or not. In the freedom of this decision, which was not always positive, he preserved his autonomy. Asked whether he was observing a certain *mitzvah* his answer might be: no, not yet. He had not only to be willing, but also to be able, morally and intellectually, to accept the *mitzvot* or any of them. He rejected the description of them as laws. Law demands unquestioning compliance. *Mitzvah*, for Rosenzweig, was a request, a demand, a direct personal approach. But man could do no more than was "humanly possible." Accepting the historical view of revelation, he believed that his own generation, as well that which went before, had a share in the God of Israel—according to its ability, conditioned by its particular historical circumstances and setting. As a Jew he felt himself a member of the Jewish community as well as a link in the chain of a tradition borne and passed on by preceding generations. While recognizing the compulsive element which lies in this double involvement, he nevertheless postulated for the individual a certain elbow room of autonomous freedom of decision. This intensely individualistic approach is open to many obvious objections. But it may still be a modus vivendi of sorts vis-à-vis a religious problem which confronts a certain type of modern Jew, a way which has the merit of keeping the doors open for many who wish to return and keep some attachment to Torah and *mitzvot* without having to accept the all or nothing alternatives which systems such as Hirsch's place before the perplexed but searching Jew of our time.

The foregoing survey—in many ways sketchy and inadequate—of one of the most pressing problems of religious man, of the Jew who loves and believes with all his heart and soul in the Torah, has led us through the four principal periods of our spiritual history: the biblical, the talmudical, the medieval-philosophical—

all abutting on this modern age. In all of these we found the
problem of theonomy either adumbrated or discussed with various
solutions or accommodations proffered or implied. Much of this
was ephemeral, conditioned by transient circumstances, but below
the surface there flowed a strong current of a conflict that is
perennial. Modern Jew, no less than his predecessors, must return
to the Bible and Talmud as the reservoir of living waters from
which to draw the elements of both question and answer. The
masters of the Middle Ages and their pupils not only brought
the clarity and articulation of philosophy to an age-old problem,
but it was their merit to have assured, once and for all, the legitimacy of the inquiring human mind facing what is superhuman
and supernatural. The age which we call modern has broadened
this intellectual freedom into the moral and social freedom of
man who is called to master and mold not only himself but also
his environment. We moderns have learned, as the logical result
of that new freedom, to see in history humanity's striving towards
its God-given goals and the dynamism of the human spirit to
which God has entrusted the unfolding and consummation of His
Revelation.

Modern times have more than any other age made man conscious of this hard-won inner freedom. But how is he to use it?
Some of us are only too eager to surrender it forthwith and to
accept freely and eagerly the shackles of theonomy, of the heteronomous way of thought and life as it is found in the self-
contained and timeless teachings of our masters, past or present.
Others, the great majority, have cast off the yoke and arbitrarily
break or fulfill God's law according to their hearts' desire. And
there are those who strive to find the inner balance and harmony
of the religious, God-serving man without having to jettison the
freedom that they feel is theirs, the judgment of the heart and of
the mind that makes them accept "every day anew" what was
commanded of old. They feel that they live in today's world, not
yesterday's or that of the day before, and as such have to shoulder
the Jewish man's burden. Theirs is the harder road but, in this
writer's opinion at least, the only one that is neither a cul-de-sac
nor one that leads into outer darkness but to the broad uplands
of a great future.

NOTES

1 See Dr. Grunfeld's Introduction to *Horeb*, p. LXXVII.
2 I Samuel, 15:22.
3 Ex. 24:7.
4 *Shabbat* 88a.
5 *Sifra*, Lev. 20:22.
6 See also Malbim to *Sifra*, i.e. and 11:44, 45.
7 Or, of "revelation" (Klatzkin, *Thesaurus IV*, p. 133; so also Rosenblatt in his translation of Saadia, p. 145); or, of "obedience" (Guttmann, *Die Philosophie des Judentums*, p. 80).
8 *Yoma* 67b and *Sifra*, Lev. 18:2; *Pesikta de'R. Kahana* (Buber, p. 40b) and parallels.
9 S. R. Hirsch, *Horeb*, 396–479, ed., Grunfeld, II, p. 279 ff.
10 *Kiddushin* 31a.
11 *Bava Kamma* 38a.
12 *Lifnim mishurat hadin* or *me'kadesh et atzmo b'mutar lo.*
13 Moritz Lazarus, *Ethik des Judentums*, I, p. 225 ff. and additional note no. 32.
14 J. Guttmann, *op. cit.*, p. 91.

BIBLIOGRAPHY

JULIUS GUTTMAN. *Die Philosophie des Judentums*, Munich, 1933, (Hebrew edition, Jerusalem, 5711; English edition, *Philosophies of Judaism*, Jewish Publication Society, Philadelphia, 1963).

ISAAC HEINEMANN. *Ta'amey Hamitzvot be-Sifrut Yisrael*, 1st vol., 3rd revised edition, Jerusalem, 5714, II; Jerusalem, 5715.

I. GRUNFELD. *Introduction to the English translation of S. R. Hirsch, Horeb*, I, London, 1962.

MAX WIENER. *Jüdische Religion im Zeitalter der Emanzipation*, Berlin, 1933

JOSEPH WOHLGEMUTH. *Das jüdische Religionsgesetz in jüdischer Beleuchtung*, II, Berlin, 1912, 1919.

JUDAISM CONFRONTS THE WORLD

JOSEPH B. SOLOVEITCHIK

*

Confrontation

ONE

1

THE BIBLICAL account of the creation of man portrays him at three progressive levels.

At the first level, he appears as a simple natural being. He is neither cognizant of his unique station in the cosmos nor burdened by the awareness of his paradoxical capability of being concurrently free and obedient, creative to the point of self-transcendence and submissive in a manner bordering on self-effacement. At this stage, natural man is irresponsive to the pressure of both the imperative from without and the "ought" from within—the inner call of his humanity surging *de profundis*—ממעמקים. For the norm either from within or from without addresses itself only to man who is sensitive to his own incongruity and tragic dilemma. The illusory happy-mindedness of natural man stands between him and the norm. Natural man, unaware of the element of tension prevailing between the human being and the environment of which he is an integral part, has no need to live a normative life and to find redemption in surrender to a higher moral will. His existence is unbounded, merging harmoniously with the general order of things and events. He is united with nature, moving straightforwards, with the beast and the fowl of the field, along an unbroken line of mechanical life-activities, never turning around, never glancing backwards, leading an existence which is neither fraught with contradiction nor perplexed by paradoxes, nor marred by fright.

וכל שיח השדה טרם יהיה בארץ וכל עשב השדה טרם יצמח... ואדם אין לעבד את האדמה. ואד יעלה מן הארץ והשקה את כל פני האדמה. וייצר ה׳ א׳ את האדם עפר מן האדמה ויפח באפיו נשמת חיים ויהי האדם לנפש חיה.
"And every plant of the field was not yet in the earth and every

herb of the field had not yet grown, . . . and there was no man
to till the ground. But there went up a mist from the earth and
watered the whole face of the ground. And the Lord God formed
the man of the dust of the ground and breathed into his nostrils
the breath of life and the man became a living soul" (Genesis
2:5–7).[1]

Man who was created out of the dust of the ground, enveloped
in a mist rising from the jungle, determined by biological immediacy and mechanical necessity, knows of no responsibility, no
opposition, no fear, and no dichotomy, and hence he is free from
carrying the load of humanity.

In a word, this man is a non-confronted being. He is neither
conscious of his assignment vis-à-vis something which is outside
of himself nor is he aware of his existential otherness as a being
summoned by his Maker to rise to tragic greatness.

2

When I refer to man at the level of naturalness, I have in mind
not the *Urmensch* of bygone times but modern man. I am speaking not in anthropological but typological categories. For non-
confronted man is to be found not only in the cave or the jungle
but also in the seats of learning and the halls of philosophers and
artists. Non-confrontation is not necessarily restricted to a primitive existence but applies to human existence at all times, no
matter how cultured and sophisticated. The *hêdoné*-oriented, egocentric person, the beauty-worshipper, committed to the goods
of sense and craving exclusively for boundless aesthetic experience,
the voluptuary, inventing needs in order to give himself the opportunity of continual gratification, the sybarite, constantly discovering new areas where pleasure is pursued and happiness found and
lost, leads a non-confronted existence. At this stage, the intellectual gesture is not the ultimate goal but a means to another end—
the attainment of unlimited aesthetic experience. Hence, non-
confronted man is prevented from finding himself and bounding
his existence as distinct and singular. He fails to realize his great
capacity for winning freedom from an unalterable natural order
and offering this very freedom as the great sacrifice to God, who

wills man to be free in order that he may commit himself unreservedly and forfeit his freedom.

Beauty, uncouth and unrefined but irresistible, seducing man
and contributing to his downfall, emerges in the Biblical arena
for the first time—according to the Midrash quoted by Nachmanides (Genesis 4:22)—in the person of Naamah (the name
signifies pleasantness), the sister of Tubal-Cain.

ומדרש אחר לרבותינו שהיא האשה היפה היא מאד שממנה טעו בני
האלהים והיא הנרמזת בפסוק ויראו בני האלהים את בנות האדם.

"Our sages offered another Midrashic interpretation, that
Naamah was the fairest of all women, who seduced the sons of
the mighty, and it is she who is referred to in the verse: 'and the
sons of the mighty saw the daughters of man that they were fair.'"
Her seductive charms captivated the sons of the mighty and led
to their appalling disregard for the central divine norm enjoining
man from reaching out for the fascinating and beautiful that does
not belong to him. The sons of the mighty yielded to the hedonic
urge and were unable to discipline their actions. They were a
non-confronted, non-normative group. They worshipped beauty
and succumbed to its overwhelming impact.

Naamah, the incarnation of unhallowed and unsublimated
beauty, is, for the Midrash, not so much an individual as an idea,
not only a real person but a symbol of unredeemed beauty. As
such, she appears in the Biblical drama in many disguises. At
times her name is Delilah, seducing Samson; at other times she
is called Tamar, corrupting a prince. She is cast in the role of a
princess or queen, inflicting untold harm upon a holy nation and
kingdom of priests whose king, the wisest of all men, abandoned
his wisdom when he encountered overpowering beauty. The Book
of Wisdom (Proverbs) portrays her as the anonymous woman
with an "impudent face" who "lieth in wait at every corner" and
the Aggadah—also cited here by Nachmanides—as the beautiful
queen of the demons tempting man and making him restless.

No less than their seductress, the sons of the mighty also represent a universal type. Non-confronted man—whether he be a
primitive caveman, the king depicted in *Ecclesiastes*, or a modern
counterpart—is dominated by two characteristics: he can deny

himself nothing, and he is aware of neither the indomitable opposition he is bound to meet in the form of a restrictive outside,
nor of the absurdity implied in man's faith that the beautiful is
a source of pleasure rather than one of frustration and disillusion-
ment. The aesthete of today, like the aesthete of old, is prisoner
of—no matter what her name—beauty unethicized and unre-
claimed from aboriginal immediacy. He enjoys a sense of oneness
with the natural scheme of events and occurrences and his transient successful performance encourages him to strive for the
absurd—an unopposed and uncontradicted hedonic *modus
existentiae.*

ויטע ה' א' גן בעדן מקדם וישם שם את האדם אשר יצר. ויצמח ה' א'
מן האדמה כל עץ נחמד למראה וטוב למאכל ועץ החיים בתוך הגן ועץ
הדעת טוב ורע.

"And the Lord God planted a garden eastward in Eden and there
he put the man whom He had formed. And out of the ground the
Lord God caused to grow every tree that is desirable to the sight
and good for food; the tree of life in the midst of the garden and
the tree of knowledge of good and evil" (Genesis 2:8–9).[2]

Man depicted in these verses is hedonically-minded and pleasure-
seeking, having at his disposal a multitude of possibilities of sense-
gratification. Before him stretches a vast garden with an almost
endless variety of trees desirable and good, tempting, fascinating,
and exciting the boundless fantasy with their glamorous colors.

3

At the second level, natural man, moving straightforwards,
comes suddenly to a stop, turns around, and casts, as an outsider,
a contemplative gaze upon his environment. Even the most abandoned voluptuary becomes disillusioned like the king of Ecclesiastes and finds himself encountering something wholly other than
his own self, an outside that defines and challenges him. At this
very moment, the separation of man from cosmic immediacy,
from the uniformity and simplicity which he had shared with
nature, takes place. He discovers an awesome and mysterious
domain of things and events which is independent of and disobe-

dient to him, an objective order limiting the exercise of his power and offering opposition to him. In the wake of this discovery, he discovers himself. Once self-discovery is accomplished, and a new I-awareness of an existence which is limited and opposed by a non-I outside emerges, something new is born—namely, the divine norm. "ויצו ה' א' על האדם", "And the Lord God commanded the man." With the birth of the norm, man becomes aware of his singularly human existence which expresses itself in the dichotomous experience of being unfree, restricted, imperfect and unredeemed, and, at the same time, being potentially powerful, great, and exalted, uniquely endowed, capable of rising far above his environment in response to the divine moral challenge. Man attains his unique identity when, after having been enlightened by God that he is not only a committed but also a free person, endowed with power to implement his commitment, he grasps the incommensurability of what he is and what he is destined to be, of the ויהי and יהי.

God, in answer to Moses' inquiry, gave His name as אהי' אשר אהי' —I am what I am. God is free from the contradiction between potentiality and actuality, ideal and reality. He is pure actuality, existence par excellence.[3] Man, however, is unable to state of himself אהיה אשר אהיה since his real existence always falls short of the ideal which his Maker set up for him as the great objective. This tragic schism reflects, in a paradoxical fashion, human distinctiveness and grandeur.

Simultaneously with man's realization of his inner incongruity and complete alienation from his environment, the human tragic destiny begins to unfold. Man, in his encounter with an objective world and in his assumption of the role of a subject who asks questions about something hitherto simple, forfeits his sense of serenity and peace. He is no longer happy, he begins to examine his station in this world and he finds himself suddenly assailed by perplexity and fear, and especially loneliness. ויאמר ה' א' לא טוב היות האדם לבדו "And the Lord God said: 'It is not good that the man should be alone.'" The I-experience is a passional one and real man is born amid the pains of confrontation with an "angry" environment of which he had previously been an integral part.

Confronted man is called upon to choose either of two alternatives:

1) To play an active role as a subject-knower, utilizing his great endowment, the intellect, and trying to gain supremacy over the objective order. However, this performance is fraught with difficulty because knowledge is gained only through conflict, and the intellectual performance is an act of conquest.[4] The order of things and events, in spite of its intrinsic knowability and rationality, does not always respond to human inquiry and quite often rejects all pleas for a cooperative relationship. The subject-knower must contest a knowable object, subdue it, and make it yield its cognitive contents.[5]

2) Man may despair, succumb to the overpowering pressure of the objective outside and end in mute resignation, failing to discharge his duty as an intellectual being, and thus dissolving an intelligent existence into an absurd nightmare.

Of course, the Torah commanded man to choose the first alternative, to exercise his authority as an intelligent being whose task consists in engaging the objective order in a cognitive contest. We have always rejected the nirvana of inaction because the flight from confrontation is an admission of the bankruptcy of man. When man became alienated from nature and found himself alone, confronted by everything outside of him, God brought the "animal of the field and every fowl of the heaven unto the man to see what he would call it . . . and the man gave name to all the beasts and the fowl of the heaven and to every animal of the field."

וייצר ה' א' מן האדמה כל חית השדה ואת כל עוף השמים ויבא אל האדם
לראות מה יקרא לו... ויקרא האדם שמות לכל הבהמה ולעוף השמים
ולכל חית השדה.

Man no longer marched straightforwards with the brutes of the field and the forest. He made an about-face and confronted them as an intelligent being remote from and eager to examine and classify them. God encouraged him to engage in the most miraculous of all human gestures—the cognitive. Confronted Adam responded gladly because he already realized that he was no longer a part of nature but an outsider, a singular being, endowed with intelligence. In his new role, he became aware of his loneliness and isolation from the entire creation. ‏ולאדם לא מצא עזר כנגדו‎. "And for the man [God] had not found a helpmeet opposite him." As a lonely being, Adam discovered his great capacity for facing and dominating the non-human order.[6]

4

The Book of Genesis, after describing the four rivers which flow from the Garden of Eden, offers us a new account of the placing of Adam in this garden.

‏ויקח ה' א' את האדם וינחהו בגן עדן לעבדה ולשמרה.‎ "And the Lord God took the man and placed him in the Garden of Eden to cultivate it and to keep it." This sentence in Genesis 2:15 is almost a verbatim repetition of Genesis 2:8, yet the accounts differ in two respects.

First, in the second account, the Bible uses a verb denoting action preceding the placing of man in the Garden of Eden— "And God *took* (‏ויקח‎) the man and placed him"—whereas in the previous account, the verb "he placed", ‏וישם‎, is not accompanied by any preliminary action on the part of the Almighty. The expression ‏ויקח‎ does not occur in the first account. Second, there is no mention in the previous account of any assignment given to man while this account does specify that man was charged with the task of cultivating and keeping the garden.

The reason for these variations lies in the fact that the two accounts are related to two different men. The first story, as we have previously indicated, is of non-confronted man carried by the mighty tide of a uniform, simple, non-reflective life, who was placed in the Garden of Eden for one purpose only—to pursue pleasure, to enjoy the fruit of the trees without toil, to live in ignorance of his human destiny, to encounter no problem and to be concerned with no obligation. As we stated previously, non-confronted man is a non-normative being. The second story is of confronted man who began to appraise critically his position vis-à-vis his environment and found his existential experience too complex to be equated with the simplicity and non-directedness of the natural life-stream. This man, as a subject-knower facing

an almost impenetrable objective order, was dislocated by God
from his position of naturalness and harmonious being and placed
in a new existential realm, that of confronted existence. Confronted man is a displaced person. Having been taken out of a
state of complacency and optimistic naivete, he finds the intimate
relationship between him and the order of facticity ending in
tension and conflict. The verb ויקח signifies that God removed
man from one dimension and thrust him into another—that of
confronted existence. At this phase, man, estranged from nature,
fully aware of his grand and tragic destiny, became the recipient
of the first norm—"ויצו ה' א' על האדם". "And the Lord God commanded the man." The divine imperative burst forth out of infinity and overpowered finite man.

Alas, not always does creative man respond readily to the divine
normative summons which forms the very core of his new existential status as a confronted being. All too often, the motivating
force in creative man is not the divine mandate entrusted to him
and which must be implemented in full at both levels, the cognitive and the normative, but a demonic urge for power. By fulfilling
an incomplete task, modern creative man falls back to a non-
confronted, natural existence to which normative pressure is alien.
The reason for the failure of confronted man to play his role fully
lies in the fact that, while the cognitive gesture gives man mastery
and a sense of success, the normative gesture requires of man surrender. At this juncture, man of today commits the error which
his ancestor, Adam of old, committed by lending an attentive ear
to the demonic whisper, "Ye shall be as God, knowing good and
evil."

5

There is, however, a third level which man, if he is longing for
self-fulfillment, must ascend. At this level, man finds himself confronted again. Only this time it is not the confrontation of a
subject who gazes, with a sense of superiority, at the object beneath
him, but of two equal subjects, both lonely in their otherness and

uniqueness, both opposed and rejected by an objective order, both craving for companionship. This confrontation is reciprocal, not unilateral. This time the two confronters stand alongside each other, each admitting the existence of the other. An aloof existence is transformed into a together-existence.

ויאמר ה' א' לא טוב היות האדם לבדו אעשה לו עזר כנגדו... ויבן
ה' א' את הצלע אשר לקח מן האדם לאשה ויבאה אל האדם.

"And the Lord God said, It is not good that the man should be alone. I will make a helpmeet opposite him . . . And the Lord God made the rib which He had taken from the man into a woman and brought her unto man" (Genesis 2:18, 22). God created Eve, another human being. Two individuals, lonely and helpless in their solitude, meet, and the first community is formed.

The community can only be born, however, through an act of communication. After gazing at each other in silence and defiance, the two individuals involved in a unique encounter begin to communicate with each other. Out of the mist of muteness the miraculous word rises and shines forth. Adam suddenly begins to talk—ויאמר האדם—"And the man said." He addresses himself to Eve, and with his opening remark, two fenced-in and isolated human existences open up, and they both ecstatically break through to each other.

The word is a paradoxical instrument of communication and contains an inner contradiction. On the one hand, the word is the medium of expressing agreement and concurrence, of reaching mutual understanding, organizing cooperative effort, and uniting action. On the other hand, the word is also the means of manifesting distinctness, emphasizing incongruity, and underlining separateness. The word brings out not only what is common in two existences but the singularity and uniqueness of each existence as well. It emphasizes not only common problems, aspirations, and concerns, but also uniquely individual questions, cares, and anxieties which assail each person. Our sages, in explaining the graphic difference between the open and closed *mem,* spoke of מאמר פתוח and מאמר סתום—the enigmatic and the clear or distinct phrase. They felt that the word at times enlightens, at times, confounds;

at times, elucidates, and at other times, emphasizes the unintelligible and unknowable.

When Adam addressed himself to Eve, employing the word as the means of communication, he certainly told her not only what united them but also what separated them. Eve was both enlightened and perplexed, assured and troubled by his word. For, in all personal unions such as marriage, friendship, or comradeship, however strong the bonds uniting two individuals, the *modi existentiae* remain totally unique and hence, incongruous, at both levels, the ontological and the experiential. The hope of finding a personal existential equation of two human beings is rooted in the dangerous and false notion that human existences are abstract magnitudes subject to the simple mathematical processes. This error lies at the root of the philosophies of the corporate state and of mechanistic behaviorism. In fact, the closer two individuals get to know each other, the more aware they become of the metaphysical distance separating them. Each one exists in a singular manner, completely absorbed in his individual awareness which is egocentric and exclusive. The sun of existence rises with the birth of one's self-awareness and sets with its termination. It is beyond the experiential power of an individual to visualize an existence preceding or following his.

It is paradoxical yet nonetheless true that each human being lives both in an existential community, surrounded by friends, and in a state of existential loneliness and tension, confronted by strangers. In each to whom I relate as a human being, I find a friend, for we have many things in common, as well as a stranger, for each of us is unique and wholly other. This otherness stands in the way of complete mutual understanding. The gap of uniqueness is too wide to be bridged. Indeed, it is not a gap, it is an abyss. Of course, there prevails, quite often, a harmony of interests—economic, political, social—upon which two individuals focus their attention. However, two people glancing at the same object may continue to lead isolated, closed-in existences. Coordination of interests does not spell an existential union. We frequently engage in common enterprise and we prudently pursue common goals, travelling temporarily along parallel roads, yet our destinations are not the same. We are, in the words of the Torah, an

עֵזֶר —a helpmeet to each other, yet at the same time, we experience the state of כנגדו—we remain different and opposed to each other.[7] We think, feel and respond to events not in unison but singly, each one in his individual fashion. Man is a social being, yearning for a together-existence in which services are exchanged and experiences shared, and a lonely creature, shy and reticent, fearful of the intruding cynical glance of his next-door neighbor. In spite of our sociability and outer-directed nature, we remain strangers to each other. Our feelings of sympathy and love for our confronter are rooted in the surface personality and they do not reach into the inner recesses of our depth personality which never leaves its ontological seclusion and never becomes involved in a communal existence.

In a word, the greatness of man manifests itself in his dialectical approach to his confronter, in ambivalent acting toward his fellow-man, in giving friendship and hurling defiance, in relating himself to and, at the same time, retreating from him. In the dichotomy of עֵזֶר and כנגדו we find our triumph as well as our defeat.

Modern man, who did not meet to the fullest the challenge of confrontation on the second level, does not perform well at the level of personal confrontation either. He has forgotten how to master the difficult dialectical art of עֵזֶר כנגדו —of being one with and, at the same time, different from, his human confronter, of living in community and simultaneously in solitude. He has developed the habit of confronting his fellow man in a fashion similar to that which prevails at the level of subject-object relationship, seeking to dominate and subordinate him instead of communicating and communing with him. The wondrous personal confrontation of Adam and Eve is thus turned into an ugly attempt at depersonalization. Adam of today wants to appear as master-hero and to subject Eve to his rule and dominion, be it ideological, religious, economic, or political. As a matter of fact, the divine curse addressed to Eve after she sinned, והוא ימשל בך —"and he shall rule over thee," has found its fulfillment in our modern society. The warm personal relationship between two individuals has been supplanted by a formal subject-object relationship which manifests itself in a quest for power and supremacy.

TWO

1

We Jews have been burdened with a twofold task; we have to cope with the problem of a double confrontation. We think of ourselves as human beings, sharing the destiny of Adam in his general encounter with nature, and as members of a covenantal community which has preserved its identity under most unfavorable conditions, confronted by another faith community. We believe we are the bearers of a double charismatic load, that of the dignity of man, and that of the sanctity of the covenantal community. In this difficult role, we are summoned by God, who revealed himself at both the level of universal creation and that of the private covenant, to undertake a double mission—the universal human and the exclusive covenantal confrontation.

Like his forefather, Jacob—whose bitter nocturnal struggle with a mysterious antagonist is so dramatically portrayed in the Bible—the Jew of old was a doubly confronted being. The emancipated modern Jew, however, has been trying, for a long time, to do away with this twofold responsibility which weighs heavily upon him. The Westernized Jew maintains that it is impossible to engage in both confrontations, the universal and the convenantal, which, in his opinion, are mutually exclusive. It is, he argues, absurd to stand shoulder to shoulder with mankind preoccupied with the cognitive-technological gesture for the welfare of all, implementing the mandate granted to us by the Creator, and to make an about-face the next instant in order to confront our comrades as a distinct and separate community. Hence, the Western Jew concludes, we have to choose between these two encounters. We are either confronted human beings or confronted Jews. A double confrontation contains an inner contradiction.

What is characteristic of these single-confrontation philosophers is their optimistic and carefree disposition. Like natural Adam of old, who saw himself as part of his environment and was never assailed by a feeling of being existentially different, they see themselves as secure and fully integrated within general society. They do not raise any questions about the reasonableness and justification of such an optimistic attitude, nor do they try to discover in the deep recesses of their personality commitments which transcend mundane obligations to society.

The proponents of the single-confrontation philosophy (with the exception of some fringe groups) do not preach complete de-Judaization and unqualified assimilation. They also speak of Jewish identity (at least in a religious sense), of Jewish selfhood and the natural will for preservation of the Jewish community as a separate identity. As a matter of fact, quite often they speak with great zeal and warmth about the past and future role of Judaism in the advancement of mankind and its institutions. However, they completely fail to grasp the real nature and the full implications of a meaningful Jewish identity.

2

This failure rests upon two misconceptions of the nature of the faith community. First, the single-confrontation philosophy continues to speak of Jewish identity without realizing that this term can only be understood under the aspect of singularity and otherness. There is no identity without uniqueness. As there cannot be an equation between two individuals unless they are converted into abstractions, it is likewise absurd to speak of the commensurability of two faith communities which are individual entities.

The individuality of a faith community expresses itself in a threefold way. First, the divine imperatives and commandments to which a faith community is unreservedly committed must not be equated with the ritual and ethos of another community. Each faith community is engaged in a singular normative gesture reflecting the numinous nature of the act of faith itself, and it is futile to try to find common denominators. Particularly when we speak of the Jewish faith community, whose very essence is expressed in the halakhic performance which is a most individuating factor, any attempt to equate our identity with another is sheer absurdity. Second, the axiological awareness of each faith community is an exclusive one, for it believes—and this belief is indispensable to the survival of the community—that its system of

dogmas, doctrines, and values is best fitted for the attainment of
the ultimate good. Third, each faith community is unyielding in its
eschatological expectations. It perceives the events at the end of
time with exultant certainty, and expects man, by surrender of
selfish pettiness and by consecration to the great destiny of life, to
embrace the faith that this community has been preaching throughout the millenia. Standardization of practices, equalization of
dogmatic certitudes, and the waiving of eschatological claims spell
the end of the vibrant and great faith experience of any religious
community. It is as unique and enigmatic as the individual himself.

The second misconception of the single-confrontation philosophy consists in not realizing the compatibility of the two roles. If
the relationship of the non-Jewish to the Jewish world had con-
formed to the divine arrangement for one human being to meet the
other on the basis of equality, friendship and sympathy, the Jew
would have been able to become fully involved together with the
rest of humanity in the cosmic confrontation. His covenantal
uniqueness and his additional mandate to face another faith community as a member of a different community of the committed
would not have interfered in the least with his readiness to and
capability of joining the cultural enterprise of the rest of humanity.
There is no contradiction between coordinating our cultural activity with all men and at the same time confronting them as
members of another faith community. As a matter of fact even
within the non-Jewish society, each individual sees himself under
a double aspect: first, as a member of a cultural-creative community in which all are committed to a common goal and, at the
same time, as an individual living in seclusion and loneliness.

Unfortunately, however, non-Jewish society has confronted us
throughout the ages in a mood of defiance, as if we were part of
the subhuman objective order separated by an abyss from the
human, as if we had no capacity for thinking logically, loving
passionately, yearning deeply, aspiring and hoping. Of course, as
long as we were exposed to such a soulless, impersonal confrontation on the part of non-Jewish society, it was impossible for us
to participate to the fullest extent in the great universal creative

confrontation between man and the cosmic order. The limited role we played until modern times in the great cosmic confrontation was not of our choosing. Heaven knows that we never encouraged the cruel relationship which the world displayed toward us. We have always considered ourselves an inseparable part of humanity and we were ever ready to accept the divine challenge, מלאו את הארץ וכבשה "Fill the earth and subdue it," and the responsibility implicit in human existence. We have never proclaimed the philosophy of *contemptus* or *odium seculi*. We have steadily maintained that involvement in the creative scheme of things is mandatory.

Involvement with the rest of mankind in the cosmic confrontation does not, we must repeat, rule out the second personal confrontation of two faith communities, each aware of both what it shares with the other and what is singularly its own. In the same manner as Adam and Eve confronted and attempted to subdue a malicious scoffing nature and yet nevertheless encountered each other as two separate individuals cognizant of their incommensurability and uniqueness, so also two faith communities which coordinate their efforts when confronted by the cosmic order may face each other in the full knowledge of their distinctness and individuality.

We reject the theory of a single confrontation and instead insist upon the indispensability of the double confrontation. First, as we have mentioned previously, we, created in the image of God, are charged with responsibility for the great confrontation of man and the cosmos. We stand with civilized society shoulder to shoulder over against an order which defies us all. Second, as a charismatic faith community, we have to meet the challenge of confronting the general non-Jewish faith community. We are called upon to tell this community not only the story it already knows—that we are human beings, committed to the general welfare and progress of mankind, that we are interested in combatting disease, in alleviating human suffering, in protecting man's rights, in helping the needy, *et cetera*—but also what is still unknown to it, namely, our otherness as a metaphysical covenantal community.

3

It is self-evident that a confrontation of two faith communities is possible only if it is accompanied by a clear assurance that both parties will enjoy equal rights and full religious freedom. We shall resent any attempt on the part of the community of the many to engage us in a peculiar encounter in which our confronter will command us to take a position beneath him while placing himself not alongside of but above us. A democratic confrontation certainly does not demand that we submit to an attitude of self-righteousness taken by the community of the many which, while debating whether or not to "absolve" the community of the few of some mythical guilt, completely ignores its own historical responsibility for the suffering and martyrdom so frequently recorded in the annals of the history of the few, the weak, and the persecuted.

We are not ready for a meeting with another faith community in which we shall become an object of observation, judgment, and evaluation, even though the community of the many may then condescendingly display a sense of compassion with the community of the few and advise the many not to harm or persecute the few. Such an encounter would convert the personal Adam-Eve meeting into a hostile confrontation between a subject-knower and a knowable object. We do not intend to play the part of the object encountered by dominating man. Soliciting commiseration is incongruous with the character of a democratic confrontation. There should rather be insistence upon one's inalienable rights as a human being, created by God.

In light of this analysis, it would be reasonable to state that in any confrontation we must insist upon four basic conditions in order to safeguard our individuality and freedom of action.

First, we must state, in unequivocal terms, the following. We are a totally independent faith community. We do not revolve as a satellite in any orbit. Nor are we related to any other faith community as "brethren" even though "separated." People confuse two concepts when they speak of a common tradition uniting two faith communities such as the Christian and the Judaic. This term may have relevance if one looks upon a faith community under an historico-cultural aspect and interprets its relationship to another faith community in sociological, human categories describing the unfolding of the creative consciousness of man. Let us not forget that religious awareness manifests itself not only in a singular apocalyptic faith experience but in a mundane cultural experience as well. Religion is both a divine imperative which was foisted upon man from without and a new dimension of personal being which man discovers within himself. In a word, there is a cultural aspect to the faith experience which is, from a psychological viewpoint, the most integrating, inspiring, and uplifting spiritual force. Religious values, doctrines, and concepts may be and have been translated into cultural categories enjoyed and cherished even by secular man. All the references throughout the ages to universal religion, philosophical religion, et cetera, are related to the cultural aspect of the faith experience of which not only the community of believers but a pragmatic, utilitarian society avails itself as well. The cultural religious experience gives meaning and directedness to human existence and relates it to great ultimates, thus enhancing human dignity and worth even at a mundane level.

Viewing the relationship between Judaism and Christianity under this aspect, it is quite legitimate to speak of a cultural Judeo-Christian tradition for two reasons: First, Judaism as a culture has influenced, indeed, molded the ethico-philosophical Christian world-formula. The basic categories and premises of the latter were evolved in the cultural Judaic orbit. Second, our Western civilization has absorbed both Judaic and Christian elements. As a matter of fact, our Western heritage was shaped by a combination of three factors, the classical, Judaic, and Christian, and we could readily speak of a Judeo-Hellenistic-Christian tradition within the framework of our Western civilization. However, when we shift the focus from the dimension of culture to that of faith— where total unconditional commitment and involvement are necessary—the whole idea of a tradition of faiths and the continuum of revealed doctrines which are by their very nature incommensurate and related to different frames of reference is utterly absurd, unless one is ready to acquiesce in the Christian theological claim that Christianity has superseded Judaism.

As a faith individuality, the community of the few is endowed with intrinsic worth which must be viewed against its own metahistorical backdrop without relating to the framework of another faith community. For the mere appraisal of the worth of one community in terms of the service it has rendered to another community, no matter how great and important this service was, constitutes an infringement of the sovereignty and dignity of even the smallest of faith communities. When God created man and endowed him with individual dignity, He decreed that the onto-logical legitimacy and relevance of the individual human being is to be discovered not without but within the individual. He was created because God approved of him as an autonomous human being and not as an auxiliary being in the service of someone else. The ontological purposiveness of his existence is immanent in him. The same is true of a religious community, whose worth is not to be measured by external standards.

Therefore, any intimation, overt or covert, on the part of the community of the many that it is expected of the community of the few that it shed its uniqueness and cease existing because it has fulfilled its mission by paving the way for the community of the many, must be rejected as undemocratic and contravening the very idea of religious freedom. The small community has as much right to profess its faith in the ultimate certitude concerning the doctrinal worth of its world formula and to behold its own eschato-logical vision as does the community of the many. I do not deny the right of the community of the many to address itself to the community of the few in its own eschatological terms. However, building a practical program upon this right is hardly consonant with religious democracy and liberalism.

Second, the *logos*, the word, in which the multifarious religious experience is expressed does not lend itself to standardization or universalization. The word of faith reflects the intimate, the pri-vate, the paradoxically inexpressible cravings of the individual for and his linking up with his Maker. It reflects the numinous char-acter and the strangeness of the act of faith of a particular com-munity which is totally incomprehensible to the man of a different faith community. Hence, it is important that the religious or theo-logical *logos* should not be employed as the medium of communi-cation between two faith communities whose modes of expression are as unique as their apocalyptic experiences. The confrontation should occur not at a theological, but at a mundane human level. There, all of us speak the universal language of modern man. As a matter of fact, our common interests lie not in the realm of faith, but in that of the secular orders.[8] There, we all face a powerful antagonist, we all have to contend with a considerable number of matters of great concern. The relationship between two communities must be outer-directed and related to the secular orders with which men of faith come face to face. In the secular sphere, we may discuss positions to be taken, ideas to be evolved, and plans to be formulated. In these matters, religious communities may together recommend action to be developed and may seize the initiative to be implemented later by general society. However, our joint engagement in this kind of enterprise must not dull our sense of identity as a faith community. We must always remember that our singular commitment to God and our hope and indomitable will for survival are non-negotiable and non-rationalizable and are not subject to debate and argumentation. The great encounter between God and man is a wholly personal private affair incomprehensible to the outsider—even to a brother of the same faith community. The divine message is incommunicable since it defies all standardized media of information and all objective categories. If the powerful community of the many feels like remedying an embarrassing human situation or redressing an historic wrong, it should do so at the human ethical level. However, if the debate should revolve around matters of faith, then one of the confronters will be impelled to avail himself of the language of his opponent. This in itself would mean surrender of individuality and distinctiveness.

Third, we members of the community of the few should always act with tact and understanding and refrain from suggesting to the community of the many, which is both proud and prudent, changes in its ritual or emendations of its texts. If the genuinely liberal dignitaries of the faith community of the many deem some changes advisable, they will act in accordance with their convictions without any prompting on our part. It is not within our purview to advise or solicit. For it would be both impertinent and unwise for an outsider to intrude upon the most private sector of the human existential experience, namely, the way in which a

faith community expresses its relationship to God. Non-interference
with and non-involvement in something which is totally alien to
us is a *conditio sine qua non* for the furtherance of good-will and
mutual respect.

Fourth, we certainly have not been authorized by our history,
sanctified by the martyrdom of millions, to even hint to another
faith community that we are mentally ready to revise historical
attitudes, to trade favors pertaining to fundamental matters of
faith, and to reconcile "some" differences. Such a suggestion
would be nothing but a betrayal of our great tradition and heritage and would, furthermore, produce no practical benefits. Let us
not forget that the community of the many will not be satisfied
with half measures and compromises which are only indicative of
a feeling of insecurity and inner emptiness. We cannot command
the respect of our confronters by displaying a servile attitude.
Only a candid, frank, and unequivocal policy reflecting unconditional commitment to our God, a sense of dignity, pride and
inner joy in being what we are, believing with great passion in the
ultimate truthfulness of our views, praying fervently for and ex-
pecting confidently the fulfillment of our eschatological vision
when our faith will rise from particularity to universality, will
impress the peers of the other faith community among whom we
have both adversaries and friends. I hope and pray that our friends
in the community of the many will sustain their liberal convictions and humanitarian ideals by articulating their position on
the right of the community of the few to live, create, and worship
God in its own way, in freedom and with dignity.

4

Our representatives who meet with the spokesmen of the community of the many should be given instructions similar to those
enunciated by our patriarch Jacob when he sent his agents to meet
his brother Esau.

ויצו את הראשון לאמר כי יפגשך עשו אחי ושאלך לאמר למי אתה ואנה
תלך ולמי אלה לפניך ואמרת לעבדך ליעקב מנחה היא שלוחה לאדני לעשו
והנה גם הוא אחרינו. ויצו גם את השני גם את השלישי גם את כל ההלכים
אחרי העדרים לאמר כדבר הזה תדברון אל עשו במצאכם אתו׃

"And he commanded the foremost, saying: 'When Esau my brother meeteth thee and asketh thee, saying: whose art thou and whither goest thou? And whose are these before thee? Then thou shalt say they are thy servant Jacob's; it is a present sent unto my lord Esau, and behold he also is behind us.' And he commanded also the second, and the third and all that followed the droves, saying: 'in this manner shall ye speak unto Esau when ye find him' " (Genesis 32:18–20).

What was the nature of these instructions? Our approach to and relationship with the outside world has always been of an ambivalent character, intrinsically antithetic, bordering at times on the paradoxical. We relate ourselves to and at the same time withdraw from, we come close to and simultaneously retreat from the world of Esau. When the process of coming nearer and nearer is almost consummated, we immediately begin to retreat quickly into seclusion. We cooperate with the members of other faith communities in all fields of constructive human endeavor, but, simultaneously with our integration into the general social framework, we engage in a movement of recoil and retrace our steps. In a word, we belong to the human society and, at the same time, we feel as strangers and outsiders. We are rooted in the here and now reality as inhabitants of our globe, and yet we experience a sense of homelessness and loneliness as if we belonged somewhere else. We are both realists and dreamers, prudent and practical on the one hand, and visionaries and idealists on the other. We are indeed involved in the cultural endeavor and yet we are committed to another dimension of experience. Our first patriarch, Abraham, already introduced himself in the following words: "I am a stranger and sojourner with you"—"גר ותושב אנכי עמכם" Is it possible to be both—גר ותושב—at the same time? Is not this definition absurd since it contravenes the central principle of classical logic that no cognitive judgment may contain two mutually exclusive terms? And yet, the Jew of old defied this time-honored principle and did think of himself in contradictory terms. He knew well in what areas he could extend his full cooperation to his neighbors and act as a תושב, a resident, a sojourner, and at what point this gesture of cooperation and goodwill should terminate, and he must disengage as if he were a גר, a stranger.

He knew in what enterprise to participate to the best of his ability
and what offers and suggestions, however attractive and tempting,
to reject resolutely. He was aware of the issues on which he could
compromise, of the nature of the goods he could surrender, and
vice versa, of the principles which were not negotiable and the
spiritual goods which had to be defended at no matter what cost.
The boundary line between a finite idea and a principle nurtured
by infinity, transient possessions and eternal treasures, was clear
and precise. Jacob, in his instructions to his agents, laid down the
rule:

כי יפגשך עשו אחי ושאלך לאמר למי אתה ואנה תלך ולמי אלה לפניך ?

"When Esau my brother meeteth thee and asketh thee, saying:
whose art thou, and whither goest thou and whose are these before
thee?" My brother Esau, Jacob told his agents, will address to you
three questions. "Whose art thou?" To whom do you as a metaphysical being, as a soul, as a spiritual personality belong? "And
whither goest thou?" To whom is your historical destiny committed? To whom have you consecrated your future? What is
your ultimate goal, your final objective? Who is your God and
what is your way of life? These two inquiries are related to your
identity as members of a covenantal community. However, Jacob
continued, my brother Esau will also ask a third question: "And
whose are these before thee?" Are you ready to contribute your
talents, capabilities, and efforts toward the material and cultural
welfare of general society? Are you ready to present me with gifts,
oxen, goats, camels, and bulls? Are you willing to pay taxes, to
develop and industrialize the country? This third inquiry is focused
on temporal aspects of life. As regards the third question, Jacob
told his agents to answer in the positive. "It is a present unto my
lord, even unto Esau." Yes, we are determined to participate in
every civic, scientific, and political enterprise. We feel obligated
to enrich society with our creative talents and to be constructive
and useful citizens. Yet, pertaining to the first two questions—
whose art thou and whither goest thou—Jacob commanded his
representatives to reply in the negative, clearly and precisely, boldly
and courageously. He commanded them to tell Esau that their
soul, their personality, their metaphysical destiny, their spiritual
future and sacred commitments, belong exclusively to God and

His servant Jacob. "They are thy servant Jacob's," and no human power can succeed in severing the eternal bond between them and God.

This testament handed down to us by Jacob has become very relevant now in the year 1964. We find ourselves confronted again like Jacob of old, and our confronters are ready to address to us the identical three questions: "Whose art thou? Whither goest thou? Whose are these before thee?" A millennia-old history demands from us that we meet the challenge courageously and give the same answers with which Jacob entrusted his messengers several thousand years ago.

NOTES

1 While the Biblical phrase נפש חיה refers to natural man, Onkelos' רוח ממללא is related to a typologically more advanced stage.

2 Maimonides translated טוב ורע into aesthetic terms as "pleasing and displeasing". Paradisical man, violating the divine commandment by eating from the tree of knowledge, suspended the ethical and replaced it with the aesthetic experience (*Guide of the Perplexed*, I, 2).

3 See *Guide of the Perplexed*. I, 63.

4 The Latin *objectus* derived from *objicere*, to oppose, the German *Gegenstand*, denoting something standing opposite, the Hebrew חפץ having the connotation of something intensely desired but not always attainable, are quite indicative of the element of tension which is interwoven into the logical subject-knower knowable-object relationship.

5 The element of tension in the subject-object relationship is a result not of sin but of the incongruity of "attitudes" on the part of the confronters. The attitude of man is one of dominion while the "attitude" on the part of the objective order is one of irresponsiveness. The knowable object refuses to surrender to the subject-knower. The result of man's sin was not the emergence of tension and resistance—since this state of affairs prevailed even before man's expulsion from Paradise—but the change from tension to frustration, from a creative, successful performance to defeat. In imposing this metaphysical curse upon man, God decreed that the latter, in spite of all his glorious achievements, be finally defeated by death and ignorance. Judaism does not believe that man will ever succeed in his bold attempt to unravel the *mysterium magnum* of being and to control nature as a whole. The human cognitive and technological gestures, Judaism maintains, have a chance to succeed only in small sectors of reality. וקוץ ודרדר תצמיח לך—"Thorns and thistles shall it bring forth to thee."

6 See Nachmanides (Genesis 2:9).

7 The interpretation of כנגדו as "opposing" was accepted by our Talmudic sages. See *Yebamot*, 63a.

8 The term "secular orders" is used here in accordance with its popular semantics. For the man of faith, this term is a misnomer. God claims the whole, not a part of man, and whatever He established as an order within the scheme of creation is sacred.

ADDENDUM

[*The following statement formulated by Rabbi Soloveitchik appeared in the* Rabbinical Council Record *for February, 1966.*]

ON INTERFAITH RELATIONSHIPS

The Jewish religious tradition expresses itself in a fusion of universalism and singularism. On the one hand, Jews are vitally concerned with the problems affecting the common destiny of man. We consider ourselves members of the universal community charged with the responsibility of promoting progress in all fields, economic, social, scientific, and ethical. As such, we are opposed to a philosophy of isolationism or esoterism which would see the Jews living in a culturally closed society.

On the other hand, we are a distinctive faith community with a unique commitment, singular relationship to God and a specific way of life. We must never confuse our role as the bearers of a particular commitment and destiny with our role as members of the family of man.

In the areas of universal concern, we welcome an exchange of ideas and impressions. Communication among the various communities will greatly contribute towards mutual understanding and will enhance and deepen our knowledge of those universal aspects of man which are relevant to all of us.

In the area of faith, religious law, doctrine, and ritual, Jews have throughout the ages been a community guided exclusively by distinctive concerns, ideals, and commitments. Our love of and dedication to God are personal and bespeak an intimate relationship which must not be debated with others whose relationship to God has been moulded by different historical events and in different terms. *Discussion will in no way enhance or hallow these emotions.*

We are, therefore, opposed to any public debate, dialogue or symposium concerning the doctrinal, dogmatic or ritual aspects of our faith vis à vis "similar" aspects of another faith community. We believe in and are committed to our Maker in a specific manner and we will not question, defend, offer apologies, analyze or rationalize our faith in dialogues centered about these "private" topics which express our personal relationship to the God of Israel. We assume that members of other faith communities will feel similarly about their individual religious commitment.

We would deem it improper to enter into dialogues on such topics as:

Judaic monotheism and the Christian idea of Trinity; The Messianic idea in Judaism and Christianity; The Jewish attitude on Jesus; The concept of the Covenant in Judaism and Christianity; The Eucharist mass and Jewish prayer service; The Holy Ghost and prophetic inspiration; Isaiah and Christianity; The Priest and the Rabbi; Sacrifice and the Eucharist; The Church and the Synagogue—their sanctity and metaphysical nature, etc.

There cannot be mutual understanding concerning these topics, *for Jew and Christian will employ different categories and move within incommensurate frames of reference and evaluation.*

When, however, we move from the private world of faith to the public world of humanitarian and cultural endeavors, communication among the various faith communities is desirable and even essential. We are ready to enter into dialogue on such topics as War and Peace, Poverty, Freedom, Man's Moral Values, The Threat of Secularism, Technology and Human Values, Civil Rights, etc., which revolve about religious spiritual aspects of our civilization. Discussion within these areas will, of course, be within the framework of our religious outlooks and terminology.

Jewish rabbis and Christian clergymen cannot discuss sociocultural and moral problems as sociologists, historians or cultural ethicists in agnostic or secularist categories. As men of God, our thoughts, feelings, perceptions and terminology bear the imprint of a religious world outlook. We define ideas in religious categories and we express our feelings in a peculiar language which quite often is incomprehensible to the secularist. In discussions we apply

the religious yardstick and the religious idiom. We evaluate man
as the bearer of God's Likeness. We define morality as an act of
Imitatio Dei, etc. In a word, even our dialogue at a socio-
humanitarian level must inevitably be grounded in universal religious categories and values. However, these categories and values,
even though religious in nature and biblical in origin, represent the
universal and public—not the individual and private—in religion.

To repeat, we are ready to discuss universal religious problems.
We will resist any attempt to debate our private individual
commitment.

ELIEZER BERKOVITS

*

An Integrated
Jewish World View

I

IT IS with a sense of intellectual discomfort that one approaches the theme of this article. It is deeply embarrassing that in our time it is still necessary to discuss the relationship between *limudei kodesh* (religious studies) and *limudei chol* (secular studies) with a view to justifying their integration within a wholesome and complete form of Jewish education. There are still many individuals as well as substantial groups who, in the name of Judaism, question the religious propriety of teaching Jewish youth secular subjects. Grudgingly, they put up with the prevailing situation in Jewish Day Schools, in which secular subjects are taught side by side with religious ones, but they object to higher forms of secular studies at colleges and universities. One must count it among the frustrating anachronisms of our days that in *yeshivot* in this country as well as in the State of Israel, teachers and students often violently reject the idea of a higher professional secular education as being contrary to Jewish religious faith and piety. I know of a young man, studying at one of the great *yeshivot* in Eretz Israel, who wrote to his younger brother in this country advising him to throw all his secular books out and to concentrate on nothing else but his talmudic studies. The reason given for such a radical suggestion was: let *Goyim* be physicians; for a Jew there is nothing else but the study of Torah. The young man overlooked, of course, the fact that even in the famous *Cherem* (interdict) that the *Rashba* and his *Bet Din* invoked for the duration of fifty years against any one who in their congregations would read "in the books of the Greeks," one finds the following exception: "We have excluded from our interdict the science of medicine even though it is based on nature; for the Torah gave the physician permission to heal." *

It should not be difficult to show, even halakhically, that the same exception applies to all other scientific disciplines, which are *lekuchot min ha-teva*, based upon the study of nature, and whose pursuit is no less essential for the maintenance of life than that of medicine itself. Needless to say that in the present state of the close interrelation of all branches of science, the science of medicine is inconceivable without the sciences of physics, chemistry, biology, zoology, and many more. One cannot pursue any scientific discipline effectively without having scientists carrying out research in numerous related areas. But it is not our intention to discuss the question from its halakhic angle. We believe that the *Halakhah* in this case has been decided by life itself, not in the sense that life, as so often, ignoring *Halakhah*, has gone past it; but there are certain fundamental requirements of life which *Halakhah* cannot ignore and without whose adequate satisfaction *Halakhah* itself becomes impossible. The living example of the State of Israel offers the most compelling proof of our point. It is inconceivable that the Jewish people could exist in the State of Israel for a single day without effective mastery of those sciences which form the foundation of present day civilization! Since it is the intention of the Torah that there be a people of the Torah, living in the land of Israel, it must also be the intention of the Torah that Jews be physicians, engineers, physicists, mathematicians, men of creative search and practical application in every field of human endeavor, without whose knowledge and skill no nation can survive. This is obvious in our own days, and the situation was undoubtedly the same whenever Israel lived as a people in its own land. Agriculture, commerce, industry, national administration and defense, whether on an advanced modern level or during the periods of the First or Second Temple, have always required education and training in those disciplines called *limudei chol* (secular studies). The very existence of the State of Israel demonstrates that the raising of the question of permissibility of

* והוצאנו מכלל גזרתנו חכמת הרפואות אע״פ שהיא לקוחה מן הטבע לפי
שהתורה נתנה רשות לרופא לרפאות. תשובות הרשב״א סי׳ תט״ו.

secular studies, as if a question of *Halakhah* were involved, is one of the sickly manifestations of the *Galut* mentality. Only in the Diaspora could the fantastic idea have arisen that scientific knowledge and education was only for the Gentiles, whereas a Jew should occupy himself only with the Torah. When one views the matter from the perspective of the life interest of the Jewish people in its historic normalcy, the idea of limiting Jewish education to the "four cubits of the law," to the exclusion of all secular and worldly knowledge, vanishes in its own meaninglessness.

In the well-known letter which he addressed to the rabbis of Marseilles, Maimonides complains that our ancestors "did not occupy themselves with learning the arts of war and conquest." Speaking of this mistake, Maimonides continues: "This is what caused the loss of our Kingdom, the destruction of our sanctuary, the length of our exile, and brought us to our present condition. Our fathers have sinned, but they are no more." [1] If one tried to express the thought of Maimonides in the form of a general principle, one would have to say that the neglect of any branch of learning which is essential for the survival of the Jewish people is an anti-religious act, directed against Judaism itself. In this sense, the pursuit of scientific inquiry and the acquisition of scientific techniques, upon the application of which the survival of the Jewish nation in a Jewish land depends, is not only to be tolerated but must be considered a religious demand that emanates from the very intention and purpose of the Torah itself.

I I

While, in our opinion, there is no question of *Halakhah* involved in the issue before us, we are certainly confronted with a question of ideological consistency. The problem may be felt most intimately in the realm of Jewish education. It is a fact that in Jewish primary and secondary schools, as well as at higher institutes of learning, at Jewish colleges and universities, in this country as well as in the State of Israel, our educational effort is divided into two branches, one secular, the other sacred. Most of the time, there is hardly any connection between the two. Each stands under its own independent authority. Our youth is being educated in the intellectual climate of two worlds that do not recognize each other. But can the two worlds ignore each other in the heart and in the mind of the student, too? There can be no education without an educational philosophy, and consistency is the main requirement of such a philosophy. This, of course, means that all subjects must conform to the basic educational purpose: the educational goal must be reflected in the teaching of all the subjects. Such an educational philosophy may only be conceived on the basis of a philosophy of Judaism which in the name of Judaism itself is able to formulate a world-view within which the sacred and the secular become harmonized in a more fundamental unity.

We believe that in classical Jewish thought there is a rich treasure of relevant material which may guide us in formulating such a comprehensive Jewish view. For the sake of illustration we shall choose some significant ideas from the works of some of the great teachers in Israel.

There is, at least, one concept which has specific importance in relationship to knowledge in general no less than in relationship to the study of the Torah itself; it is the concept of truth. Without truth, there is no Torah; without truth, there is no knowledge of any kind. The question of truth may be asked epistemologically; it may also be asked ontologically. One may inquire about the means by which we reach the knowledge of truth; and one may investigate the essential nature of truth, its contents. Concerning the epistemological question, Saadia Gaon, in the introduction to his *Emunot ve'Deot*, maintains that there are three sources for the knowledge of truth: sense perception, immediate rational insight, and inference by means of logical necessity. There is, however, also a further source of knowledge, i.e., reliable tradition. Our acceptance of the Torah is based on such tradition. It is noteworthy that, in the name of Jewish monotheism, Saadia Gaon most determinedly rejects skepticism regarding the original three sources of knowledge. Since our acceptance of the Torah depends on a *Haggadah Ne'emenet* (reliable tradition), the question cannot be avoided: How does a tradition become reliable? Saadia Gaon's answer is that, like any other knowledge, tradition too must be validated by the three basic sources of truth. If sense

perception is not to be trusted, then *Ma-amad Sinai* itself could
be no witness to *Matan Torah;* if reason is not to be relied upon,
we should of course not be able to grasp the contents and meaning of the Torah either. Thus, Saadia concludes that the validity
of the *Haggadah Ne'emenet* is established "by reason of the fact
that it is based upon the knowledge of the senses as well as that
of reason . . ."

For Saadia Gaon, the epistemological question, "how do we
know?," is solved in a comprehensive manner. For him, there
is no two-fold epistemology, one for matters sacred and another
one for matters secular. All truth must ultimately be validated
by sense perception and by reason. In this respect, the concerns
of Judaism and of the sciences are identical. One may, of course,
disagree with Saadia and see in the act of revelation a way of
reaching the truth which is essentially religious and different
from other sources of knowledge. Such indeed, was the position
adopted by Yehudah Halevi. However, the difference would only
apply to those to whom revelation is actually granted. Undoubtedly, our acceptance of the Torah is based on *Ma-amad
Sinai.* But we know *Ma-amad Sinai* not by means of revelation
but by what Saadia calls *Haggadah Ne'emenet.* Thus we are
back to the question: How does tradition become *Ne'emenet?*
How is it to be validated? One need not accept Saadia's epistemol-
olgy, but one cannot escape his conclusion that the question
can only be answered within a general theory of knowledge
within which no distinction can be made between secular and
sacred. Such a comprehensive theory of knowledge is a religious
necessity. Without it, the floodgates are opened for *Emunot
Tefeilot* (superstitions) of all kinds, which are bound to distort
and to degrade genuine religion. Without due respect for a
sound theory of knowledge, even the famous leap of faith may
be a form of tumbling into darkness and futility. This is the
ultimate significance of Halevi's repeated statement: God forbid
that there should be anything in the Torah which is contrary
to reason. For the sake of religion itself, religion dare not ignore
those requirements for the validation of truth to which all human
inquiry is subject. Truth, as such, is a religious value.

I I I

As to the ontological character of truth, the actual nature of the object of knowledge for which it stands, differences in the importance between the various disciplines of knowledge are obvious. The statement that last winter saw more snow in Chicago than any other winter in the past twenty-five years may be true, but it is far less exciting than that in the beginning God created heaven and earth. No doubt, from the point of view of the value and significance of the truth taught, there is ample room for distinguishing between knowledge and knowledge. Nevertheless, there are also such among the teachers of Israel who, on the strength of the truth contents of the various disciplines of knowledge, were able to recognize a harmonious pattern between them, subserving a superior concept of unity. The outstanding one among these men was, of course, Maimonides. According to him, the purpose of man on this earth is to know God, and the goal of Judaism is to lead men to the knowledge of God. This knowledge Maimonides identifies with the knowledge of the supreme truth. But how can one reach it? How can one reach God, how can one know Him? As is well known, according to Maimonides, the essence of God remains forever unknown to human nature. Man can know God only from His deeds and from His handiwork. Since it is man's purpose on earth to know God, he must search in His works for Him. Only from the knowledge of the creation can one know the Creator. He lays down, therefore, the rule: "It is thus necessary to examine all things according to their essence, to infer from every species such true and well established propositions as may assist us in the solution of metaphysical problems (without which the knowledge of God is impossible)." The truth in Nature points to the supreme truth which is above Nature. Thus, in order to know God, one must be familiar with the natural sciences. These, however, are based on certain auxiliary disciplines like mathematics and logic. Maimonides has occasion to declare: ". . . he who wishes to attain to human perfection must therefore first study Logic, next the various branches of Mathematics in their proper order, then Physics, (i.e., the sciences of nature), and lastly Metaphysics." [2] Even the commandment "Thou shalt love the Eternal One, thy God, with all your heart . . ." (Deuteronomy 6:5) he explains in the light of this thought. Only a person who understands the nature of the universe and is able to meditate on God's wisdom revealed in it is capable of loving God with all his heart.[3] One may see in Maimonides the most extreme proponent of the concept of unity. Truth is one because all reality is one—the creation of the one God. All knowledge and all wisdom leads to the knowledge of the One. In the realm of truth, there is no distinction between the secular and the sacred. Truth is, as the Talmud teaches, "the seal of the Holy One, Blessed be He"; all truth leads man to its source, to God.

It is worth noting that even Bachyah ibn Pakuda, whose *Chovot Halevavot* is highly valued in the *yeshivot* as a work of *Mussar*, adopts a position very similar to that of Maimonides. As he states in the *Shaar ha-Bechinah* of his work, it is through our meditations that we come to appreciate "the manifestations of God's wisdom in all created things . . . For all wisdom is one; even though its signs vary among the things created, in its foundation and essence it is all one. . ."[4] There is a certain intellectual boldness in this concept of the essential unity of all knowledge which derives from our knowledge of the universe and which in its various partial manifestations adds up to the one divine truth. Because of that, Bachyah declares it to be man's duty to study God's creation in order to come nearer to His wisdom. In another passage, elaborating the idea further, he practically develops a plan for the scientific study of nature, inspired by the purely religious motivation of coming closer to God.[5]

It may be difficult to accept the extreme rationalistic position of Maimonides. Yet, he and Bachyah ibn Pakuda have prepared the ground for us for a religious approach to a scientific investigation of all reality and to the evaluation of the truth which it may reveal. The basic principle is that this world is God's world: and all truth has its source in God. The laws of nature are God's laws; and the wisdom in the creation is of His wisdom. The truth revealed in God's creation and the truth revealed in the Torah are akin to each other—both have their origin in the same *emet ha-elyonah* (higher truth), to use the terminology of

Maimonides. Trying to establish that it is man's duty to study the nature of all creation in order to understand God's wisdom, Bachyah quotes the words of the Talmud: "Had the Torah not been given to Israel, we could have learned modesty from the cat, chastity from the dove, conduct from the rooster, and respect for the property of others from the ant." [6] According to him, the saying shows that in the opinion of the teachers of the Talmud one may find Torah in the wisdom revealed in creation, too.[7] In this sense, Maimonides occasionally emphasizes that Nature and Torah emanate from the same source.

Before concluding this part of our discussion, we should like to refer to the views of another one among the thinkers and teachers in Israel, to those of the Maharal of Prague. The Maharal would, of course, not accept the opinion that "all wisdom is one." He recognizes a difference in essence between knowledge grasped by the human intellect as the result of human endeavor and the knowledge that comes from God in the form of revelation. The truth of God is inaccessible to man unless it be revealed to him in God's Torah. Nevertheless, he considers it a religious duty, incumbent on every Jew, to occupy himself with the study of those man-made disciplines of knowledge which try to penetrate the nature of reality in order to understand the existence of the universe. He finds a basis for his contention in the well-known saying of the Talmud: "Rabbi Joshua, son of Levi, said in the name of Bar Kappara: 'He who knows how to calculate the turn of the seasons and the motions of the planets but does not do it, concerning him the verse (Isaiah 5:12) says: But they regard not the work of the Eternal One, neither have they considered the operation of His hands.'" [8] Rabbi Shemuel Bar Nachmani even adds that to make the astronomical computations of the motions of the planets is a commandment of the Torah, which he derives from the words of the Bible: "This is your wisdom and understanding in the sight of the peoples" (Deuteronomy 4:6). The originality of the Maharal's interpretation consists in seeing clearly that this statement of the Talmud should not be limited to the study of astronomy alone, but that it applies to every type of human knowledge that investigates God's creation. This, of course, is supported by the verse from Isaiah, which serves as the justification of the original talmudic opinion, "But they regard not the work of the Eternal One, neither have they considered the operation of His hands." In keeping with the wider meaning of this verse, a man should not only meditate on the revolutions of the planets, but is obligated to penetrate to the understanding of all works of the Creator. Thus, the Maharal sums up his position in the following words: "From this we may learn that a man ought to study everything that will enable him to understand the essential nature of the world. One is obligated to do so, for everything is God's work. One should understand it all and through it recognize one's Creator." [9]

I V

We have then before us a classical tradition of Jewish thought which in our own days may serve as a guide in the development of a Jewish-religious world view that will embrace the whole of reality and relate all human knowledge to the focal point of all Jewish-religious affirmation and commitment. We are, of course, still far removed from such a comprehensive and consistent world outlook. The foremost intellectual challenge of our generation is to create such an outlook. It is inconceivable that Jews as individuals and Israel as a nation should make practical use of successful scientific inquiry and yet the genius of Judaism should ignore the fact that the same scientific disciplines carry within themselves certain insights or suggestions which are not without consequences for religious faith and for that ultimate truth which is God's own seal. In the continuous progress of human knowledge and search for the truth, there is ever present a spiritual challenge that influences the life of man in its entirety.

A scientific understanding of certain biological processes, interpretations of laws of nature, understanding of historical developments may often tend to undermine some forms of established religious faith. How is Judaism to meet such challenges? By closing its eyes to them? The problems will not go away. The attitude of *bitul* (disdain) toward all secular knowledge, which is propagated in certain circles, is based on a profound ignorance of what it despises and rejects, and, far from being a solution,

is in fact a sign of spiritual incompetence and intellectual cow-
ardice. If religious faith is joined by intellectual honesty, it must
find the idea intolerable that the truth of religion should be
defended by such questionable means. What is worse, a truth
so defended must itself become questionable. If any branch of
human knowledge poses problems to religion, then out of religious
zeal for the truth and for the truthfulness of religion itself, religion must take such problems seriously. It will meet such problems effectively, or at least live with them comfortably, not by
rejecting secular knowledge but by mastering it. All so-called
limudei chol (secular studies) are now within the scope of Jewish
religious interest and concern. Without a knowledge of their
premises, methods, and conclusions by the believing Jewish
scholar, a comprehensive world-view of Judaism cannot be formulated.

We have yet to mention the most hazardous consequences
of failure to integrate the entire scope of human knowledge
within the framework of religious concern. Earlier in this paper
reference was made to a talmudic passage which quotes the verse,
". . . for this is your wisdom and your understanding in the sight
of the peoples." Most medieval Jewish philosophers justify on
the basis of this text the demand for a rationally meaningful
interpretation of Judaism. Maimonides quotes the verse to prove
that even *chukim* are to be interpreted rationally.[10] It would be
wrong to assume that the intention of the afore-mentioned was
to impress the nations with the wisdom of the Torah. Their
efforts in interpreting Judaism were inward-directed to the Jews,
not outward, to the Gentiles. What they wanted to emphasize
was that the truth of Judaism has universal meaning and applicability. Because of its universal import, it must be, at least potentially, recognizable as "your wisdom and your understanding in
the sight of the peoples." It must retain its ability to deal meaningfully with the human situation, even though only the Jew
must accept its pronouncements as binding for himself. The
moment Judaism loses this ability, it ceases being a world religion
and degenerates into a marginal sect. This is, however, the danger
if we turn away from the challenges of the various branches of
human knowledge. A negative attitude to secular knowledge will

not only prevent "the peoples" seeing in Judaism "our wisdom
and our understanding," it will not even allow the Jewish people
to gain a comprehensive Jewish world-view. It may lose us the
historic Israel and replace it by a handful of life-estranged Jewish
sectarians.

There are, of course, dangers and pitfalls along the path we
are required to take. One must tread carefully. But the challenge
must not be ignored and the responsibility cannot be avoided.
Our faith that Judaism's intellectual and spiritual power is equal
to the task is identical with our faith in the inexhaustible vitality
and eternal validity of the Torah. In the world of the spirit one
need not fear the truth; as to the untruth, one must know it in
order to defeat it. Undoubtedly, the secular disciplines have often
served as the basis of philosophies of life which the believing
Jew cannot accept. Yet, when confronted with the challenge of
overcoming an untruth, one must understand the source of its
strength. The powerful grip which secular and materialistic
philosophies hold on the modern mind is in large measure due to
the truth-contents of the sciences upon which they are based.
But it must be remembered that each of the sciences may bring
into relief only one facet of the truth. Philosophy often turns
the partial aspect of the truth that is uncovered in some domain
of knowledge into an absolute concept; this is the lie in such
philosophy. The power of such a lie is at times frightening, but
only because it has its root in something that is valid and true.
In order to meet the spiritual challenge of our age, we must learn
how to evaluate the truth-contents of all those disciplines of
human knowledge that to a large extent determine the fabric of
our civilization. Only thus shall we succeed in formulating that
comprehensive Jewish world-view which will make manifest the
truth-contents in the various disciplines of human knowledge as
a part of a meaningful pattern which derives its validity and value
from the truth which is of God.

Through the ages, Jews, as individuals, have greatly enriched
every branch of human knowledge. However, in most of the separate branches a partial truth reigns supreme. And man's world
is broken. With the rise of the State of Israel the Jewish people
have been called by historic necessity to become a people of sci-

ence in the widest sense of the word. For the religious Jew who
sees in Israel's return to the land of its fathers the hand of God,
the historic necessity for scientific effectiveness imposed by the
return becomes a divine command. We interpret it as meaning
that Israel, the people of the Torah, must acquire mastery in the
realm of worldly knowledge and weave the pattern of unity between fact and value, faith and reality, between life and Torah.
"For this is your wisdom and your understanding in the sight
of the peoples."

NOTES

1 *Igrot ha-Rambam, Teshuvot le-Chakhmei Kehal Ir Marselia.*
2 Maimonides, *Guide for the Perplexed*, Part 1, Chapter 34.
3 *Ibid.*, Part 3, Chapter 28.
4 Bachyah ibn Pakuda, *Chovot Halevavot, Shaar ha-Bechinah*, Chapter 1.
5 *Ibid.*, Chapter 3.
6 *Eruvin* 100b.
7 Bachyah ibn Pakuda, *op. cit.*, Chapter 2.
8 *Shabbat* 75a.
9 *Kitvei Maharal mi-Prague*, Mossad Harav Kook, vol. 2, pp. 119–120.
10 Maimonides, *op. cit.*, Part 3, Chapter 31.

WALTER S. WURZBURGER

*

Alienation and Exile

MUCH OF current thought revolves around the theme of alienation and estrangement—and for good reason. Modern
man has been subjected to a relentless process of de-personaliza-
tion in the pressure chambers of a technological society whose
operations are geared to mass production and standardization.
Moreover, to cope with the increasing complexities of an age of
automation, ever more delicate methods of control have become
necessary. Thus, paradoxically, the more control man is capable
of exerting over his environment, the more he himself becomes
enmeshed in a network of pressures and forces against which he
feels too helpless to assert himself. Far from enhancing man's
sense of importance, his spectacular technological triumphs have
actually left him with a gnawing feeling of impotence. Dimin-
ished in stature, he has become a thing rather than a person, an
object rather than a subject, an "it" rather than a "thou."

Small wonder, then, that in artistic, literary, and philosophical
circles, one encounters steadily mounting anxiety over the fate of
the individual. It has even been said that the entire existentialist
movement basically represents a reaction to the sense of alienation that has gripped modern man.[1]

Concern over self-alienation is by no means a monopoly of the
intellectual elite. Revolutionary mass movements such as social-
ism and communism derive much of their messianic fervor from
the Marxian ideology which held out to the disillusioned and
frustrated the promise not only of a redistribution of worldly
goods but of a society in which the light of a new social gospel
would redeem mankind from the blight of alienation.

Other influential thinkers—both secular and religious—have indicated with varying effectiveness that our deep-rooted anxieties
arise not merely out of social or economic dislocations, but out
of the spiritual condition of modern man. In this view, self-

estrangement is but the final phase in the long process of disintegration that began with the erosion of the religious basis which previously provided the foundation for our structure of values and ideals.

I

Yet, not all thinkers share this aversion to alienation. Far from it! In many quarters a certain degree of alienation, instead of being viewed with apprehension as a major threat to man's humanity, is actually enthusiastically welcomed as a prerequisite to all genuine creativity. Considerable admiration is evoked by the alienated "outsider's" inability to feel at home in the universe; for it is this state of mind which is credited with inducing the creative tensions which in turn lead to the quest for moral, spiritual, and intellectual advancement. It was perhaps on the basis of such an orientation that Matthew Arnold went so far as to define religion as a "criticism of life." What ultimately seems to matter in this view is not so much the possession of a positive, definite set of values or commitments, but rather the sense of estrangement and detachment which is engendered by a religious approach to life. Religion is singularly equipped to fulfill this function because it calls for the ability to participate in the affairs of the world with a certain sense of detachment, to immerse oneself in the currents of time while retaining the consciousness of an eternal destiny.

Any ideology that makes a virtue out of not belonging is likely to hold a special attraction for the modern Jew who even in the open and democratic society—with all its assimilationist pressures and blandishments—sooner or later experiences the frustrations of being a rejected outsider. But when one views the world from the perspective of the "outsider," the sting of bitterness is removed from the feeling of not belonging. An apparent curse is converted into a genuine blessing. Being Jewish—or better, "not being a Goy"—becomes equated with the ideal of an authentic human life: not to feel at home in the universe, because one deliberately elects to remain a foreigner, refusing to become completely naturalized into a full-fledged citizen of the world. Jewishness, in the phrase of Ben Halpern, becomes "a ticket of admission to the community of alienated intellectuals." [2]

Religiously non-observant Jewish intellectuals are especially prone to identify Judaism with such a negative stance. Intellectuals, in general, tend to be wary of specific, positive commitments. Because of their proclivity for detachment, they gravitate towards an orientation of alienation, which, as Daniel Bell put it, "guards one against being submerged in any cause, or accepting any particular embodiment of community as final." [3] And it is to be expected that the Jewish intellectual will project this mentality into his approach to Judaism. Understandably, his views on Judaism are bound to reflect the predilections of those who constitutionally seem to shy away from all positive commitments. Since the intellectual finds it so much easier to identify with a Judaism that is couched in negative terms, he is apt to define Jewishness as the negation of the pretensions of other cultures and religions.

For leading intellectuals such as Milton Konvitz,[4] Leslie Fiedler, Arthur Cohen [5] Will Herberg,[6] it is the consciousness of living in Galut that emerges as the defining characteristic of being Jewish. To be a Jew is synonymous with being in exile—the experience of a sense of alienation. In the words of Leslie Fiedler, once Jews become "insiders, they cease to be Jews." [7]

There can be no doubt that the ever-present awareness of living in a state of *Galut* (both physically and metaphysically!) has etched itself deeply in the consciousness of the genuine Jewish personality. For that matter, the yearning for Messianic redemption constitutes a vital ingredient of our religious faith. We must not forget this—even at the moment of gaiety and merriment. This is why at a wedding ceremony, a note of sadness is injected: a glass is broken to remind us that no joy can be complete until the dawn of the ultimate redemption.[8] Since only *"then* shall our mouths be filled with laughter" (Psalms 126:2), it is not permissible nowadays to abandon oneself completely to unrestricted hilarity. When one is conscious of the intrinsic limitations of Galut existence, one cannot embrace a philosophy of "letting go" and lose oneself completely in momentary thrills. He who yearns for ultimate redemption cannot help but maintain a cer-

tain degree of reserve and detachment—no matter how intense
the satisfaction of the moment and however rewarding the immediate task at hand may be.

One must not, however, jump to the conclusion that Judaism
basically represents a principle of negation. Purely negative definitions of Jewishness, as Aharon Lichtenstein has already noted,[9]
amount to distortions of the true character of the Jewish people.
It is, of course, true that since the days of Abraham it has been
the historic destiny of the Jew to function as the *Ivri*—the one
who stands in opposition to the rest of the world.[10] Indeed, a good
case could be made that the Jew personified what Tillich has
called the "Protestant Principle"—the refusal to absolutize the
relative. Throughout history Jews have protested against the various idolatries that have held sway. Time and again they have
refused to worship at the shrine of the false gods. Yet, notwithstanding some prominent theologians, there is more to Judaism
than the struggle against mythology. The smashing of idols—
and for that matter, the breaking of a glass—does not exhaust
the meaning of Jewish existence. Judaism is not merely a classic
exercise in cool, critical detachment; there is ample provision for
the romance of whole-hearted "engagement" with the fiery ideals
of Torah. Torah was never conceived purely as a criticism of life;
it was life itself! Those who concentrate purely on the critical
function of Judaism without considering adequately its positive
commitments end up not with a picture, but a caricature.

I I

One of the most interesting illustrations of the distortions that
are bound to occur whenever Judaism is forced into a strait jacket
of purely negative thinking is provided by Ahad Ha'am's famous
description of the nature of Jewish ethics, which played such a
decisive role in the making of the modern Jewish mind. It was
largely due to the impact of this influential thinker that so many
Jews were prepared to repeat uncritically the Christian cliché
that Jewish ethics is one of justice and not of love. It must be
borne in mind that only very flimsy "evidence" is adduced by
Ahad Ha'am in support of his sweeping thesis that Jewish ethics

is based exclusively upon justice. His case rests on the fact that Hillel, in his classic formulation to a prospective convert, reduced the "essence" of Torah to a commentary on the maxim "Do not unto your neighbor what you would not have him do unto you."

For Ahad Ha'am, it is of crucial importance that Hillel did not express the golden rule in positive terms. Why could not Hillel simply have quoted the biblical verse "Love thy neighbor as thyself" (Leviticus 19:18)? Ahad Ha'am [11] concludes that Hillel was compelled to paraphrase the biblical verse in order to forestall misunderstanding on the part of the heathen. It had to be spelled out clearly that the Jewish interpretation of "Love thy neighbor as thyself" does not call for the cultivation of benevolence, kindness, or altruism. Love, so Ahad Ha'am contends, really does not figure in the Jewish scale of values. Insofar as Jewish ethical thinking is concerned, nothing but absolute justice truly matters.

It can readily be seen that this doctrine roughly represents the equivalent of the Kantian categorical imperative. As Max Scheler [12] and others have pointed out, the Kantian scheme is essentially not a positive formulation of ethical precepts or maxims, but rather a principle of criticism which can serve as a criterion for the *rejection* of certain attitudes or actions. The Kantian morality is not a system of *material* content, but a purely *formal* principle which enables us to deny the propriety of certain types of motivation.

It could be maintained with a high degree of plausibility that Ahad Ha'am's formulation—and for that matter many other positions which reflect preoccupation with purely negative aspects of Judaism—arises out of the matrix of Kantian rather than genuinely Jewish categories of thought. Otherwise, how would it have been possible for him to gloss over such a pivotal concept as *Chessed* (loving-kindness), which plays such a primary role in Jewish religious and ethical thought?" [13] In view of the continued emphasis upon love in both biblical and rabbinic literature, there is not the slightest shred of evidence to support the contention that, because of its preoccupation with absolute justice, Judaism is completely indifferent to the cultivation of altruistic sentiments. What has happened to such concepts as compassion and mercy which in rabbinic literature are defined as the tell-tale mark of the Jew? Are we not supposed to balance justice with mercy?

It is, of course, true that without the restraint of justice, the blind application of love can lead to morally disastrous consequences. But this merely indicates that we cannot dispense with justice as a *regulative* principle, not that justice is superior to love. Notwithstanding Ahad Ha'am, who spoke of the preference of Judaism for abstract principles, there is ample room within the Jewish ethical and religious scheme for personal sympathetic involvement in the fate of one's fellow-man. It is simply not correct to speak of Judaism as a cold, detached scheme that eliminates "subjective attitudes" because it is only concerned with the application of something "abstract and objective." Justice, to be sure, is essentially a negative concept; it rules out inequalities of treatment. But it is theoretically possible to devise rules of behavior which are equally bad for all parties concerned. Though satisfying the criterion of equality, they could hardly be termed just. Hence, even justice transcends considerations of equality. Moreover, it is highly questionable whether justice is the fundamental ethical concept. Kabbalistic doctrines (e.g., the primacy of *Chessed* over *Gevurah* in the order of *Sefirot*) could be cited to buttress Professor Tillich's contention that not justice, but love is primary and that justice must be defined in terms of the proper distribution of love.[14]

I I I

The claim that the "essence" of Judaism lies in the *negation* of all pretensions to finality [15] rather than in the affirmation of specific positive values may be buttressed by citing the *prima facie* kinship of this position with the world view of Maimonides. After all, Maimonides did not merely formulate a "negative theology" in his "theory of attributes," but even his ethical ideal of the "middle road" appears to be primarily an attempt to negate any form of extremism. At first sight, the advocacy of a middle course on the part of Maimonides strikes one as a sort of *caveat* prescribed by a detached sage who views with skepticism any manifestation of unbridled radicalism. Such counsel

of moderation is to be expected from the classical philosopher
who looks askance at the excesses of romanticism and warns us
not to go emotionally overboard in the pursuit of any specific
value. But, in reality, Maimonides is far from espousing a prudential morality of compromise. His views cannot be attributed
to the "outsider's" reluctance to become completely "engaged"
with any specific ideal or goal. Anyone who has read his moving
account of love for God which is couched in such passionate
terms [16] will be unable to label Maimonides a reserved, detached,
or even disillusioned philosopher who out of his disenchantment
put the brakes on any genuine emotional involvement. As a matter of fact, notwithstanding its obvious resemblance to the Aris-
totelean "golden mean," Maimonides' ideal of the "middle
road" [17] does not reflect so much the classic aversion to any form
of imbalance ("Nothing in excess") but a fundamental Jewish
religious ideal of striving to "walk in the ways of God." [18] In
the Maimonidean scheme, choosing the middle road ceases to
be an exercise in prudential morality; it becomes the fulfillment
of a most positive religious imperative: "the imitation of God."
It is to the extent that man succeeds in harmonizing polar values
that he emulates his Creator; for, according to rabbinic theology,
it was through the fusion of love and justice, mercy and righteousness, truth and peace, that God—both immanent and transcendent—created the universe. Thus the "middle of the road" approach
as espoused by Maimonides does not at all amount to a negation
of any specific value. What it does reflect is an awareness of the
need for creative tension between polar values. Conceived in this
fashion, the middle of the road is far from being a state of
equilibrium. It is a *road* in the fullest sense of the term calling
for dynamic movement and engaging man's total moral and intellectual resources.

It must be noted that this creative tension, which is so indispensable to all genuine human progress, need not be induced—as
so many modern intellectuals suggest—by a sense of alienation
and estrangement. As Maimonides seems to imply, creative tension may have its source in the spiritual restlessness which grips
those who experience a sense of genuine relatedness and commitment to God. Veering between polar values, at once drawn

to God in love and recoiling from Him in fear, the righteous have
ample cause for the restlessness which, as the Talmud asserts, is
their eternal lot.[19]

For a proper appraisal of Maimonides' position, it must also
be borne in mind that, with all his emphasis upon the essentially
negative character of all theology, the Guide concludes on a most
affirmative note. The ideal to which man is summoned calls not
merely for the purely intellectual endeavor to master the doctrine
of negative attributes. The knowledge that God is Wholly Other
—the very apex of the entire philosophical quest—must be counterbalanced by imitatio dei, the attempt to emulate the ways of
God in a relentless quest for loving-kindness, justice, and charity.
Lest the consciousness of God's utter transcendence give rise to
a sense of total alienation, man is bidden to pattern his conduct
after the divine "attributes of action," which enable him to "walk
in His ways."

IV

It may, of course, be argued that the very ideal of holiness
entails a sense of alienation from the world. The very concept of
kedushah (holiness) denotes "separation." In talmudic language, holiness implies geder ervah (the limitation imposed
upon the libido.) The contrast between natural inclinations and
holiness is stressed in Numbers 15:39, where we are admonished
to submit ourselves to the discipline of the mitzvot instead of
following the inclinations of our own "hearts and eyes."

Yet, we are not justified in concluding that holiness stands in
irreconcilable opposition to the natural. Within Judaism there
is no antithesis between nature and spirit, for both are religiously
neutral. It is for this reason that Judaism aims not at the suppression but the utilization of the natural in the service of the
Creator—the Author of both nature and spirit. The network of
the mitzvot provides a formula designed to enable man to fulfill
a supernatural but not un-natural vocation. Through the performance of the mitzvot, the domain of the mundane can be
hallowed and endowed with supernatural significance.

The attainment of this goal is by no means an easy task. It

unquestionably demands a good measure of self-control and discipline. But the further man advances in his spiritual quest, the less resistance he encounters. He may even reach the point where he can identify himself with the divine task, because Torah ceases to be merely imposed from without. It is at this stage that Torah truly becomes his own—part and parcel of his very personality. At this ideal level, man becomes really free; for he is fully "engaged" in Torah. He is no longer merely an object manipulated by all sources of internal or external pressures. He is a subject in the fullest sense of the term, actively molding his existence in keeping with a divine purpose. Thus, for the *Tzaddik*, in the Chabad scheme, all struggle has been overcome. He is completely liberated from the sway of forces that restrict his inner freedom. Or, as Rabbi Kook put it, man is truly his own "natural" self to the extent that he is suffused with the love of God.

It should be noted that the emphasis upon estrangement, aloofness, and detachment from the "world," which is so characteristic of modern Jewish thought, has largely been the result of thinkers who have "emancipated" themselves from the yoke of the *mitzvot*. Having stripped Judaism of all traditional practices and belief, they were left with only one facet of Jewish existence: the state of living in Galut. To be a Jew was to be different, different for the sake of being different. Accordingly, the Galut was no longer looked upon as a dismal blight. It became the highest type of Jewish existence, providing conditions where Judaism could shine in the brightest colors. It was felt that only the Galut could fully reveal the uniqueness of the Jewish people, a uniqueness which was defined in purely negative terms: a stance of critical non-conformity and alienation with respect to the "natural." [20] Thus, by a strange twist, the tragic necessity of the Galut was converted into a supreme religious virtue.

Obviously, this kind of orientation is incompatible with Halakhah-centered Jewish thought. How can the Galut be enthusiastically endorsed as the apex of Jewish spirituality, when so many vital areas of Halakhah are inoperative in the Diaspora? Galut dealt a crippling blow to Jewish religious life. Gone is the opportunity to practice *mitzvot ha-teluyot ba-aretz* (*mitzvot* which can be observed only in the land of Israel) and to fulfill the numerous laws that are applicable only under "normal" conditions, when the Jewish people settled in its natural habitat rallies around a central *Bet Hamikdash* (Temple) as the abode of the *Shekhinah*.

From the standpoint of Halakhah, the abnormal Galut existence is not a desideratum, but a serious handicap. To be sure, Jewish piety has been able to flourish even under such adverse conditions. By the same token, under "normal" conditions there loom certain dangers to the spiritual integrity of the Jew who may crave that "the house of Israel be like all the nations." The Jew possesses no natural immunity protecting him against the spiritual diseases that so frequently strike the *body politic* of all types of communities.

Twice in our history it became necessary for the Temple to be destroyed because the Jewish people was on the verge of completely perverting its religious ideals. But the resulting Galut was viewed as a *punishment*, not as the emergence of a "higher" or more rewarding form of spirituality. To overcome the alienation of the Galut (both in the physical and metaphysical sense) became the beckoning goal for the Jew. The plight of Galut was bearable only because there abided in the Jewish heart the hope for a more "natural" life, when to be a Jew will not mean to be an "outsider" but to be involved in temporal affairs and to be engaged with mundane matters in a society that bears witness to the Kingdom of God; in short, a world where the *Shekhinah* will no longer be in exile.

NOTES

1 F. H. Heinemann, *Existentialism and the Modern Predicament*, Harper Torchbooks, New York, 1953.

2 Ben Halpern, "A Theological Jew," *Jewish Frontier*, February 1964, p. 13.

3 Daniel Bell, The End of Ideology, N.Y., Macmillan, 1962, pp. 16, 17.

4 Milton R. Konvitz, "Zionism: Homecoming or Homelessness," *Judaism*, Summer 1956, pp. 204–211.

5 Arthur Cohen, *The Natural and The Supernatural Jew*, New York, 1962.

6 Will Herberg *Judaism and Modern Man*, New York, 1951, pp. 275–281.

7 *New York Times*, June 9, 1963.

8 *Berakhot* 31a; see *Tosafot ad loc.*

9 Aharon Lichtenstein, "The Jewish Fraternity," *Judaism*, Summer 1963, p. 279.

10 *Bereshit Rabbah* 42:13.

11 Ahad Ha'am, *Essays, Letters, Memoirs*, Oxford, 1946, pp. 130–137.

12 Max Scheler, *Der Formalismus in der Ethik und die Materiale Wertethik*, Halle, 1921.

13 See David S. Shapiro, "The Concept of Hessed in Judaism," *Yavneh Studies*, Fall 1962, pp. 27–45.

14 Paul Tillich, *Love, Power and Justice*, London, Oxford University Press, 1954.

15 For a striking illustration of this position see Leo Baeck's statement "Absence of the supporting crutch of dogma is in the very nature of Judaism" (*The Essence of Judaism*, p. 16). Equally revealing is the following passage: "The price Judaism paid for the possession of a philosophy was the sacrifice of certainty, of a formula of creed" (ibid., p. 12).

16 *Hilkhot Teshuvah* 10:6.

17 *Hilkhot Deot* 1:5.

18 My interpretation of Maimonides' "middle road" can in some measure be attributed to my recollection of a lecture delivered by Rabbi Soloveitchik in Detroit at the 1954 convention of the Rabbinical Council of America. As I recall, Rabbi Soloveitchik demonstrated how the Kabbalistic doctrine of the *Sefirot* with its emphasis upon the synthesis of *Chessed* and *Gevurah*, or of *Netzach* and *Hod*, which result in the emergence of *Tiferet* and *Yesod* respectively, parallels Maimonides' notion that the middle road is the road of God.

19 *Berakhot* 64a.

20 Thus, for Leo Baeck, "The special task of Judaism is to express . . . the ethical principle of the minority . . . it stands for the enduring protest of those . . . who assert their right to be different . . ." (*op. cit.*, p. 273). See also David Riesman's "A Philosophy for 'Minority' Living," *Individualism Reconsidered*, New York, 1955, pp. 48–66.

SIMEON L. GUTERMAN

*

Separation of Religion and State

THE HISTORICAL PERSPECTIVE

THE PROBLEM of "Church and State" is a legacy of the
breakup of the Roman Empire. It was at that time that
Christianity first rent the unity of the state by proclaiming a distinction between the duties due God and those due Caesar, and
that Constantine annexed the church to the Empire. The two
powers thus linked but not merged have made uneasy partners
ever since, with each one contending for superiority. Their struggle has filled the annals of history with sound and fury, but it
has also been responsible for political liberty and representative
institutions in the modern world. Only in the last century and
a half, however, has the problem of the relations of Church and
State received solutions compatible with democratic and liberal
ideas.

Israel's recent history highlights the question of Church-State
relations in that country. The First Amendment to the Constitution of the United States, adopted in 1791, declares that "Con-
gress shall make no law respecting an establishment of religion
or prohibiting the free exercise thereof." The French Separation
Law of 1905 states: "The Republic neither recognizes nor salaries
nor subventions any cult." Is the American or the French legislation applicable to Israel? Are the American, French, and Israeli
situations comparable? These questions have been debated with
great feeling in recent times and it is as a contribution to their
clarification that this paper is presented. The approach will be
historical, and the point of view and criterion that of the modern
principle of religious liberty.

I

The United States and France offer a sharp contrast in regard to the real purposes of Separation. In one country Separation was designed to promote religion, in the other it has been accused of aiming at the dechristianization of France. Separation is simply a device to regularize a pre-existent social situation, not an end in itself. The term "Separation" has had a flexible meaning in the United States. Not until 1917 did Massachusetts adopt an amendment to its constiution ending state aid to ecclesiastical establishments. In the 1920's there was still one state of the Union in which only Protestants might hold the highest offices. A regime of Separation of Church and State must recognize the underlying religious interests of the people or, if need be, their lack of religious interest. As Professor Holcombe puts it, "ours is a secular commonwealth in principle and a religious commonwealth in practice." There are no *a priori* reasons for favoring Separation over other arrangements independently of the social needs the system serves.

Similarly, Jurisdiction (a system in which one or several religious bodies are linked to the state) serves the purpose of formalizing or translating into political terms the basic religious needs of a community in which a majority of the people adhere to one church, and in which, for other reasons, a laissez-faire attitude would be regarded as socially harmful.

If Separation is suited to the United States, Jurisdiction seems to suit England and the Scandinavian countries. Separation is favorable to organized religion; Jurisdiction is favorable to unorganized, individual beliefs or disbelief. Hence in jurisdictionalist countries there exists freedom *from* religion as well as *of* religion. Privileges accorded by these countries to the established church or churches are *odiosa* as well as *favorabilia*, meaning that they impose responsibilities as well as confer rights.

In certain respects it has even been claimed that individual religious liberty is better protected in jurisdictional than in separationist countries. Ruffini, the distingushed Italian historian of religious liberty, writing in the first decade of the present century, makes this point with great force.

The Law of Guarantees of 1871 has not prevented a Jew, Luzzati, from becoming President of the Council of Ministers . . . In America, the character . . . Christian . . . Protestant makes it impossible . . . that a Catholic, let alone a Jew, should regard himself as capable of becoming president.

But contrast in the United States the inordinately powerful position given by New York State to the Catholic Church in 1895, unthinkable in Italy; so that the iron absolutist hierarchy of the Catholic Church is recognized and protected in the United States in such a manner as rigidly to exclude any democratic or representative velleity of the lay element . . . in a manner which has no parallel in the European states unless one goes back to the Middle Ages.

If public sentiment today had the same ideas about witchcraft as it had during the seventeenth century, severe laws against witchcraft could be expected in a separationist no less than in a jurisdictionalist country. There is no substitute for an enlightened public opinion under either system. But there is one advantage which a jurisdictionalist regime has from the point of view of religious minorities. This is in its commitment to the recognition of religious values. One may ask whether a proper concern with the religious needs of the Jewish Community would have deterred Switzerland, in which Church and State are separated, from outlawing *shechitah* by constitutional referendum in the 1890's. Switzerland divides her enmities. The Jesuit Order is still banned there, at least by law.

Anyone familiar with developments in France and Italy knows how much difficulty both countries have experienced in dealing with the Church-State problem. In both countries the overwhelming majority of the population belonged to the Roman Catholic Church. In both countries, a strong anti-clerical movement existed. Anti-clericalism of the Latin type embodies hostility to the influence of the Roman Catholic Church in particular. In Italy the government had no alternative, when the Law of Papal Guarantees was rejected by Pope Pius IX and his successors, but to act on the assumption that Church and State were separate. This led to a crop of evils which were only solved by the Lateran Treaty of 1929 which made the Roman Catholic Church the "official" church of the Italian people while recognizing the rights of other religious groups including the Jews. In spite of its Fascist genesis the treaty was made part of the Constitution of the new Italian Republic adopted after the war, indicating the value attached by Italian statesmen to a suitable relationship with the church of the majority of the Italian people.

France, after living under the Napoleonic Concordat since 1801, with some changes under the various regimes which succeeded one another, proceeded in 1905 to separate Church and State. Several considerations influenced French statesmen to take this step. There were political causes stemming from the opposition of some churchmen to the Third Republic as well as the involvement of several of the religious orders in the anti-republican campaign that accompanied the Dreyfus Case. There was also the idea of the Lay State which had been growing during the nineteenth century and which involved the triumph of the doctrine of State sovereignty with its accompaniment of the Concession Theory. This meant the subjection to State power, the sole *legal* power in society, of all religious associations. Only religious groups authorized by the government were permitted to remain in France; all others were expelled. A third motive was undoubtedly an anti-religious or at least a rationalistic attitude on the part of some of the promoters of the Separation Law. It will suffice to mention Combes and Briand.

The Separation Law of 1905 followed a diplomatic break with the Papacy. The disturbed situation created by this law in the relations between devout Catholics and the government was not conducive to a normal political life. This was demonstrated during and after the first World War by the restoration of diplomatic relations between France and the Papacy. The Law of Separation continued to regulate France's relations with the Church but with modifications or rather interpretations of some of its provisions calculated to allay criticism by the Church.

Germany in the decade of the 1870's was also in the throes of a Church-State conflict, the *Kulturkampf*. In Germany, however, the Catholic Church, though it represented majority sentiment in Bavaria and the southern parts, was a minority group in the Empire as a whole. In spite of these disadvantages the members of the Catholic Church in Germany forced Bismarck "to Canossa" and obliged the Iron Chancellor to revoke the May Laws of 1873 and 1874.

There is enough in the experience of the European nations to justify the following characterization of the basic problem of Church-State relations by Professor Holcombe:

But when Church and State are separated in deference to the principle of complete toleration, the sovereignty of the Church-State is divided between the two organizations. One, the state, retains political sovereignty; the other, the church, acquires the supreme power in purely spiritual affairs, unrestrained by civil laws. In the last analysis the authority of Church and State alike is what men believe it to be. The boundary between them cannot be determined once for all upon any universal, logical principle. It must be determined in each case by the conscience and will of the body of people directly concerned.

I I

I have compared the two systems of regulating the relations of the secular and the religious powers, known respectively as Separation and Jurisdiction, without particularizing further about either system. Separation and Jurisdiction can in actual practice, as well as in law, vary from one country to another. Jurisdiction, for example, may take the form of an Established Church, State Church, Dominant Church, or National Church which may in turn be Anglican, Lutheran, Calvinist, or Orthodox; sometimes it assumes the form of a single Establishment, and at other times that of Parity of confessions. But all these arrangements have this in common, that they are capable of being harmonized with the modern conception of religious liberty.

What we now need is a definition or characterization of religious liberty which will make clear in historical terms the meaning of the modern achievement of freedom of conscience and of worship. The methods by which the goal was approached also reveal a few paradoxes worthy of note and expose a fallacy or two that have had the sanction of long acceptance.

Liberty of *conscience* has been described as a negative right because a man's conscience is inaccessible to human scrutiny.

But it has its positive side in that it protects the individual from being forced to perform acts or rites against his religious convictions. Violation of freedom of conscience is sometimes charged to certain laws such as Sunday observance or those providing for the reading of verses from the Bible in the public schools. The same criticism has been made of the oath required in courts of law, but this has been met by the provision for the taking of an affirmation instead of the oath. Though freedom of the conscience may in strict principle be infringed in some of these instances, there is not much doubt that the principle is substantially recognized by the law of State and Nation.

Much more vital is freedom of *worship* or, as Europeans would call it, liberty of the cult. The recognition of the private cult accorded by Spain does not satisfy the modern requirement which calls for liberty of public worship. This right is recognized explicitly in the French law of 1905 which declares that "the Republic guarantees the free exercise of the cults, under the sole restrictions appended hereto in the interest of the public order." This freedom is now recognized in all democratic countries with some restrictions, as in Italy and elsewhere, in the name of "public order." Generally also this important form of religious liberty means not only the liberty of specified groups, but also of individuals. It is true that the freedom enjoyed in the United States is often regarded as partial and incomplete, as recent cases in Pennsylvania and Maryland have demonstrated, but to expect it to be perfect in the eyes of all men is to be blind to the complexities of human nature and society. Basically it is a question of more or less, not all or nothing.

With these criteria in mind it will be useful to review a few historic situations which offer a contrast to the modern systems based on the recognition of the principle of religious liberty. One relationship which involved the complete subordination of the Church to the State is known as "Caesaropapism" and prevailed in the later Roman Empire, in Charlemagne's day, and, under the name of "Byzantinism," was transmitted by the Eastern Roman Empire to Russia. Another relationship, called "theocracy," really the exercise of the *direct power* of the Pope over the temporal ruler, was realized under Innocent III and his immediate successors, but actually only achieved in a fully theocratic sense in the government of the Papal States. Neither of these conditions obviously suits a modern state nor satisfies the elementary requirements of political and religious liberty. It is true that Caesaropapism shades into modern regalism and may have logical ties with the legal union of Church and State or Jurisdiction; but logic, as suggested above, is no guide to politics or religion. It is also conceivable that theocracy could develop out of Jurisdiction, but the modern state is too strong and historically grounded in the Roman tradition for this development to take place.

In this connection we must also exclude the Roman Catholic conception of the relationship of religion and politics, even in the form of the *indirect* power of Church over State advocated by Aquinas, Bellarmin, and Suarez. It is based on a number of ideas —the Christian State, exclusive salvation, a theory of persecution inherited from St. Augustine, and a dogmatic system—not easily reconcilable with the modern democratic state, and lacking in Judaism. It must be noted in passing, however, that the Catholic Church in our day makes a distinction between *thesis* and *hypothesis*. In the thesis only a Christian State is supportable; under the hypothesis a schismatic or heretical establishment or even Separation is tolerable. In *principle* and philosophically, however, a Christian State, even heretical, is preferable to a secular State divorced from any religion.

The contrast between modern systems of regulating the relations of Church and State and the traditional order of Islam, in which temporal and religious functions were united in the Caliph, is striking. Authority in Islam, as a result, went unchecked by any other power. Yet since the system lacked a real legislative organ capable of introducing needed reforms, the progress that might have been secured by such an organ was lacking. Historic Islam has lacked a genuine State tradition. Its political system embodied the old oriental ethos with its emphasis on religion. (The modern State of Israel, contrariwise, not only represents the fulfillment of a religious ideal, but it incorporates the State and secular traditions of the Western peoples in its national life. It is the offspring of Rome as well as of Jerusalem, and its religious and secular institutions, though distinct, work together to give it a strength lacking in any of the Arab States.)

In reading our history and drawing lessons from it, we must avoid being victimized, however, by the theory of legal sovereignty —an invention of the lawyers which would subject all activities including religion to the will of the State. We must think of the State and Law, as Goodhart urges, in terms of obligations accepted by the citizen rather than of authority imposed by the State. Obligation has essentially religious roots. But even state authority must somehow be legitimized by religion. There is only one way of legitimizing authority—by sentiment; and religion is one form of such sentiment. It is public opinion, to recur to an earlier theme, that determines the limits between two such necessary institutions as State and Church (or Synagogue), not some meaningless formula that takes no account of political and social realities. Religion is a force that the State cannot ignore either by pretending that it does not exist or by attempting to subjugate it to its own purposes. History demonstrates that a healthy social organism is built on religious as well as more strictly political foundations, to mention only two factors of social life. If England escaped the ordeal of a social and poltical upheaval in the period following the French Revolution it was because of the action of Methodism and the new Evangelical Movement in diverting popular discontent into constructive legislative activity, as Halevy has demonstrated in his classic work on England in the Nineteenth Century.

The history of the modern movement of religious liberty conveys a sense of paradox extremely disturbing to those who would like to stretch history on a Procrustean bed. It may seem extraordinary to such people that Separation originated in fanaticism while Jurisdiction was the system advocated by the first promoters of religious freedom in Western Europe.

The Anabaptists, for example, advocated Separation of Church and State, but only as an alternative to an Anabaptist theocracy. Their ideas flowed into Holland where they mingled with and influenced those of English refugees fleeing from James I's Anglicanism. The Pilgrim Fathers brought from their stay in Scrooby,

Holland, a determination to hold to their own religious ways. If they could not impose them on the Anglican Church they were prepared to advocate Separation of Church and State in England. But when they reached Plymouth they established a complete theocracy in which freedom of dissent was suppressed. Out of the Reformation conflicts also emerged the Sozzini brothers, founders of the Unitarian movement, which is undoubtedly the first Christian denomination to uphold religious liberty for its own sake. But Faustus and his brother Laelius also advocated a union of Church and State and hoped to see genuine liberty realized under such a system rather than under a separate organization of the two. What a paradox, at least to Americans of the present day: fanatical Anabaptists advocating Separation, purely as a lesser evil but an evil just the same; while liberal Socinians defend Jurisdictionalism and oppose Separation, because the former was more likely to restrain fanaticism, promote comprehension, and protect religious liberty from the violence of sectaries!

But the tale is not done. The two diverse streams converged, the Socinian emphasis on religious freedom and the Anabaptist recourse to Separation, to produce the typical American solution, freedom of religion under Separation, in the colony of Rhode Island in 1636. Roger Williams had "imbibed" from the Dutch Arminians, the liberal element in the Calvinist church, the idea of a commonwealth in which the magistrates dealt only with civil matters and exercised no authority in religion, thus allowing complete freedom of conscience to all believers, even Jews, though at first the latter did not qualify for citizenship in Rhode Island. Driven out of Massachusetts for advocating such views, he founded Providence and lived to see Rhode Island receive a charter from Charles II in 1663. Roger Williams anticipates the Fathers of the Constitution and inaugurates that fusion of liberty and Separation which is typically American.

Just as Roger Williams inaugurated the American solution, a French thinker of the eighteenth century became the principal advocate of religious freedom in France. This was Voltaire, who was neither an orthodox churchman nor a democrat after the modern fashion. Paradoxically, he advocated toleration under a system in which Church and State were united. In a real sense

Voltaire represents the continental tradition and practice of Jurisdiction.

In the light of these developments it is not surprising that the theory of religious persecution, which was extremely long lived, has had some of its most ardent defenders among English freethinkers who, following in the footsteps of the medieval sceptic, the Emperor Frederic II, supported the crown and advocated the most rigorous control of religious belief by the State. Such was Thomas Hobbes who, in his *Leviathan* and other writings, worked out with marvelous logic a theory of sovereignty that left nothing outside the scope of State control. Such also were Hume and Bolingbroke. The contrast with John Locke is striking; for the latter, a devout churchman, advocated religious toleration as well as civil liberty and implied his readiness to accept Separation of Church and State if these fundamental freedoms were protected.

Lecky concludes that political and religious liberty in England was created by men of a definitely religious cast of mind while the champions of the same movement in France were sceptics, like Voltaire. It is worth noting that scepticism or "philosophy," as it was called in eighteenth century France, did not necessarily guarantee a commitment to religious liberty. Rousseau, for example, advocated a civic religion to be imposed on all citizens, and the disciples of the master sought to establish such a system during the French Revolution.

In brief, religious liberty has been advocated by religious men as well as by sceptics under a jurisdictional as well as a separationist system.

III

It is sometimes assumed that countries living under a system of Separation, like the United States, are free from the difficulties attending jurisdictional regimes. While there is no doubt that Separation is the only arrangement possible in the United States with its multiplicity of sects, it cannot be denied that problems of a serious nature beset the American system. These problems are a result of changing social and religious conditions which have altered the traditional relationships of religious denominations to one another and to governments of State and Nation. The Protestant groups, which at one time divided the religious loyalties of the American people, are now confronted by a competitor whose whole official outlook, political as well as social, is directly antithetical to all that Protestantism has stood for. In 1790 there were perhaps 30,000 Roman Catholics in the United States out of a total population of almost 4,000,000. By 1950 there were, by Catholic estimates, over 25,000,000 Roman Catholics out of a population of 150,000,000.

When one group with the solidarity of the Catholic Church becomes so numerous, the effect in a separationist, unlike a jurisdictionalist, country is that no adequate control or restraint on that Church exists other than that provided by public opinion. When the trusts toward the close of the nineteenth century threatened the freedom of economic life, public opinion was aroused; but it was the legislation enacted as a result of this popular feeling that placed a check upon the inordinate growth of business combinations. The effect of public opinion even within the membership of the Catholic Church in restraining the hierarchy has in the eyes of competent and impartial observers not thus far proved palpable. At the same time, as the examples in the following few paragraphs show, there is considerable influence exerted by the Catholic Church on legislation. Whether or not the community at large exercises pressure on the Church, there is little doubt that the hierarchy does exert great influence on legislators.

The New York State Law of 1895 is the crowning example of the special treatment of religious corporations, not in accord with common law rules, which the Catholic Church was able to secure. By this law a Roman Catholic Church is put in an entirely different legal category from a Protestant or Jewish Congregation: it is not subject to popular election of officers and trustees, and its members cease to have control of it after its establishment. The author recalls the interesting case of a non-Roman church in Pennsylvania which wished to withdraw from the jurisdiction of Rome after having unwittingly accepted it with a new priest. The judge's decision rendered abortive the action of a majority of the members in voting to withdraw from the Roman Communion.

The extent of Catholic influence on legislation is revealed in the Massachusetts law forbidding interreligious adoptions, thus stamping a child with an indelible religion. It is revealed in the restraint of divorce legislation in New York in spite of the patent frauds employed under the present law and the curious use of annulment to beat the devil around the bush.

It would be idle to undertake a repertory of Catholic influences on legislation. There is no question of the right of the Church to promote legislation favorable to its ideology, but there is serious question about the existence of a situation which allows enormous power to be exercised by a hierarchy without moral or legal responsibility to either its members or the community at large. This was the burden of Professor La Piana's complaint against the Catholic Church in the lectures delivered several years ago at Butler University on the subject of an "Authoritarian Church in a Democratic Society."

There is danger that because of these developments the era of laissez faire in religion may end, just as laissez faire of trusts ended and just as laissez faire of labor unions threatens to end. Inequality apparently has been the result of an original equality in law. All this need not mean a calamity for American democracy, but it may well mean a decline of certain traditional institutions. One of the victims of this movement in the meantime may well be the public schools which are finding the competition of Catholic parochial schools in many communities difficult to sustain.

I V

What are the lessons from all this to be pondered by a legislator in Israel, or any other country, seeking to find the right road in adjusting the relations of Church and State? His first duty is clear. The system he adopts must guarantee individual liberty of religion. But if his people in majority have a commitment to religion and to one religious organization in particular, he must also be concerned with another liberty, ecclesiastical liberty. This kind of freedom entails a special regime for large aggregates of religious people who might otherwise upset the balance of religious forces and disrupt the life of the State.

In Israel this arrangement can only mean the union of Synagogue and State. Religious groups other than Jewish would be similarly recognized. Such a system is in keeping with the regime inherited from the British and the Turks which has built religious status into the legal system.

But there are more compelling reasons why Jurisdiction is desirable in Israel and why Separation would be unworkable.

There are a great many questions which the government of the State, assuming a commitment to Judaism of most of Israel's people, must submit to ecclesiastical authority. Jewish law must be permitted to rule on such questions and Jewish law can only be expounded under these circumstances by an official body. The *ius respondendi* is as necessary to Israel as it was to Rome in the days of Augustus and Tiberius. The alternative is religious anarchy and this could only bring grief to the State. The decisions rendered by an official Rabbinate will not only develop Halakhah but promote the interests of the State. Synagogue and State must work together. Ancient Judaism was inconceivable without a political or social organization. Part of the difficulties faced by modern Judaism in the *Galut* are traceable to the absence of such an authority. In the State of Israel there is an opportunity and necessity to overcome this deficiency.

But there may be a question in the minds of many whether Jurisdiction may not promote intolerance and even fanaticism. The experience of the European peoples definitely refutes this fear, as in fact does the recent history of the Israeli community itself. It is Separation that would arm fanaticism. Jurisdiction would promote responsibility, moderation, and comprehension. Sliver groups will probably always exist and they should be given every right to exist. But the great majority of Jews will find their religious needs served by an Establishment which will carry on the tradition of historic Judaism and not of the sects which divide it.

Liberals will recognize that under such a jurisdictional system the Synagogue and the State will mutually check the other's pretensions and allay the danger of that totalitarianism which has been gnawing at the vitals of free states throughout the world. And with Ruggiero, the liberal will recall that "the deepest significance of the struggle between Church and State lies in the conflict itself, not in the respective claims of the contestants, because it facilitated the free development of the individual conscience."

BIBLIOGRAPHICAL NOTE

The following brief list of books will, it is hoped, partially compensate for the absence of detailed references to the sources of information of many of the statements made above.

A. Bouche-Leclercq, *L'Intolerance Religieuse et La Politique*, 1911.

J. Bryce, *Studies in History and Jurisprudence*, Vol. II, 1901.

J. B. Bury, *History of Freedom of Thought*, 1913.

E. Chenon, *Le Role Social de l'Eglise*, 1928.

S. Z. Ehler, J. B. Morrall, *Church and State: Historic Documents*, 1954.

A. Esmein, *Elements de Droit Constitutionnel*, T. II, 7e edition, 1921.

A. N. Holcombe, *Foundations of the Modern Commonwealth*, 1923.

A. Latreille, A Siegfried, *Les Forces Religieuses et la Vie Politique*, 1951.

W. E. H. Lecky, *History of the Rise and Influence of the Spirit of Rationalism*, 1865.

J. Lecler, *The Two Sovereignties*, 1952.

F. Ruffini, *Religious Liberty*, 1912.

G. De Ruggiero, *History of European Liberalism*, 1927.

A. P. Stokes, *Church and State in the United States*, 1950, 3 vols.

HOWARD I. LEVINE

*

The Non-Observant Orthodox

O NE OF the most momentous of the struggles that have emerged in modern Israel between secularists and religionists has been about the issue "Who Is a Jew?" On no other issue have traditional Jews shown such complete agreement, for on the answer to this question hinges the very life of our faith and our people.

American Jewry faces a related issue which will perhaps play no less crucial a role in the determination of its future. Merely amend the question to read "Who is an Orthodox Jew?" and you have before you a most critical question of practical policy confronting our Torah leadership. Inasmuch as we equate Orthodox Judaism with the true Judaism of the past and of the future, it is vital that we determine which Jews in the present are the links in the eternal chain of our existence. This spiritual community constitutes the soil and the seed which will, with adequate nurture, bear the fruit of our future existence.

It is therefore necessary that we answer the fundamental question: "Who is an Orthodox Jew?" Is an Orthodox Jew defined by his *acts* or by his *beliefs*? What is the status of the non-observant Jew who identifies himself with the Orthodox community? What is the exact definition of an Orthodox synagogue and an Orthodox rabbi? Is separate seating or *mechitzah* the line of demarcation of Orthodoxy? When does a deviationist synagogue lose its Orthodox character?

We should not commit the fundamental error of considering the answers to these questions as being arbitrary matters of opinion. On the contrary, they are matters of fundamental *Halakhah*—Law. While these answers may not always meet with complete agreement they must be based upon the authoritative sources of Torah doctrine. Halakhah pertains not only to matters of ritual and worship but to people and their basic world-outlook as well.

Moreover our approach cannot be dictated by the purely utilitarian policy as to which policy is calculated to produce the greatest loyalty to Orthodox Jewish institutions. Not only is a parochial approach no substitute for the truth of Torah teaching, but we operate in the faith that in an ultimate sense the pursuit of truth is synonymous with the practical success of Orthodoxy.

In this view we approach our task. It is the aim of this article to defend the place of the non-observant Jew in the Orthodox body; that is, to show that Orthodoxy, while strongly advocating maximum observance, yet recognizes that even the non-observant who desire this identification belong to its religious community. Furthermore, it is our purpose to present the case to the non-observant Jew for his joining hands with Orthodoxy despite his close correspondence to the level of observance demanded of him by Conservative or Reform Judaism. In addition we shall endeavor to show that deviationist synagogues and rabbis within the framework of Orthodoxy should not, despite shortcomings, be excluded from our ranks at the present time.

It is our firm conviction that no greater harm could be done to our cause than the severance of these Jews and synagogues from our main body. We can hardly commit a graver error than that of categorizing non-observant Jews as "Conservative" or "Reform." It is sad enough that many Jews mistakenly call themselves by these names without realizing the implication in terms of ultimate commitment to Torah. We dare not add to this error and accelerate a process of dissolution.

It is related that Rabbi Elijah, the Gaon of Vilna, happened to be at an inn with a companion. During mealtime the two venerable rabbis sat together at one table, while at another table was seated another Jew who was obviously completely non-observant. He neither washed before the meal nor did he recite any blessing over his food. Yet at the conclusion of the meal the Gaon invited this Jew to join in a *mezuman*—the special blessing immediately preceding the Grace after meals, which requires a quorum of three adult males. The reply was in a tone of scoffing ridicule: "Don't you see that I am an *apikores* (disbeliever)? I have nothing to do with *mitzvot* and blessings." To which the Gaon answered, "That you did not wash and did not recite a blessing and call yourself an *apikores* does not change the fact that you are a Jew. You have just finished eating; as a Jew, you are obligated to bless God. All your past transgressions cannot erase your present obligation to join in our *mezuman.*" The narrative concludes that the words of the Gaon made such a deep impression, that they ultimately brought about this man's *teshuvah* (repentance).

The point is that every Jew, no matter what his designation, still "belongs." Torah's claim is upon all Jews. We cannot accept the resignation of any Jew from Torah life. Certainly we should not force the resignation of any Jew from the historic Jewish community by giving him a new name to hide behind.

We recognize only one Torah, one Judaism, and one historic Jewish community. We cannot recognize the legitimacy of the division of American Judaism into three branches. Moreover, this division, at least from the viewpoint of the layman, is not a genuine ideological one. Many lay people, in calling themselves "Reform" or "Conservative," are merely describing a certain level of observance and are not indicating a denial of basic Jewish belief in Torah. To the extent that such is the case, we have not three branches of Judaism, but three variations of one type of Judaism, which might be rephrased as Orthodox-Orthodox, Conservative-Orthodox, and Reform-Orthodox. Only to the extent that genuine difference in ideology exists do we see a defection from the ranks of Orthodoxy. The vast bulk of American Jewry is guilty of no such defection. By and large, Orthodoxy speaks to all Jews for all Jews.

Let us, however, disregard entirely the matter of numbers in order to clarify the basic Orthodox position in the Jewish community. The prophets of Israel never spoke in the name of the majority position of the Jewish people—yet they were more truly representative of the genuine Jewish community than any other leaders of their day. They represented the true and inviolable claims of the historic Jewish Torah community. Similarly, Orthodoxy does not represent a clearly delineated group with its own special interests. Our claim is not on the basis of a voting bloc—certainly not that of a minority group asking for the protection of its rights within the Jewish people, in the name of our Torah. We do not ask all Jewish organizations to observe *Shabbat* and *Kashrut* in their public functions out of consideration for their Orthodox members and their sensibilities. Even if an organization does not have a single observant Jew our claim is just as insistent. *Kelal Yisrael*, that collective conscience of the historic Jewish community which has taken upon itself the yoke of the Divine imperative, always constitutes the one and only true Jewish majority. Orthodoxy views itself as the heir of historic Judaism rather than as a faction within Judaism or as a spokesman for a particular type of synagogue architecture.

It is true that were Orthodoxy to constitute itself a separatist group it might enjoy many short-range benefits. It could build its ranks firm and strong. It could to a large degree shut out the disturbance of an outside world. It would not need to dissipate its energies on behalf of outside groups. It could be narrow and single-minded, unchallenged and unyielding. It could, under those conditions, feel self-righteous and superior and live up to the role of its self-image.

It is not at all surprising that a small minority within Orthodoxy has succumbed to this temptation. But this can never be the genuine position of Orthodoxy because it is not consistent with the truth of Judaism. Our Torah is one. Our people is one. No devout wish or strategy can efface that reality. Neither the narrow institutional interests of Conservative and Reform Judaism nor the parochialism of minority elements within Orthodoxy can sustain the myth of the division of Judaism into branches. Judaism, in any ultimate sense, cannot abide denominationalism.

An exceptionally clear and authoritative decision on this matter is rendered by the eminent talmudist Rabbi Naphtali Tzevi Yehuda Berlin, *Rosh Yeshivah* of the renowned Volozhiner Yeshiva that flourished in the past century, in his collection of responsa.[1] In this responsum, the *Netziv* (as he is called) expresses his difference of opinion with the position stated in a periodical issued by German Orthodox Jews that Judaism can be split into three divisions and that Orthodoxy should separate itself from the non-observant elements in Jewish life and thereby strengthen its position. The *Netziv* differs sharply with this point of view and presents the following arguments against Orthodox separation:

"This advice is as fatal as a sword wound in the body of our nation," he warns. First, a sharp line of demarcation between the observant and the non-observant will not only separate the Orthodox from other groups, but it will also divide Orthodox against Orthodox. An atmosphere of excessive suspicion and zeal will prevail and any deviation whatever in practice or custom will cause the doer to be branded a heretic—and to be treated accordingly. There is no end to the harm that will be caused even to pious Orthodox Jews once the attitude of exclusion reigns.

Secondly, we Jews in the Diaspora vitally need the unity of our people in order to protect our group existence. Only when the Jews are all united will we succeed in withstanding the onslaughts of hostility to the Jews from the outside world.

Thirdly, separation is against human nature. We see the tremendous attraction of non-Jewish society for the Jews, which results in inter-marriage and assimilation, and which can be resisted only by great conscious effort. How much more so would it be unnatural to expect one Jew to be estranged from his brothers. Human nature will never allow it.

The *Netziv* goes on to offer an alternative solution to the problem of Orthodox survival. The spread of Torah learning in all quarters is the only answer. Torah should be taught even *shelo li-shemah*, even if the motives for its study are not of the highest religious order, of "learning for its own sake." He adds "if not in his own life time, at least his children will come to realize the higher ideal," citing a statement of the Talmud.[2] Even if Torah must be taught in combination with secular studies we should gladly do so, rather than drive away our youth from our midst. It is preferable that secular studies be conducted under religious auspices and in a religious atmosphere than have our youth leave our fold completely. (A prophetic statement of the effectiveness of the Yeshivah movement in America!) The study of Torah will also diminish controversy amidst our people and join all Jews together in a closer bond.

Thus we see that the policy of separatism is foreign to authentic Jewish teaching as articulated by the *Netziv*. Orthodoxy cannot separate itself as a group and divorce itself from other groups in Jewish life. A distinction, however, must be made at this point. There is a difference between *relatedness* and *inclusiveness*. Ortho-

doxy *relates* itself to all Jews, is concerned for the totality of the
Jewish people, and aspires to *include* all Jews in the future. It does
not, however, at the present *include* all Jews. Were this the case
Orthodoxy would be amorphous and its designation a meaningless
term. It cannot possibly accomplish its purpose without some
form and structure.

We therefore turn now to the question: which Jews are actually,
and not potentially, part of the Orthodox community? On what
grounds can the non-observant Jew belong to Orthodoxy? If his
level of observance does not disqualify him for membership in this
community, how can Orthodox belief, alone, accomplish this
identification in view of our knowledge that Judaism is primarily
a religion of *Mitzvot Maasiyot* (practical observances) and not a
religion of dogma?

Happily we have available a most authoritative source—the
Mishnah, which upon proper interpretation offers a solution to
our problem. It is the unqualified view of the Mishnah, that it is
Jewish *belief* above all that determines the membership or belonging of an individual in the Jewish spiritual community called
Kelal Yisrael. By the latter phrase is meant a community not
necessarily identical with the Jewish people in its totality. It is a
community to which is attached a special state of spiritual grace
which the Mishnah describes by telling us that all in it have a
share in the world-to-come—notwithstanding the serious breaches
of observance of such individuals as may comprise this group.
Thus we read in the Mishnah: [3] "All Israelites have a share in
the world-to-come, as it is written, 'And your people are all righteous, they shall possess the land for ever, the shoot of my planting,
the work of my hands, in whom I glorify.' The following, however,
have no share in the world-to-come: He who says that resurrection
of the dead is not the teaching of the Torah, that the Torah is not
from Heaven, and the heretic."

Maimonides, in his commentary on the Mishnah, states clearly,
the implication of this doctrine:

When a person believes in all of the fundamental Jewish doctrines
. . . he is part of *Kelal Yisrael* and we are commanded to love him,
have mercy upon him, to fulfill all of the commandments based on
love and brotherhood which God bade us observe in relation to our

fellow Jews. No matter what sins this individual may have committed, because of sinful appetite and base passion, though he will be duly punished for his transgression, he nevertheless has a share in the world-to-come . . . But if an individual renounces his belief in these foundations of Judaism he is no longer part of *Kelal Yisrael*—he has denied the fundamentals and is considered as a heretic and *apikores*. . . .

Upon careful analysis we see that Maimonides in his explanation resolves an apparent contradiction in the Mishnah. The Mishnah first states without qualification that all Israelites have a share in the world-to-come. The Mishnah immediately afterwards seemingly modifies the initial broad, all-inclusive statement by saying "the following have no share in the world-to-come." Maimonides solves this problem by pointing out that it is the clear implication of the Mishnah that disbelievers are not part of *Kelal Yisrael*; hence the first statement in the Mishnah, "All Israelites have a share in the world-to-come," stands without qualification. We have here then, in the Mishnah, not only a statement as to who has a share in the world-to-come but also an exact definition as to who is part of *Kelal Yisrael*—the Jewish spiritual community.

There emerges from the study of the Mishnah yet another significant point. The saving power does not pertain to belief in dogma as such, but to one's attachment to the Jewish people—*Kelal Yisrael*. Righteousness and blessing are the qualities that adhere to the Jewish people as such, and by being included in *Kelal Yisrael*, one partakes of these qualities by virtue of his membership in the larger body. However, belief, in itself, has no power to save. It is only the means whereby we maintain our true attachment to *Kelal Yisrael*—which in turn is the source of spiritual blessing. R. Menachem Meiri in his comment on the Mishnah emphasizes this point: "In order to teach us that an idolater, or an atheist, or anyone guilty of sin with regard to the foundations of Judaism and religion does not have a share in the world-to-come, the Mishnah adduces its proof from the verse 'And your people are all righteous'; that is to say, that *insofar as one shares in these beliefs he is still part of the Jewish people* and he is thus not entirely excluded from the category of the righteous despite his many individual sins."

Hence it follows that an individual who believes and observes but does not identify himself with *Kelal Yisrael* has no share in the world-to-come. The Talmud [4] explicitly lists, together with the disbelievers previously mentioned, "those who separate themselves from the ways of the community." Maimonides [5] explains this category as follows:

He who separates himself from the ways of the community, even though he has committed no transgression, but remains apart from the Jewish people and does not perform *mitzvot* in their midst and does not share in their sorrow or join in their fasts, but follows his own way as if he were a stranger and not one of them, has no share in the world-to-come.

The intimate connection between one's attachment to the Jewish people and the Jewish religion is of the very essence of Judaism. It is, one might say, the most basic concept of Judaism—the concept of Covenant. Even more so than the Torah or the *mitzvot*, it is the Covenant (*Berit*) which relates the Jewish people to God. The particularly Jewish relationship of man to God is not Man—God nor even Man—Torah—God but is Man—Israel—Torah—God. Israel on many occasions in its history has entered into a covenant with God to keep the Torah; we, as part of Israel, therefore have a share in Torah and are thereby related to God.

The Covenant relationship is the central reality of Jewish history because it is the Covenant which simultaneously defines and establishes our relationship to God and Torah. We are the people of God only by virtue of the *Berit*, as the Scriptures state (Exodus 19:5): "Now therefore if you will hearken unto My voice indeed and keep My covenant, then you shall be Mine own treasure from among all people; for all the earth is Mine and you shall be unto Me a kingdom of priests and a holy nation." The implication of this teaching is that a Jew approaches God and Torah first through attachment to his people. Thus we find that the formula in marriage is *Harei at mekudeshet li ke'dat Mosheh ve'Yisrael*, "Behold thou art betrothed unto me in accordance with the *Law of Moses and Israel*." It does not suffice that the marriage is contracted on the basis of the laws of the Torah—it must also be based on the consent of *Kelal Yisrael* as a living entity. Hence we find that if a woman violates *dat yehudit*, the Jewish traditions of modesty, though she has not violated explicit Torah Law, there are grounds for divorce. Similarly we find that in certain cases extraordinary powers are granted to the extant Torah authorities to nullify a marriage because, as the Talmud teaches, "Every person marrying does so with the understanding that his act meets with the consent of the Rabbis." [6]

It should be understood that the authority of the Rabbis here derives from their position as the articulate spokesmen of the conscience of *Kelal Yisrael*—the living Jewish spiritual community.

It follows then that our attachment to Torah is a twofold one. The Torah contains not only the commandments of God to us, but it also contains the historical record of our reiterated agreement as a people to live by these laws. Not only at Sinai but also at *Ohel Moed*, the Tent of the Meeting, after the Tabernacle was erected, and at the plains of Moab before entering the land of Israel, did the entire Jewish people bind themselves and their children to keep the Torah.[7]

So too in the times of King Josiah (6th century B.C.E.) was the Torah reaffirmed as the constitution of the Jewish people. Even again in the times of Ezra and Nehemiah (5th century B.C.E.) was allegiance pledged anew by the leaders of Jewry to abide by the Torah.

Consequently the Torah is not only the religion of the Jewish people—it is its legal constitution. The Covenant is by its very nature a legal relationship. It is basically a form of contractual agreement between God and the Jewish people with the Torah as the instrument of this contract. To deny the validity of the Torah is tantamount to destroying the conventional relationship between God and Israel because the Torah is the very contract of this agreement. The first requirement of a Jew is to give allegiance to the Torah and to recognize its validity even as the first requirement of a citizen is to give his allegiance to the Constitution and to recognize its authority. Violating any specific law is a wrong but does not constitute treason, whereas denying the validity of the constitution is clearly an act of treason, resulting in a loss of citizenship. Similarly, a Jew who violates individual commandments remains in *Kelal Yisrael*, whereas a Jew who denies the total validity of Torah is guilty of an act of treason resulting in his severance from *Kelal Yisrael.*

The analogy of Torah and constitution warrants further development. A constitution cannot exist without a recognized judicial body to interpret it. It would be meaningless for a person to say "I uphold the integrity of the constitution but I do not recognize the right of the courts to interpret it. I shall follow another interpretation." So too a Jew cannot say "I believe in the Torah but I do not recognize the right of one recognized central rabbinic body to interpret it. I shall follow another interpretation." Either one believes in the Torah and *one* valid judicial body that can interpret it or one's allegiance to Torah becomes meaningless. Nachmanides, in commenting on the biblical verse (Deut. 17:11) "Thou shalt not turn aside from the sentence which they shall declare unto you, to the right hand nor to the left," remarks:

Rashi quotes the talmudic teaching "even if they declare the right to be the left and the left to be the right!" This means that even if you in your heart are convinced that the Court is wrong and their error is as clear to you as the difference between your right hand and left hand, you should nevertheless follow the direction of the Court. . . . You should say: thus has God given me the *mitzvot* that I should fulfill them as the Sanhedrin directs and in accordance with their understanding—*though they err.* The need for this command is exceedingly great. For the Written Torah is amenable to many interpretations and unanimity cannot be easily achieved. Thus controversy would prevail and the one Torah would split up into many Torahs. Therefore it is God's will that we follow the Torah as interpreted by the authority of the Sanhedrin. . . . Moreover we have reason to have faith that they are teaching that "the right is the right."

We may derive from the above the important truth that even above the principles of reason and conscience stands the principle of the validity of Torah and its due judicial process of interpretation. Obviously this teaching applies not only to the Sanhedrin but to the central religious authority that exists in all ages. The Talmud in its entirety has been recognized by *Kelal Yisrael* as such an authority.

In applying this criterion of belief (rather than one of practice) to the American Jewish community we have every reason to be encouraged. Studies of religious attitudes in America reveal a remarkable record of belief in God and in the Bible.

What do Americans believe? Most emphatically they believe in God. 97 percent according to one survey, 96 percent according to another, 95 percent according to a third." [8] They believe in prayer: about 90 percent say they pray on various occasions. They hold the Bible to be an inspired book, the word of God. 86 percent regard it as divinely inspired, the word of God; a survey conducted by the British weekly gives the figures for Americans who regard the Bible as divinely inspired as 86.5 percent.[9]

One may legitimately conclude that the non-observant Jew in America is in quite a different category from the once non-observant Jew in Europe. Whereas in the latter case non-observance was very often associated with an outright rejection of religion and with a materialistic ideology, the non-observant Jew of America is by no means characterized by blatant atheism and materialism.

It can be argued, as indeed it has been, that this commitment of belief is quite superficial when we compare performance in deed to profession of belief. As Herberg writes,

Yet it is only too evident that the religiousness characteristic of America today is very often a religiousness without religion, a religiousness with almost any kind of content or none, a way of sociability or belonging rather than a way of re-orienting life to God.[10]

Granting his place in the vast twilight zone between true belief and disbelief, we nevertheless maintain that the American Jew is by and large ranged on the side of Jewish belief and is not to be excluded on that ground from genuine religious affiliation with *Kelal Yisrael*. Here we must draw an essential distinction in our definition of the obligation to believe as required by Judaism. It can be defined positively or negatively. In its positive sense, belief entails complete awareness, absence of doubt, and decisive conviction. It is in this sense that the thirteen principles of faith were formulated by Maimonides and are recited daily by many worshippers. In its negative sense, however, it is merely non-denial—

tacit acceptance with the possibility of intermittent doubt and weakness of conviction. There is a great difference between the two approaches.

If we accept the negative approach, our community of believers will include the numerous persons who are in the neutral zone between belief and disbelief, those lacking in positive faith but who yet are not heretics and disbelievers.

Significantly, the Mishnah of Sanhedrin does not require belief in the sense of positive avowal but only condemns the denial of fundamental Jewish doctrines. It was the innovation of Maimonides to expand and put in positive form the doctrinal teachings of the Mishnah. Classical Judaism, however, has contented itself with the negative formulation, for it maintains, as we explained before, that the avowal of belief in itself cannot endow one with saving grace. The way of blessedness for the individual lies in his attachment to *Kelal Yisrael*. This attachment itself is the true beginning of the road to ultimate faith, which is a long and arduous one. It is one thing to say "I believe the Torah is Divine" and quite another to learn its contents carefully, practice its precepts, and thereby gain strength of conviction. One can begin his attainment of faith by assent to the doctrine that God controls all events in the universe, but will only free himself from worldly concern and worries after a long process of growth in religious maturity. Assent to belief and the gaining of real conviction are two stages of one protracted process. The requirement of Judaism is that a person begin on the road to faith by not severing himself from Torah ideals. Attachment to *Kelal Yisrael* and its living experiences will accomplish the rest.

The late Chief Rabbi of Israel, Rabbi Kook, of blessed memory, makes this entire point explicit in a letter to a disciple.

Though it is a certain prohibition and a festering sore for one to even cast a doubt concerning the truth of the content of our perfect Faith, nevertheless we do not find our Sages adjudging such individuals as atheists or *apikorsim*. Only one who definitely denies, that is, who decides that the very opposite of our faith is true, is included in this category. A categoric denial cannot possibly emanate from any Israelite who is not outright sinful and consciously distorting the truth. For the most that irreligion can do is to sow doubt in people of weak

conviction. Therefore, one who arrogantly denies without mental
reservations is sinful beyond question. This is clear: whoever is aware
that even extreme irreligion, if it is honest, can at most stake itself in
a position of doubt, and this only as a result of absence of knowledge,
weakness of sensibility, and want of guidance—will certainly on due
reflection of this, become more perfect in his own faith and more
richly endowed with true piety. The more such an individual will
attach himself to men of learning, to true seekers after God, the more
will he progress in his attainment of a firm faith that will be rooted
in knowledge and wisdom.[11]

One might add that unquestionably doubt is no excuse for
breach of observance. He who violates *Shabbat* or *Kashrut* because
of weakness of faith is no longer in a position of doubt. He has
reached the existential decision to divorce religion from his life.
He bet his life against the premise of religion, as Pascal has
expressed it in his famous wager. No human being can persist in
a state of perpetual doubt. The human psyche could not abide the
burden of continuous indecision. The person who ceases to observe the *mitzvot* on ideological grounds has clutched at a position
of certainty. It is only the person who observes, though weak in
conviction, who can be considered as an individual in doubt. This
latter type, Rabbi Kook explains, can transcend his state of doubt
in his attachment to Torah personalities, and thereby deepen and
strengthen his faith.

A further point ought be made at this juncture. The division of
ethics and religion is a secular distinction. Authentic Judaism
recognizes no essential difference between ritual and ethics—all
are commandments of the same God. Consequently, we should
not disregard the ethical observances of the "non-observant" Jew.
He too is observant, to an appreciable degree, in his fulfillment
of such *mitzvot* as honoring one's parents, honest behavior, and
the giving of charity. Being part of *Kelal Yisrael*, his deeds take
on the aspect of Jewish religious observances: *mitzvot*. We have
no right to conclude that because he is negligent in the observance
of basic ritual *mitzvot* and is primarily keeping only the ethical
laws of civilized living, that these observances are accountable to
him *qua* universal human being, not *qua* Jew. On the contrary,

our Sages have always viewed such ethical behavior as being peculiarly Jewish. "For I have known him [Abraham] to the end that he may command his children and his household after him that they may keep the way of the Lord to do righteousness and justice." (Gen. 18:19).

The Talmud [12] teaches: "The people of this nation have three characteristic traits: they are merciful, modest in behavior, and readily perform acts of lovingkindness."

It is a striking phenomenon in Judaism that the Prophets berated the Jewish people mainly for their ethical misdeeds, rather than for neglect of ritual observances of our religion. Reform Judaism, together with Christianity, unfortunately draws from this the erroneous conclusion that ethics and social justice are the essential content of prophetic religion and that the prophets were opposed to ritual observances. The refutation of the Reform position should not lead us to commit the opposite fallacy of reducing religion primarily to ritual. Judah Halevi gives us the correct evaluation of the relationship that exists between the ritual and ethical commandments:

The rational laws (i.e. ethics), being the basis and the preamble of the divine law (i.e. ritual), precede it in character and time and are indispensable to the administration of every human society. Even a gang of robbers must have a kind of justice among them if their confederacy is to last. When Israel's disloyalty had come to such a pass that they disregarded rational and social principles . . . but held fast to the sacrificial worship and other divine (i.e. ritual laws) . . . it was told to them 'Would that you might observe those laws which rule the smallest and meanest community, such as refer to injustice, good actions and recognition of God's bounty.' For the divine law cannot become complete till the social and rational laws are perfected.[13]

It would therefore be improper to ignore a person's ethical observance in our evaluation of his Jewishness. On the contrary, such persons should be made to feel that in their ethical behavior they are fulfilling basic Jewish *mitzvot* which culminate in the fulfillment of the sacred ritual observances of Judaism.

Above all our approach to the non-observant Jew must be based on a fundamental Jewish outlook which can be called our faith in faith. By this we mean that we have unshakeable faith in the native Jewish endowment of the capacity for faith.

The Midrash teaches us that when Moses lost confidence in the success of his mission to save the Jewish people from bondage and complained of his flock "But they will not believe me," he was censured for lack of faith in the faith of the Jewish people. "They are believers and children of believers." *Emunah* (Faith) is the natural endowment of the Jewish people. As Maimonides writes in his letter of encouragement to the Jews of Yemen,

Our Creator, blessed be He, has long ago assured—just as a man re-assures his fellow, and certainly His reassurances will suffice us—that all who were present at Mt. Sinai will have faith in the prophecy of Moses and in the prophecy of his successors, they who were present and their children and their children's children to all generations. For thus said He, "And also in you shall they always trust."

This approach to our people is basic. It is God Who gives man faith and sustains him in faith. It is God Who has chosen Israel and not Israel which has chosen itself. It is God Who has implanted in the Jewish people its faith in Torah and prophecy. This faith is not the precious possession of the few to be guarded from the insensibilities of the many. All Jews are given this most precious of all spiritual gifts which Judah Halevi calls *ha-inyan ha-e-lohi*, the Divine influence.

Furthermore, a Jew has faith not as a result of his will. He believes though sometimes he may not wish to believe, even though his belief frustrates the free expression of his will and desires. Jewish *emunah* is, as R. Schneur Zalman of Lodi expresses it in his classic *Tanya*, "beyond the range of taste or intellect." Only in this fashion, he points out, can we explain the ready martyrdom for the sake of the Unity of God's Name, even of Jews who up to the last moment flagrantly violated the most fundamental Jewish observances. Morality is a matter of free will —belief is not. The individual is free either to act or not to act in accordance with faith in Torah. He is not, however, existentially free to believe or not to believe. When the test of final commitment to belief in God comes, the Jew is not free to ignore his innermost faith. There is a dormant power of true faith in the soul of every Jew. It is, in the language of the *Tanya*, "the natural love of God, in the Divine Soul, that is found in *Kelal Yisrael*."

It is fitting therefore that we welcome the non-observant Jew with greater faith in his faith. We dare not exclude such Jews from our ranks. They are in every sense *our* Jews—part and parcel of the historic Jewish religious community.

As long as a Jew maintains his tie with the Jewish people and the Torah, though he be not fully observant, he is our brother and compatriot. The doors of his soul are open to receive inspiration. There is hope that his children well receive a more intensive Torah education and will be more observant than the parents. Experience in our *Yeshivot* and Day Schools abundantly proves that this can and does frequently happen. People who desire more Judaism for their children than they embody in their own lives are the kind of Jews of whom we can be proud. It requires courage of a parent to give his child this extra measure of education. It requires courage of a Jew to join an Orthodox synagogue though he is not observant by Orthodox standards. He at least keeps open the channel of communication to the higher ideals of Torah. He does not merely seek approval of his way of life which he might well find in non-Orthodox synagogues. He seeks the truth of Torah—though it is not always pleasing and approving. He therefore deserves true Orthodox fellowship and encouragement.

At this point another serious objection may be raised with regard to the inclusion of the non-observant in our religious community. One might argue: is it not true that disbelief can express itself in action as well as in words? Does not the Torah expressly say that the Sabbath is a sign of the Covenant between God and Israel?

Wherefore the children of Israel shall keep the Sabbath, to observe the Sabbath throughout their generations, for a perpetual covenant. It is a sign between Me and the children of Israel for ever; for in six days the Lord made heaven and earth, and on the seventh day He ceased from work and rested. (Ex. 31:16,17)

Hence, as our Rabbis teach us, a person who brazenly desecrates the Sabbath thereby excludes himself from *Kelal Yisrael*.

Admittedly this is a very difficult and delicate problem—one with which the rabbinic leaders of our era have been grappling. The entire matter hinges on the qualification "brazenly." It appears that this characterization does not apply to Jews who, though guilty of Sabbath desecration in public, are unaware of the gravity of their offense as a result of inadequate Jewish training and knowledge. It also would not include a Jew who is aware of the gravity of the Sabbath and in view of this attempts to keep *Shabbat*, at least to some degree, and feels remorseful for his lack of fuller observance. Rabbinic Judaism does not condone breach of observance even under these conditions but yet is extremely reluctant to exclude such Jews from *Kelal Yisrael*. Thus, Rabbi Jacob Etlinger, one of the outstanding rabbinic authorities of recent times, writes:

With regard to desecrators of the Sabbath in our day, it is difficult for me to decide as to their status. The plague is so widespread that many individuals are not aware of the seriousness of their offense. . . . Some individuals recite their Sabbath prayers and say the *Kiddush*, and then proceed to commit biblical and rabbinic prohibitions of labor . . .

Now the reason that a Sabbath desecrator is considered a heretic is only because it is tantamount to denial of the fact of creation by the Creator. However, these people acknowledge these beliefs in their prayers and in their recitation of the *Kiddush*. Certainly their children, raised in such an environment and therefore unaware of the laws of Sabbath observance, are similar in their status to the Sadducees who, though they desecrate the Sabbath, are not considered as heretics because they are merely "continuing the ways of their fathers." They are like innocent children brought up by non-Jews (and are therefore not considered sinners), as it is stated in the *Shulchan Arukh, Orach Chayim* sec. 365.[14]

Herein we see how true Orthodoxy strives towards the goal of greater inclusiveness. Without sacrificing its principles in any way, it is able to view with tolerant understanding those who neglect fundamental observances due to extraneous circumstances, and does not exclude them from the ranks of *Yisrael*.

Our treatment of the subject would not be complete without at least a brief consideration of the problem of Orthodox congregations and rabbis who are guilty of deviations from the Hala-khah in their seating arrangements or in other matters. Surely this is a very serious question of Orthodox policy—but the matter of basic policy is beyond the range of this article. One observation will suffice. Any individual or group within Orthodoxy has the right to question the propriety and wisdom of such deviationist practices. However, no individual or group has the right to de-clare these congregations and rabbis non-Orthodox. As long as an Orthodox Yeshivah or Orthodox congregational body or Orthodox rabbinic organization sponsors such a rabbi and congregation, they remain within the Orthodox fold. One may argue policy, one may differ, any segment within Orthodoxy can bind itself to a stricter standpoint, but no one can exclude the more liberal elements from the Orthodox community.

Our problems are numerous and complex. This is all the more reason for us to maintain a warranted degree of stability in our organizational set-up. This stability can only exist if there is a fundamental respect for the integrity of the Jewish Orthodox community in its totality despite our internal differences.

American Jewry stands at the crossroads. A bold challenge con-fronts us. Shall we be uncompromising purists and consign the non-observant Jew or congregation to camps divorced from *Kelal Yisrael?* Or shall we make every effort to retain the unfortunately too numerous group of the non-observant within the fold? We might well follow the example of the Talmud which, when faced with a similar alternative, chose the latter course.

In early talmudic times, there were many restrictive laws directed against the reliability of the *Am Ha-aretz*, the uneducated farmer, who out of ignorance and laxity of observance was not to be trusted in matters of ritual purity, in giving testimony, and in the fulfillment of other religious practices. Yet when the need arose, we find that the Talmud adopted a more lenient viewpoint towards the members of this group, a viewpoint later accepted as normative law. Thus we read in the Talmud:

Rabbi Yose said: Why is everybody held as trustworthy during the entire year (not only in holiday seasons) with regard to their observ-ance of the laws of ritual purity of wine and oil? In order that such an individual should not break off from the community and build a *bamah* (an altar on a high place) by himself. R. Pappa said: In accordance with whose view do we now accept the reliability of the testimony of the *Am Ha-aretz?* It is in accordance with the view of R. Yose.[15]

We see here how our talmudic Sages were willing, in certain cases, to forego the strict interpretation of the Law in order to prevent the trend towards sectarianism. How much more so should we be willing to foster an attitude of closeness and friendship where no change of the Law is involved.

Josephus records [16] that in the division of Pharisees and Sadducees the masses of Jewish people felt closer in spirit to the Pharisees, our spiritual ancestors. They admired their integrity, their simplicity of taste, and the true friendship and mutual respect that existed in their ranks. It was because of its closeness to the masses of Jewry that Phariseeism ultimately triumphed. Would that we be worthy of fulfilling a similar role in our generation.

There is a wisdom above and beyond our individual grasp, a wisdom taught by faith in the eternity and indestructibility of the Jewish spirit and its bearers. Somehow we must recapture the Prophetic scope, the ability, when necessary, to be a severe critic of Jewish society and yet to remain indissolubly linked with it, and to be utterly convinced that this society will be redeemed. Even more so than its quantity of belief and practice, the distinguishing feature of Orthodoxy has always been its quality of belief, its irrepressible determination to serve the God of our fathers in truth. If we but reignite the quality of true Jewish belief in Torah, which lies dormant in every Jewish soul, surely this belief will bring in its wake the renewal of Jewish observance in all its manifestations.

NOTES

1 *Meshiv Davar* I:44.
2 *Sanhedrin* 105b.
3 *Sanhedrin* 11:1.
4 *Rosh Ha-shanah* 17a.
5 *Hil. Teshuvah* 3:11.

6 *Ketubot* 3a.
7 *Sotah* 37b.
8 Will Herberg, *Protestant, Catholic and Jew*, p. 85.
9 *Ibid.*, p. 105 note 6.
10 *Ibid.*, p. 276.
11 *Igrot R'Iyah*, Vol. I, p. 20.
12 *Yevamot* 79.
13 *Ktab al Khazari* 2:48, based on trans. Hirschfeld, p. 111.
14 Responsa *Binyan Tziyon* 2:23.
15 *Chagigah* 22a. and v. *Tosafot, ad loc.*
16 *Antiquities* xiii.10, xviii.1.

EMANUEL FELDMAN

*

The American and the Jew

EQUATION OR ENCOUNTER?

ONE OF THE paradoxes of the American Jew is the fact that
despite his freedoms and his ever widening vistas of opportunity, he lives under a nameless tension. In a country which
offers him freedom to live as he desires, he is basically ill at ease.
In an environment which permits him to live, act, and think as
his non-Jewish neighbor does, the Jew, beneath the façade of
apparent conformity, is not completely comfortable. Even as he
conforms to the patterns of American life he feels himself the
perpetual outsider.

The causes of this phenomenon are many, but basic to them
all is the fact that there is a fundamental divergence between
that which is characteristically Jewish and that which is characteristically American, a polarity of views which cannot quite be
reconciled.

Of course, there are constant attempts at reconciliation. This
is perhaps the fundamental *raison d'être* of the dissenting Jewish
religious groups, and certainly of the secular agencies. From them
there issues forth a constant clatter of "Judeo-Americana": Judaism and Americanism are really very much alike; each is democratic, freedom loving, believes in social justice; even the founding
fathers looked upon themselves as the chosen people in a promised
land; the Liberty Bell contains a biblical inscription; and so forth
ad infinitum. Because of this, we are told, we have a great share
in America. We really do belong.

To this, Torah Judaism, as I understand it, submits a demurrer.
For over and above its insistence on maintaining halakhic standards and the *mitzvah* way of living, it states frankly that the
typically Jewish and the typically American are quite dissimilar.
It would be more fruitful to ascertain what the two cultures have

to say to one another rather than force them into an equation. In truth, it is precisely because they are not alike that an intelligent encounter between them is possible.

Orthodox Judaism would offer a fresh and healthful approach, one that would clear the fog of misconception, by recognizing the diverging paths of the Jewish and the American *Weltanschauung*. These are many and on all levels. We will briefly sketch here a few of the more fundamental ones.

The most obvious difference between the two traditions is that of national origins. The beginnings of Judaism are as old as history itself, whereas the sum total of American yesterdays reaches 190 odd years, a total which in Jewish history amounts to only a page and which to the Jewish consciousness is absurdly small. While it is true that America's roots antedate 1776 and can be found in Greece and Rome, it is equally true that in conduct, thought, and character, America is distinctive and unique. For despite the variegated roots of American civilization, a homogeneous national character has emerged which is peculiarly a product of the New World. And the beginnings of this national character are quite recent.

This historyless character was observed by Thomas Hardy who wrote, after his visit to America:

> I shrink to seek a modern coast
> Whose riper times have yet to be;
> Where the new regions claim them free
> From that long drip of human tears
> Which people old in tragedy
> Have left upon the centuried years.[1]

Hardy could have been thinking not only of British but of Jewish history when he spoke of "the long drip of human tears" of "a people old in tragedy."

From this contrast in the origin and type of history stems an entirely dissimilar world-view. It cannot be said of the American tradition, for example, that it has a real sense of tragedy. Fortunately, it has not been burned in the crucible of martial fire. Except for the War between the States, it has largely been spared agony and suffering. Quite the contrary, in fact. Observers have noted that "the history of America has been an epic continuity of almost unbroken success." [2] This, at least in part, accounts for an America which is "unwilling to confront a life experience which includes penalties as well as gains, failures as well as success, tragedy as well as happiness." [3] If success is the goddess, it follows that failure is the devil. It is simply not supposed to happen.

It has been the dynamic of the American tradition that progress is inevitable, success a foregone conclusion. This condition was true of the frontiersman hacking a new civilization out of the forest, and it certainly obtains in modern American life. Witness the cults of Positive Thinking, of Confidence in the Future, of Optimism at All Costs. Vance Packard has shown how business growth and political campaigns are based on the premise that any form of pessimism is evil, and that a climate of confidence must be maintained at all costs—even when things are going badly.[4] It is true that we have had a Melville, an O'Neill, and a Faulkner in our literature. But the very universal attention given them is perhaps in itself an indication that they are not typically American: the interest in them is less due to what they have to say than to the fact that these are Americans who are saying it.

A people old in tragedy is more realistic. The drip of human tears has given Judaism a keener insight into the life experience and a deeper awareness of the profundities of human existence. It is incongruous for Judaism to attempt to force itself into the mold of this ebullient forward-march. To do this is to twist and distort Jewish history. The attempts of fund-raising publicists of Israel to picture the young state as a miniature United States, with its own pioneers and frontiersmen and cowboys, are often comically pathetic. The efforts of Jewish apologists in America are similarly grotesque. Jewish patriarchs were not frontiersmen; we reckon Jacob and not Daniel Boone among our forefathers. And Judaism knows that life has tragedy and failure—Job is more than a literary image—and that man has the power to transcend tragedy and failure into a higher and nobler life.

This contrasting length of the two histories accounts in part for their disparate time-view. A civilization whose past is measurable has a more restricted view of time than one whose traditions reach into pre-history. For Judaism, the future follows the way of the past, distant and infinite. In America, too, future is like past: brief, measurable, and immediate. Thus we find America operating on a short, hurried time scale. It is more concerned with the here-and-now than with the hereafter, both in the practical and teleological sense. There is no patience for eternity. By contrast, the Jewish time scale is long and far feaching. The Jew has time. This has been celebrated in our folk lore, our humor, and even in the classic Yiddish aphorism, A Yid hat zeit. He is patient, as one who has come from the dawn of history and now waits for the Messiah must be patient. The objects of his authentic ambition are sacred rather than secular, and he does not think only in terms of the immediately attainable. Time is not a commodity which must be used. God Himself is mekadesh Yisrael ve'ha-zemanim—He Who sanctifies Israel and the seasons. Time is holy. Speed in understanding all things, rapidity of movement for its own sake, short courses in learning and in scholarship—these are foreign to the Jewish tradition.

The Jew has time, and his Book is constantly expanded: Bible to Talmud to commentaries to super-commentaries ad infinitum. The American Book is quickened, shortened: novels to pocket editions to abridgements to condensations. Characteristically, the Jew has carried his Book on his shoulders: Ol Torah, the yoke of the Torah. The American carries his book in his hip pocket.

This impatience manifests itself in the American compulsion to change for its own sake. Young, with no deep moorings in the ancient past, the American civilization has little respect for tradition, and this rootlessness accounts for her frenetic chase after newness and experimentation. The very character of America, according to Frederick Jackson Turner's classic theory, was shaped and molded by the frontier experience and born out of the American forest. A frontier is always moving. It is restless, energetic, inventive, and there is a pervading sense of experimentation. In our day, Harold Laski has shown that the "spaciousness of the United States as a physical entity makes the idea of unlimited horizons, of constant discovery, of novelty that is always imminent, part of the background against which each American is set." [5] (How do Americans greet one another?—"What's new?") Even today the phrase "American experiment" is part of our daily vo-

cabulary, for the character of the restless frontier did not cease to
exist when the frontier was conquered. Modern American civilization still retains this restless experimentalism. "The characteristic
American is always on the move. He is always willing to try something new. He is skeptical of anything that expresses itself as
permanent or absolute." [6] And David Riesman has even viewed
the American search for newness as a modern manifestation of
the explorer, and the suburbs as a counterpart of the old frontier
town.[7]

Even the arts have been forced to keep pace with this constant
motion and its search for infinite variety. Music, always an accurate index of any civilization, provides a characteristic illustration.
The truest American musical idiom is found in jazz. This is America's most important national musical style, and reflects more
than any other art form the experimentalism and the search for
novelty of which we speak. It places a premium on improvisation.
It is inventive. It is restless. It is mobile. It is the embodiment of
an experimental literature, an amorphic architecture, a formless
painting, a casual speech. It is, in a word, thoroughly American
and a mirror of its innovating culture.

For Judaism, events are seen *sub specie aeternatis*. For while
Judaism is dynamic and moving, its dynamism is expressed in
the key word *Halakhah*, a "going," a movement along a certain
path without constant forays into the backroads of experimentation and innovation. The structure of the Halakhah is absolute
and eternal. But the key phrase of America is found in "nothing
is here to stay." New structures have in them a built-in transiency and impermanence, and Detroit builds "dynamic obsolescence" into its automobiles.

For further contrast, consider the poets of the two traditions.
Could any Jewish poet have written in the wild enthusiasm and
self-deification of a Walt Whitman:

> I celebrate myself and sign myself,
> And what I assume you shall assume,
> For every atom belonging to me as good belongs to you. . . ?

Can any Jewish poet boast of his own land as Whitman boasts
of America: ". . . born here of parents born here of parents the

ext::

same, and their parents the same . . . ?" Conversely, could an American poet have written in the prophetic cadences of a Bialik, who was a contemporary of the modern Whitman and not an ancient:

> If you wish to know
> The eternal strength of my people . . .
> Seek out the *Bet Ha-midrash*
> And there you will see,
> Bent over the Talmud,
> A figure swaying, swaying . . .

Or consider the folk literature, in which a deeper split is found. Contrast the American folk tale, with its hyperbole and self assurance (the "tall story") with the Jewish folk tale and its understatement and self-deprecation. Jewish folk heroes are quite dissimilar from Paul Bunyan, logger de luxe, and Billy the Kid or Jesse James, outlaws. (Again the frontier is visible.)

The American spirit is the song of the open road: the past is known, the future charted. American history is clear, factual, documented. Perhaps as a consequence of this we find in American life little of mystery or symbolism. In truth, the very attraction which ritual and mystery hold out for Americans is an indication of its absence from daily life. Witness the fascination with which America observed the Queen's coronation ritual several years ago, or the powerful appeal of exotic organizations:

To belong to a secret order and be initiated into its rites, to be part of a "Temple" with a fancy Oriental name, to parade dressed in an Arab fez or burnoose, to have high-sounding titles of potentates of various ranks in a hierarchy: all this has appeal in a nonhierarchical society *from which much of the secrecy and mystery of life have been squeezed out.*[8]

It has even been suggested that the United States Constitution is achieving the status of sacred symbol because the openness of American history has resulted in a society bereft of symbolism of a mystical nature.[9]

The Jew is rooted in something less open and tangible. His beginnings and his destiny are shrouded in the unknown, and

Jewish life is replete with symbol, with ritual, and with mystery. We need only compare the respective holiday celebrations. Passover, for example, is taught to many Jewish children as the "Jewish Fourth of July." Externally, both occasions celebrate independence and freedom from oppression. But they are celebrated quite differently. Pesach is typically Jewish. It brims with symbol: *matzah*, *maror*, the Seder, the Haggadah: the Pesach cup of ritual runneth over. But Fourth of July observances are frequently diluted into nothing more than noise, fireworks, and patriotic speeches.

Because of the intrinsic clarity of the American tradition, its thinking concerning some of the basic issues of life is expressed in the pragmatic: that is good which succeeds, that is evil which fails. There is a concurrent admiration for the concrete and particular as against abstract ideas. A leading American historian states that "the American felt instinctively that philosophy was the resort of the unhappy and the bewildered, and he knew that he was neither." [10] The authentic American is not a thinker, but one who gets things done. He believes in tangibles; intangibles make him suspicious, for, in Turner's words, "American democracy was born of no theorist's dream. God Himself, to the American mind, was not so much a supernatural Being as a kindly older brother." In Commager's words, "Americans naturalized God, as they naturalized so many other concepts." [11] The American is a technical man who is concerned with *how* and not *what* or *why*. His thought is therefore often tentative and fragmented, and he is "anxious to do rather than be." [12]

Judaic thought, however, is based on concepts less utilitarian. To William James the "good is the maximum satisfaction of demand," but for the Jew the quest is not for the good but the holy. For him, that is holy which is godly, that is profane which is ungodly. His concern is not the satisfaction of a demand but the satisfaction of a command—God's. The Jewish concept is absolute and unswerving. Torah, prayer, Messiah are not useful in immediate life. Their value can be known only at some future point in eternity. But the American mind, rooted in the now, cannot wait until eternity for results.

We have attempted to point out several of the key differences between the American and Jewish experiences. Some of these differences, of course, obtain in any discussion concerning secular and religious traditions. But this is precisely the issue: that an equation between the two cannot be made. If some of the characteristics of the two traditions have been simplified, we have done so not to disparage but to present archetypes so as to crystallize our theme that America represents an unfamiliar rhythm and a strange tempo for the Jew. If Judaism has thus far been able to survive in this milieu it is less an indication of the essential compatibility of the two than of the viability of Torah in all cultures.

This is not to say that the two are mutually exclusive, but simply that the issue should not be one of reconciling the two civilizations. This is not necessary, or even desirable.

The credo of authentic Judaism is this: creative Jewish thinking must do more than merely make feeble attempts to force Judaism's compatibility with every current doctrine. Apologetics are less important than self-understanding, and Judaism must be true to, and consistent with, nothing but itself. In so doing it best serves the majority culture in which it may find itself at any given time. Particularly is this true in America, where the unmistakable signature of the Jewish experience can serve as a benign control on some of the more disturbing aspects of living.

The constant clatter of Judeo-Americana serves only to confuse. America is open to all points of view, to the Jewish no less than any other. The divergent world-views here adumbrated are an indication of some of the areas in which the American Jew, by being a standard bearer of his own unique tradition, can contribute to the American experience and enrich it with his own perspective and heritage.

NOTES

1 Thomas Hardy, "On an Invitation to the United States" in *Collected Poems* (New York: Macmillan, 1926).

2 Max Lerner, *America as a Civilization* (New York: Simon & Shuster, 1957), p. 947.

3 *Ibid.*, pp. 949, 951.

4 Vance Packard, *The Hidden Persuaders* (New York: David McKay, 1957), p. 230.

5 Harold Laski, *The American Democracy* (New York: Viking Press, 1948), p. 5.

6 *Ibid.*, p. 716.

7 David Riesman, *Individualism Reconsidered* (New York: Anchor Books, 1954), pp. 138ff.

8 Lerner, *op. cit.*, p. 635. Italics are mine.

9 *Ibid.*, p. 30.

10 Henry Steele Commager, *The American Mind* (New Haven: Yale U. Press, 1959), p. 9.

11 *Ibid.*, p. 164.

12 Laski, *op. cit.*, p. 39.

THEOLOGICAL PERSPECTIVES

NORMAN LAMM

*

The Unity Theme and Its Implications for Moderns

THE ONENESS of God is universally acknowledged as the foundation stone of Judaism and its main contribution to the world. The theme of the *Shema*, "Hear O Israel, the Lord is our God, the Lord is One," underlies every single aspect of Jewish life and thought, and permeates every page of its vast literature. So powerful is this vision of God's unity that inevitably it must express the corollary that the divine unity is the source of a unity that encompasses all existence.[1]

Nowhere is the idea of *yichud ha-shem*, the Unity of God, given more poignant and intense expression than in the Kabbalah. In Jewish mysticism, the Unity of God is not only one of the mightiest themes, but it becomes a living reality—perhaps the only reality. God's unity is taken not alone as an arithmetic proposition, but as the unification of all existence, in all its awesome diversity, through God. It is symbolized, in the Kabbalah, by the unity within God Himself. It is this unity—elaborated, explained, enhanced, and expounded by kabbalists from the Zohar through the late Rav Kook—of which our modern world stands in such desperate need. If it was ever necessary to reaffirm that theme, with its conscious rejection of all conflict, multiplicity, and fragmentation, it is today, when mankind stands poised, ready to blow itself to bits both physically and conceptually.

In this paper we shall examine the treatment of the Unity of God in one expression of the Jewish spirit, the Kabbalah—particularly in the Zohar and in the works of its most recent exponent, the late Rav Kook, Chief Rabbi of the Holy Land; in one sacred institution of Judaism, the Sabbath; and in one famous hymn of the Prayerbook, the *Lekhah Dodi*, a kabbalistic poem which celebrates the Sabbath. Our purpose is not a historical presentation of the Unity Theme, but rather to see what it can yield for us in the way of instruction: its implications for moderns.

The reader who is unacquainted with the atmosphere and terminology of the Kabbalah should be aware of the fact that mystical concepts, by their very nature, are incapable of precise, descriptive articulation. They can be expressed only suggestively, in symbolic form often quite complex in structure. The terms used may therefore sometimes sound absurd and unreal, even when they strive to grasp the very essence of reality itself. The reader who will regard the discussion of the Kabbalah as too recondite, may safely begin with the section entitled "The Implications."

THE WORLD OF DISUNITY

The Zohar, the source book of Kabbalah, regards our mundane world as the *alma de'peruda*, the World of Disunity or Diversity. The unification of existence, the overcoming of this fragmentation, is to be sought in the establishment of the *alma de'yichuda*, the World of Unity which is the higher unity within God Himself.[2] The true unity, beyond all others, is that of *Kudesha Berikh Hu*, the "Holy One, Blessed be He," and His *Shekhinah*, His "Presence" or "Indwelling." The apparent divorce of one from the other is what accounts for all that is wrong with the world. The failure of mankind is to be found in this World of Disunity. The function of man on earth is to help overcome this *perud* of schism and reestablish the primordial divine harmony of the Holy One and His Shekhinah, God in His transcendence and His immanence—the World of Unity.

This passion for the Unity of God, for the healing of the breach within Him, was given expression in the most powerful metaphor available. In human life it is the erotic urge which is the most intense symbol of union and oneness. Hence, erotic imagery was freely used in representing the drive for unity and the overcoming of the World of Disunity. (Parenthetically, it is in place to mention Prof. Scholem's observation that rarely did the Zohar ever use this kind of symbolism to express the urge for *devekut*, for the *unio mystica*, between God and man, as did the Christian mystics. It was almost exclusively used to designate the *yichud* or unification within God Himself.) The Holy One was considered the male element, and the Shekhinah almost always the female element. Shekhinah is thus known by a variety of names, all emphasizing its feminine quality. By thus assigning genders to these different aspects of the Creator, the Kabbalah was able to tap the deepest wells of human experience to express its overwhelming yearning for the *yichud* of God and the firm establishment of the World of Unity.

THE ROLE OF MAN

This reestablishment of the World of Unity was not considered, by the Kabbalah, an independent divine activity in which man is merely a passive observer who can do no more than exercise theosophic insight. Man is deeply involved with God in this drama of unification. The breach is not intrinsic; that would be a serious departure from the pure monotheism of all Judaism. God is, of course, absolutely one. It is, rather, only apparent. The error and failure that brought about this breach can be traced to man, not God.[3] It is, therefore, man who must initiate the reunification, and the ascendancy of unity in God is both to be reflected in and caused by unity in man's own life.

The act of *perud* (breach or separation), the conception of the Shekhinah as a *truly* separate entity rather than just an *apparent* distinction in the Godhead, was recognized by the Kabbalah as a danger to monotheism and identified as the primal mystical sin of man. The division introduced between Shekhinah and the Holy One was called, by the Zohar, The Cutting of the Plants (*ketzitzah bi'netiot*), the "Plants" symbolizing the Sefirot. This was the crime of Elishah ben Abuyah, the sage turned heretic, whom the Talmud described as a "cutter of plants" (*kotzetz bi'netiot*). This too was the original sin of Adam. By the act of eating of the forbidden fruit, primordial man separated the Shekhinah (represented by the Tree of Knowledge) from the rest of the Sefirot (i.e. the Holy One, represented by the Tree of Life). The punishment for this dualism, the divorce of the Shekhinah from the Holy One, is the silencing of Shekhinah

(God's immanence) which now becomes known as "speech without sound" (*dibbur beli kol*) or personified as "the lonely woman" (*ishah galmudah*), and the ordaining of death for mankind. Death was not a new decree issued by God, thus external to man. It is inherent in man in potential, and is awakened by his sin. Death is, in the Kabbalah, also represented by a tree: the *ilana de'mota*. This Tree of Death lies dormant within the Tree of Knowledge and is inactive as long as there is no disruption between the Tree of Knowledge and the Tree of Life—that is, the Holy One and His Shekhinah. But once the separation is effected, the Tree of Death emerges from the Tree of Knowledge which has been cut off from the Tree of Life. Man must die when he upsets the harmony of the divine unity. His life must therefore be dedicated to the reestablishment of the World of Unity.

In many other ways does the Kabbalah express the idea that the drama of *perud* and *yichud*, of separation and unification, is not a purely theocentric plot, but includes man as a major protagonist in its grand sweep. The Zohar refers to man as the *diyukna de'kalil kula*, the synthesis of all the spiritual forces that went into the work of creation. Man in his pure, pre-sin state reflected the hidden organism of God's own life. In that pure state, according to the author of *Shaarei Orah* (p. 9a), there was a free interchange between the higher and lower worlds. When Adam sinned, order turned into chaos; the Shekhinah was, so to speak, cut loose from the Holy One, and only through the act of redemption will the exiled Shekhinah be reunited with the Holy One in a return to the original divine harmony. Further, human effort, the "impulse from below," evokes a corresponding "impulse from above." The whole unification of God takes place in the soul of man, which is absorbed in the ultimate *yichud*. Hence the remarkable appellation of man as the "Lower Shekhinah" (*Shekhinah Tataah*). The union of Shekhinah and the Holy One which is regarded as taking place, as we shall later explain in greater detail, every Sabbath eve, has its corresponding effect on human life: the scholar is expected to cohabit with his wife on Sabbath eves. Every true marriage, maintains the author of *Iggeret ha-Kodesh* (Joseph Gikitila, later ascribed to Nachmanides), is a symbolic realization of the union of the Holy

One and His Shekhinah. Man is thus the active partner of God
in the whole process of *yichud*. An agent of the original disruption of universal harmony, he must become the agent of its redemption, restoring the unity of God's Name. The purpose of
the performance of every *mitzvah* is, therefore, the act of restoration. Hence, every religious performance is to be introduced by
the formula "for the sake of uniting the Holy One and His Shekhinah . . ." This restoration by means of Torah, *mitzvot*, and
prayer, with its many mystical intentions (*kavvanot*), becomes
the task of man and his function in the universe.

THE SABBATH

The quest for *yichud* found particularly strong articulation in
the Kabbalah's treatment of the Sabbath. We need not emphasize
the importance of the Sabbath in Kabbalah as in all of Judaism.
In the Kabbalah, the "Additional Soul" of the Sabbath day became not only an additional capacity for intellectual attainment,
as it did with Maimonides and the Jewish rationalists, but a
heightened religious sensitivity, an added spiritual dimension "on
the pattern of the world-to-come." The Sabbath, according to
the Zohar, is the source of all blessings for the six work days. The
author of *Shnei Luchot ha-Berit* speaks for the whole kabbalistic
tradition when he represents the week diagrammatically as the
menorah or candelabrum in which the middle flame which points
straight upwards symbolizes the Sabbath, and the two sets of
three flames each, which point towards the middle one, are the
week-days.

This Sabbath is the day par excellence of *yichud*. We have
already mentioned that Friday night is the time of union of the
Holy One and His Shekhinah or, as it is otherwise put, the King
and His Matron. But in this grand *yichud* the Kabbalah saw
many other elements absorbed. All of time is united in the Sabbath. The concentrated essence of the Sabbath, called the "Holy-
Point" (*nekudah kaddishah*), is indeed present during the week,
but it is obscured. There is no absolute distance between the holy
days and the profane days, for by the agency of Sabbath observance—"all those who occupy themselves with holiness during the

whole Sabbath day"—the weekdays become absorbed in the Holy
Sabbath-Point. On this day the Point is revealed to man as it
ascends upward, in the form of the Shekhinah, to be united with
the King (or Holy One). Man's whole life, even his ordinary
workdays, is thus included in the *yichud* of the Sabbath. Man's
participation in this unification of time is further emphasized by
the Zohar's description of the Lower Point (*nekudah tataah*), a
sort of counter-point to the Higher Point (*nekudah ilaah*) and a
symbol of human involvement in the Sabbath. It is this Lower
Point that banishes all woe and worry on the Sabbath and re-
places sadness and anger with the joy that makes it possible for
the Additional Soul to arrive. The unification within God on
the Sabbath is reflected in a corresponding unification within
man on the Sabbath. To this day Hassidim, who follow the Sephardic version of the liturgy, recite, on Friday nights, the passage from the Zohar beginning *ke'gavna* . . . "even as they unite
above in the One, so is there a unification below . . . one corresponding to one . . ."

Not only Sabbath and weekdays, the horizontal aspect of time,
but also past and present are united on the Sabbath for the Jew.
The Patriarchs are participants in the Jewish Sabbath, representing all of the past and uniting with the present. The Hebrew word
Shabbat— שבת —is divided by the Zohar into its component letters. The last two letters spell בת, daughter, which stands for
the Holy Sabbath Point: the united essence of the whole week,
or the Shekhinah with which it is identified. The first letter   ש
is interpreted orthographically, each of the three bars of the letter
representing a different one of the three Patriarchs. The unity
that prevails on the Sabbath, the Zohar implies, belies any abrupt
discontinuity between the sacred past and the mundane present.
All history is one continuum of holiness.

Even the material must be united with the spiritual in order
to involve the totality of existence in the great *yichud* on the Sabbath—for disembodied spirituality is itself a fragment, a result of
perud. Hence the importance of eating on the Sabbath, especially
the three meals, called by the Zohar the Meals of Faith (*seudata
di'mehemenuta*), each involving the participation of another one
of the Patriarchs.

All these unifications are but aspects of the central and ultimate *yichud* of the Holy One and the Shekhinah. The erotic metaphor is, therefore, most appropriate to this transcendent union. A number of kabbalists have even compared the Sabbath to a wedding ceremony. Both at a wedding and in the Sabbath Amidah, seven blessings are recited. In each there is a declaration of sanctity (*kiddush* in one case, *kiddushin* in the other) over wine. The opening verses of the central portions of the Amidahs of the Sabbath have similar significance: "Thou hast sanctified" (*atta kiddashta*) stands for the sanctification of the nuptials (*kiddushin*); "Let Moses be happy" for the happiness of the wedding; the "Additional" prayer (*musaf*) for the additional jointure of the bride's settlement (*tosefet ketubah*); and "Thou art One" (*atta echad*) for the coming together (*yichud*) of bride and groom following the ceremony.

LEKHAH DODI

This Unity Theme on the Sabbath is most beautifully expressed in the popular hymn chanted on Friday nights, the *Lekhah Dodi* ("Come my beloved, let us meet the bride, let us welcome the Sabbath"). The poem was composed in the sixteenth century by R. Solomon Alkabetz, the teacher and brother-in-law of R. Moses Cordovero; these, together with R. Isaac Luria (who encouraged Alkabetz to write the hymn), are the leaders of the great school of Safed Kabbalists. The hymn is vastly popular. A measure of its wide acceptance can be seen in the remarkable number of melodies composed for it. Mr. Jakob Michael, a friend of the writer and member of his congregation, has 540 melodies in his private collection. The Birnbaum collection at the Hebrew Union College contains another 700 *Lekhah Dodi* melodies, with an estimated total of 1300 to 2,000 different tunes having been composed for it—so that if a new one were chanted every Friday night, one would not exhaust his repertoire for about forty years! Felicity of style and esthetic excellence can only partially account for the hymn's universal popularity amongst all Jews. It seems that a more basic explanation is the innate and unstudied response to the hymn's major mystical themes,[4] to the poetry of the soul rather than the poetry of the pen. The praying public may retain or reject a *new* prayer, especially one whose precise mystical symbolism is clear only to initiates, without being consciously aware of the nature or causes of its reaction. The worshippers unconsciously respond to the broad themes, the real essence of the prayer which, like the moon obscured behind the clouds, exerts a hidden but inexorable influence upon the ebb and tide of their religious experience in the deepest subterranean channels of their souls. So does the secret of the success of *Lekhah Dodi* lie in the magnificent sweep of its esoteric Unity Theme.

The Symbols

The symbols in Alkabetz's poem are not always constant. The Sabbath may sometimes be the "bride"—the Talmud already speaks of Sabbath as bride and queen. The groom or beloved (*dodi*) may be Israel. In a famous Midrash, the Sabbath complains to God that while each of the other days has its mate she is being left an old maid—an all too human complaint—and God presents her with her groom, Israel. But no doubt these are secondary to the primary "wedding" or *yichud*: that of the Holy One and His Shekhinah, the true *dodi* and *kallah* of the hymn. On Sabbath the Shekhinah (the Zohar's Holy Point which during the weekdays is in the lower worlds, obscured from both God and man) rises to meet her divine lover, the Holy One. It should be emphasized that not only is Sabbath the time during which the unification is effected, but *Shabbat* is itself identified with Shekhinah, the bride of the Holy One.

An Interpretation of the Halakhah

The first stanza explicitly repeats the Unity Theme. Since the Holy One and His Shekhinah have already been united, God is referred to as the *E-lha-meyuchad*. This union means that God's Name—the first two and last two letters of the Tetragrammaton which represent, respectively, the Holy One and the Shekhinah has been reunited, hence: "the Lord is One and His Name is One."

The first phrase of this same stanza is of particular importance to us. *Shamor ve'zakhor be'dibbur echad hishmianu*—"observe" and "remember" were spoken in one word. The poet here refers to the well known Agadah that that both commandments relating to the Sabbath, in each of the two versions of the Decalogue, were given simultaneously. Both "observe the Sabbath day to keep it holy" and "remember the Sabbath day to keep it holy" were uttered by God at one moment, but were heard separately by the Israelities. In the Halakhah, "remember" represents the positive commandment—the *kiddush* or sanctification of the Sabbath —while "observe" is the negative, the warning to refrain from the thirty-nine categories of *melakhah* or labor. It would not be amiss to say that here, too, in the context of the whole hymn, we have the *yichud* theme and an implicit rationale for the prohibition of *melakhah* on the Sabbath. If Sabbath is the time for and of the essence of *yichud*, then the positive commandment, "remember," is, of course, to be understood as the means for the achievement of this union. But since "observe" and "remember" are but two aspects of a single divine command, then the negative expression of the divine will—the "observe," the refraining from labor—must also contribute to the unification in God. This is indeed understandable in terms of the Halakhah's treatment of the biblical prohibition of *melakhah* (labor) on the Sabbath. The breakdown of the *melakhah* prohibition to thirty-nine separate major categories, with untold numbers of *toledot* or minor categories subsumed under them, signifies the fragmentized nature of the profane days. The unsanctified days are the real World of Disunity. Man's involvement with nature requires of him to atomize his experience in the various arts and crafts by which he sustains himself physically and economically. The fragmentization of his activity is indicative of the inner disintegration of his own personality and spirit. On *Shabbat*, by refraining from any intrusion into the normal processes of nature, he protects, in a negative manner, the integrity of his own personality. He is in a position to pursue the goal of *yichud*, by way of "observing" the Sabbath, without interference and breakdown. During the six workdays mundane life has broken up man's human experience into a spectrum of thirty-nine colors; but Judaism, through the Sabbath, reunites and reintegrates the diverse colorations of experience into the pure white light of the unique, undivided Creator. The abstention from *melakhah* thus enables man to overcome the World of Disunity and participate in the Sabbatical unification of the Holy One and His Shekhinah. The Halakhah, which normally presumes a pluralistic universe because it operates in the "real" World of Disunity, thus reveals in its treatment of the Sabbath its ultimate monism.

The Future

The middle and last stanzas of *Lekhah Dodi* speak of the themes of Messiah, the redemption, and peace. The relationship of these to the idea of Unity is obvious. The Shekhinah is in exile together with Israel; the Kabbalah often refers to Shekhinah by the name *Knesset Yisrael*, the Congregation of Israel. The redemption of Israel signifies the reunion of Shekhinah with the Holy One, the beloved. The time we welcome the Sabbath as the occasion for the meeting of the Holy One and His Shekhinah is therefore most appropriately the occasion for waiting and hoping and praying for the national *yichud* of which the union of the Holy One and Shekhinah is paradigmatic. *Shalom*, peace, is the state at which *yichud* aims, the condition of complete and utter universal harmony and unity. R. Loewe of Prague (the *Maharal*) declares, in a similar vein, that the present mundane world is that of diversity, whereas the world-to-come is that of oneness —thus extending the principle from Messianic to eschatological times.

THE IMPLICATIONS

It now remains for us to investigate some of the implications of this idea for modern Jews—modern in a chronological sense only, for the implications we shall draw are valid for us only as long as we locate ourselves ideologically in the context of the Jewish tradition which gave birth to the Kabbalah and especially the Unity Theme. In order to do this we shall move from the esoteric and mystical world of the Kabbalah to contemporary, exoteric modes of thought, and follow some of the consequences of the *yichud* idea in terms relevant to our own current predicament, dealing with problems which are, at most, only penultimate to the transcendent *yichud* of which the Kabbalah speaks.

Disintegration

Modern man and the complex society he has built for himself are in a state of progressive inner disintegration. Psychologically, socially, and spiritually, he has re-formed himself on the pattern of his new industrial economy. With the obsolescence of the artisan who fashioned the whole vessel, the Whole Man has faded into obscurity. The division of labor, which is indigenous to our modern economy, has begotten many other divisions in many other fields of human endeavor. In professional life, narrow specialization has replaced general practice. Culturally, the expert dominates over men of broad knowledge and general culture. Literature, which should strive for the wholeness of man, has merely reacted to our inner atomization and put under the literary microscope man's baseness and degradation in which only unrelated pieces of fractured experience are regarded as real, and in which wholeness and higher integrity are considered meaningless abstractions. Literary criticism has turned upon the Bible and replaced its unity with a Documentary Hypothesis which has made of Scriptures a haphazard collection of disparate fragments. Philosophically, the extreme logical positivism of some modern thinkers and their reduction of all issues to linguistic analysis is symptomatic of the same tendency. Man's spiritual and religious life has become a true World of Disunity. Long before the atom bomb struck Hiroshima, the modern world sustained a historic atomization, the fission and dis-integration of man's heart and soul and mind, and the beginning of the end of his *universe*.

Indeed there is a deeper relation between the splitting of the atom and the fragmentation of the Self. The tendency to view existence as divided, in pieces or dualities, in "over-against" terms, must inevitably have a deteriorating effect upon the integrity not only of man's ideological orientation but ultimately also his social existence. It was Philo who traced war and peace to man's intellectual activity, particularly to his conception of the Deity. War, he said, stems from paganism which, in its elaborate mythology, saw gods locked in combat with each other, spying, stealing, and betraying in order to gain victory. The pagan's theology influenced his anthropology, his view of man. His social *anschauung* was thus compatible with constant conflict and war—a true *imitatio dei*. The monotheist, who knew of only One God Who embraces all existence in His unity and Who prefers the state of peace which is the end result of unification, naturally sought peace in his own social and political relationships. A recurrent verse in our liturgy is: "May He Who makes peace up above make peace for us and for all Israel." A divided society and fragmented polity is the natural result of a World of Disunity.

Yet we are not here addressing ourselves primarily to the obvious fact of the divisiveness of the world politically and militarily, consequential as it is to our very existence. We are emphasizing, rather, the inner peace without which there can be no outer peace, for a fragmented world is merely fragmented man writ large. It is this inner fragmentation of both experience and man's beliefs and attitudes that must be overcome as the World of Disunity if the social and political integration of mankind into one brotherhood is to be achieved.

It was Rabbi Abraham Isaac Hakohen Kook, the famed Chief Rabbi of the Holy Land (d. 1936), who gave the Unity Theme its greatest development in modern times. Rav Kook's concern with man's atomizing tendencies, and his deep passion for unity throughout all existence, are apparent in almost every page of his writings. Himself a kabbalist of the first order who was very much aware of the modern world, he bridges the gap between the Kabbalah's mystical yearning for *yichud* and the need for unity in human affairs. In the following paragraphs we shall draw upon many of his works, but primarily upon the first volume of his *Orot ha-Kodesh*, published in Jerusalem in 1938.

Knowledge

Rav Kook sees the need for *yichud* in the transcending of human epistemological limitations. Every act of cognition, he writes, implies an area of error (*tzel* or shadow). The view of the whole, in proper perspective, must become distorted in the very act of reduction and withdrawal from the whole to the part or specific, a process which is indigenous to the very act of cognition. The more isolated and refined the area of knowledge, the greater the error or *tzel*. The only way to overcome this inherent defect in man's cognitive life, the only way the shadows can be dispersed and the breach in his intellectual organism healed, is through communion with God Who comprehends all knowledge in His transcendent *yichud*.

The same striving for *yichud* in a spiritual context, or at least an awareness of the severe limitations of our World of Disunity, is the solution not only to the problem of epistemology, but to a related problem in our modern culture: the phenomenon of specialization. The more we are involved in one branch of knowledge, the more we tacitly assume its self-sufficiency, and the more we ignore its relatedness to and dependence upon other branches. Rav Kook was especially annoyed by the specialist's haughty disdain, his willful, transcendental ignorance of other disciplines. This is the way of error and confusion, he taught. All knowledge must be accepted as interrelated, reflecting the fundamental unity of the Creator, if specialization is to yield the desired creative results.

In the same vein, Rav Kook refuses to see an unbridgeable chasm separating religion and science. Religious and scientific knowledge are really one in an objective sense; they stand in contrast only subjectively. Spiritual insight, as opposed to intellectual comprehension, is characterized by a total view, by grasping all at once; the latter by its nature deals with specifics, with fragments. The practical progress of the world requires quantification rather than the total, unifying grasp of spiritual insight. Yet spiritual cognition and scientific knowledge are only apparently contradictory. It is a psychic gap that separates the religionist's striving for the over-all from the the scientist's critical eye for detail. It requires genius to be able to overcome this abyss, this division, and arrive at their underlying oneness, recognizing that obectively both forms of knowledge are one.

The *yichud* of knowledge is extended by Rav Kook to the study of Torah. Torah cannot abide artificial distinctions between the inner life of man and the world at large, between human individuality and universality. The emphasis on the Prophets and Writings, as opposed to the Pentateuch, represents an imbalance

in favor of inwardness, an imbalance he regards as one of the
"great pains of exile." Both the element of Prophecy (and Aggadah) and the legal element that predominates in the Pentateuch
must be integrated with each other. (This is a somewhat oblique
criticism of the Christian—and Emancipation's—usurpation of
the post-Pentateuchal portions of the Bible and their spirit-against-
letter and love-against-law dualisms.)

Similarly, Rav Kook is unhappy with the chasm that separates
Aggadah from Halakhah. Superficially there is a difference between them. The Holy Spirit responsible for the Written Law is
different in quality from the Holy Spirit of the Oral Law or Halakhah. Prophecy and Aggadah derive from what might be translated as "idealistic dignity" whereas Halakhah issues from "royal
strength." But the world can be set right only when they are
united in the soul of the Jew, for the strangeness of the halakhist
in Aggadah and the aggadist in Halakhah is destructive of spiritual
growth. The *yichud* we perform between them merely reveals the
preexistent, original identity of Halakhah with Aggadah: they are
one and the same. The attempt at integration must proceed by
searching for the halakhic norms in the Aggadah, and the fundamental aggadic themes of Halakhah.

Yichud in the world of knowledge, therefore, applies to Torah
as well as to all other branches of wisdom, demanding the integration of all knowledge and the abandonment of artificial barriers
in order to achieve a more wholesome view of life, a unified
world-view which will be built on the specialized sciences and
yet transcend them. It should be indicated in passing that in many
disciplines, especially the natural sciences, a more integrated, total
view is now beginning to find acceptance. In quantum physics,
statistical predictions based on group phenomena have replaced
the study of individual particles; the motion of a single particle
is not examined except in relation to others. Biology has veered
towards a more organismic approach, as we shall have occasion
to mention again later, and psychology is leaning more and more
to a gestalt position. Whether field theory, gestalt, organismic
approach, or holism, when the scientific terms are translated into
the vocabulary of the Kabbalah, you have: *yichud*—not, of course,
the great and transcendent *yichud* of the Holy One and the She-

khinah, but the first baby steps, as it were, leading ultimately to the integration of all knowledge and experience in the oneness of God.

Personality

More serious than the fragmentation of knowledge is the disintegration of personality. And the personal break-down of modern man, his inability to grasp more than a multiplicity of isolated aspects of life and his failure to unify his experiences in a comprehensive point-of-view, is reflected most clearly in the *study* of personality. In the sciences devoted to the study of man and society we usually work from the parts to the whole; we analyze discreet items and then add them together. This emphasis on discreet entities has a long history in Western thought. If Aristotle was unable to fit a new observation into a predetermined category, he created a new one. Hume, setting the prototype for modern positivism, maintained that man can know "nothing but a bundle or collection of different perceptions." On this basis he denied the possibility of knowing the Self. Following him, John Stuart Mill treated all psychological problems as soluble by an atomistic psychology. Hobbes saw society only as an aggregate of self-contained individuals, assimilated through external instruments. One writer, Dorothy Lee (cited in Helen Merrell Lynd's *On Shame and the Search for Identity*), has seen in this attitude a fundamental pattern of thinking characteristic of Western man. She calls this preoccupation with proceeding from the parts to the whole a "lineal codification of reality," in contrast to the non-lineal approach of other cultures; a difference being, for example, whether we conceive of society as a plurality of independent individuals, or of the individual as a differentiated member of society.

Fortunately, the pendulum seems now to be swinging from an affirmation of the World of Disunity to a quest for the World of Unity, if we be permitted to use these terms freely. Some psychologists now believe that the differences between atomistic and holistic psychology are being resolved in favor of holistic or gestalt concepts, of "molar" as opposed to "molecular" terms. Even Freud, who with his concentration on specific biological needs and his splitting of the Self into Id, Ego, and Super-ego seemed to enhance the fragmentation of personality, nevertheless contributed to a holistic or molar approach by bringing into the scope of investigation many other heretofore neglected areas of the Self and treating them all as a continuity. One renowned researcher working on the biology of nervous systems has concluded that only the sick or damaged personality can be understood by examining its parts in isolation; its relation to the world can best be described in segmented, additive terms. A fully functioning person, however, can be described only in holistic terms. The *yichud* theme, understood exoterically and anthropocentrically, is thus a striving for a higher sanity, an escape from the psychosis of the World of Disunity. The *yichud* within God requires a corresponding *yichud* within man, including, as Rav Kook writes, a "merging of intellect and emotion," and the "integration of reason and will"—a reintegration of man's personality in which his mental oneness will be paralleled by a spiritual unity.

Theology

In his theological thinking, too, modern Western man behaves atomistically rather than holistically. He is heir to a number of dualisms, which he usually accepts uncritically, that have come to him from the ancient Greeks via Christianity, especially the Church Fathers. Thus the distinction between the body and soul, which in Judaism is essentialy a diagnostic way of explaining the ethical tensions of man, is for Christianized Western man a stark reality. When the Kabbalah unites, as it does in its interpretation of the Sabbath, the spiritual and material, it denies the bifurcation of man's Self into body and soul as two independent and antagonistic entities. The same can be said for the dichotomy of religious endeavor into faith and works, of religious experience into *eros* and *agape*, or, for that matter, into love (*ahavah*) and fear (*yirah*.) All such distinctions are merely apparent. Underneath, they are one, even as the Holy One and the Shekhinah are one. The kabbalistic formula recited before the performance of a *mitzvah*, to which we referred previously, includes the phrase *bi'dechilu u'rechimu*—in fear *and* love. The Kabbalah, with its deep and passionate striving for *yichud*, cannot abide a bifurcated view of life which accepts *perud* as a permanent and inherent quality of all existence.

Of even greater moment is the distinction between sacred and profane. At first glance it would seem as if the very existence of these two categories, not only sanctioned by Torah but crucial to its whole outlook, conveys a sense of *perud*, an absolute distance between the two, so that there can be no underlying unity comprehending the both of them. Yet the truth is that in a religion which did not make of the Devil an independent personality pitted against the beneficent God, thus providing for separate sanctions for the domains of the sacred and profane, but saw Satan as only one of the created angels commissioned by God to execute His Will, there can be no *absolute* distance between holy and unholy. A distinction there certainly is—the concept of *havdalah* with all its profound ramifications attests to this— but it is accidental rather than essential, apparent rather than real, extrinsic rather than intrinsic. This is the gist of Rav Kook's intention when he remarks that the "foundation of the holy of holies" comprehends both the "subject [or element] of the sacred and that of the profane." Even more poignant expression was given to this idea in a profound homiletic observation by R. Isaiah Halevi Horowitz, the author of *Shnei Luchot ha-Berit*. In the Havdalah service which marks the end of the Sabbath, he remarks, we proclaim the distinction between sacred and profane, light and dark, Israel and the other nations, and Sabbath and weekday. The first two and the last are appropiate to the occasion. But what is the relevancy of the *havdalah* between Israel and the other nations in this context? He answers that there is a difference not only between Jew and non-Jew, but between the Jewish and non-Jewish understanding of the whole concept of *havdalah*. The Gentile conceives of an *absolute* separation between the sacred and the profane. The Jew, contrariwise, understands that the gulf between sacred and profane is introduced not to signify a permanent and irreconcilable dualism, but to allow the sacred to be confirmed in its strength and purity so that it might return and sanctify the profane. From this point of view there is no holy and unholy; there is just the holy and the not-yet-holy. This is identical with Rav Kook's assertion that the holy of holies includes the sacred *and* the profane.

Basically, this insight pertains most strongly today. We modern Jews have, in our daily life and habit, adopted the *havdalah* concept of the non-Jewish world. We have conducted our affairs on the unspoken presupposition that there is an unbridgeable gap between the two categories, each isolated in its own cubicle. We go about life as if the American political doctrine of the separation of church and state were a metaphysical dogma. The modern Jew factually confines the expression of his religious convictions to several holy places and holy moments, not to the entire week and every place. The "Holy Sabbath-Point" of the American Jew's Sabbath, unlike that of the Zohar, has no relationship with the six workdays. Despite his clearly defined occasions of holiness, which may be sincerely intended and genuinely experienced, he permits himself spiritual vulgarity, or spiritlessness, in the material endeavors of life. Emotionally he is unrelated to his spiritual dimension. We are different things to different people, different people to ourselves. Finding ourselves, when within the large area of the profane, thoroughly insulated from the influence of the holy, we are not only at an infinite distance from God, but broken and fragmentized within, our knowledge unrelated and our experiences unintegrated. Our entire world is as much in danger from mankind's internal fission as it is from the fission of the atomic nucleus. The powerful secularism of our day, which recognizes the sacred only so long as it promises not to encroach upon the privileged domain of the secular, is a reassertion of the non-Jewish concept of *havdalah*, a theology which we, in our *yichud*-obsessed world-view, cannot accept lest it disarm and emasculate the very essence of holiness whose function it is to fructify the profane and secular.

This position on the basic, underlying relationship and dialectic of sacred and profane implies a critical revaluation of the whole educational structure and philosophy of most of Orthodoxy today. Modern Orthodoxy has good reason to be proud of its herculean educational achievements. It has raised a generation of American Jews who have benefited from both a religious and secular upbringing. This is not the first time in history that this has occurred, but the number of Jews receiving a training in both and retaining a commitment to Torah is unprecedented. The whole edifice of traditional Judaism in this country today rests upon this dual educational foundation. It is of interest to observe, therefore, that by and large we may be guilty of a cultural schizophrenia in our attitude to secular and religious studies, equivalent to what, in *Shnei Luchot ha-Berit*, is regarded as the theological schizophrenia in the non-Jewish understanding of the two categories themselves. Whether we relegate the sacred studies to an hour on a Sunday morning as Reform does, or strive for the minimum secular studying required by state law as the Hassidic schools do, or somehow try to accommodate both on an approximately equal schedule as modern *yeshivot* do, the common denominator of all three in practice is that the two courses of study are departmentalized, unrelated, and merely coexist in splendid isolation from each other within the individual student. The differences between the above systems thus seem to lie in the quantitative distribution of the time allotted for each discipline. Yet this is decidedly not in keeping with the thesis we have been developing.[5] As long as this unrelatedness continues, we are guilty of wasting the resources of the sacred for the profane. State law or economic necessity or social needs are not an answer sufficient to define a consistent philosophic position. The real answer—and this is the real meaning of the "synthesis" of which Yeshiva University speaks and for which it stands—is the qualitative accommodation of both studies. The secular studies are not inherently and eternally unholy. And the sacred studies are sterile unless they have something other than the sacred to act upon. There is no blurring of the distinctions between sacred and secular. But there is an appreciation of the function of the sacred in relation to the secular. The secular studies are important not *despite* the fact that they are not holy, but *because* this is the way in which all life, all knowledge, all existence is ultimately integrated in the great *yichud* of the Holy One and His Shekhinah. Eventually all that is profane (not-yet-holy) is to be found in and sanctified through the Torah, for which reason—according to Rav Kook—it is called *de'kullah bah* ("containing everything") and is regarded as the fulfillment of

God's blessing of Abraham *ba-kol* ("with everything"—Genesis
24:1).

CONCLUSION

We have seen how the theme of the oneness of God, fundamental to every expression of Judaism, is expanded by the Kabbalah—especially in its treatment of the Sabbath and beautifully
expressed in the *Lekhah Dodi*—to an overwhelming, burning
passion for the unification of all life and existence, in all its multifarious aspects, in the unity of God. Where the earlier kabbalists,
as in the Zohar, were satisfied in articulating this theme in purely
mystical terms, as the union of the Holy One and the Shekhinah,
its later exponents, and especially Rav Kook, increasingly applied
this thesis to the current, real world, the World of Disunity.
Man, as an active participant in the *yichud*, must exert himself
mightily in order to overcome the disintegrating tendencies of
life and society. We have seen how the modern manifestations
of the striving for unity, the transcending of petty dualisms and
fragmentizations, are gradually making themselves felt. Philosophically, psychologically, theologically, we must begin to move
from an atomistic to a holistic position.

What of the future? We must again return to Rav Kook in
whose life and works are so magnificently combined substance
and charm, power and elegance, the sudden insight of the kabbalist and the responsible thinking of the intellectual—the per-
sonification of the *yichud* which he preached and for which he
yearned. *Bo yavo*, Rav Kook proclaims. It shall come. It must
come. For the Jew—who cannot by his nature bear disunity in
his soul—it will appear in his people's redemption. The Diaspora,
the national realization of fragmentation and disunity, is only
ephemeral and basically unreal; sooner or later, Israel shall become "one nation upon earth." And *yichud* will come for all mankind. The future unification of all knowledge, all peoples, all
existence is inevitable. Redemption for Israel and peace for all
men will mark the World of Unity which is surely coming, and
which can be brought on even faster by our own efforts.

"And the Lord will be King over all the earth; on that day the Lord will be One and His Name will be One."

BIBLIOGRAPHICAL NOTE

1. KABBALAH.

Reference was made to many passages in the Zohar, particularly on the appropriate verses in the portions of *Be'shalach*, *Yitro*, and *Va-Yakhel*. Readers who wish to pursue the topic further may refer to Gershom G. Scholem's *Major Trends in Jewish Mysticism* (New York: Schocken Books, 1946), especially pp. 225–235, and in Hebrew to P. Lachover and Yeshayahu Tishbi, *Mishnat ha-Zohar* (Jerusalem, Hashiloah Press, 1949), pp. 219–263.

2. LEKHAH DODI.

Chemdat Yamim (Leghorn: 1763) I, 41.
A. Z. IDELSOHN, *Jewish Liturgy and its Development* (New York: Henry Holt & Co.).
Otzar ha-Teffilot, Anaf Yosef.

3. RAV KOOK.

As mentioned in the body of this essay, most of the references to Kook are from his *Orot ha-Kodesh* (Jerusalem: 1938), I. The theme is also alluded to by Rav Kook in his letters and in his *Olat Re'iyah* (Jerusalem: Mosad Harav Kook, 1939), his commentary on the prayerbook. Jacob B. Agus, in his *Banner of Jerusalem* (New York: Publishing, 1946), discusses Kook's mystical monism in general without going into detail.

4. HALAKHAH.

The place of Halakhah in the monistic scheme is quite complex. We have mentioned that Halakhah must presume a pluralistic universe, yet accept an ultimate monism. For a fuller development of this most significant theme, see Part III of the *Nefesh ha-Chayyim* of Rabbi Chayyim of Volozhin.

5. GENERAL.

Much of the material used is excellently summarized in Helen Merrel Lynd's *On Shame and the Search for Identity* (New York: Harcourt, Brace & Co., 1958). See also the Everyman edition of David Hume's

Treatise on *Human Nature*, vol. I, pp. 238–40. A theme similar to ours, but in a non-Jewish and non-theistic form, has been pressed in recent years by a number of Western Orientalists, notably Aldous Huxley.

NOTES

1 Amongst Jewish rationalists, Maimonides is the first to assert the unity of existence as flowing from the unity of the Creator: "Know that this Universe, in its entirety, is nothing else but one individual being . . . The variety of its substances . . . is like the variety of the substances of a human being: just as, e.g., *Said* is one individual, consisting of various solid substances such as flesh, bones, sinews, of various humours, and of various spiritual elements . . . You must therefore consider the entire globe as one individual being living through the motion of the sphere, which is endowed with life, motion, and a soul. This mode of considering the universe is . . . indispensable, that is to say, it is very useful for demonstrating the unity of God; it also helps to elucidate the principle that He who is One has created only *one* being . . . There also exists in the Universe a certain force which controls the whole, which sets in motion the chief and principal parts, and gives them the motive power for controlling the rest. Without that force, the existence of this sphere . . . would be impossible. It is the source of the existence of the Universe in all its parts. That force is God, blessed be His name!" (*Guide to the Perplexed*, 1:72). Cf. Yehudah Even Shmuel's (Dr. Y. Kaufman) Introduction to his edition of the *Guide* in Hebrew, Vol. I p. xlii–xliii—*Moreh Nevukhim*, (Jerusalem: Mosad Harav Kook, 1959). The Kabbalists, of course, greatly elaborated on this theme. See, for instance, Part III of *Netzach Yisrael* by Rabbi Loewe of Prague (the *Maharal*) and Part III of *Nefesh ha-Chayyim* by Rabbi Chayyim of Volozhin.

2 The World of Unity is that of the ten Sefirot which in the Kabbalah are not, as are the Neoplatonists' emanations, static steps mediating between the Absolute God and the phenomenal world. They exist, rather, within God; they are the "unified universe" of God's life.

3 This holds true for the Zohar. For Luria, "the breaking of the vessels" implies a disarray in the world(s) that preceded the creation of man.

4 It is interesting that the same mystical content was responsible for the initial hesitation in accepting the hymn as a part of the service. Many Sephardic, and some Ashkenazic—especially German—congregations, were opposed to the chanting of *Lekhah Dodi* because of the general sensitivity to Kabbalah following the Sabbatian heresy. I am informed that the cantor in the *klaus* in Frankfort a.M. would remove his *tallit* for the chanting of *Lekhah Dodi*.

5 For a more elaborate development of this theme, see my "Two Versions of Synthesis" in *The Leo Jung Jubilee Volume* (New York: The Jewish Center, 1962).

WALTER S. WURZBURGER

*

Pluralism and the Halakhah

O F LATE it has become fashionable to view atomic fission as the symbol of a disintegrating civilization. Our atomic misery makes for strange bedfellows. Spokesmen for science and religion vie with each other in decrying the ills of atomization and fragmentation—the villains blamed for the weird array of psychological, social, and political ailments that plague modern man.

Amidst such a climate of opinion, we are prone to ignore the intellectual and psychological hazards that can result from preoccupation with the other extreme—the craving for absolute unity —that is so often regarded as the hallmark of religious orientation.[1] We tend to forget that without division, separation, and specialization, all significant human thought must come to a standstill. Moreover, it must be borne in mind that the Platonic emphasis upon the *essential* unity that underlies all *existential* diversity has given rise to various political systems that swallow up the individual in an ocean of collectivity. Similarly, the grandiose attempt of Hegel to reduce Reality to the One Absolute unfolding itself in a logic of history has led (via its Marxian adaptation) to the emergence of modern communism with its utter contempt for the rights of the individual. By the same token, Higher Criticism—the fantastic attempt to undermine the authority of the Bible, especially of the Pentateuch, by stigmatizing the canonical writings as clumsy hodgepodges of assorted passages from numerous authors—does not at all reflect the influence of atomization or fragmentization. On the contrary, the methods of Higher Criticism, as Professor Kaufmann[2] has shown, were inspired either by Hegelian notions concerning the unfolding of the Absolue in history or by the totally unwarranted extension to the domain of religious thought of Darwinian notions concerning the evolution of the species. In either case, the fragmentization of the Pentateuch can be traced back to the overzealous search for unity—manifesting itself in the obsession to find a single master formula for the understanding of all of reality.

It may be contended that these arguments discredit only certain brands of monistic philosophies but do not affect the validity of the so-called "unity theme." [3] It will therefore be the purpose of this paper to show that for cogent reasons Judaism held in check its monistic trends and assigned priority to the pluralism inherent in the halakhic approach.

I

Kabbalistic thinking, though composed of a variety of strands, is marked by a strong bent towards a radical monism. Drawing upon this conceptual framework, Rabbi Lamm portrays a masterful picture of a world view that regards all forms of separation as a cosmic tragedy—relieved only by the comforting realization that with the fulfillment of our eschatological hopes all divisiveness would be overcome.

This standpoint is akin to the orientation of the mystic to whom any form of separation from the ultimate One is intolerable. Hence, escape from the illusory world of appearance and union with the ultimately Real become the only worthwhile goals of life.

Significantly, many of the foremost halakhic thinkers displayed a proclivity for this mystic approach. Even such a staunch advocate of a rigorous Halakhah-centered orientation as Rabbi Chayyim of Volozin could not completely suppress his monistic longings. They come to the fore in a passage in which the illusory character of all existential diversity is unabashedly admitted. Developing the kabbalistic notion of the "Higher Unity" to its logical conclusion, Rabbi Chayyim acknowledges that, metaphysically speaking, Absolute Reality is constituted of undifferentiated oneness. "In truth, from His side, all of existence is filled with His being, without any separations, distinctions, or divisions, as if creations had not taken place at all." [4] Rabbi Chayyim is, of course, quick to recognize that such an attitude is completely incompatible with any form of normative Judaism. This is why he immediately proceeds with the important proviso: "We are neither capable nor permitted to contemplate this fact at all, but must seek to perform His *mitzvot* in the world that is revealed to our understanding." [5]

Obviously, the very foundation of the Halakhah would collapse if all distinctions were merely of an illusory character. Large segments of Jewish law presuppose the reality of spatial and temporal distinctions. Even more disastrous would be another corollary of viewing the world from the perspective of the "Higher Unity." If God's Presence permeates equally all reality, then the very difference between the sacred and the profane, the pure and the impure, between good and evil itself, would be completely obliterated. The implications of the position would lead to such a radical antinomianism that even the excesses of the Sabbatian heresy would by comparison pale into insignificance.

Rabbi Chayyim could not brook any world view that would assign only relative importance to halakhic norms. In a manner so characteristic of the essentially pluralistic approaches of halakhic Judaism, he does not even attempt to resolve the tension between his mystic, monistic leanings and his halakhic, pluralistic orientation. Instead, he pragmatically postulates the existence of finite, individual entities as indispensable to the functioning of the halakhic process. [6]

In marked contrast to this position, Rabbi Lamm, in his quest for unification, invades the very stronghold of pluralism—the Halakhah. While he concedes the essentially pluralistic outlook of the Halakhah as a whole, he nonetheless contends that Judaism's penchant for absolute unity comes to the fore in one of the most pivotal areas of the Halakhah—the laws of the Sabbath.

From Rabbi Lamm's brilliant presentation, the various halakhic injunctions and regulations concerning the Sabbath emerge as an eloquent protest against man's involvement in the world of nature. Since all creativity in the world of nature depends upon processes utilizing atomization and fragmentization, the abstention from creative work on the Sabbath is designed to remove man from the "World of Disunity" and lead him towards a higher plane of existence where all separation and division are surmounted.

This poetic description of the higher symbolic function of the Sabbath—as a manifestation of the "Higher Unity" towards which

Judaism aspires—has a deeply moving quality. But it cannot be adduced as evidence for the unity thesis. For nowhere can it be shown that this interpretation reflects halakhic categories of thought. In point of fact, the argument has employed purely kabbalistic notions to provide a rationale for Sabbath observance. As a matter of fact, it could easily be shown that this essentially mystic explanation clashes with numerous other halakhic norms which look upon creativity in the world of nature not as a necessary evil but as the realization of the religious duty to become a partner with the Holy One, Blessed be He, in the process of creation." [7] Those who are not privileged enough to share the same proclivity for mystic thinking are free to adopt an entirely different rationale for Sabbath observance. Admirers of Samson Raphael Hirsch, for example, would find in the Sabbath not a protest against man's involvement with the mundane but rather an enthusiastic endorsement of human creativity. Accordingly, we link ourselves with the divine scheme of creation when, in conscious imitation of the Creator, we, too, interrupt our own creative efforts on the Sabbath.

Halakhic thinking, as a general rule, is marked by a far more affirmative attitude towards uniqueness and individuality than is suggested by the broad espousal of monism. Judaism does not strive for Nirvana—the dissolution of all individuality and particularity in the ocean of undifferentiated oneness. The verdict "it was good" was pronounced by God, so the Book of Genesis (1:31) informs us, not before, but after the process of separation had been initiated and distinctions had made their appearance in the world of creation. The Psalmist certainly was not embarrassed by the manifold. He made no attempt to discover any underlying unity. On the contrary, he exclaimed: "How manifold are thy works, O God!" (Psalms 104:24). The absolute Unity of the Creator does not at all imply the oneness of the creation. Moreover, it is precisely in the lower world of creation, not in the higher regions of Being, that, according to a well known Midrash, the Divine Presence has its main abode.[8]

Judaism has, of course, its share of mystic thinkers who yearn passionately for redemption from the world of disunity and disintegration. Thus Maimonides extolls *mitat neshikah* (death as a kiss) which enables the soul to become reunited with God.[9] A contemporary mystic, Professor Heschel, sums up his philosophy of life with the statement, "For the pious man it is a privilege to die." [10]

But it must be borne in mind that such attitudes do not arise out of the matrix of halakhic thinking. Instead, they reflect points of view that relegate the Halakhah to a peripheral position. In the case of Maimonides, we should note that his glorification of *mitat neshikah* as the liberation of the soul from the prison of finite limitation goes hand in hand with other non-halakhic trends such as the downgrading of the role of the *mitzvah*,[11] a stringent asceticism, and the advocacy of philosophical reflection as a means to mystical union with God. Obviously, these views do not express halakhic categories of thought, but attest to the powerful influence which Neo-Platonism exerted on Maimonides. Insofar as Professor Heschel's position is concerned, it is hardly necessary to point out that he represents a school of thought in which the Halakhah plays only a very subordinate role.

As opposed to these flights from earthly realities, the halakhist's attachment to the world of existential diversity is typified by Rabbi Hayyim's trenchant observations concerning the proper motivation for Torah study. In the Hassidic scheme, the study of Torah was looked upon as a means to communion with God. This view is rejected by Rabbi Chayyim who insisted that *Torah Lishmah* was to be taken literally as the study of the Torah for its own sake.[12] Superficially, the argument rests on solid, practical ground. It is, of course, impossible to concentrate upon involved and intricate talmudic problems if concern for mystical union with God diverts one's attention from the legal question at hand.

In reality, however, the issue goes far deeper than the requirements of the psychology of learning which call for a maximum of undivided attention for the attainment of optimum results. The very ideal of losing oneself in the all-embracing One clashes with the spirit of the Halakhah which emphasizes serving the One in and through a pluralistic world. Hence, we should study Torah to comprehend the divine will as it relates to man's task on earth, not to reach the mystic goal of *bittul ha-yesh* (the obliteration of individuality in the union with God).[13]

I I

Because halakhic thinking veers away from the ultimate implications of any system that revolves around the absolute Unity of Reality as a whole, it represents the very antithesis of what has been described by William James as the typical religious attitude. To quote a particularly revealing passage in *The Varieties of Religious Experience*, "the abandonment of self-responsibility seems to be the fundamental act in specifically religious, as distinguished from moral, practice." [14] That religion lends itself to this kind of interpretation was demonstrated by Dr. Servatius in a specially shocking manner during the Eichmann trial. In a ridiculous attempt to shift the onus of guilt from his client to Divine Providence, Eichmann's lawyer implied that the extermination of six million Jews formed an integral part of a divine design for human history. The absurdity of such an obnoxious defense maneuver should not blind us to the fact that the so-called religious attitude, unless counterbalanced by halakhic components, may in fact lead to an evasion of moral responsibility. If evil and suffering are parts of a cosmic scheme that "as a whole" is good, why not resign oneself to the prevalence of tragedy in the comforting faith that the calamities of our fellow man contribute to the ultimate goodness of the universe? [15] Why struggle against moral lapses if seemingly discordant notes constitute part of the higher harmony of an orchestra directed by a Divine Conductor?

Such attitudes of resignation and passivity are completely foreign to halakhic Judaism. In its scheme, man is not merely a creature, but also co-creator, "God's partner in the creative process." [16] Jewish tradition pins upon every individual the responsibility for the very survival of the cosmos. We must so act as if our action were to decide the very existence of the universe.[17] Thus religion leads, not to the evasion, but to the accentuation of personal responsibility.

Unlike the Stoic philosopher, the religious Jew cannot be indifferent to the suffering of his fellow man. Judaism advocates a philosophy of involvement—not detachment. It may be granted that from the standpoint of "Reality-as-a-whole" or, as Spinoza put it, "under the aspect of eternity," the suffering of the individual may vanish in the total good. The Midrash [10] goes so far as to credit death and suffering with winning for the universe the stamp of divine approval contained in the phrase, "God saw everything that He had made, and, behold, it was very good" (Gen. 1:31). Yet, this does not entitle any individual to adopt a "philosophical" attitude towards *preventable* suffering, especially that of his fellow man.

As human beings, we must come to grips with individual situations and specific problems. We cannot act with reference to "Reality-as-a-whole." All significant human action would come to a standstill if we were to proceed upon the assumption that all our distinctions are meaningless because they are transcended in the infinite. Our ethical behavior and social action must be predicated upon the admittedly limited perspective of finite, mortal creatures who catch only a partial (and probably even distorted) glimpse of the truth. But any attempt to rise above such a limited standpoint will only end up with a vicious relativism (even moral solipsism) where all distinctions between good and evil, right and wrong, become completely blurred.

With this proviso, we can wholeheartedly accept many spiritual benefits that spring from the "religious" attitude. When personal tragedies are accepted as necessary to the good of the whole, the burden of sorrow can be borne with a measure of equanimity. By stepping beyond our self-enclosed frame of reference, we can remove the sting of bitterness from much of our pain. A Hassidic sage expressed this in a striking comment on the Biblical verse, "God blessed Abraham with all" (Gen. 24:1). It was Abraham's ability to regard each isolated event as part of an over-all scheme that made his life the blessing it was.[19] In a similar vein, the same Hassidic leader read a profound insight into the Talmudic dictum, "All that God does is for the good" (*Berakhot* 6ob). If we look upon events not as isolated units but as parts of an all-embracing Whole, we shall discern that, all appearances to the contrary, they are really for the good.[20] It was this kind of faith that came to the fore in the moving statement of R. Israel Baal Shem Tov: "Because I am conscious of God, all things are of equal value to me."[21]

As one among the many strands that form the fabric of a pious life, such an attitude is highly commendable. But the situation is altogether different when absorption in the Whole becomes the dominant, let alone exclusive, feature of religiosity. Judaism is far too concerned with the fate of the individual to invite cavalier solutions to the problem of evil. The suffering of the individual remains a problem (witness the Book of Job!) in spite of the most idealistic systems human fancy can construct. The goodness of the system as such does not answer the needs of the individual in the throes of anguish and sorrow. Religion should deepen our sense of compassion, not provide a glib metaphysical pseudo-solution that explains away the very problem of evil.

Characteristically, the Halakhah is too realistic to recommend the adoption of an ultimate metaphysical perspective as a solution of the problem. True, we are required to bless God both for good and evil.[22] But the content of the respective blessings is altogether different in both cases. Good news we receive by hailing God as the dispenser of goodness; sad news prompts us to acknowledge Him as the "True Judge." Significantly, even when there is reason to expect that in the long run the present calamity may turn out to be a blessing in disguise, we still are not permitted to gloss over the immediate tragedy. Even momentary anguish cannot be dismissed lightly as something utterly inconsequential. This is why the Halakhah stipulates that no matter what the ultimate consequences of a given event may be, we must judge it in terms of the present and pronounce whatever benediction is warranted in the light of immediate circumstances.[23]

Refusal to draw a sharp line of demarcation between metaphysical good and evil (viewing the latter as something apparent rather than real) can easily result in confusion in the moral sphere as well. In all fairness, it must be pointed out that this is not a necessary corollary of metaphysical monism. It is quite possible to uphold the distinction in the moral sphere, while rejecting it in the realm of metaphysics. But there can be no doubt that metaphysical monism tends to spill over into the ethical domain. This need not take such extreme formulations as the Sabbatian and Frankian heresies. There are many Hassidic doctrines that tend to blur the absolute distinction between right and wrong. The justification of *averah lishmah* (the sin which is committed with the express purpose of serving God), especially on the part of the *Tzaddik*, represents a specially telling example. The views of the late Rabbi Kook at times also gravitate in this direction. As Pinchas Rosenbluth pointed out in a recent essay, if the lights of holiness shine forth from the most secular and even atheistic manifestations of culture, if all of reality is "holy and divine," and all evil purely illusory, then we are deprived of all significant criteria for moral evaluation.[24] Indeed, an element of goodness (a spark of holiness) may possibly be found in even an immoral act as the most moral human act may be tainted with some evil (due to the intrinsic limitations imposed upon everything finite). But unwillingness to make any distinction at all will undermine the very structure of all morality. No crime can be justified on the ground that in the long run it has proved a boon to mankind. Pharaoh's brutalities against the Jewish people cannot be defended on the ground that they were necessary as background for the exodus from Egypt which forms such a keystone of Judaism. To revert to the criticisms levelled by Pinchas Rosenbluth,[25] Rabbi Kook's thought, at times, seems to confuse the ideal with the real, the ultimate Messianic perspective with the requirements of the harsh present-day realities in all their ugliness and baseness.

The same kind of confusion comes to the fore in Rabbi Lamm's powerful plea for the re-evaluation of our attitude towards secular studies. His view aspires to a synthesis that knows no essential gulf between the sacred and the secular, because "all knowledge is . . . ultimately integrated in the great *yichud* of the Holy One and His Shekhinah."[26]

Here again we must fall back upon the vital distinction between the temporal and eternal, the immediate and the ultimate. The categories of normative Judaism are geared to the requirements, not of a Messianic era in which all differences are transcended, but of our present world that abounds in existential diversity. The fact that secular knowledge can also serve a religious purpose by no means detracts from the singular and unique importance of Torah in the narrower sense of the term.

At this point it will be of special importance to remember that Judaism attaches a great deal of weight to distinctions even within the domain of the sacred itself. Considerable attention is paid to

different forms and degrees of holiness. Within halakhic thought,
particular emphasis is placed upon the lines of demarcation between the various branches and aspects of Torah. Legal principles
governing ritual questions need not necessarily apply to civil law,
and, conversely, the standards of civil law cannot be automatically
extended to the ritual law.[27]

Far more fundamental is the distinction between Halakhah
and Aggadah. Methods and processes appropriate to the one are
completely irrelevant to the other. To fuse the two, in accordance
with Bialik's recommendation,[28] would only result in a confusion
of languages. We would end up in a Babel of confusion, similar
to the one that would arise out of the mixing of the language of
poetry with that of science.

In keeping with this emphasis upon the autonomy of the various areas of religious thought, the Halakhah is hermetically sealed
off against intrusion of all elements that interfere with the canons
and procedures of strictly halakhic reasoning. According to a well
known talmudic episode, the rabbis, in the midst of a very heated
debate, not only refused to be swayed by the "evidence" of miracles, but categorically objected to heeding a heavenly voice that
seemed to substantiate a minority opinion. Rabbi Eliezer was
overruled—in spite of the supernatural support he was able to
marshal for his point of view, for "Torah was no longer in
Heaven." [29] Rabbi Joseph Karo did not fare any better when he
sought acceptance for some of his rulings on the ground that they
were vouchsafed to him by his heavenly mentor (the *Maggid*). For
that matter, only the Pentateuch—no other part of the Bible—can
serve as the basis for the derivation of laws.[30] When it comes to
questions of laws, "the scholar is superior to the prophet." [31] The
notion of "progressive revelation," which plays such a dominant
role in Conservative and Reform theology, is completely strange
to traditional Judaism. For interpretations of the law we rely
exclusively on the following two sources: 1) The content of the
Sinaitic revelation as recorded in the Pentateuch and 2) the principles of interpretation of the Oral Torah. It must be borne in
mind that subsequent prophetic revelations are completely devoid
of authority in matters affecting the proper elucidation of the
intent of the Law.[32]

III

Respect for the autonomy of the diverse fields of religious knowledge represents not merely an indispensable methodological principle, violation of which would result in intellectual chaos or disastrous confusion of languages. Within the Halakhah itself, there is noticeable a marked accent upon diversity and a deeply ingrained aversion to all types of *reductionism*. In sharp contrast to many other religious systems, there is no single mood, emotion, or attitude, be it love, faith, or self-surrender, that can claim a monopoly in the Jewish religious economy. Variety is the order of the day. According to the Talmud, the biblical verse "in *all* thy ways thou shalt acknowledge Him" (Proverbs 3:6) best sums up the sweeping range over which Jewish piety holds sway.[33] There are innumerable avenues of service to God; every psychological drive can be harnessed in the process.

We are, of course, bidden to love God. But, for that matter, we are also supposed to fear Him. We are neither in love with love, nor in fear of fear. Both sentiments represent solid pillars supporting the arch of Jewish piety. The daily liturgy reflects this all-embracing attitude in the prayer, "unify our hearts to love and fear Thy name," [34] Notwithstanding all the scathing theological attacks directed against us on this score, during the "Days of Awe" we unabashedly continue to turn to God with the request, "and thus place Thy *fear* upon us." [35] We seek, not the conquest of fear, but its proper use.

It has become fashionable to ridicule what Walter Lippmann has branded "lower forms of religion" in which appeals to self-interest are sanctioned.[36] But Judaism maintains that every attitude can be hallowed (not merely sublimated) in the service of God. In this scheme, there is room for self-regarding as well as altruistic motives, for the Freudian *libido* as well as the "death-instinct," for self-realization as well as self-surrender. All the components of our complex psychological make-up can be channeled into the service of God.

To cite a typical example, the Talmud approves of charity, even if it is inspired by such a strictly prudential mentality as expressed in the proverb "charity is the salt (preservative) of money." [37] Now it may be argued that the talmudic sages were so preoccupied with the communal benefits accruing from the practice of charity that they were completely uninterested in the motive of the giver. But it would hardly be proper to impute to the sages of old the kind of mentality associated with a certain type of professional fundraiser, to whom nothing matters but the success of a campaign. There is clear-cut evidence that the rabbis were most definitely concerned with the propriety of the motive. They went so far as to negate altogether the value of any donation that was motivated by any form of haughtiness.[38] Nietzsche was by no means original in his discovery that, at times, charity springs from resentment rather than love.[39] The talmudic sages were astute enough depth-psychologists to recognize how frequently base emotions are concealed behind the veneer of charity. They might even concur with many of Nietzsche's biting denunciations of certain types of charity. Yet—and here an unbridgeable chasm separates the two points of view—insofar as the rabbinic position is concerned, only what transpires at the conscious level need be taken into consideration in the evaluation of the worthwhileness of a philanthropic act. Charitable giving is condemned only when it serves as a vehicle for the expression of haughtiness or similar attitudes—e.g., when a "philanthropist" relishes the feelings of superiority over his "inferior" fellow man who must depend upon him for sustenance. In cases like these, when philanthropy represents a deliberate act of self-aggrandizement rather than an expression of loving-kindness, it must be regarded as a spiritual liability. But the rabbis could not go along with Nietzsche in cases where charity arises out of a *sublimated* sense of resentment. What takes place on the subconscious level cannot detract from the spiritual merits of an act. On the contrary, the transformation of an undesirable psychological trait into a wholesome quality would be regarded as a spiritual triumph of the highest order. Man fulfills his task to the extent that he succeeds in the sublimation of immoral drives by harnessing them into the service of his Creator.[40]

Owing to the intrinsic limitations besetting human nature, this ideal can never be fully realized. The rabbis, therefore, encouraged the performance of good deeds, even if prompted by ulterior motives. This realistic approach was justified on the ground that, eventually, the habit of performing good deeds may gradually transform our mentaility and ennoble our character to such an extent that we may reach a level of religiosity where the good deed is inspired only by the sublime desire to serve God. Although many scholars maintain that such completely disinterested service is within the reach of man, Rabbi Chayyim of Volozin, in espousing a rigorous halakhic approach, considerably tones down what he considers to be extravagant claims for the efficacy of this approach. What emerges is a far less idyllic picture of man's capacity for selfless service. Rabbi Chayyim anticipates no miracle cure from selfishness and ego-centeredness. All he expects is that, as the result of the repeated performance of good deeds, our character may become sufficiently refined so that at least *some* of the motives prompting our good deeds will stem from the desire to serve God.[41] But this ideal motive can, in point of fact, co-exist with numerous other purely selfish and even base drives and urges. Reinhold Niehbuhr and other neo-orthodox Christian theologians may be completely right in their analysis of the selfishness that mars so much of what parades as selfless love. But Judaism suffers from no perfectionist pretensions. Granted that even our noblest sentiments and finest actions are tainted by residual traces of selfishness, resentment, and even outright hostility, we still are not justified in repudiating altogether the worthwhileness of moral effort. In the Jewish scheme, the recognition of our imperfections leads, not to a Pauline obsession with "original sin," but to a design for the "ultimate sanctification" of all the elements comprising our psychological and biological make-up. We end up—not with a vicious perfectionism where the damned and doomed individual will depend for his redemption upon a gratuitous act of "grace" to be bestowed upon those who possess "faith"—but with a wholesome stress upon moral responsibility, manifesting itself in a never-ending quest towards self-perfection.

IV

The ultimate objective of such incessant striving obviously will mirror the peculiar structure of Jewish piety with its accent upon ethical and psychological pluralism. We do not seek the exclusive cultivation of any one or even a select set of "ideal" attitudes, accompanied by the repression of other "lower" drives. Our pattern for man's unification is woven out of a variety of strands. It is through integration rather than reduction of psychological capacities that we aim for unity. We are by no means embarrassed by the staggering psychological riches with which we are endowed—even though they cannot be neatly listed in an inventory and categorized in a ready-made system of classification.

The highways and byways of thought are strewn with the wreckage of all sorts of grandiose attempts to arrive at comprehensive ethical systems based upon over-simplified versions of human motivation. Thus the hedonists deluded themselves that with the discovery of the pleasure principle they had found the magic key to the complexities of life; the utilitarians, though rightly diagnosing the limitations of hedonism, did not escape similar pitfalls when it came to the formulation of their own criteria for moral evaluation. For Spencer and other evolutionists, ethics was to be based upon sheer "survivalism," while Nietzsche espoused—with such tragic consequences for the twentieth century—the "will to power." Freud, at least in his early period, suffered from a pan-sexualist approach to human behavior, and the younger Huxley till this day has not overcome his fascination with an unadulterated evolutionist ethics.

Some of the most obnoxious features of the Kantian morality provide especially telling illustrations of the inevitable pitfalls besetting systems of morality that are committed to the universal applicability of any one absolute principle. Thus, for Kant, a lie cannot be sanctioned—even to save a human life! Similarly, suicide would be condoned for a woman who was violated. For a rigid formalist like Kant the sanctity of life cannot be preserved in a person in whom immorality has become objectified! Kant is so enamored of consistency that in the formulation of the categorical imperative all other considerations are brushed aside. The outcome of such one-sidedness is not a system of love, but love of a system. If necessary, Kant would echo the sentiments of the gruesome Roman proverb: "Let justice be done, even though the world may perish!"

Judaism shies away from all attempts to do violence to the

complexities of ethical issues. Working through any category *ad nauseam*—be it in the realm of normative ethics or descriptive psychology—will produce only dizziness and confusion. Moral balance can be achieved only through the careful weighing of the diverse factors that enter into our ethical dilemmas. This is why the Jewish formula for spiritual and moral equilibrium prescribes that justice be tempered with mercy, the quest for truth be reconciled with that for peace, and the sense of duty be supplemented with such sentiments as compassion, love, etc.

Christian theologians, especially Niebuhr and Tillich, have introduced into modern thought the awareness of the self-contradictions and absurdities that arise when the implications of ethical principles are developed to their ultimate conclusions. But the fact that moral and ethical intuitions lead to antinomies does not warrant the adoption of a purely antinomian attitude. There is no need to resort to a purely "situational" ethics, let alone to a renunciation of the intrinsic worth of all moral endeavor. As Rabbi Rackman demonstrated so convincingly in his incisive essay "The Dialectic of the Halakhah," [42] the halakhic structure manages to incorporate divergent and even antithetical values within a system of law. The attainment of this objective is due to the ingenious use of a system of checks and balances, preventing any one principle from completely dominating the sphere of morality. Thus the Halakhah succeeds in combining a stress upon moral laws with an awareness that all moral principles must be handled with care, lest their rigorous application, without counterbalancing safeguards, yield a harvest of moral paradoxes and absurdities.

Perhaps an analogy from the history of philosophy might be helpful at this point. Although Kant has compiled an impressive list of antinomies which arise from the employment of our rational faculties in the realm of metaphysics, the logical consequences to be drawn from this premise is that we must proceed with extreme caution and restraint in the exercise of reason—not to throw it to the winds altogether. By the same token, our awareness of the limitations assailing ethical norms does not warrant utter despair over the moral enterprise. The road of morality may be fraught with grave perils—the abyss of ethical absurdity gaping on both sides. But instead of frantically searching for "salvation" "through faith" and "grace," the Jew traverses the narrow ridge over the abyss, holding on to the guiding rail provided by the checks and balances imbedded in the halakhic system.

Proceeding under halakhic guidance, we can safely uphold the infinite worth and dignity of the human individual without risking a plunge into the abyss of self-idolization. Since the Halakhah protects us from confusing freedom with autonomy, there is no danger that we may become so intoxicated with the idea of self-emancipation as to reject with Kant any law that is grounded upon divine authority (i.e., revelation) as unworthy of a free moral creature. For the Halakhah, the road to freedom does not lead over the repudiation of all heteronomous ethics. On the contrary, true freedom, in the halakhic scheme, is born out of the union of self-surrender with self-emancipation. There can be no freedom, so the rabbis assert, "unless man is engaged in Torah." [43]

Yet, this engagement does not imply any withdrawal from reason. However spacious the intellectual mansion of Judaism may be, it simply has no room for the debunking of reason and the denigration of all humanistic aspirations that is so characteristic of much of modern existentialism. Professor Leibowitz ignores many vital areas when he describes the Halakhah as being completely indifferent to humanistic values such as the search for justice, truth, peace, etc.[44] Actually, the halakhic approach is by no means so one-sided, narrow, and formalistic as to banish from its domain everything but blind submission to the rules of the Law. After all, man is bidden "to walk in His ways" and to strive for moral perfection. Judaism demands far more than merely a set of specific observances. As Nachmanides pointed out, a commandment such as "Ye shall be holy" (Leviticus 19:2) goes far beyond the sum total of individual precepts.[45] In quest of such a beckoning ideal, man must develop his admittedly very limited moral and intellectual capacities—not blunt them as an expression of "ontological despair." Though the Halakhah—as a legal code—revolves primarily around external acts, the inner life of man (his hopes, aspirations and values) is by no means irrelevant to the religious ideal.

It must be borne in mind that the Halakhah merely provides

the objective basis upon which the individual must build his own personal quest for holiness. Undoubtedly, adherence to halakhic norms will stimulate the growth of such sentiments as piety, compassion, justice, love, etc. Self-surrender in the service of God—the hallmark of the halakhic approach—does not reduce man to a lowly creature cringing in the dust of moral unworthiness and intellectual insignificance. On the contrary, the Halakhah shows the way to human freedom, which must not be confounded with idolatrous self-emancipation smacking of self-deification. Far from crushing the inner life of man under the steamroller of uniformity and conformity, the Halakhah paves the way for the maximum development of individuality in a world rich in variety and diversity. For in the final analysis, the Halakhah points beyond itself—beyond a uniform and objectively valid religious code—to the manifold approaches that are available to man in his quest for a life of holiness.

NOTES

1 It is, of course, true that the religious personality gravitates towards the ultimate Unity that lies beyond all empirical diversity. Abraham, the Jewish "knight of faith," is described in the Midrash as the religious genius who through his discovery of God restored the original unity of the world "in the same manner as a tailor sews together a garment that has been ripped apart" (*Bereshit Rabbah*, 39:3).

2 Walter Kaufmann, *Critique of Religion and Philosophy* (New York: Doubleday and Company, 1961), pp. 379 ff.

3 *Norman Lamm*, "The Unity Theme and Its Implications for Moderns," *Tradition*, Fall 1961, pp. 44–64, reprinted in this volume.

4 *Nefesh ha-Chayyim*, by Rabbi Chayyim of Volozin, Part III.

5 *Ibid.*

6 *Ibid.*

7 *Sabbath* 119b; cf. also Rabbi Joseph B. Soloveitchik, "Ish ha-Halakhah" (*Talpiot*, 1944), pp. 710–18.

8 The fundamental differences between the halakhic and the kabbalistic attitudes are clearly formulated in Rabbi Joseph B. Soloveitchik's classic study, "Ish ha-Halakhah" (*Talpiot*, 1944, pp. 651–735). This pioneering work is indispensable to an understanding of the philosophy of Halakhah.

9 *Guide For the Perplexed*, 3:51.

10 A. J. Heschel, *Man is not Alone; A Philosophy of Religion* (Philadelphia: Jewish Publication Society, 1951), p. 296.

11 See *Guide for the Perplexed*, Part 3, Chapter 51, where the religiously

observant, but philosophically naive individual is compared by Maimonides to a person who, while anxious to enter the palace of a king, has not even seen it. In all fairness to Maimonides we should, however, remember that the concluding chapter of the *Guide* implies a far more positive attitude towards religious practice.

12 Rabbi Chayyim of Volozin, *op. cit.*, Part IV.

13 For similar reasons, Rabbi Chayyim objected to excessive emphasis upon Mussar (pietistic literature) at the expense of halakhic literature. Our main objective in life is not simply to seek communion with God, but to understand His will as it relates to our specific tasks in all sorts of situations (see *Nefesh Chayyim*, Part IV).

14 William James, *The Varieties of Religious Experience* (New York: New American Library, 1958), p. 229.

15 Cf. the grotesque distortion of the religious attitude contained in Daniel Bell's "Reflections on Jewish Identity" (*Commentary*, June 1961, p. 472): "Orthodoxy leads to quietism, suffering is the badge, one accepts it as the mark of fate."

16 *Sabbath* 119b.

17 *Kidushin* 40b.

18 *Bereshit Rabbah* 9:9–13.

19 Rabbi Zushah of Hanipol, quoted in *Al Ha-Torah*, by Rabbi Mordecai HaKohen (Jerusalem: Orot, 1956), vol. 1, p. 63.

20 *Ibid.*

21 Quoted in *Keter Shem Tov*, by Aaron of Apt.

22 *Berakhot* 54a.

23 *Ibid.*, 60a.

24 Pinchas Rosenbluth, "Ha-mashber ha-Ruchani shel ha-Yahadut ha-Modernit le-Or Tefisato shel ha-Rav Kook u-Teguvato" (*Deot*, Tishri 5721), pp. 13–21.

25 *Ibid.*

26 Norman Lamm, *op. cit.*, p. 63.

27 Cf. *Kidushin* 3b, *Ketuvot* 4b, et al.

28 Cf. Ch. N. Bialik's essay, *Halakhah ve-Aggadah* in *Kol Kitvei Bialik*, (Tel Aviv: Dvir, 5715), pp. 207–13.

29 *Bava Metzia* 59b.

30 *Chaggigah* 10b; *Bava Kamma* 2b; *Niddah* 23a.

31 *Bava Batra* 12a.

32 We refer here only to authoritative interpretations of the Law, not to temporary suspensions or other measures dictated by *Horaat Shaah* (emergency regulations necessitated by the exigencies of the moment were within the scope of prophetic competence).

33 *Berakhot* 63a.

34 *Ahavah   rabbah . . . Ve-yached   le-vaveinu le-ahavah   u-leyirah   et shmekha.*

35 *U-vekhen ten pachdekha . . .*

36 A *Preface to Morals,* by Walter Lippmann (Boston: Beacon Press, 1960).

37 *Ketuvot* 66b.

38 *Bava Batra* 10b.

39 Cf. *The Genealogy of Morals,* by Friedrich Nietzsche (New York: Doubleday, 1956), esp. 3:18; cf. also *Also sprach Zarathustra,* (Leipzig: Kröner, 1918), pp. 88–90 and pp. 127–130.

40 This point of view differs sharply from that expressed by Max Scheler in his celebrated "Das Ressentment im Aufbau der Moralen" (*Vom Umsturz der Werte,* [Bern: A. Francke, 1945], pp. 33–131). Approaching the subject from a Christian perspective, Scheler discounts the value of any form of charity that is grounded on any other emotion but love. In Scheler's scheme, charity, as opposed to mere philanthropy cannot have its ultimate root in any undesirable psychological trait. The Jewish standpoint is altogether different. However pre-eminent a position we assign to altruistic love in our scale of values, we must reckon with other psychological factors. Given sufficient self-discipline and self-control, other psychological drives and urges can be sublimated and eventually channeled into religiously approved outlets. To illustrate our point concretely, Scheler disparages the moral worth inherent in the selfless actions of a nurse who chose her profession out of a subconscious delight in watching suffering at close range. Judaism, instead of harboring disdain for this nurse, would credit her with a colossal spiritual victory. To have sublimated an ugly urge to the extent that it becomes the driving force behind a life of selfless service is deserving, not of sneering derision, but of wholehearted admiration.

41 Chayyim of Volozin, *op. cit.,* appendage to Part 3; Chapter 3.

42 Emanuel Rackman, "The Dialectic of the Halakhah," TRADITION, Spring 1961, reprinted in this volume, *supra.*

43 *Avot (Kinyan Torah)* 6:2.

44 Isaiah Leibowitz, "The World and the Jews," *Forum,* v. 4, Spring 1959, pp. 83–90.

45 Nachmanides, commentary to Leviticus 19:2.

ELIEZER BERKOVITS

*

What Is Jewish Philosophy?

I

SEVERAL years ago, a reviewer of a standard work on Jewish philosophy took its author to task for not having included Spinoza in his presentation as one of the major links in the chain of the philosophy of Judaism. Such criticism is a far cry from the days in the past century and in the early part of the present one when Jewish scholars refused to speak of Jewish philosophy and saw in the thoughts of a Saadia Gaon and a Maimonides only variations on the themes of the Kalam and Arabic Aristotelianism. A resurgent national pride of our own days is only too willing to claim as Jewish the achievements of any great man of Jewish descent; just as the spineless assimilationism of the past generation was only too anxious to disclaim characteristic marks of Jewishness wherever it could be done with the least semblance of plausibility. However, the question as to the authentic criteria of Jewish philosophy cannot be answered by the varying moods of the contemporary Jew. Whatever the significance of the mood of a time may be, it requires no thorough investigation to know with certainty that, for example, the inclusion of Henri Bergson in a survey of Jewish philosophy, as was done a few years ago by the editors of a massive volume about Jews, is a sign of emotional coarseness and intellectual confusion.

No doubt a case may be made out for the Jewish elements in the thought of Spinoza and even in that of Bergson; just as an even stronger case may be made out for the assertion that most of the key ideas in the philosophy of Maimonides were borrowed from Arabic Aristotelianism. Yet, there can be no question that Maimonides was a Jewish philosopher, whereas the same thing will not be so readily affirmed about either Spinoza or Bergson. At times, the thoughts of a man may betray Jewish origins, but his path will hardly be recognizable as that of a Jewish thinker; at others, the thoughts may well be of foreign extraction, yet the path of the man will be unquestionably Jewish.

An extremely intriguing example of this latter possibility is the case of Ibn Gabirol. For centuries his philosophical work was known only in a Latin translation as *Fons Vitae*. The name of the author having been corupted into Avicebron, the work served as a kind of textbook of Christian scholasticism. The contents of the work revealed no recognizable Jewish traits. Not until the middle of the nineteenth century was it discovered that the mysterious Avicebron was none other than the genius of Jewish poetry, Shlomo Ibn Gabirol. How are we to relate this undoubtedly great Jewish soul to a philosophy bearing so little signs of Jewishness that for many centuries its author was thought to have been either a Christian or a Moslem or—perhaps—a pious heathen?

The truth, of course, is that the history of Jewish philosophy reflects the philosophies of all ages and of all lands in which the Jewish people lived and thought. From the philosophy of Plato to the latest fashion in existentialism, the various schools of thought are all represented in Jewish philosophy, as they are also represented in every other national or regional philosophy of the Western world. In a way, this is unavoidable. Philosophical inquiry is a human pursuit and man is always time-and-place conditioned. Any Jew who ever attempts to give a philosophical account of Judaism cannot but work with the philosophical equipment of his own times. He must make use of the tools of logic which are at hand, of the epistemological concepts and metaphysical ideas which are accessible to him. When, in the tenth century, Saadia Gaon set out to provide intellectual certitude for the traditional doctrines of Judaism, he could only do so by making use of the philosophy he knew; just as many centuries later, when Hermann Cohen wrote his *The Religion of Reason* etc., notwithstanding his deep admiration for Maimonides, he could not be expected to offer a philosophy of Judaism in terms of the outdated categories of Aristotle. It was inescapable that his *chef d'oeuvre* on Judaism should be conceived in terms of a Kantianism which he himself considered the valid philosophical system of the day.

We are faced here with a paradoxical situation. The very ambition of the thinker to provide a true and convincing philosophy of Judaism makes his work always relative, i.e. temporal, and, therefore, of only passing validity. Notwithstanding Hegel, there is no final and eternal philosophy. Every thinker in the history of Jewish philosophy interpreted Judaism in the categories of thought of his own generation. All Jewish philosophies are subjective. They make sense in a certain time, in a certain situation, for certain people. They are always the words of men, not the word of God.

II

At this juncture of our discussion two questions would seem to be appropriately raised.

First, if the Jewish philosopher applies contemporary methods and concepts to the interpretation of Judaism, wherein lies the specific quality of his Jewishness? Or as we may also put it: if all the philosophies of Judaism are time-and-place conditioned, what is it they have in common that justifies the adjective Jewish? What is their common Jewish denominator?

Secondly, if, as we have maintained, all the philosophies of Judaism are essentially subjective and, therefore, of only passing validity, if all of them eventually become antiquated, what is their value as interpretations of Judaism?

Let us turn to the question of the common denominator. Before anything else, there is a limiting factor that circumscribes the search and the efforts of the Jewish thinker which all ages have in common. No Jewish thinker can ever start from the beginning. Judaism is always already given when he starts his inquiry. Descartes became the founder of modern philosophy by his decision to start anew, by throwing overboard all acknowledged certainties and applying the method of the radical doubt. He allowed himself to be led by nothing else but by clear and critical reasoning. In a way, this is the ideal method for all non-committed thinkers to follow. This, however, is the method that a Jewish thinker cannot adopt. The Jewish philosopher does not create Judaism as Descartes created modern philosophy. When he arrives on the scene, Judaism is already a given fact. His thinking always has a partner, Judaism. It is true, every philosophy of Judaism is essentially subjective; but this subjectivity is tempered,

it is circumscribed, fenced in, and controlled by the factual given-
ness of Judaism itself, which forever confronts the Jewish philosopher.

The path of the Jewish philosopher is determined by one element that it is variable and another that is constant. The variable
is the intellectual, scholarly equipment that each thinker uses in
building his own philosophy. This is, as we have maintained,
time-conditioned and passing. All these philosophies are the
thoughts of men; they are Jewish because they attempt to render
Judaism intellectually meaningful. Implied in such a position is,
of course, the insight that Judaism is not identical with a philosophy or a theology. If it were, we should be moving around in a
circle. The philosophy, the theology, the metaphysics, are the
variables. Judaism contains the element of constancy because it
is founded not on ideas but on certain facts and events. These
facts and events do have their philosophical, theological, and
metaphysical relevance. But such relevance is always a matter of
interpretation and as such subject to change. The events themselves having occurred, the facts having entered into history, are—
as such—unalterable and irrevocable. What happened happened,
and what is does exist. No matter to what philosophical school a
person may belong, the event of the exodus from Egypt will not
be affected by it. Whatever metaphysical ideas a person may en-
tertain, the revelation at Sinai remains forever the revelation at
Sinai. Even a *mitzvah* is an event and not an idea. Its essential
quality lies in the fact that it was actually addressed as a command of God to the Jewish people. This was an event that occurred in history at a definite moment and at a definite place.

If we wished to list the events which, because of their centrality,
might be considered the constants of Judaism, we could well make
use of the traditional formula *Kudesha Berikh Hu, Yisrael,
ve'Oraita*—God, Israel, and Torah. In the context of Judaism the
three terms stand for historic events. God, in the Bible, is not an
idea. He is not the First Cause or the metaphysical Absolute. He
is the living God, who addresses Himself to people, who revealed
Himself to Israel, who acts in history and is known to men by the
events of His manifestations. The task of a Jewish theology is to
interpret the intelligible and conceptual implications of the events

in which the living God makes Himself known to men. And so it is with the Torah. The Torah is not just a very clever book containing a great store of wisdom. It is the word of God addressed to Israel. This is its essential nature. As such, the Torah is a fact, a historic event that happened between God and Israel. In this connection, the Jewish people too should be understood in its dynamic, eventful stance in history, as the people who is actually addressed by God and whose existence evolves under the impact of the Word. The conceptual interpretations of these facts is Jewish philosophy. The concepts may change with the times, the events remain forever.

III

We are now in a position to say more clearly how the variables and the constants may combine to determine the path of a Jewish thinker. Any interpretation, from whatever foreign source it may originate, that acknowledges God, Israel, and the Torah as historic realities and attempts to provide the metaphysical or theological corollary to the facts and events for which they stand, may well be incorporated in a Jewish philosophy. On the other hand, any interpretation that attempts to substitute the idea, the metaphysics, and the philosophy for the historic reality, cannot be called Jewish.

When we read in the Bible, "And God spoke to Moses," the phrase raises problems of anthropomorphism. In its solution, different courses of interpretation are open to the investigator. He might adopt the concept of the *memra*, of the *dibbur nivra*, of Onkelos and Saadia Gaon, or he might follow the more rationalistic method of a Maimonides, as there may also be other explanations of the event. This is the variable and it depends on place and person, time and temperament. All these interpretations will be Jewish as long as the event remains an event, as long as they leave inviolate the fact that—no matter in what manner—an actual communication between God and Moses did occur. But should one maintain that "God spoke to Moses" has only symbolical significance, that God never really communicates with man, that the meaning of the phrase is that the genius of Moses grasped some supreme truth—however absolute a rational dignity one may be prepared to accord to the teachings of Moses—one would be philosophizing *outside* the realm of Judaism.

Let us now look at some of the more dubious historic examples. The first one to come to mind is, perhaps, Philo. The outstanding authorities in the field consider him the originator of theology and mysticism for all monotheistic religions. Yet for many centuries he remained unknown in the midst of his own people and his writings were preserved by Christian theologians. Even though a contemporary of Hillel, he had to wait till the sixteenth century to be discovered for Jews. For this there was a valid reason. His concept of the Logos, the mediator between God and creation, was so conceived that it readily lent itself to serve as the metaphysical basis for a central Christian dogma. It was a concept which, offered as an interpretation of Judaism, the Jewish consciousness had to ignore. But was the path of the man, Philo's own personal predilection for problems of philosophy and metaphysics, Jewish or not? We believe that the answer should be given unhesitatingly in the affirmative. Attempting to harmonize the philosophical concept of the Absolute, as it was understood in Greek philosophy, with that of the personal God of Judaism, he was led to the concept of the Logos. For him, it explained the "technique" by which the Absolute was in contact with the cosmos. The concept itself is purely subjective and as such, characteristic of the man, Philo. It signifies the personal way of Philo in Jewish philosophy. It may be readily rejected by other Jews. Yet the concept itself, as understood by Philo, does belong in the realm of Jewish philosophy, because with its help the thinker was endeavoring to give expression to the intellectual significance of the events represented by God, Israel, and the Torah. Nevertheless, the same concept as it was later developed and understood by the theologians of the Church, is outside the realm of Jewish theology because it is meant to invalidate the constants of Judaism.

We may now, once again, consider the cases of Gabirol and Spinoza. A great deal of the criticism to which Abraham Ibn Daud subjected Gabirol was, of course, justified. One may rightly say that Neo-Platonism, the philosophical system adopted by

Gabirol, is not only foreign, but antithetical to Judaism. Emanation is the opposite of creation; the Absolute One negates the
concept of the living God revealing Himself to man. For some
reason or other, Neo-Platonism appealed to Ibn Gabirol. He made
it his own metaphysics. However, while we are not really in a
position to judge fully his personal philosophy—an essential part
of it which, at the end of the *Mekor Chayyim*, he promised to
give us in another volume which we do not have—we are able
to discern the inconsistency of his Neo-Platonism. Between the
One and the world he interposed the *retzon ha-Shem*, the will
of God. By using this classical term of Judaism, Gabirol replaced
the Neo-Platonic One with the God of his fathers. By introducing
the idea of the Will of God, he made room for the concept of
creation beside that of emanation. One might well say that this
is poor metaphysics. The grafting of the "Will of God" on to
the trunk of Neo-Platonism is, perhaps, a metaphysical monstros-
ity. Poor Plotinus! The entire emanation theory was conceived
in order to eliminate the need for a divine will, which could not
be harmonized with the idea of the Absolute. How did this metaphysical monster, a hybrid between emanation and creation, come
about? Neo-Platonism assumed the function of the variable in
Ibn Gabirol's philosophy. But there were also the constants of
Judaism. Where the two clashed, the Jew Gabirol submitted his
Neo-Platonism to be manipulated by his more fundamental commitments to Judaism. The result was a purely individual and subjective effort, but one which has its rightful place in Jewish
philosophy.

On the other hand, Spinoza provides us with the opposite example. There is a certain similarity between Spinozism and Neo-
Platonism. Both are pantheistic; both recognize only the Absolute
One. But whereas with Neo-Platonism the cosmos exists as the
emanation of the One, Spinozism eliminates the dynamic element and with it the cosmos itself. Being, for Spinoza, is static.
There is only the One, the Infinite Substance, and whatever exists
is either attribute or mode of the Infinite. Within the framework
of such acosmic pantheism there is no room left for individual
existence. But just because of that, because this system knows
only God and nothing else beside Him, it is not Jewish. The

constants of Judaism have no place within such a philosophy. The concepts of a divine will, of revelation, of a living God making Himself known to men, are not tolerated by Spinoza. Within his system there is no room for history; how much less for the historic events of the intercourse between God and Israel. His is not only a non-Jewish, but an anti-Jewish philosophy.

This does not mean that pantheistic elements may not be incorporated in authentic Jewish thought. In fact, some of the most characteristic insights of the Kabbalah often show an extremely uncomfortable affinity with pantheistic trends with which we are familiar from gentile sources. Kabbalistic writers, however, make use of such ideas in order to render the historic facts on which Judaism is based—God, Israel, and Torah—more meaningful and more challenging for the individual Jew. The result is a more intimate personal commitment to the living God, His Word, and His people. The Ari ha-Kadosh is a good example of how, as long as these constants were not lost sight of, even gnostic ideas could be included within the scope of a kabbalistic Jewish philosophy.

IV

However, the relationship between the subjective factor in every Jewish philosophy and the permanent facets of Jewish religious reality has its significance far beyond what we have thus far been able to indicate. It has its epistemological as well as its metaphysical implications. All Jewish philosophies are subjective and relative because an absolute and eternal philosophy is inconceivable. Philosophers and theologians often indulge in speaking about the eternal verities of a universal reason or the divine truths of religion. Even Kant, who warned against the transcendental usage of reason, still believed that its conclusions had absolute validity. The *connaissance des vérités necessaires et éternelles*, as Leibniz defined it, has a long and respected tradition in the history of human thought. The truth, of course, is that the human mind is incapable of grasping the absolute. Whatever is affirmed by human reason cannot have absolute validity. Whatever logical necessity a judgment may have, it will be the logical necessity as comprehended by the finite intellect of a human being. Applying these insights to the theological field, one might say with even greater conviction that one can speak of divine truth only rhetorically. No divine truth has ever been conceived by a human mind. If God wanted to communicate such a truth to man, he would first have to transform the finite human intellect into a divine one. This, of course, would be the end of man, and the creation of a non-human, divine being. This is an insight to which the teachers of the Midrash and the Talmud drew our attention. Of the revelation at Sinai they said that the Torah was received, *le'fi kocho shel kol echad ve'echad,* according to the human limitations of each individual. Even Moses received the revelation *le'fi kocho,* according to his personal capacity. This is the meaning of the talmudic statement that the fiftieth gate of wisdom remained closed even to Moses. The highest and most authoritative understanding of the Torah is bound to be lacking in absolute validity owing to limitations of our humanity.

How then can the Absolute, the Eternal, communicate with man? Not by means of ideas and intellectual insights, but by events. He may reveal His presence, His intention, His will for man in events. Facts have the unique quality of being true, i.e., even if they are not understood. The revelation at Sinai remains the same majestic supernatural occurrence in the history of Israel even though, generation after generation, its significance for man can only be understood commensurately with our human capacity and limitation. Theologians may wrestle with the problem of the divine attributes. Their deepest insights will—at best—be pointers toward God. Man's knowledge of Him will ultimately be based on the fact of His revelation. So it is also with that important theological issue of the *taamei ha-mitzvot,* the reasons for the commandments. There can be no interpretation of the divine commandments that has absolute validity. But the Word of our God stands forever. There is no contradiction in the fact that Maimonides in the *Moreh Nevukhim* gave a historic interpretation for most of the *mitzvot,* yet in the *Yad ha-Chazakah* he considers them as timeless Halakhah. The reason offered by Maimonides in his explanation of the sacrifices may no longer satisfy the twentieth century Jew; the *mitzvah* as such does not become outdated. For, as we saw, the essence of a *mitzvah* is not the communication of an idea, which once absorbed by a human mind has only conditional validity, but the fact of the divine command directed to Israel. There is no perennial Jewish philosophy; but Judaism itself is eternal.

Let such a position not be misunderstood as skepticism. To be aware of the finitude of human reason is the only rational attitude toward reason. And to acknowledge the reality of factual experience is ordinary common sense. Indeed, one might say that the combination of these insights is the very foundation of modern science. Modern science began when the human intellect finally realized that it could not ignore what Galileo called "irreducible and stubborn facts" and that, on the contrary, its task was to seek to understand and to interpret them. The reverend gentleman who refused to look at Jupiter through Galileo's "Tuscany glass" was, of course, a rationalist. This, however, did not reduce Galileo to a skeptic. Judaism too has its "irreducible and stubborn facts." We have called them the constants of Judaism. The man who refuses to use a telescope because what is not supposed to be there cannot be there, is not a scientist. The Jew who does not acknowledge the "irreducible and stubborn facts" of Judaism remains a Jew, of course, and he may even be a thinking Jew; but he is not a Jewish thinker.

V

We may now take up the question which we have posed earlier. Having maintained that all philosophies of Judaism were essentially subjective creations of passing validity, we inquired after their value as interpretations of Judaism.

We believe that the question has already been answered, at least partially. In this world, one gains understanding only by way of the mind and the heart of man. The result will never be of eternal significance. There is no other way for man to understand anything except in terms of his finite humanity. And so it is with our understanding of Judaism too. There is no other way of interpreting intelligibly the "irreducible stubborn facts" of

Judaism, which are the core of its eternity, except by way of time-conditioned and subjectively limited Jewish philosophies. Nevertheless, these philosophies are not irrelevant even in terms of the divine truth, which, forever hidden from the human intellect, communicates its presence and its will to man in these "stubborn facts." We have noted how the subjective efforts of the philosophical inquirer are kept in check, as it were, by the necessity of interpreting the elements of constancy in Judaism. The interpretation should, therefore, yield a measure of objectivity in terms of Judaism. Our discussion of Ibn Gabirol showed how the constants may modify the subjective elements and urge the philosophical spirit of the day to correct itself in the direction of "Jewish objectivity." The variable becomes oriented toward the permanent and eternal.

There are numerous examples illustrating the same point in the history of Jewish philosophy. One of the most difficult problems with which Maimonides had to wrestle in the *Moreh Nevukhim* was that of *hashgachah* or divine Providence. On the basis of Aristotelian metaphysics, Providence could not be associated with the Godhead. The Supreme Form thinks only that which is most noble, i.e. the Supreme Form itself. In other words, the Aristotelian God thinks only himself; he knows only himself and is wholly unaware of a world beside him. He is, of course, incapable of exercising providence for a world whose very existence is unknown to him. But what is God without *hashgachah!* At this point the variable, Aristotelianism, was in conflict with the reality of divine existence as known to Judaism. Maimonides does solve the problem in a manner adequate for himself. Preserving the idea of *hashgachah*, he modifies Aristotelianism. He deals in a similar way with such issues as creation versus the Aristotelian idea of an uncreated universe, and the conflict between divine foreknowledge and the freedom of the human will. The solutions to the problems are found by making a time-conditioned philosophy face the permanent and take due cognizance of the intellectual implications of its existence. The constants of Judaism were also the determining factor in Hasdai Crescas' criticism of Aristotle and his turning away from both Maimonides and Gersonides. The conflict with the "irreducible facts" served for him as the incentive to seek a different approach for himself. The elements of constancy in Judaism not only control and limit the philosopher, they also influence and guide him. The intensity of the orientation of the variable and subjective elements toward the constants determines the quality of Jewishness in a philosophy. The result of such orientation represents the "objective" significance of a philosophy in the history of Jewish thought. To be sure, the realization of objectivity proper is never to be accomplished. The "irreducible facts" of Judaism which reveal the divine presence and the divine will in relationship with Israel do testify to the reality of the divine in its absoluteness, yet in their absolute meaning and depth they remain forever inaccessible to man. Interpreting the constants of Judaism, Jewish philosophy does not reach pure objectivity, but neither does it remain within the scope of pure subjectivity; it becomes a pointer to the Absolute, the Eternal. What is being accomplished might, perhaps, be called a form of subjectivity which has validity in the presence of the Eternal. My understanding of Judaism, as my understanding in general, is limited by the condition of my individual humanity. Yet it is valid for me in the presence of God as the only pointer to God which is accessible to me. This is not to be confused with either relativism or pragmatism. The Jewish philosopher accepts the discipline imposed by the facts and events which, in Judaism, make manifest absolute meaning and value. He can only interpret. In terms of the relativity of his own personal existence, he interprets the historic reality of the Absolute. His interpretation lends validity to his individual insights not because "it works" for him, but because for him it represents the only relevant pointer to the Absolute.

The ultimate need for Jewish philosophy is a religious one. Rabbenu Saadia Gaon, in defining the purpose of his *Emunot ve'Deot*, says he undertakes the inquiry "so that what we have learned from the prophets of God as a matter of belief may be clarified for us in actuality." What Saadia Gaon has in mind is to embrace by an act of intellectual penetration what has originally come to us on the authority of divine revelation. What a man holds to be true on the authority of tradition alone, though having its source in revelation, he owns passively. It is imposed upon him, as it were, from without. If he wants to make it his very own, he must acquire it by some vital intellectual effort. One way or another, he must be able to clarify it for himself, *be'fo'al,* as the Gaon says, i.e. in the actuality of his own personal life and understanding. This is a requirement of religious life. If the intellect has no share in one's religious affirmation, one cannot be involved in them with the wholeness of one's humanity. Objectivity may be the goal of scientific inquiry; subjective commitment is the very essence of religious life. The deeper the involvement of the personal element in one's philosophy of Judaism, the more religiously meaningful the affirmations and the more real the commitment to which they lead. Rabbenu Saadia Gaon's demand for clarifying in actuality what has been revealed to us by the prophets amounts to rendering individually meaningful the constants of Judaism. That a person can hear the word of God only *le'fi kocho,* without ever being able to fathom it in its origin in the Absolute, is of course due to the limitations of his human condition; that he *should* hear it *le'fi kocho,* in the full actuality of his human condition, is of the very essence of religious life. Only if he does absorb the "objective" meaning of the constants of Judaism, assimilating it and making it part of the most intimately individualistic aspect of his being, will such meaning become for him a significant pointer to the Eternal.

For the sake of the sincerity of its Jewish affirmations and the wholeness of its religious commitment, each generation needs its Jewish philosophy, validated in the light of Judaism. To be sure, the philosophy itself may become outdated, yet as long as it did point in the direction of the Eternal even for a single soul, it deserves the attention of all those who seek to interpret for themselves meaningfully the irreducible religious realities of Judaism. The writing on the pointers may become faded and vague, hardly legible and no longer quite convincing. But as long as they ever oriented a searching mind toward eternity, they remain pointers for all of us.

SHUBERT SPERO

*

Is Judaism
an Optimistic Religion?

Two particular intellectual currents have been the favorites of Jewish theological surf riders in recent years. One is the existentialist wave of pessimism, the sense of human helplessness and the futility of human reason, ridden mainly by estranged intellectuals returning to Judaism. The second is the "know thyself" current of depth psychology and psychiatry ridden mainly by leaders of Liberal or Reform Judaism. Presumably, Orthodoxy can get to the beach on its own motive power and needs the help of neither current. Certain interesting issues, however, have arisen as a result of conflicting views on Judaism emerging from the two aforementioned groups.

Ever since the publication of *Peace of Mind* fifteen years ago, publicists of Liberal Judaism have not tired of pointing out the affinity between the counsel of psychiatry and the insights of Judaism. The secret of happiness, it is asserted, lies completely within the human being and his ability to accept a new morality which will overcome inner anxieties, teach us how to love, accept death with courage, and become mature, responsible adults. God is to be encountered in a "good friend, a wise father, a loving mother, and in general in the love, sympathy and relationships of the world." [1] Man is a responsible co-worker with God who must persist in his confidence in eternal progress and social victory. Peace of mind, so understood, seemed to have primarily negative connotations, i.e., the ability to accept life's disappointments, rejections, and death without becoming inwardly tormented, emotionally unhappy, or developing any recognizable neuroses or anxieties. [2] The underlying premise peculiar to this entire tendency is the notion that with the eradication of all mental illness and social evils, life in its "natural healthy state" justifies itself and will itself generate fulfillment and satisfaction.

Related to this view and indeed presupposed by it, is the oft repeated notion that Judaism is an optimistic religion. Speaking of the exaggerated pessimism of existentialists, a leader of Liberal Judaism tells us "this is diametrically opposed to Judaism which does not build God's absolutism on man's nothingness. Man can, to a large degree, make his own world and man has, to a large degree, made it." [3] And again, we are told, "Judaism's faith is suffused with optimism and therefore reactions against tendencies towards varieties of asceticism among Jews were bound to set in, for they were not at heart native or intrinsically Jewish. The life-loving and optimistic spirit of Judaism was certain to resist it." [4]

It appears to the present writer that much of the discussion on this subject has failed to maintain the distinction between optimism as the quality of a metaphysics and optimism as the subjective state of an individual temperament. There can be no question that Judaism as a system of thought is metaphysically optimistic. Our view of the unity of God, the doctrine of *creatio ex nihilo*, the perfectability of man, the relative character of evil, and the promise of a Messianic future all reflect an over-all view which pronounces "good" upon the world and promises ultimate victory for the forces of divinity. However, it does not necessarily follow from this that the individual Jew, the devout believing Jew, was therefore endowed with a sustained optimistic mental attitude. The very contrary can be shown to be the case.

I disagree with the thesis which holds that historical lapses from "natural Jewish optimism" are to be explained in terms of persecution and suffering which darkened the cheerful Jewish spirit. ("Bruised spirits in dark hours might give way.") If persecution and suffering make for pessimism, then it would be more correct to say that by now pessimism has become "natural" for the Jew. Moreover, pessimism has more often been the result of repletion and satiety than of want and deprivation. Kohelet was written by Solomon and not by Bar Kochba!

What I wish to assert is that any attempt to take God and Judaism seriously must involve profound, life-long anxieties and not peace of mind in any usual sense of that term; that meta-physical optimism notwithstanding, the more accurate descrip-tion of the Jewish religious temperament is probably pessimism; that in spite of the fact that the Torah does not forbid us to enjoy life, it does not follow that the thinking Jew therefore necessarily does enjoy it. The origin of Liberal Judaism's bias in the direc-tion of optimism is to be found in a weakness traditionally asso-ciated with the liberal position.[5]

It would be futile to attempt to demonstrate the optimistic or pessimistic character of Judaism solely by an appeal to appro-priate passages in Scripture and in the Talmud. Let us assume that one could amass an impressive collection of references in support of either view. Of course, the very ability to do this would suggest a rather comfortable hypothesis. Perhaps, Judaism *qua* Judaism is "beyond pessimism and optimism" and is something which lends itself to free will, to the determination of individual temperaments and historical epochs.[6]

Indeed, William James, in one of the earliest analyses of the psychology of religion, distinguishes between what he calls "the religion of healthy-mindedness" and "the religion of the sick soul." [7] The former is an expression of a religious sentiment which is happy, optimistic, and usually extroverted. It sees the good in all things, looks upon evil and misfortune as an "accident," and greets the dawn of each new day with cheer and joy. The latter road is the opposite of all this. The religion of the "sick soul" is pessimistic and is given to periods of melancholy and depres-sion. This type of religious sentiment senses the dark side of things, suffering, and death and sees little in life to be cheerful about. As students of the psychology of religion have pointed out, it is doubtful whether the majority of individuals fall into the categories represented by the extreme poles of these two ap-proaches. More likely, one is apt to discover a continuum of characteristics.[8] However, if these categories are in any way de-scriptive of basic human types, then one can maintain that Juda-ism in its rich moodal variety lies before the devotee and that the "sick soul" opts for those elements conducive to his tempera-ment, while the "healthy minded" appropriates those aspects suitable to his emotional structure.

While one may find occasional references which appear to support this approach, nevertheless I believe that a careful examination of the sources will reveal a structured view which leans in the direction of pessimism. Of the two broad outlooks on life, pessimism or optimism, the former represents the more realistic and the more Jewish view. Elsewhere, James rejects the view that answers the question "is life worth living?" with the rejoinder "it depends upon the liver!" [9] and casts his vote in favor of pessimism. Says he, "We are bound to say that morbidmindedness ranges over the wider scale of experience . . . the method of averting one's attention from evil and living simply in the light of the good is splendid as long as it will work. But it breaks down impotently as soon as tragedy comes." [10] Of course, asserts James, there are the lucky few who live their years unscathed and appear to escape the frustrations and the failures, the catastrophies and the sudden death. However, even the most healthy minded of men must surely know what life *can* have in store. "The fact that we *can* die, that we *can* be ill at all, is what perplexes us; the fact that we now for a moment live and are well is irrelevant to that perplexity. We need a life not correlated to death, a health not liable to illness, a kind of good that will not perish, a good that flies beyond the goods of nature." [11] As James astutely observes, "The luster of the present hour is always borrowed from the backgrounds of possibilities it goes with." Once a person's eyes are opened to the radical contingency of human life, the breath of the sepulchre will forever be present. Hence, "they [the morbid experiences of life] may be after all the best key to life's significance and possibly the only openers of our eyes to the deepest levels of truth."

From another direction, Freud, too, confirms the basic unfriendliness of life to the program of the pleasure-principle. From three pervasive quarters there constantly arise experiences which run counter to "happiness" construed in its narrow sense: from our own bodies, where anxiety and pain are danger signals of decay and dissolution; from the outer world with its forces of destruction; and from our relations with other men. Concludes Freud, "the intention that man should be 'happy' is not included in the scheme of 'creation.' "[12]

I should like to call this realistic view which sees much of man's existence as characterized by suffering, anxiety, and frustrations as "first order pessimism." This type of pessimism has been incorporated in the philosophies of despair cultivated by the Stoics and the Epicureans. As James rightfully observed, Stoics and Epicureans should be considered not merely as historical schools, but as a "typical attitude marking a definite stage in the development of the sick soul." [13] One can clearly see this kind of attitude reflected in the writings of many thinkers today who adopt the sober position of naturalism. While committed to a transcendent pessimism, they nevertheless advocate a philosophy which possesses at least courage and dignity. Sidney Hook, for example, recently pointed out that "pragmatism avoids the romantic pessimism of Bertrand Russell's free man shaking his fist in defiance of a malignant universe by being melioristic, not optimistic." According to Hook, "pragmatism is an attempt to make it possible for men to live in a precarious world of inescapable tragedy . . . by the arts of intelligent social control . . . It may be a lost cause. I do not know of a better one." [14]

These views represent what James calls "the highest flight of purely natural man."

Let us examine the claims of the advocates of Jewish optimism and the Jewish love of life and attempt to comprehend how this is achieved. The thesis has been suggested that the Jewish way of life with its Sabbaths, holidays, and ceremonials give to the Jew a "zest for life" by simply developing his faculty "to get more joy than sorrow out of life." "Although the cup of Jewish suffering was virtually always running over, the cup of Jewish joys was yet fuller." [15] This is a rather strange notion. Does the concept of *simchah shel mitzvah*, and the fact that Jewish tradition bids us to enjoy life, imply that the resulting joy to the Jew is so intense that he will, to a greater degree than others, affirm life and tenaciously cling to it, "never be gloomy even in the most tragic periods," and "savor life as long as there is breath in one's nostrils?" What shall we say to Rabbi Judah the Prince who, at his death, called upon Heaven as witness that he did not enjoy this world even to the extent of his small finger? [16]

An alternate explanation is one which shifts the grounds of

the Jewish will-to-live from an egoistic, subjective hedonism to
the concept of a transcendent "happiness." That is to say, Judaism as a system of values, irrespective of the joys it may give
or not give, is considered meaningful and worthwhile. "Judaism
fills the Jew rooted in the traditions of his people with the certainty of significant self-fulfillment before which even the harsh-
est sufferings pale." [17] This is, of course, something entirely different. Such a view of the Jewish affirmation of life simply draws
the implications of its metaphysical optimism and assigns to life
values and meaning which are beyond the reach of the vicissi-
tudes of our worldly existence. But then, what is unique about
this? There are countless philosophies of life, including the classic
formulations of ancient Greece, which equate man's "happiness"
with the fulfillment of his particular *telos* or end, each differently
conceived. Such abstract "happiness," however, does not necessarily entail cheerfulness rather than sadness, joy rather than depression.

Upon consideration, it appears that the initial effect of a religious consciousness upon the outlook and feeling tone of an individual is in the direction of pessimism. James, for example,
maintains that pessimism is essentially a religious disease. "It
consists in nothing but a religious demand to which there comes
no normal religious reply." On the basis of mere animal existence, the expression of first order pessimism can perhaps be overcome by the resignation and courage of the Stoic approach. Man
is a small part of a cosmic process. This is life and there is no
more. Let us make the best of it.

But if, as a result of a religious orientation, man encourages
attitudes which attribute a supreme worth to the human spirit
and to certain values and which see a Spirit beyond reality and
posit intrinsic good, then the sheer contradiction between the religious evaluation of things and the harsh reality of existence
plunges him into a nightmarish pessimism of a far deeper nature.
Precisely because life is good, intrinsically good, transcendentally
good—is its negation bad. To the extent that the religious outlook invests life with tremendous spiritual opportunities, to that
extent must it look upon every frustration of these opportunities
with increased horror and a heightened sense of tragedy. Thus

we arrive at a "second order pessimism" which has, as its reflective source, religious sentiment.

Whenever Judaism has been taken seriously, this element of pessimism has been apparent. Perhaps its clearest expression is to be found in the Talmud, where is recorded an issue debated for two and one half years between the House of Hillel and the House of Shammai. The House of Hillel maintained, "better was it for man to have been created than not to have been created," while the House of Shammai maintained "better would it have been for man not to have been created than to have been created." The issue was called to a decision and it was concluded that "better would it have been for man not to have been created, but now that he has been created, let him examine his behavior." [18] What we have here does not contradict the accepted view of the metaphysical optimism of Judaism. "And the Lord saw everything that He had made and behold it was very good." Creation gives man an opportunity he would otherwise not have. Nevertheless, looked at existentially, as part of my own individual, personal being, the possibility (no matter how small) of not achieving the goal, the possibility of succumbing to sin and plunging into the abyss, the possibility that my fate might be "death and evil," can well engender the reaction: "neither thy sting nor thy honey," better that I not be given this crushing responsibility, better not to have been created!

Indeed, the truly righteous person will constantly question and be critical of his own deeds and behavior and will be forever anxious about the state of his relationship with God. Does not the Bible itself record that Jacob, in his hour of peril, "was sorely afraid" lest his sins be the cause of a suspension of God's providence? [19] Does not the Talmud stipulate that hints of the esoteric wisdom may be revealed only to him "whose heart worries inside of him?" [20] There can be no question but that the individual who takes the absolute demand of his religion seriously will develop profound anxieties of guilt concerning the quality and validity of his religious response. The modern Mussar movement in particular stressed the need for constant vigilance and constant tension on the part of the God-fearing person. Rabbi Israel Salanter taught: "Man may be compared to a bird. It is within the power of the bird to ascend ever higher on condition that it continue to flap its wings without cessation. If it should stop flapping for a moment, it would fall into the abyss. So is it with man." [21]

Psychologists have observed the conditional quality of even the most ego-bolstering of Jewish concepts. One of them remarks rather perceptively, "The Jews have very often been in situations which have caused them to doubt . . . the love of their God . . . All their trials and tribulations have been regarded as sent by God as punishment for their sins, but also as special proof of His love, since only through suffering could they be made worthy of a Covenant with Him . . . the Jew's self esteem has none of the serenity of certainty. It is restless and based on doubt." [22] A recent sociological study of the *Shtetl* finds evidence of "intense and unremitting anxiety" in spite of strict observance of the Law. The very elements which Liberal Judaism sees as making for optimism are seen here as conducive to anxiety:

> The combination of the two concepts, free will and predestination, discourages fatalism and fosters anxiety. God has decreed the circumstances of each man's life but the individual alone is responsible for what he does with them. There are so many opportunities for failure in fulfillment of the commandments, in the amount of effort one expends on earning a livelihood, in all one's activities and relationships. Ignorance of circumstances may be an excuse, but ignorance of the Law is not, and there is no excuse for ignorance due to oversight or negligence. Obligations are so many, opposite God, family, and fellows, that no matter how much one does, it is never really enough. There is always the burden of undischarged duty. [23]

There is yet another aspect to this issue. The existentialist analysis of man as a creature beset by a natural anxiety stemming from his awareness of his own finitude affords us an opportunity to restate the authentic Jewish view on a metaphysical level. Existentialist literature abounds with analyses of man's growing anxiety and sense of alienation. To call our time an "age of anxiety" has become almost a truism. Alienation is a fact. Undoubtedly all of the sociological explanations are relevant—the breakdown of the family, the impersonalism of modern industry, the uncontrollability of political events, the element of infinitude in the new cosmological image. Alienation is a multi-dimensional phenomenon. Religious thinkers, however, have asked whether modern man's estrangement is merely "the itch of personal neuroses" to be overcome by the wisdom of the Fromms and Peales, or whether it is perhaps revealing of human existence as it really is. The latter view holds that there are forms of anxiety which belong to existence *as such* and are to be distinguished from an abnormal state of mind, such as in neurotic anxiety. This notion is already implicit in the account of Genesis where man is described as having been created in a condition of freedom, a condition of sheer possibility in which he can negate as well as affirm, destroy as well as create. This condition of indeterminate potentiality with its awful responsibilities is already a condition of anxiety. Finitude, temporality, selfhood, and sexuality are aspects of the grandeur of creation. But we rarely encounter them in this unspoiled condition. "Sin lieth at the door and its desire is unto thee but thou canst rule over it." [24]

Kierkegaard, and Tillich after him, have raised the phenomena of guilt, fear, despair, the prospect of one's own death, and the prospect of salvation, beyond the sphere of purely psychological considerations into aspects of metaphysical thought, which is what what they have always been for traditional Judaism. Kierkegaard maintains that the self is a synthesis of the infinite and the finite, the eternal and the temporal, freedom and necessity.[25] Man is thus not self-sufficient and can achieve true selfhood only by being related aright to God. Whether man is aware of it or not, God is both the criterion and the goal of selfhood. Hence, whoever has no God has no self, and who has no self is in despair which is a specific illness of man as spiritual being. Despair, to Kierkegaard, is any imbalance in the relationship of the self to itself. Any attempt by man to separate himself from the power which created him, or to neglect what is eternal in him, or fight his spiritual nature, will result in despair. Kierkegaard goes on to analyze the different types of despair such as the "despair of weakness" and the "despair of defiance" which correspond to well known types in the Jewish gallery of the godless. There is little here that Jewish theology could not agree with. Even Tillich's formulation [26] of the basic types of anxieties—the anxiety of death, the anxiety of meaningless, and the anxiety of guilt—are implicit in traditional accounts of repentance.[26a]

Another approach, also not without interest to traditional Jewish thinking, sees as basic in current analyses of the dynamics of anxiety a positive urge which is somehow frustrated.

This view maintains that the experience of anxiety has a certain constant structure. Whether described by Catholic mystic, agnostic existentialist, or atheistic psychoanalyst, it exhibits a specific character. "That character is anxious longing. The experience itself is constituted by a polar tension between fear and longing. Anxiety is desire aware of a threat to its fulfillment." [27]

Could we not therefore understand anxiety as the consequence of a genuine desire for God, the longing for the elements of goodness and divinity and at the same time a reflection of the impediments faced by this finite creature in responding to this call? The anxiety of the sinner is thus his tendency to erect false gods and encounter inevitable frustration as he seeks to satisfy the soul's thirst for God with imperfect substitutes of the things of this world.

The Psalms do not lack for expressions of the soul thirsting after God. Rabbi Joseph Albo taught, "Everything has a desire for that which is of the same nature as and similar to itself . . . so the mind desires to fulfill the will of God because it is natural to do so." [28] Rabbi Nissan Ben Reuben adds the thought: "Just as man's sense of touch fears the fire because it is contrary to its nature, so does the mind fear to violate the commands of the Almighty because its very nature requires compliance." [29] It remains for us to draw the implications and with them formulate an hypothesis in explanation of the empirical phenomena of anxiety and alienation. Indeed, Saadia already saw this as an intimation of the "world-to-come"—"I find furthermore that none of God's creatures known to me feel secure and tranquil in this world, even when they have reached the most exalted ruling position and the highest station therein. Now this feeling is not something natural to the soul. It is due, rather, to its consciousness of the fact that there is reserved for it an abode that is superior to all the excellence of its present dwelling. That is why its eyes look forward longingly to it. Were it not so, the soul would have felt secure and have been at rest." [30]

It appears, therefore, that traditional Judaism possesses all the ingredients making for a doctrine of human nature which could incorporate the phenomenon of existential anxiety and offer an explanation for man's growing sense of alienation.

We stated earlier that the initial effect of the religious outlook is in the direction of pessimism. The religious person is in a position to develop a fuller recognition of the terror and insecurity of ordinary human life, of the blackness of sin and, as far as one's own strength goes, of the possibility of slipping back into evil and nothingness. Indeed, it has been rightly said that the religious outlook does not give peace of mind but simply substitutes the right anxieties for the wrong anxieties. This is reflected in a teaching of Rabbi Nachman of Bratzlav: "Man is afraid of things that cannot harm him and he knows it, and he craves things that cannot be of help to him and he knows it; but in truth the one thing man is afraid of is within himself, and the one thing he craves is within himself." [31]

Is this, however, the ultimate condition, or can we perhaps find in Judaism some final turn, some higher level of feeling which bespeaks joy? I believe that the key to the teaching of Judaism on this point lies in the phrase "serve the Lord with fear and rejoice in trembling." [32] Thinkers as diverse as Rabbi Joseph Albo and Rabbi Judah Loew of Prague are one in their understanding of this passage.[33] Both agree in describing man's initial awareness of himself as a creature subject to contingency and temporality in terms of fear and sadness which cause the heart "to tremble and grieve." Rabbi Loew specifically points to what we have called the "first order pessimism" of the creature as he faces death and also the "second order pessimism" which takes hold of man as he contemplates the rigors of ultimate judgment. This is the fear of God which is not only the beginning of wisdom but the disposition which leads to immortality of the soul and ultimate salvation. This state of fear and trembling is prior to any other and constitutes "the fundamental spirit of service." As a more recent thinker has put is, "All religious reality begins with what biblical religion calls the 'fear of God.' It comes when our existence between birth and death becomes incomprehensible and uncanny, when all security is shattered through the mystery. This is not the relative mystery of that which is inaccessible only to the present state of human knowledge and is hence in principle discoverable. It is the essential mystery, the inscrutableness of which belongs to its very nature; it is the unknowable." [34]

However, once man reaches the state of "fear of God" he can, as he contemplates his trembling, find cause for joy "because he realizes that he fears that which is deserving of fear—an indication of spiritual perfection and health on his part." [35] This "joy in trembling" is neither the hedonistic "zest of life" described above nor the healthy-minded optimism which believes it can, by positive thinking and talking, blind itself to the grim realities of life. This Jewish joy is instead a tempered optimism, a "holy insecurity" which recognizes that existence has meaning under God not *in spite* of its tragedies and sufferings, but perhaps *through* its tragedies and sufferings, *by means of* the trivial and the prosaic. Kierkegaard has observed with great sensitivity that Abraham, who attained the level of faith, unlike one who has merely achieved the level of resignation, does not lose the finite but rather regains it.[36] "After passing through the dark gate the believing man steps forth into the everyday which is henceforth hallowed as the place in which he has to live with mystery." [37] The believing Jew has looked sadness in the face. He knows that wife, the family, career, the daily tasks are not the ultimate "answer." But precisely because he has accepted their contingency can they have for him freshness and be a source of tempered joy. We can indeed experience the simple joys of life if we know their limitations beforehand. The cry of "vanity of vanities, all is vanity" comes as no surprise because we did not strain the simple joys with a burden they are not equipped to bear. We did not ask them to justify life for us. "Serve the Lord with fear and rejoice in trembling."

In summation: Judaism as a metaphysical system is optimistic, yet it recognizes fully the tragic character of human existence. On the existential level, it fosters sobriety and shifts the locus of anxieties to the areas that count—concern for the state of one's soul and one's relationship to God. Those who repress their thirst for the spirit expose themselves to futile frustrations and suffer the unmitigated consequences of man's naturally anxious condition. The mature religious personality who fixes his gaze on the infinite can, however, regain the finite in tempered joy.

NOTES

1 Joshua Loth Liebman, *Peace of Mind* (New York: Simon & Shuster, 1946) pp. 165, 171.

2 *Ibid.* p. 202.

3 Abba Hillel Silver, *Where Judaism Differed* (New York: Macmillan, 1957) p. 179.

4 *Ibid.* p. 210.

5 Walter Houston Clark, *The Psychology of Religion* (New York: Macmillan 1958) p. 159.

6 H. Rose, "Beyond Pessimism and Optimism" in *Judaism*, Spring 1957.

7 William James, *The Varieties of Religious Experience* (New York: Modern Library) pp. 77–163.

8 Clark, *op. cit.*, p. 155.

9 William James, *The Will to Believe* (New York: Dover Publications, 1956) p. 32.

10 James, *Varieties*, p. 160.

11 *Ibid.*, p. 137.

12 Sigmund Freud, *Civilization and Its Discontents* (London: Hogarth Press, 1930) Chap. 2.

13 James, *Varieties*, p. 141.

14 Sidney Hook, "Pragmatism and the Tragic Sense of Life" in *Commentary*, August 1960.

15 T. W. Rosmarin, *Jewish Survival* (New York: Philosophical Library, 1949) p. 207.

16 *Ketubot* 104a. See commentaries of Rashi and Tosafot.

17 Rosmarin, *op. cit.*, p. 210.

18 *Eruvin* 13b.

19 Genesis 32:8.

20 *Chagigah* 13a.

21 Dov Katz, *Tenuat Ha-Mussar* (Tel Aviv: Beitan Ha-Sefer, 1946) p. 269.

22 Rudolph M. Loewenstein, *Christians and Jews* (New York: Int. Universities Press, 1952) p. 139.

23 M. Zborowski and E. Herzog, *Life Is With People* (New York: Int. Universities Press, 1952) p. 411.

24 Genesis 4:7.

25 Soren Kierkegaard, *The Sickness Unto Death* (New York: Doubleday, 1954) pp. 182–207.

26 Paul Tillich, *The Courage to Be* (New Haven: Yale University Press, 1952) p. 35.

26a "Despair of weakness" is the unwillingness to be oneself which results in the life of "pure immediacy." In this condition, the person looks at others in order to discover what he himself is and "recognizes himself by his dress." He becomes "an imitation, a number, a cipher in the crowd." He flees reflection, plunges into the outgoing, active life, and takes his cue from external circumstances. If he ever experiences self-reflection, it is thrust into forgetfulness or attributed to the instability of youth. In "despair of defiance" man wills to be himself but tries to overcome finitude on his own power. He attempts to create his "self" to his own specifications by sheer assertion of will. This is "the despairing abuse of the eternal in the self to the point of being despairingly determined to be oneself." In its final desperate form, this defiance turns into demonic rage in which the despairer wills to be himself with his torment, which he believes constitutes a proof against the goodness of existence and thus he revolts and protests against the whole of existence. He will not hear of any help because comfort now "would be the destruction of him as an objection against existence and would rid him of his justification for being what he is." From this psychological analysis, Kierkegaard moves forward to theological considerations and asserts that "sin is the potentiation of despair before God."

These analyses apply quite readily to well-known types in our own literature. The "despair of weakness" may well explain the "Disciples of Balaam" with their "evil eye, haughty spirit, and excessive desire" (*Avot* 5:22), or even he who "blesses himself in his heart saying, I will have peace" (Deut. 29:18), or the *kesil* who has all the knowledge but is lost in his "immediacy" (see commentary of *Malbim* on Proverbs 1:22), or those "whose stomachs have become their gods, and their clothing their Torah" (*Chovot ha-Levavot, Shaar ha-Perishut*, Ch. 2). Those afflicted with the "despair of defiance" have a recognized niche in Jewish thought. This genre starts with Nimrod who "knows his Master but deliberately revolts against Him" (see *Rashi* on Gen. 10:9) and continues with the "stiff-necked ones" who persist in their ways though there be "proof to the contrary" (see *Seforno* on Deut. 9:6), and concludes with the "wicked ones who refuse to repent even on the threshold of Gehinnom" (*Eruvin* 19a).

According to Tillich man's "ontic self-affirmation" as a created being is threatened from three directions by "non-being." Awareness of this three-fold threat is anxiety appearing in three forms: threat of death; threat of emptiness or loss of meaning; threat of condemnation or guilt. In all of these the anxiety is existential, i.e., it belongs to man's nature. If we accept this analysis, then making man aware of his anxieties and the sources of his anxieties can perhaps bring him to the realization that he can overcome these anxieties only by "grounding himself in God."

It is not difficult to see that the Rabbis have consistently appealed to these three kinds of anxieties in attempting to bring about the experience of repentance. The entire Book of Kohelet is an appeal to the emptiness of man's existence if it is lived only "under the sun." (*See Shaarei Teshuvah* of R. Jonah Gerondi, *Shaar* 2, paragraphs 19 and 20). Remembrance of the day of one's death is suggested as a most potent stimulus for *teshuvah* (*Berakhot* 5), while the constant theme of the Prophets is to point to Israel's obligation, both collectively and individually, to God as "liberator from Egypt," as "Father and as Master," as "the Rock that begot thee," and "the God Who made thee," and the ingratitude with which Israel has responded. The purpose of all of this is, of course, to generate a sense of guilt and remorse which is the first step towards Repentance (Maimonides *Hil. Teshuvah* 2:2).

It is quite plausible that these three anxieties are implied in the dictum of R. Akavya ben Mahalalel: ". . . You come from a fetid drop"—your existence, due essentially to egoistic sexuality, is thus meaningless. "You are going to a place of dust and worms"—the anxiety of death. And "before Whom are you destined to give judgment and reckoning—before the Almighty"—the anxiety of guilt (*Avot* 3:1).

27 Fred Berthold, Jr., *Fear of God* (New York: Harper, 1959) pp. 75, 90, 92.

28 Joseph Albo, *Sefer ha-Ikkarim* (Philadelphia: Jewish Publication Society, 1930) Vol. III p. 301.

29 Rabbenu Nissim, *Shneim Assar Derushim* (Jerusalem: 1955), *Derush* 10, p. 69.

30 Saadia Gaon, *The Book of Beliefs and Opinions* (New Haven: Yale University Press, 1948) Treatise IX, Ch. 1, p. 324.

31 Martin Buber, *The Tales of Rabbi Nachman* (New York: Horizon Press, 1956) p. 37.

32 Psalms 2:11.

33 Albo, *op. cit.*, p. 307; Judah Loewy, *Netivot Olam* (Tel Aviv: Pardes, 1956) Netiv Halitzanut, p. 167. See also the discussion in *Berakhot* 30.

34 Martin Buber, *Eclipse of God* (New York: Harper, 1952) p. 50.

35 Albo, *loc. cit.*

36 Soren Kierkegaard, *Fear and Trembling* (New York: Doubleday, 1954) p. 46.

37 Buber, *loc. cit.*

HALAKHAH AND
CONTEMPORARY
SOCIETY

ISADORE TWERSKY

*

Some Aspects
of the Jewish Attitude
Toward the Welfare State*

IMUST confess that although I found the proposed subject interesting and imaginative and although I knew that this conference was important and distinguished, my acceptance of the
invitation was accompanied by sustained apprehensiveness. First
of all, my professional ineptitude was a serious deterrent: I am
not a social worker and have never been initiated into either the
pragmatic or conceptual aspects of social work. Secondly, the
treatment of such a theme is beset with "occupational" or topical
hazards; it can imperceptibly pass from the carefully lined note-
book of the historian or analyst to the supple and suggestive text
of the preacher or partisan. Welfare, social justice, acts of loving-
kindness, humanitarianism are not neutral terms that can be
handled with frosty detachment. T. S. Eliot already observed that
"social justice" is a much abused phrase; its rational content is
often replaced by an emotional charge.[1] This could be especially
applicable in our case, for the Jewish tradition of social welfare
contains much vitality, virtuosity, and relevance and can easily
beget impassioned rhetoric. If, as Whitehead aphorized, all of
western thought is a footnote to Plato, one might suggest that
western *humanitas* is a footnote to the Bible—and then proceed
indolently to luxuriate in this flattering fact.

In planning this paper (and in an attempt to avoid generalities

* Based upon a lecture to the Annual Conference on the Relationship of
the Rabbi to the Jewish Social Worker, sponsored by The Commission on
Synagogue Relations of the Federation of Jewish Philanthropies of New York,
December 1962.

which could intensify the kind of abusiveness just mentioned),
I undertook to answer three questions which presumably provide
a matrix for comprehensive analysis of the issue under consideration. I should like to emphasize that I have tried only to fulfill
the function of a cartographer and plot the conceptual-historical
terrain. The general scheme, worked out in terms of halakhic
categories and in light of historic experiences, needs thoughtful
elaboration and patient application to the many details of the
problem.

The three questions may be formulated as follows:

(1) What is the metaphysical foundation or ideological root
of charity? Into what conceptual-axiological framework does the
practice of philanthropy fit? And let me hasten to add that this
is not a purely speculative matter, for, as is always the case, the
Halakhah consistently translates metaphysical postulates into
practical conclusions.

(2) Is charity, as conceived and motivated in halakhic thought,
an integrated-unified act on the part of the individual or is it
polaric and tense? Is it a simple, one-dimensional deed or a complex, dialectical performance? In other words, just how much—in
quantity and quality, objectively and subjectively—does philanthropy demand from the individual?

(3) Is charity a particularistic performance of the Jew—like
Sabbath observance—or is it a universal expression of the basic
dignity of man and the concomitant sense of reciprocal helpful-
ness? On the practical level, this question revolves around the
historic position of Judaism vis-à-vis non-Jewish philanthropic enterprises. It eventually asks how activities of a welfare state fit into
this framework.

Let us eliminate the third question for the time being—because
of limitations of time and endurance—and concentrate on the
remaining two.

I

The Jewish theory of philanthropy (*tzeddakah; chesed*)—or
humanity, i.e., helping those who need help [2]—has often been
discussed, sometimes analyzed.[3] Its centrality in Jewish life and

its concomitant importance in Jewish literature,[4] starting in the Biblical period and continuing through talmudic times into the modern era, is copiously documented.[5] Many rabbinic statements which stress, with much verve and persuasiveness, the axial role of *chesed* are frequently quoted [6]; for example, the dictum that "charity is equivalent to all the other religious precepts combined" (*Bava Batra* 9a) or that "he who is merciful to others, mercy is shown to him by Heaven, while he who is not merciful to others, mercy is not shown to him by Heaven" (*Shabbat* 151b). I have no intention of reviewing all this. My aim is simply to describe the metaphysical foundation of charity and underscore a few basic concepts, whose implications for Jewish social justice and welfare are as profound as they are pervasive, by interpreting one striking talmudic passage.[7] This is presented as a dialogue between the second century sage R. Akiba and the Roman general Turnus Rufus who was governor of the Judean province. This historical fragment embodies the quintessence of a Judaic social ethic: (a) the special role of man (in the world) resulting from his practice of philanthropy and (b) the relation of men to each other.

It has been taught: R. Meir used to say: "The critic [of Judaism] may bring against you the argument, 'If your God loves the poor, why does He not support them?' If so, answer him, 'So that through them we may be saved from the punishment of Gehinnom.' This question was actually put by Turnus Rufus to R. Akiba: 'If your God loves the poor, why does He not support them?' He replied, 'So that we may be saved through them from the punishment of Gehinnom.' 'On the contrary,' said the other, 'it is this which condemns you to Gehinnom. I will illustrate by a parable. Suppose an earthly king was angry with his servant and put him in prison and ordered that he should be given no food or drink, and a man went and gave him food and drink. If the king heard, would he not be angry with him? And you are called "servants," as it is written, *For unto me the children of Israel are servants.*' R. Akiba answered him: 'I will illustrate by another parable. Suppose an earthly king was angry with his son, and put him in prison and ordered that no food or drink should be given to him, and someone went and gave him food and drink. If the king heard of it, would he not send him a present? And we are called "sons," as it is written, *Sons are ye to the Lord your*

God.' He said to him: 'You are called both sons and servants. When you carry out the desires of the Omnipresent, you are called "servants." At the present time you are not carrying out the desires of the Omnipresent.' R. Akiba replied: 'The Scripture says, *Is it not to deal thy bread to the hungry and bring the poor that are cast out to thy house.* When "dost thou bring *the poor who are cast out to thy house?"* Now; and it says [at the same time], Is it not to deal thy bread to the hungry?' "

(1) The first premise to emerge from this dialogue is that *chesed* is that distinctive function which legitimatizes our worldly existence and adds a new dimension of purposiveness to life. It constitutes a special challenge and unique prerogative [8] for man by establishing him as a very powerful agent and delicate instrument in the conduct of human affairs. God has abdicated part of a function of His in order to enable man to continue and extend creation.[9] It is our practice of kindness which enables us to continue God's creative plan, elevates our life from brutishness to sensitivity, and extricates us from chaotic, vacuous biological existence. Indeed, man was created only on the assumption that he would passionately pursue *chesed* [10] and this, in turn, saves him from damnation and perdition.

This axial role of *chesed* is underscored in many other ways, among which the following is probably the most notable. While all religious-ethical actions are based on the principle of "imitation of God" (*imitatio dei* or *mimesis theou*), of walking in His ways and assimilating His characteristics,[11] this is especially true of *chesed* in its broadest sense. *Chesed* is the most emphatic of God's attributes (*rav chesed*); the world came into existence because of *chesed*; the majority of God's actions toward man are characterized by *chesed*.[12] The Torah begins and ends with lovingkindness as a divine act.[13] The practice of *chesed* thereby becomes man's "most God-like act." [14]

However, this is not the complete picture. Aiding the needy in all forms is not only a fulfillment of *imitatio dei* but it is comparable to aiding God Himself (!). The same R. Akiba, whose dialogue with Rufus we are trying to interpret, dramatically deepens the social ethos of Judaism by equating charity to the poor with a loan to God![15] We are accustomed, on the basis of halakhic terminology and conceptualization, to thinking of God as the ultimate "recipient" or "beneficiary" of all things "consecrated" for the Temple or other religious causes, all priestly gifts (tithe, heave-offering, etc. . . . .). God (usually designated as גבוה) is the juridical personality that is the "owner," agent, or trustee and all legal procedures are based on this fact. Now, in R. Akiba's homily, God appears also as the ultimate "beneficiary" of gifts to the poor.[16] This involvement of God is certainly the noblest endorsement of that loving-kindness practiced between men.

(2) Now, let us return to the second feature of the dialogue. At issue between the two discussants is the point of departure for determining human relationships. For R. Akiba, we are all brothers, because we are all children and, therefore, completely equal before God.[17] The brotherhood of man and fatherhood of God are inseparable. Any system which denies the common origin of man in God eviscerates the idea of brotherhood. Any system which affirms it must logically and inevitably sustain its corollary. The coordinates of the human system, in this view, are both horizontal and vertical and together create a relationship which results in mutual responsibility and overlapping concern for each other. Even in a period of disgrace, disenchantment, or repudiation (such as exile or impoverishment), this relationship is not nullified and its demands not relaxed. Our identity as children and brothers is never obscured.[18] It is notable that the author of this statement, the great martyr who witnessed and experienced persecution and bestiality, was the one who articulated: "Beloved is man who was created in the image of God." His ethical objectivity was unaffected by oppression, his view of man and hierarchy of values was firm. Man was a unique figure.

For Rufus, on the other hand, only one aspect of the *vertical* relationship between man and God is determinative: that of submission and slavery. And did not Aristotle already proclaim that "slaves are like animals"? And had not Plato defined the slave as a "species of tame animal"?[19] If, then, the world—in this case the Jewish community—is a large household inhabited by a mass of

unrelated individuals, mere biological atoms, there can be no
community of interests and responsibilities, no compassion and
cooperation.

(3) Implicit in R. Akiba's exchange with the Roman governor
of Palestine is also a realistic-pragmatic view of the human situation, a view which is sensitively attuned to suffering and privation
and earnestly questing for improvement and fulfillment. The discussion here is not oriented to metaphysics; it is geared to ethics,
to concrete social problems—something which is characteristic of
talmudic discussion generally. It implies that one cannot con-
veniently fall back upon religious assumptions in order to justify
passivity and resignation when confronted with social and ethical
indignities. We must not look upon trouble impassively, whether
the motivation be determinism (this is God's decree) or con-
descension (some people are irretrievably singled out for subjection) or contemptuousness (physical-carnal matters are insignificant).[20] Poverty and inequality are pervasive—and will perhaps
endure forever [21]—but they must be incessantly condemned and
combatted. Judaism insists that man is obligated to mitigate injustice and alleviate suffering. There is, if you like, something antithetical in this situation. Poverty or sickness may be viewed as
divine punishment or a form of retribution just as wealth and
health may be construed as signs of divine favor or reward.[22] Indeed, given a theocentric-teleological view of life, every episode or
situation—exile, death—is divinely purposive.[23] Man, however,
must not sit in judgment from such a theistic perspective; it is not
for him to approach poverty or sickness as predetermined criminal
or punitive situations. A providential view of history is no excuse
for quietism or pretext for withdrawal.

(4) Similarly, it seems to follow that one cannot dismiss a
destitute person with a counterfeit expression of faith: "Rely on
God, your father and king! He will help you." The cherished
virtue of *bitachon*, trust, is something with which to comfort
yourself in a time of depression, but it is not a pain-killing drug
to be callously prescribed for others. If Reuben is starving, Simeon
must provide food—not sanctimony. It is true that Reuben must
live with hope and courage, but Simeon must act with dispatch
and compassion. God's inscrutable benevolence is not a substitute

for man's tangible benevolence. As R. Bachya ibn Pakuda ob-serves,[24] bitachon has a multiplicity of implications: to the im-poverished person it conveys the need for tranquillity, patience, and contentment with one's portion, while to the man of means, it suggests the obligation of sustained and gracious liberality.

Our cursory analysis of these concepts enables us, in conclu-sion, to pinpoint the unique feature of chesed, in contradistinction to other philanthropic systems. It would be gratuitous—and chau-vinistic—to give Judaism an exclusive monopoly over the practice of charity; the rabbis, as a matter of fact, never denied that other nations were charitable.[25] Judaism's contribution is a new motive for philanthropy: the religious-humane motive, which means act-ing for the sake of humanity because of religious conviction and obligation. Humanity is an expression of piety ("Everyman who is endowed with loving kindness is without doubt a God-fearing man," Sukkah 49b); the two are absolutely inseparable. Commit-ment to God is inconceivable in Judaism without compassion for man. "Whoever turns his eyes away from [one who appeals for] charity is considered as if he were serving idols." [26] Philo de-scribes philanthropy as "the virtue closest akin to piety, its sister and its twin," for "the nature which is pious is also humane, and the same person will exhibit both qualities of holiness to God and justice to man." [27] One cannot claim to be God-intoxicated with-out having an unquenchable thirst for social justice. Indeed, theo-logical postulates sundered from their practical consequences are powerless, and—perhaps—purposeless. They are mutually supple-mentary and independently fragmentary.[28]

This motive should be the propelling force of federation activ-ities and should determine its welfare program.

I I

Halakhah is a tense, vibrant, dialectical system, identifiable by its beautiful blend of romanticism and classicism. This is both cause and consequence of the halakhic insistence upon norma-tiveness in action and inwardness in feeling and thought. The historic achievement of Halakhah was to move beyond theoretical principles of faith to a minutely regulated code of religio-ethical behavior—to give concrete and continuous expression to theological ideals, ethical norms, and historical concepts. It is based upon the conviction that abstract belief, even an intensely personal or charismatic one, will be evanescent and that religious insight which is not firmly anchored down by practice is unreal. Its goal is spirituality together with conformity—"the saturation and transfusion of everyday life with the thought of God" (the felicitous phrase of a 19th century theologian, Bousset). This insistence upon the "coincidence of opposites" (call it law and prophecy, if you like, or institution and charisma, everyday life and the thought of God) creates the "dialectical pull" or tension which is characteristic of so many root principles and fundamental beliefs of Judaism.

A favorite example of this creative tension is the institution of prayer, which attempts to balance inward experience with routinized performance, to avoid an anarchic liturgy and at the same time not to produce a spiritless stereotype. In other words, the Halakhah takes a thesis—spontaneity of prayer, manifest in a genuinely dialogic relationship between man and God—superimposes upon it an antithesis—standardization and uniformity of prayer—and strives to maintain a synthesis: a devotional routine.

I would like to suggest that the institution of tzedakah—charity —provides an equally attractive illustration of this dialectical structure. The Halakhah undertook to convert an initially amorphous, possibly even capricious act into a rigidly defined and totally regulated performance. It made charitable contributions, usually voluntary in nature, obligatory, subject to compulsory assessment and collection. However, while objectifying and concretizing a subjective, fluid state of mind, it insisted relentlessly upon the proper attitude, feeling, and manner of action. It hoped to combine the thesis of free, spontaneous giving with the antithesis of soulless, obligatory contribution and produce a composite act which is subjective though quantified, inspired though regular, intimate yet formal. As is the case with prayer and other products of such dialectical synthesis, the tension is very great, for the breakdown of the synthesis is always an imminent and immanent possibility. The pattern of behavior may become atrophied and de-spiritualized or else the standardized practice may be overthrown. Here the tension is even reflected semantically in the term *tzedakah* which means both righteousness and charity, an act based on one's moral conscience as well as an appropriate course of action spelled out in detail by the law.[29]

Within the practical-halakhic framework of philanthropy, this polarity comes to the surface in two main areas. First of all, there is the constant interplay betwen the individual and the community with regard to the responsibility for and awareness of philanthropic needs. A study of the laws of charity yields paradoxical conclusions. On the one hand, it seems that the central figure is the individual: to him are the commandments addressed, he is enjoined to engage unstintingly in charity work, and assiduously to help his fellow man. He is the hero of philanthropy, seeking exposure to needy people and responding effusively to their requests. On the other hand, it is surprising to find that the Halakhah has assigned an indispensable, all-inclusive role to the community. The community acts not only as a supervisory, enforcing agency but occupies the center of the stage as an entity possessed of initiative and charged with responsibility. One may persuasively argue that the Halakhah makes of philanthropy a collective project; philanthropic endeavor, long-term aid (*kupah*) as well as immediate, emergency relief (*tamchuy*), is thoroughly institutionalized. Responsibility for the care of the needy—sick, poor, aged, disturbed,—is communal. The individual makes his contribution to the community chest and with this he apparently discharges his obligations. He acts mechanically, almost anonymously, by responding to the peremptory demands of the collectors "who go about among the people every Friday soliciting from each whatever is assessed upon him" (*Mishneh Torah, Hilkhot Matenot Aniyim*). *Tzedakah* thus emerges as an individual obligation which is fulfilled corporately. And it should be noted that this is a premeditated arrangement. The community does not step in and assume responsibility ex post facto, after individuals have shirked their duty or failed to manage matters properly. The community initially appears as a modified welfare city-state, with its special functionaries who collect the compulsory levy and act as trustees for the poor and needy.

This is the first expression of polarity between the individual and community.

Whoever continues to acquaint himself with *Hilkhot Tzedakah* in the *Shulchan Arukh* or *Matenot Aniyim* in the *Mishneh Torah* comes across another basic antithesis inherent in the very concept of charity. On the one hand, the Halakhah is interested only in the objective act, the amount given, meeting the challenge, and relieving the needs of the destitute. This is a complete, self-contained, determinate act. On the other hand, we are confronted by an exquisitely sensitive Halakhah, very much concerned not only with *what* but *how* the act of charity is implemented. Not only the outward act is important but the experiential component is significant. One need not rely upon the preacher's eloquence or the moralist's fervor to underscore the importance of motivation and attitude in the halakhic act of charity.

This correlation of the objective and subjective components within the individual act is the second area of tension and polarity.

Let us take up these two points briefly and concretize them somewhat. We may illustrate the polarity of the community-individual partnership by introducing a few specific laws.

For example, the Mishnah states that twelve months' residence is required before a man is counted as one of the townsmen and is obliged to support communal projects. The Talmud, however, goes on to cite another passage which differentiates between various levies. "A man must reside in a town thirty days to become liable for contributing to the soup kitchen, three months for the charity box, . . . and twelve months for contributing to the repair of the town walls." [30] The reason for the distinction between charity and communal enterprises is clear. Only after a man has become a full-fledged resident and has submitted to communal jurisdiction does he become liable to abide by communal ordinances (*takkanot bene ha-'ir*) and share communal expenses. Charity, though, is an individual obligation and one need not come under communal jurisdiction to be liable. The community, however, serves as the executive branch which organizes and implements and distributes.

The sense of communal involvement is projected even more in the following laws. "If the inhabitants of a city impose a charitable levy upon a visiting merchant, the contribution belongs to the poor of the city visited. If, however, the levy be imposed upon a visiting group of people, the contributing is done in the city visited, but the sum collected is conveyed, by the returning visitors, to the city of their origin that the poor of the latter city may be aided with that money." [31] Again, the reason for the differentiation between a wayfaring individual and an itinerant company is apparent. The individual relates to his immediate communal framework and his charitable contribution is absorbed and disbursed there. A group of people are considered to have affiliations with both communities. They contribute immediately to demonstrate their solidarity with the new group and remove suspicion that they are tax dodgers, but return the money for distribution to their original community. What is significant is the permeative involvement with the community on all levels—the strong, ineradicable sense of community action.

So far the enterprising community is in the center and the timid individual is on the periphery. It would almost appear as if a man's obligation is terminated when he weighs the gold pieces or signs a check—and then, losing his identity, just fades away into the shadows of the community. Now let us see how the relationship shifts gear and hear the Halakhah insist that there are aspects of the commandment concerning charity which transcend the basic levy exacted by the community. The institution of *kupah* relieves only one's minimal, quantified duties but other individual, contingent obligations are not superseded.

For example, the obligation of charity is based on both positive and negative commandments: "open thy hand unto him"; "thou shalt not harden thy heart nor shut thy hand" (cf. Leviticus 25:35; Deuteronomy 15:7-8). The nature of the relationship between such mutually reinforcing formulations—a *mitzvat 'aseh* and a *mitzat lo ta'aseh*—presents an halakhic problem. Some interpretations submit that the two are completely commensurate and the negative one has no intrinsic significance; it relates only to the omission of the positive—the failure to contribute. According to many Talmudic authorities, however, the negative commandment not to harden one's heart relates exclusively to one's mental-emotional attitude when confronted with distress. It is addressed only to the individual and stipulates that the individual should not be insensitive and non-responsive to the plea of an indigent person—"a poor person in search of help." The positive commandment is in no way contingent upon the plea or request of the poor, while the negative commandment relates not only to the omission of the positive but is also an act of commission: of callously refusing the poor, of consciously hardening one's heart and thwarting one's inclination to kindness.[32]

What is more, if one has already given charity, even over-subscribed his quota, there is an additional law which states: "It is forbidden to turn away a suppliant poor person empty handed, though one grant no more than a single berry." This is based on Psalm 74:21: "Let not the oppressed turn back in confusion." [33]

The emphasis upon the individual responsibility is thus un-equivocal. However, if you are not convinced, we might go further and submit that according to the social ethos of Judaism, the individual can never really isolate himself from the needy, *especially* in times of euphoria, pleasure and indulgence. The very nature of rejoicing and festivity includes sharing with others. This axiom of kindness was formulated by Maimonides as follows. "While one eats and drinks by himself, it is his duty to feed the stranger, the orphan, the widow, and other poor and unfortunate people, for he who locks the doors to his courtyard and eats and drinks with his wife and family, without giving anything to eat and drink to the poor and the bitter in soul—his meal is not a rejoicing in a divine commandment, but a rejoicing in his own stomach . . . Rejoicing of this kind is a disgrace to those who indulge in it." [34]

It is noteworthy that in many cities—one of the earliest records is from Hamburg—a communal ordinance required every towns-man to have two guests for the Sabbath.[35] Personal contact with and exposure to the needy was of the essence. "There was a cer-tain pious man with whom Elijah used to converse until he made a porter's lodge (gatehouse) after which he did not converse with him any more" (because the poor men were shut out from the courtyard).[36] Sharing the companionship of the poor and making them socially equal is a highly sensitive performance which merits special blessing. "He who lets poor people and orphans partake of food and drink at his table shall call upon the Lord and find, to his delight, that the Lord will answer (Is. 58:9).[37]

So, although the balance may be delicate and tense, corporate responsibility does not eclipse individual awareness and should not dull individual sensitiveness. This would remain true even if communal funds were somehow to become inexhaustible; individual obligations never cease.[38]

Let us return to the second expression of polarity—the objective act vis-à-vis the inner experience and accompanying attitude. As a general principle we may study the assertion that "the reward of charity depends entirely upon the extent of the kindness in it." [39] The cold, formal, objective act does not suffice; it must be fused with warmth and loving-kindness. From an objective point of view, the giving of charity is not subject to qualifications; if you give, that's that and the amount is the only thing that counts. From a subjective point of view, the same act may well be shoddy and meretricious. There can be such a thing as "defective charity." The difference is, if you like, whether there is a heart of flesh or a heart of stone behind it. Allow me to suggest perhaps that the difference expresses itself in the two expressions we have for this act: "giving charity" and "doing charity." "Doing" relates to the method and quality of "giving." "Giving' is concrete and limited; you give ten dollars or one hundred dollars. Doing is how you go about it.

A late source gives this apt illustration.[40] "The giving is tzedakah. The doing is the trouble to bring it to the poor man's house, or the thoughtfulness on the part of the giver that it should be most useful . . . in short, being preoccupied with the good of the poor recipient." The key terms here are tirchah and tirdah which denote constant concern and abiding interest—continuous commitment rather than fleeting attention. The same idea of mental and emotional preoccupation is underscored by the recurrent idiom osek be-Torah u'vigemilut chasadim. Osek suggests a resilient, incompressible quality of attention and dedication; it negates the idea of a perfunctory, quantified act.[41]

III

There are a number of specific *subjective* features which may be collated under this general principle—that "the reward of charity depends entirely upon the extent of the kindness in it." Many of these features are embodied in Maimonides' original, well-known classification of the "eight degrees of benevolence, one above the other." Instead of reproducing this classification here, it might be more useful to abstract from it and related source material a few characteristics and tendencies, which identify the experiential component of charity.

(1) Most important is to approach the needy prudently and tactfully and graciously. "Happy is he that considereth the poor" (Psalm 41:2). The ultimate aim of this approach is to get the poor one to take a loan or else think that he is taking a loan, to accept him into business partnership or help him find employment. This completely eliminates or deftly camouflages humiliation and degradation. It rehabilitates rather than aids and avoids the most objectionable influences of pauperism.[42] In other words, it is not only ethically correct but is also economically sound. Is not this the ideal of all philanthropic federations?

(2) If the humiliation attendant on receiving charity cannot be eliminated, it should be reduced as much as possible. This expresses itself above all in the secrecy and privacy of giving. "He who gives alms in secret is greater than Moses" (*Bava Batra* 9a).[43]

(3) Another basic principle, which may be most relevant to our experiences, is the insistence upon individual consideration of the needy rather than indiscriminate handling of them as so many "faces in the crowd." The indigent remains a dignified individual, with his own needs and drives, his own sensibilities and rights, strengths and weaknesses. The essence of the religious commandment is "to assist a poor person according to his needs" —in other words, selectively not uniformly. Regimentation or massive institutionalization are not in keeping with this spirit. You might find here an inferential endorsement of the case-method of social work, being careful not to de-personalize the individual client or blur his identity by mechanically bracketing him. If you like, we have here the social-philanthropic repercussions of the

metaphysical idea of the dignity, worth, and uniqueness of each individual.

(4) Also imperative is prompt, courteous attention, with little or no "red tape," bureaucratic inefficiency or personal procrastination. Delay in responding to a request may blemish the entire act or even tragically obviate its need. You know the "confession" of the sorely afflicted Nachum ish Gamzu, who was "blind in both his eyes, his two hands and legs were amputated, and his whole body was covered with boils." He had wished this state upon himself after, in his own words, "a poor man stopped me on the road and said, 'Master, give me something to eat.' I replied: Wait until I have unloaded something from the ass. I had hardly managed to unload something when the man died." [44]

(5) The benevolent act should be gracious from beginning to end and should not display half-heartedness or impatience. It is in this light that we understand one of the commandments subsumed under the precept "Love thy neighbor as thyself," namely the obligation to "escort the strangers and departing guests." "Hospitality to wayfarers is greater than receiving the Divine Presence . . . but escorting guests is even greater than according them hospitality . . . Whoever does not accompany guests is as though he would shed blood." [45] It would appear that hospitality without escorting is like throwing a bone to a dog—a begrudging concession of kindness, an intrinsically benevolent act which is vitiated by its rudeness.

(6) Most striking because it is most intangible and "supra-legal" is the stipulation that actual giving be accompanied by sympathy, sharing the recipient's troubles, talking with him, relieving him psychologically. It calls for a genuine sense of commiseration. "He who gives a small coin to a poor man obtains six blessings, and he who addresses to him words of comfort obtains eleven blessings." [46] Maimonides sharpens this sentiment even more: "Though one were to give a thousand pieces of gold, one forfeits, yea, one destroys the merit of one's giving if one gives grudgingly and with countenance cast down." On the contrary, "one should give cheerfully and eagerly. One should grieve with the poor person over his misfortune (Job 30:25) and should address to him words of solace and of comfort" (Job 29:13). [47]

The receiver must feel that there is a living human voice behind the grant, not a hollow, impersonal one. The donor should never lose sight of the fact that *tzedakah* is as much a "duty of the heart" as it is a "duty of the limb."

Without these subjective elements, the objective act is deficient and sometimes even worthless.

Even though we have expanded its scope and insisted upon the place of subjectivity in it, we have been examining *tzedakah* almost exclusively. However, we should not fail to note that there is within the scope of *chesed* an entire area of acts of kindness where the personal subjective attitude is not only relevant but is of exclusive significance. This may be designated as "mental hygiene" (as distinct from physical aid and rehabilitation). Of the several categories of kindness referred to in the Talmud, two belong to this area: visiting the sick, comforting the bereaved. These acts could also conceivably be regulated—e.g., stipulating by communal ordinance that the sick should be visited right after the Sabbath morning service [48]—but clearly the physical act of entering the sick room, unlike the physical act of signing a check, is worthless. For these are "the deeds of loving-kindness performed in person and for which no fixed measure is prescribed." (*Hilkhot Avel* 14:1). The subjective moment is paramount.

Old-age care and consideration is another area in the realm of kindness and social welfare where the attitude outweighs or at least conditions the act.

This is true with regard to parents as well as aged people generally. We are obliged "to rise up before the gray-haired and honor the face of the old man." (Leviticus 20:32) There is nothing material in this. Financial assistance to poor old people is to be viewed from the general vantage point of charity. The specific obligation is the reverential attitude: to stand, to make respectful gestures. With regard to one's parents, the material assistance, when required, is probably also to be viewed from the vantage point of charity.[49] Indeed, the Halakhah states that honoring one's parents means providing them with food and drink, clothing and covering, but the expense is to be borne by the parents. What counts, on the part of the son, is the zeal and quality of service.

In other words, the fulfillment of "honoring thy father and mother" and "ye shall fear, every man, his mother and father" is not contingent upon finance. Indeed, since it was emphatically maintained that the honoring of parents was on a level with the honoring of God,[50] this could not be, in essence, a materially-conditioned act. In socially ideal situations, where the parents have independent resources, the duty of honor and reverence is unimpaired and their scope unrestricted. The religious-social obligations toward an old person are the same regardless whether he is independently wealthy, sustained by social security and old-age assistance, or indigent.

In this sense, welfare activities which tend to mitigate financial difficulties, cannot be looked upon as corrosive of traditional values and obligations because they do not impinge upon the core of philanthropic actions: the motif of personal service and attitude. Welfare activities are no more "dangerous" in theory than the activities of high-powered, mechanized philanthropy: both challenge the subjective element, tend to neutralize or obliterate it. The response to this challenge will have to reaffirm that if Halakhah, generally, was intended to be an ongoing education in holiness and spiritual dedication, *tzedakah* in particular was intended to be an education in kindness and all-consuming *humanitas*.

NOTES

1 T. S. Eliot, *Notes Toward the Definition of Culture* (New York, 1949), p. 89.

2 These two terms are used interchangeably by Philo; see Wolfson, *Philo* (Cambridge: Harvard University Press, 1947), II, 219.

3 The following references are representative of the treatment of our theme in modern scholarly literature; they are not intended to provide a complete bibliography. I. Abrahams, *Jewish Life in the Middle Ages* (New York: Meridian Press, 1958), chs. 17–18; S. Baron, *The Jewish Community* (Philadelphia: Jewish Publication Society, 1942), vol. II, ch. XVI; J. Bergman, *Ha-Zedakah be-Yisrael* (Jerusalem, 1944; Hebrew); Israel Chipkin, "Judaism and Social Welfare," *The Jews*, ed. L. Finkelstein, (3rd ed., Jewish Publication Society, 1960), vol. II, pp. 1043–1075; A. Cronbach, *Religion and its Social Setting* (Cincinnati, 1933), pp. 99–157; Ephraim Frisch, *An Historical Survey of Jewish Philanthropy* (New York, 1924); K. Kohler, "The Historical

Development of Jewish Charity," *Hebrew Union College and other Addresses* (Cincinnati, 1916), pp. 229–253; S. Schechter, "Notes of Lectures on Jewish Philanthropy," *Studies in Judaism*, 3rd series (Philadelphia: Jewish Publication Society, 1934), pp. 238–277.

4 The following sources are most relevant: Mishnah, *Pe'ah*, 8:3–8 and Tosefta, *Pe'ah*, 4:9–11; Tosefta, *Megillah*, 3:4; *Bava Batra*, 8a–11a; *Ketuvot*, 67b–68a; *Kiddushin*, 30b–33a; *Bava Kamma* 36b (and especially *Sefer ha-Ma'or and Milchamot, ad. loc.*); *Shir ha-Shirim Zuta*, ed. S. Buber (Vilna, 1925), pp. 17 ff. Among the post-Talmudic codes: *Sefer ha-Eshkol*, ed. Albeck, I, pp. 164 ff; *Mishneh Torah, Hilkhot Matenot Aniyim*, chs. 7–10; *Hilkhot Mamrim*, ch. 6; *Hilkhot Melakim*, ch. 10; *Or Zaru'a*, I, *Hilkhot Tzedakah*, pp. 13–18; *Yoreh De'ah*, 247 ff. For more popular discussions or compendia of sayings, see *Sefer Hasidim* (Frankfurt, 1924), n. 857 ff. (pp. 215 ff.); n. 1713 ff. (pp. 404 ff.); *Ma'alat ha-Midot* of R. Yehiel b. Yekutiel ha-Rofe, chs. 5 and 6; *Menorat ha-Ma'or* of R. Isaac Abuhab, *Ner* III, *Kelal* VIII; *Menorat ha-Ma'or* of R. Israel ibn al-Nakawa, ed. G. Enelow (New York, 1929), I, pp. 23–90; *Netibot Olam* (Maharal of Prague), *Netib Gemilut Chesed*; R. Isaac Lampronti, *Pahad Yitzhak*, s.v. *tzedakah*. Of special interest is the *Me'il Tzedakah*, by R. Elijah ha-Kohen of Izmir.

Many of the talmudic sources have been discussed by Prof. E. E. Urbach in a very valuable article in *Zion*, XVI (1951), pp. 1–27. Mention should also be made of Prof. A. Cronbach's series of articles which appeared in the *HUCA* since 1925.

5 The latest is Harry Lurie, *A Heritage Affirmed* (Philadelphia: Jewish Publication Society, 1961).

6 Nachmanides observed: והצדקה גם כן חמורה מאד ובאו בה אזהרות רבות
והתעוררות גדול בתורה בנביאים בכתובים ובדברי רבותינו... ובדברי רבותינו אין אני
צריך להזכיר המקומות שדברו בענין הצדקה כי כל התלמוד וכל ספרי ההגדות מלאים מזה
See *Derashat ha-Ramban le-Kohelet*, ed. Z. Schwarz (Frankfurt, . . . 1913), pp. 26, 28.

7 *Bava Batra* 10a.

8 See *Midrash Rabbah, Va-Yikra*, 34:8 (ed. M. Margaliyot, p. 791); *Tanhuma, Mishpatim*, 9; *Shir ha-Shirim Zuta*, p. 18.

9 See the other dialogue between R. Akiba and Rufus. *Tanchuma Tazri'a*, 9 (ed. Buber, p. 18a).

10 *Bereshit Rabbah*, 8:5.

11 *Sotah* 14a; *Shabbat* 133b.

12 See Maimonides, *Guide for the Perplexed*, III, 53 and *Mishneh Torah, Hilkhot Megillah*, 2:17. Also Nachmanides, *op. cit.*, p. 26.

13 *Sotah* 14a.

14 The phrase is that of S. R. Hirsch, *Horeb*, vol. II.

15 *Bava Batra* 10a (in the name of R. Johanan); *Shir ha-Shirim Zuta*, p. 15.

16 This homiletical motif can even be substantiated by halakhic norms. According to many Talmudic authorities, obligating oneself for charitable

contributions conforms to the same procedure as consecrating objects to God. See Maimonides, *Hilkhot Mekhirah*, 22:15–16; Nachmanides, Commentary on Numbers, 30:3 (second explanation); and *Sefer ha-Ma'or* and *Milchamot* to *Bava Kamma* 36a. When speaking of "things which are for the sake of God," Maimonides mentions, all in the same breath, consecrating objects, constructing synagogues, and feeding the hungry; *Issurei Mizbeach*, 7:11.

17 See also *Avot*, 3:18.

18 This is the thrust of the end of the passage, emphasizing help to the poor when "they are cast out." It is also the theme of פרנסני ככלב וכעורב (*Bava Batra* 8). See also the view of R. Akiba in the Mishnah, *Bava Kamma* 8:6 ("Even the poorest in Israel are looked upon as freemen who have lost their possessions"); the concluding paragraph of Maimonides, *Hilkhot Avadim*, 9:8 (. . . וכן במדותיו של הקב״ה שצונו להדמות בהם הוא אומר ורחמיו על כל מעשיו) It is noteworthy that the Bible invariably uses the word "brother" when speaking of *tzedakah*.

Incidentally, Rufus' rejoinder probably mirrors the Christian polemic that exile is punishment, symbolizing the complete rejection of Israel. Note *Chagigah* 5b: ההוא אפיקורסא .. עמא דאהדרינהו מריה לאפיה מיניה.

19 Aristotle, *Politics*, 1254; Plato, *Politics*, 289b, d. See, e.g. Glenn Morrow, *Plato's Law of Slavery in its Relation to Greek Law* (Urbana, 1939).

20 Judaism, for the most part, realistically negated asceticism, monasticism or any other contemptuous rejection of worldly matters. (See E. Urbach, "Ascesis and Suffering in Talmudic and Midrashic Sources" *Baer Jubilee Volume* [Jerusalem, 1960], 48–68). There is in Judaism no exaltation or idealization of poverty, such as we find in many Christian systems of thought (see Troeltsch, *Social Teachings of the Christian Churches*, vol. I). Poverty is not adored as a blessed state; it is an ugly, demeaning situation. One is duty-bound—as far as is humanly possible—to avoid falling into such a state; he who brings it upon himself by dissipating his resources is a fool (Maimonides, *Arakhin wa-Charamin*, VIII:13). Diminution of wealth is not per se an act of piety or self-transcending religiosity (see *Kuzari*, II, 50). "Holy voluntary poverty" (a basic concept of canon law) was neither an attraction or a goal for the Halakhah. It should be stressed, of course, that this emphatic point has its counterpoint: there is in Judaism no glorification of wealth as an end in itself. As a matter of fact, the unbridled pursuit of money is most objectionable. Wealth is a trust over which man is the executor; it should be used imaginatively and wisely to uproot poverty. (*See Guide for the Perplexed*, III, 35, and 39; *Yoreh De'ah*, 247:3. The "stewardship theory" of wealth as well as the cyclical view of human resources are commonplaces.)

21 *Shabbat* 151b.

22 See *Sukkah* 29a.

23 *Chullin* 7b: אין אדם נוקף אצבע למטה אלא אם כן מכריזין עליו למעלה.

24 *Chovot Ha-levavot, Sha'ar ha-Bitachon* (Warsaw, 1875, p. 202 f.). It is noteworthy that the Karaites promulgated an inflexibly passive, quietistic

interpretation of *bitachon*; see now M. Zucker,   על תרגום רס״ג לתורה
pp. 205–207

25 The famous symposium between R. Johanan b. Zakkai and his disciples
Bava Batra 10a—focuses on this. See also S. Lieberman, *JQR*, 36 (1945–46),
pp. 357–359; E. Urbach, *Zion*, p. 4, n. 23.

26 *Bava Batra* 10a; *Koheleth Rabbah*, 7:1.

27 See Wolfson, *Philo*, II, p. 219.

28 See especially *Kiddushin* 31a, passage starting   דרש עולא... מאי דכתיב
. . .   יודך ה׳ כל מלכי ארץ כי שמעו אמרי פיך.

29 Perhaps it is this built-in tension which explains the view of those
rishonim (see *Tosafot, Ketuvot* 49b) who maintain that although charity
is obligatory, it is not enforceable in court, but can be collected only with
the help of moral suasion and social sanction. This preserves a "subjective"
element. Even more striking is an apparent incongruity in the view of Maimonides. In common with most halakhists he assumes that charity is subject
to compulsory assessment and collection. (See *Matenot Aniyim*, 7:10 and
Ketzot ha-Choshen, Yoreh De'ah, 290). Yet, in the *Moreh Nebukhim* (III,
53) he differentiates between *tzedek* and *tzedakah*; *tzedek* is legally prescribed
and regulated while *tzedakah* stems from one's moral conscience. There is an
ethical increment, something more than and different from the formalized,
purely legal act. The same problem is reflected in Jonah ibn Ganah's dichotomous definition of *tzedakah*:   ומאלה השמות מה שעניינו דין וזכות וזכות ומהם
See also *Tosafot, Shabbat* 10b,   .(423 מה שעניינו יושר והשיר. (ספר השרשים, עמ׳
'hanoten matanah,' where *tzedakah* is referred to as a present.

30 *Bava Batra* 7b, 8a.

31 *Matenot Aniyim*, 7:14; see *Or Zaru'a*, I, p. 15.

32 See *Tosafot, Bava Batra* 8b (the views of R. Tam and Ri); *Matenot
Aniyim*, 7:2   (עני מבקש);   *Sefer Yere'im, amud* 5, n. 202 (p. 182).

33 *Matenot Aniyim*, 7:7.

34 *Yom Tov* 6:18; see also *Megillah* 2:17.

35 See *Yoreh De'ah*, 256:1 and commentaries; *Menorat ha-Ma'or, Ner*
III, *Kelal* VII; Bergmann, *Ha-Tzedakah be-Yisrael*, p. 143.

36 *Bava Batra* 7b.

37 *Matenot Aniyim*, 10:16.

38 It is important for welfare workers to remember that distribution of
funds is a more exacting task than collection—no matter how important the
latter may be substantively and sociologically (as a cohesive force). Allocation
of funds, requiring serious deliberation and penetrating evaluation, is halakhically and ethically the most responsible task; allocation committees are
in the most delicate, or vulnerable, position. See the Halakhot concerning:
. . .   קופה של צדקה נגבית בשנים ומתחלקת בשלשה...

39 *Sukkah* 49b.

40 *Pachad Yitzhak*, s.v. *tzedakah*.

41 The beautiful passage (*Abot de R. Natan*, 7) which contrasts the
benevolence of Abraham with that of Job points up, in its own homiletical

idiom and cadence, the qualitative difference between bland "giving" and inspired "doing."

Now when that great calamity came upon Job, he said unto the Holy One, blessed be He: "Master of the Universe, did I not feed the hungry and give the thirsty to drink; as it is said, *Or have I eaten my morsel myself alone and the fatherless hath not eaten thereof* (Job 31:17)? And did I not clothe the naked, as it is said, *And if he were not warmed with the fleece of my sheep*" (Job 31:20)?

Nevertheless the Holy One, blessed be He, said to Job: "Job, thou hast not yet reached half the measure of Abraham. Thou sittest and tarriest within thy house and the wayfarers come in to thee. To him who is accustomed to eat wheat bread, thou givest wheat bread to eat; to him who is accustomed to eat meat, thou givest meat to eat; to him who is accustomed to drink wine, thou givest wine to drink. But Abraham did not act in this way. Instead he would go forth and make the rounds everywhere, and when he found wayfarers he brought them in to his house. To him who was unaccustomed to eat wheat bread, he gave wheat bread to eat; to him who was unaccustomed to eat meat, he gave meat to eat; to him who was unaccustomed to drink wine, he gave wine to drink. Moreover he arose and built stately mansions on the highways and left there food and drink, and every passerby ate and drank and blessed Heaven. That is why delight of spirit was vouchsafed to him. And whatever one might ask for was to be found in Abraham's house, as it is said, *And Abraham planted a tamarisk tree in Beer-Sheba*" (Gen. 21:33). Tr. by J. Goldin, (Yale University Press, 1959), p. 47.

See also *Sotah* 10b; *Shabbat* 104a.

42 This was noticed by perceptive observers. For example, Beatrice Webb concludes her description of the Jewish Board of Guardians in England as follows: "While all groundwork for the charges of pauperization is absent, we have conclusive evidence that either from the character of those who take, or from the method of those who give, Jewish charity does not tend to the demoralization of individual recipients."

43 Very beautiful is the midrashic explanation, adopted by Rashi and other commentators, of the last verse in Ecclesiastes. Whereas the standard translation reads: "For God shall bring every work into the judgment concerning every hidden thing, whether it be good or whether it be evil," the midrashic translation would read: ". . . concerning every hidden thing which is *both* good and evil." And what constitutes a "thing which is both good and evil"—giving charity publicly! See also *Chagigah* 5a.

44 *Taanit* 21a.

45 Maimonides, *Hilkhot Avel*, 14:2. See also Rashi, *Sotah* 10a, explanation of אשל.

46 *Bava Batra* 9b.

47 *Matenot Aniyim*, 10:4. See *Sefer Mitzvot Gadol.* n. 289 (לא ירע לבבך; בתתך לו). *Guide for the Perplexed*, II, 39.

48　See *Or Zaru'a*, II, 51.

49　This is a moot point halakhically. We may discern three basic views:
see *Tosafot, Kiddushin*, 31a (ד'ה כבד) and 32a (ד'ה אוזרו לה')；　R. Samson (Rash of Sens), *Pe'ah* I:1; Maimonides, *Hilkhot Mamrim*, 6:3　כפי מה)
שהוא יכול).

50　*Sifra, Kedoshim*, 86d; *Kiddushin* 30b.

NORMAN LAMM

*

Separate Pews in the Synagogue

THE PROBLEM of "mixed pews" versus "separate pews"[1] in the synagogue is one which has engaged the attention of the Jewish public for a number of years. It has been the focus of much controversy and agitation. More often than not, the real issues have been obscured by the strong emotions aroused. Perhaps if the reader is uninitiated in the history and dialectic of Jewish religious debate in mid-twentieth century America, he will be puzzled and amused by such serious concern and sharp polemics on what to him may seem to be a trivial issue. If the reader is thus perplexed he is asked to consider that "trivialities" are often the symbols of issues of far greater moment. Their significance often transcends what is formally apparent, for especially in Judaism they may be clues to matters of principle that have far-reaching philosophic consequences.

In our case, the *mechitzah* (the physical partition between the men's and women's pews) has become, in effect, a symbol in the struggle between two competing ideological groups. It has become a *cause célèbre* in the debate on the validity of the Jewish tradition itself and its survival intact in the modern world. The *mechitzah* was meant to divide physically the men from the women in the synagogue. In our day it has served also to divide spiritually synagogue from synagogue, community from community, and often rabbi from layman. This division has become a wide struggle, in which one faction attempts to impose contemporary standards— whatever their quality or worth—upon the inherited corpus of Jewish tradition which it does not regard as being of divine origin, and in which the other side seeks to preserve the integrity of Jewish law and tradition from an abject capitulation to alien concepts whose only virtue is, frequently, that they are declared "modern" by their proponents. The purpose of this essay is to demonstrate the validity of the Jewish tradition in its view that separate seating for men and women ought to prevail in the synagogue.

THE LAW

The separation of the sexes at services is not a "mere custom reflecting the mores of a bygone age." It is a law, a *halakhah*, and according to many of our outstanding talmudic scholars an extremely important one. Its origin is in the Talmud,[2] where we are told that at certain festive occasions which took place at the Temple in Jerusalem great crowds gathered to witness the service. The Sages were concerned lest there occur a commingling of the sexes, for the solemnity and sanctity of the services could not be maintained in such environment. Hence, although the sexes were already originally separated, and despite the reluctance to add to the structure of the Temple, it was ruled that a special balcony be built for the women in that section called the *ezrat nashim* (Women's Court) in order to reduce the possibility of frivolousness at these special occasions. The same principle which applied to the Sanctuary in Jerusalem applies to the synagogue,[3] the *mikdash me'at* (miniature Sanctuary), and the mixing of the sexes is therefore proscribed.

Thus Jewish law clearly forbids what has become known as "mixed pews." We do not know, historically, of any synagogue before the modern era where mixed pews existed. No documents and no excavations can support the notion that this breach of Jewish Law was ever accepted by Jews. Philo and Josephus both mention separate seating in the days of the Second Commonwealth.[4] The principle was upheld as law in the last generation by such eminent authorities as Rabbi Israel Meir Hakohen (the *Chafetz Chayyim*) in Lithuania, Chief Rabbi Kook in Palestine, and Rabbi Dr. M. Hildesheimer in Germany. In our own day, it was affirmed by every one of the Orthodox rabbinical and lay groups without exception, and by such contemporary scholars as Chief Rabbi Herzog of Israel, Chief Rabbi Brodie of the British Empire, and Dr. Samuel Belkin and Rabbi Joseph B. Soloveitchik of Yeshiva University.

Of course, one may argue that "this is only the Orthodox interpretation." We shall not now argue the point that "Orthodoxy" is the name one must give to the three thousand years of normative Judaism no matter what our contemporary preference in sectarian nomenclature. But aside from this, and aside from the fact that there is abundant supporting source material, both halakhic and historic,[5] antedating the fragmentation of the Jewish community into the Orthodox-Conservative-Reform pattern, it is interesting to note the position of the Conservative group. This is the group whose leaders still feel it necessary to defend their deviations from traditional norms, and whose attitude to Jewish Law has usually been ambivalent. It is a fact, of course, that the overwhelming majority of Conservative Temples have mixed pews. But, significantly, some of their leading spokesmen have not embraced this reform wholeheartedly. Rabbi Bernard Segal, Executive Director of the United Synagogue (the organization of Conservative Temples), recently had this to say:

We have introduced family pews, organ music, English readings. Our cantors have turned around to face their congregations. In some synagogues we have introduced the triennial cycle for the reading of the Torah. *All of these were never intended to be ends in themselves or principles of the Conservative Movement. . . .* Unfortunately, in the minds of too many these *expedients* have come to represent the sum and substance of the Conservative Movement.[6]

We thus learn that Conservative leadership has begun to recognize that mixed seating in the synagogue is not entirely defensible, that it was meant to be only an "expedient" and not an in-principle reform. From another Conservative leader we learn that the Law Committee of the Rabbinical Assembly (the Conservative rabbinic group) has for years only "condoned" but not "approved" the system of family pews! The very same group that encourages its members to drive the automobile to the Temple on the Sabbath—only "condones" but does not "approve" of mixed pews! [7] And of course those who have visited the Jewish Theological Seminary in New York know that the synagogue of the Conservative Seminary itself has separate seating for men and women. We may be sure that a "mere custom" would not retain such a hold on Conservative leadership and give its members such pangs of conscience. We are dealing here with a *din*, with a *halakhah*, with a binding and crucial law, with the very sanctity of the synagogue, and religious Jews have no choice but to insist upon separate seating as an indispensable and irrevocable feature of the synagogue.[8]

The references made so far should not be taken as a full treatment of the halakhic and historical basis for separate seating. A considerable literature, both ancient and modern, could be cited as documentation of the thesis here presented. However, as the subtitle of this essay indicates, our major interest here is not in articulating the Halakhah as much as in explaining it. Our main concern is to demonstrate that the separation of the sexes at religious services makes good sense even—or perhaps especially—in America, where woman has reached her highest degree of "emancipation." What we will attempt to show is that if there were no law requiring a *mechitzah*, we should have to propose such a law —for good, cogent reasons. These reasons are in the tradition of *taamei ha-mitzvot*, the rationales ascribed to existing laws, rationales which may or may not be identical with original motives of the commandments (assuming we *can* know them), but which serve to make immutable laws relevant to every new historical period.

Because of the fact that Tradition clearly advocates separate seating, it is those who would change this millennial practice who must first prove their case. Let us therefore begin by examining some of the arguments of the innovations, and then explain some of the motives of the Halakhah (Jewish Law) in deciding against this commingling of the sexes at services.

Those who want to reform the Tradition and introduce mixed pews at religious services present two main arguments. One is that separate seating is an insult to womanhood, a relic of the days when our ancestors held woman to be inferior to man, and hence untenable in this era when we unquestioningly accept the equality of the sexes. The second is the domestic argument: the experience of husbands and wives worshipping next to each other makes for happier homes. The slogan for this argument is the well-known "families that pray together stay together." These arguments deserve detailed analysis and investigation to see whether or not they are sufficiently valid premises upon which to base the transformation of the character of our synagogues.

THE EQUALITY OF THE SEXES

Separate seating, we are told, reveals an underlying belief that women are inferior, and only when men and women are allowed to mix freely in the synagogue is the equality of the sexes acknowledged. To this rallying call to "chivalry" we must respond first with a demand for consistency. If the non-Orthodox movements are, in this matter, the champions of woman's equality, and if this equality is demonstrated by equal participation in religious activities, then why, for instance, have not the non-Orthodox schools graduated one woman Rabbi in all these years? Why not a woman cantor? (Even in Reform circles recent attempts to introduce women into such positions have resulted in a good deal of controversy.) Why are Temple Presidents almost all men, and Synagogue Boards predominantly male? Why are the women segregated in Sisterhoods? If it is to be "equality," then let us have complete equality to the bitter end!

The same demand for some semblance of consistency may well be presented, and with even greater cogency, to the very ones of our sisters who are the most passionate and articulate advocates of mixed seating as a symbol of their equality. If this equality as Jewesses is expressed by full participation in Jewish life, then such equality must not be restricted to the Temple. They must submit as well to the private obligations incumbent upon menfolk: prayer thrice daily, and *be-tzibbur*, in the synagogue; donning *tallit* and *tefillin*; acquiring their own *lulav* and *etrog*, etc. These *mitzvot* are not halakhically obligatory for women, yet they were voluntarily practiced by solitary women throughout Jewish history; to mention but two examples, Michael, daughter of King Saul, and the fabled Hasidic teacher, the Maid of Ludmir.[9] Does not consistency demand that the same equality, in whose name we are asked to confer upon women the privileges of full participation in public worship with all its attendant glory and glamor, also impose upon women the responsibilities and duties, heretofore reserved for men only, which must be exercised in private only?

We have yet to hear an anguished outcry for such equal assumption of masculine religious duties. So far those who would desecrate the synagogue in the name of "democracy" and "equality" have been concentrating exclusively upon the public areas of Jewish religious expression, upon synagogical privileges and not at all upon spiritual duties. They must expand the horizons of religious equality if it is to be full equality.

Furthermore, if we accept the premise that separate seating in the synagogue implies inequality, then we shall have to apply the same standards to our social activity—outside the *shul!* Let us abolish, then, that terribly undemocratic system whereby the men go off to engage in "masculine" recreational activities while the women segregate for their own feminine games! And let us instruct our legislations to pass laws granting women "equal privileges" in domestic litigation, thus making them responsible for alimony payments when they initiate divorce proceedings, even as their husbands must pay under present law. Of course, this *reductio ad absurdum* reveals the weakness of the original premise that separate seating is indicative of the contemptible belief in the inferiority of women.

It is simply untrue that separate seating in a synagogue, or elsewhere, has anything at all to do with equality or inequality. And Judaism—the same Judaism which always has and always will insist upon separate seating—needs no defense in its attitude towards womanhood. For in our tradition men and women are considered equal in *value*—one is as good as the other. But equality in *value* does not imply identity of *functions* in all phases of life. And our Tradition's estimation of woman's *value* transcends anything that the modern world can contribute.

The source of the value of man, the sanction of his dignity, is God. The Bible expresses this by saying that man was created in His image. But woman too is formed in the image of God. Hence she derives her value from the same source as does the male of the species. In value, therefore, she is identical with man. She is liable to the same punishment—no more, no less—that a man is when she breaks a law, and she is as deserving of reward and commendation when she acts virtuously. A famous rabbinic dictum tells us that the spirit of prophecy, the *ruach ha-kodesh*, can rest equally upon man or woman. Our people had not only Patriarchs, but also Matriarchs. We had not only Prophets, but also Prophetesses. In the eyes of God, in the eyes of Torah, in the eyes of Jews, woman was invested with the full dignity accorded to man. Equality of value there certainly was.

Furthermore, a good case can be made out to show that our tradition in many cases found greater inherent value in woman-kind than in mankind. The first man in history received his name "Adam" from the *adamah*, the earth from which he was created. His wife, Eve, has her name "Chavvah" derived from *em kol chai*, meaning "the mother of all life." Man's very name refers to his lowly origins, while woman's name is a tribute to her life-bearing functions. Moses is commanded to give the Ten Commandments first to "the house of Jacob" and then to "the house of Israel." And our Rabbis interpret "the house of Jacob" as referring to the Jewish women, while "the house of Israel" refers to the menfolk. Our Sages attribute to women greater insight—*binah yeterah*—than men. They maintain that the redemption from Egypt, the leitmotif of all Jewish history, was only *bizekhut nashim tzidkani-yot*, because of the merit of the pious women of Israel.

Of course, such illustrations can be given in the dozens. Much more can be written—and indeed, much has been published—on the Jewish attitude towards women. This is not the place to probe the matter in great detail and with full documentation. It is true, let us grant for the sake of factuality, that there are a number of statements in the Talmud and in the talmudic literature down through the Middle Ages which are not particularly flattering to the fair sex. It is almost inevitable that such derogatory remarks should find their way into a literature extending over hundreds and hundreds of years and composed by hundreds of different persons of varying backgrounds and experiences and temperaments. However, these judgments do not have the force of law nor are they the authoritative substance of the Jewish *Weltanschauung*. They are in the main atypical of the essential outlook of traditional Judaism. They are minority opinions, perhaps encouraged by prevailing social conditions at the time, and are neither normative nor authoritative.

It is useless to match statement with counter-statement, to

marshal the commendations against the condemnations. There is a far more basic criterion than isolated quotations or fine legal points by which to judge the traditional Jewish attitude to woman. And that is: the historic role of the Jewess—her exalted position in the home, her traditional standing and stature in the family, her dignity as wife and mother and individual. By this standard, any talk of her inferiority is a ridiculous canard, and the chivalry of those who today seek so militantly to "liberate" her by mixing pews in the synagogue is a ludicrous posture of misguided gallantry.

The Jewish woman, therefore, as a person and as a human being was and is regarded by authentic Judaism as anything but inferior. Judaism orients itself to women with a deep appreciation for their positions as the mothers of our generations and as daughters of God. Their position is one of complete honor and dignity, and talk of inequality is therefore absurd.

But while it is true that woman is man's equal in intrinsic value in the eyes of Torah, it is not true—nor should it be—that her functions in life are all identical with those of man. She has a different role in life and in society, and one for which she was uniquely equipped by her Creator. By nature there are many things in which women differ from men. And the fact that men and women differ in function and in role has nothing to do with the categories of inferiority or superiority. The fact that the Torah assigns different religious functions, different *mitzvot*, to men and to women no more implies inequality than the fact that men and women have different tastes in tobacco or different areas of excellence in the various arts.[10]

That modern women have suffered because they have often failed to appreciate this difference is attested to by one of the most distinguished authorities in the field, anthropologist Ashley Montagu:

The manner in which we may most helpfully regard the present relationships between the sexes is that they are in a transitional phase of development. That in the passage from the "abolition" phase of women's movement to the phase of "emancipation" a certain number of predictable errors were committed.

The logic of the situation actually led to the most grievous of the errors committed. This was the argument that insofar as political and social rights were concerned women should be judged as persons and not as members of a biological or any other kind of group. As far as it goes this argument is sound enough, but what seems to have been forgotten in the excitement, is that women, in addition to being persons, also belong to a sex, and that with the differences in sex are associated important differences in function and behavior. *Equality of rights does not imply identity of function,* yet this is what it was taken to mean by many women and men. And so women began— and in many cases continue—to compete with men as if they were themselves men, instead of realizing and establishing themselves in their own right as persons. Women have so much more to contribute to the world as women than they could ever have as spurious men.[1]

Furthermore, this selfsame confusion in the traditional roles of male and female, a confusion encouraged by this mistaken identification of sameness with equality, is largely responsible for the disintegration of many marriages. Writing in a popular magazine,[12] Robert Coughlan cites authority when he attributes the failure of so many modern marriages to the failure of men and women to accept their emotional responsibilities to each other and within the family as *men* and *women,* male and female. There appears to be a developing confusion of roles as the traditional identities of the sexes are lost. The emerging American woman tends to the role of male dominance and exploitativeness, while the male becomes more passive. Consequently, neither sex can satisfy the other—they are suffering from *sexual ambiguity.* And Prof. Montagu, approving of Coughlan's diagnosis, adds:

The feminization of the male and masculinization of the female are proving to be more than too many marriages can endure. The masculinized woman tends to reject the roles of wife and mother. In compensation, the feminized male wants to be a mother to his children, grows dissatisfied with his wife, and she in turn with him. These are the displaced persons of the American family who make psychiatry the most under-populated profession in the country.[3]

And not only are women themselves and their marriages the

sufferers as a result of this confusion of roles of the sexes, but children too are falling victim as they are increasingly uncertain of the roles they are expected to play in life. The more masculine the woman becomes, and the more feminine the male tends to be, the more are the children perplexed by what it means to be a man or a woman. It is more than a matter of a passing phase as "sissies" or "tomboys." It is a question of the whole psychological integrity of the growing child. A lot of the wreckage ends up on the psychiatrist's couch, as Prof. Montagu said. Some of the less fortunate end up in jail—only recently Judge Samuel Leibowitz attributed the upsurge in juvenile delinquency to this attenuation of the father's role in the family. So that this confusion in the traditional roles of the sexes—a confusion that has hurt modern women, endangered their marriages, and disorganized the normal psychological development of their children—is the very source of the foolish accusation hurled at the Orthodox synagogue, that its separate seating implies an acceptance of woman's inequality and hence ought to be abolished, law or no law.

FAMILIES THAT PRAY TOGETHER

The second line of reasoning presented in favor of mixed pews in the synagogue is that of family solidarity. "Families that pray together stay together," we are told day in, day out, from billboards and bulletin boards and literature mailed out both by churches and non-Orthodox synagogues. Family pews makes for family cohesion, for "togetherness," and the experience of worshipping together gives the family unit added strength which it badly needs in these troubled times.

The answer to this is not to underestimate the need for family togetherness. It is, within prescribed limits, extremely important. One of the aspects of our Tradition we can be most proud of is the Jewish home—its beauty, its peace, its strength, its "togetherness." Christians often note this fact, and with great envy. We are all for "togetherness" for the family.

Because of our very concern for the traditional togetherness of the Jewish family, we are skeptical of the efficacy of the mixed pew synagogue in this regard. If there is any place at all where the togetherness of a family must be fashioned and practiced and lived—that place is the home, not the synagogue. If a family goes to the theater together and goes to a service together and goes on vacation together, but is never *home* together—then all this togetherness is a hollow joke. That is the tragedy of our society. During the week each member of the family leads a completely separate and independent existence, the home being merely a convenient base of operations. During the day Father is at the office or on the road, Mother is shopping, and the children are at school. At night, Father is with "the boys," Mother is with "the girls," and the children dispersed all over the city—or else they are all bickering over which television program to watch. And then they expect this separateness, this lack of cohesion in the home, to be remedied by one hour of sitting together and responding to a Rabbi's readings at a Late Friday Service! The brutal fact is that the synagogue is not capable of performing such magic. One evening of family pews will not cure the basic ills of modern family life. "Mixed pews" is no solution for mixed-up homes. We are wrong, terribly wrong, if we think that the Rabbi can substitute for the laity in being observant, that the Cantor and the choir and organ can substitute for us in praying, and that the synagogue can become a substitute for our homes. And we are even in greater error if we try to substitute clever and cute Madison Avenue slogans for the cumulative wisdom expressed in Halakhah and Tradition.

If it were true that "families that pray together stay together," and that, conversely, families that pray in a *shul* with a *mechitzah* do not stay together, then one would expect the Orthodox Jewish home to be the most broken home in all of society, for Orthodox Jews have maintained separate pews throughout history. Yet it is precisely in Orthodox Jewish society that the home is the most stable, most firm, most secure. One writer has the following to say on this matter.[14] After describing the pattern of Jewish home life in the Middle Ages, with the "love and attachment of the child for his home and tradition," and the "place where the Jew was at his best," with the home wielding a powerful influence in refining Jewish character, so that "Jewish domestic morals in the Middle Ages were beyond reproach," he writes:

Particularly in those households where Orthodox Judaism is practised
and observed—both in Europe and in cosmopolitan American centers
—almost the entire rubric . . . of Jewish home life in the Middle
Ages may be observed even today.

In those homes where the liberties of the Emancipation have infil-
trated there exists a wide variety of family patterns, conditioned by
the range of defection from Orthodox tradition.

The reader should be informed that this tribute to the Orthodox Jewish home—whose members always worshipped in a synagogue with a *mechitzah*—was written by a prominent Reform
Rabbi.

So that just "doing things together," including worshipping
together, is no panacea for the very real domestic problems of
modern Jews. "Li'l Abner," the famous comic-strip character, recently refused to give his son a separate comb for his own use
because, he said in his inimitable dialect, "th' fambly whut combs
together stays together." We shall have to do more than comb
together or pray together or play baseball together. We shall have
to build homes, Jewish homes, where Torah and Tradition will
be welcome guests, where a Jewish book will be read and intellectual achievements reverenced, where parents will be respected,
where the table will be an altar and the food will be blessed,
where prayer will be heard and where Torah will be discussed in
all seriousness. Madison Avenue slogans may increase the attend-
ance at the synagogues and Temples; they will not keep families
together.

In speaking of the family, we might also add the tangential
observation that it is simply untrue that "the younger generation"
invariably wants mixed pews. The personal experience of the
writer has convinced him that there is nothing indigenous in
youth that makes it pant after mixed seating in the synagogue. It
is a matter of training, conviction, and above all of learning and
understanding. Young people often understand the necessity for
separate pews much more readily than the older folks to whom
mixed seating is sometimes a symbol of having arrived socially, of
having outgrown immigrant status. The writer happily chanced
upon the following report of a visit to a Reform Sunday School
in Westchester, N.Y.:

When the teacher had elicited the right answer, he passed on to the
respective positions of women in Orthodox and Reform Judaism.
He had a difficult time at first because the children, unexpectedly,
expressed themselves in favor of separating men and women in the
synagogue—they thought the women talked too much and had best
be segregated—but finally they were persuaded to accept the Reform
view.[15]

There is a refreshing naïvete about this youthful acceptance of
separate seating before being "persuaded" of the Reform view.

ON THE POSITIVE SIDE

Thus far the arguments of those who would do violence to our
Tradition and institute mixed pews. What now are the reasons
why the Halakhah is so firm on separating the sexes at every
service? What, on the positive side, are the Tradition's motives
for keeping the *mechitzah* and the separate seating arrangement?

The answer to this and every similar question must be studied
in one frame of reference only. And that is the issue of prayer. We
begin with one unalterable premise: *the only function of a religious
service is prayer,* and that prayer is a religious experience and *not*
a social exercise. If a synagogue is a place to meet friends, and a
service the occasion for displaying the latest fashions, then we
must agree that "if I can sit next to my wife in the movies, I can
sit next to her in the Temple." But if a synagogue is a *makom
kadosh,* a holy place reserved for prayer, and if prayer is the worship
of God, then the issue of mixed pews or separate pews can be
resolved only by referring to this more basic question: *does the
contemplated change add to or detract from our religious experience?* Our question then is: does the family pew enhance the
religious depth of prayer? If it does, then let us accept it. If it does
not, let us stamp it once and for all as an alien intrusion into the
synagogue, one which destroys its very essence.

THE JEWISH CONCEPT OF PRAYER

To know the effect of mixed seating on the Jewish religious
quality of prayer, we must first have some idea of the Jewish

concept of prayer. Within the confines of this short essay we cannot hope to treat the mater exhaustively. But we can, I believe, present just a few insights, sufficient to illuminate the question at hand.

Prayer in Hebrew is called *tefillah*, which comes from the word which means "to judge oneself." When the Jew prays, he does not submit an itemized list of requests to God; he judges himself before God, he looks at himself, as it were, from the point of view of God. Nothing is calculated to give man a greater feeling of awe and humility. The Halakhah refers to prayer as *avodah she-ba-lev*, which means: the service or sacrifice of the heart. When we pray, we open our hearts. At the moment of prayer, we submit completely to His will, and we feel purged of any selfishness, of any pursuit of our own pleasure or satisfaction. The words of the Talmud, "Know before Whom you stand," have graced many an Ark. When we know before Whom we stand, we forget ourselves. At that moment we realize how truly insecure and lonely and abandoned we really are without Him. That is how a Jew approaches God—out of solitude and insecurity, relying completely upon Him for his very breath. This complete concentration on God, this awareness only of Him and nothing or no one else, is called *kavvanah*; and the direction of one's mind to God in utter and complete concentration upon Him, is indispensable for prayer. Without *kavvanah*, prayer becomes a senseless repetition of words.

DISTRACTION

For *kavvanah* to be present in prayer, it is necessary to eliminate every source of distraction. When the mind is distracted, *kavvanah* is impossible, for then we cannot concentrate on and understand and mean the words our lips pronounce. And as long as men will be men and women will be women, there is nothing more distracting in prayer than mixed company.

Orthodox Jews have a high regard for the pulchritude of Jewish women. As a rule, we believe, a Jewess is beautiful. Her comeliness is so attractive, that it is distractive; *kavvanah* in her presence is extremely difficult. It is too much to expect of a man, sitting in feminine company, to concentrate fully upon the sacred words of

the Siddur and submit completely to God. We are speaking of the
deepest recesses of the human heart; it is there that prayer originates. And how can one expect a man's heart to be with God when
his eyes are attracted elsewhere? We are speaking of human beings,
not angels, and the Halakhah recognizes both the strength and
weakness of a man. It is simply too much to ask of a man that
he sit in the company of women, that he behold their loveliness—
and at the same time undergo a great religious experience. What
man can feel the nearness of God when if he but raises his eye
from the corner of the Siddur he finds himself attracted to more
earthly pursuits which do not exactly encourage his utter devotion
to the pursuit of Godliness? (And what woman can concentrate
on the ultimate issues of life and feel the presence of God, when
she is far more interested in exhibiting a new dress or new chapeau?
How can she try to attract the attention of God when she may be
trying much harder to attract the attention of some man?) When
the sexes are separated, the chances for such distraction are greatly
reduced.[16]

FRIVOLITY

It is not only that what one *sees* prevents one from experiencing
kavvanah, but that mixed company in general, in the relaxed and
non-business-like atmosphere of the synagogue, is conducive to a
kind of frivolity—not disrespectful, but levity nonetheless. Now,
if a synagogue is to retain its character as a holy place, it must
possess *kedushah*, or holiness. Holiness in Judaism has a variety
of meanings, but mostly it means transcendence, the willingness
to grow above one's limits, the ability to reach upwards. Holiness
is defined by many of our Sages as *perishah me-arayot*—separation
from immorality or immoral thoughts. That is why on Yom
Kippur, the holiest day of the year, the portion of the Torah read
in the afternoon deals with the *arayot*, the prohibitions of various
sexual relations, such as incest, adultery, etc. Only by transcending
one's biological self does one reach his or her spiritual stature. By
separating oneself from sensual thoughts and wants, one achieves
the state of holiness. It may be true, as modern Jews like to hear
so often, that Judaism sees nothing inherently wrong or sinful

about sex.[17] But that does not mean that it is to be regarded as a harmless exercise not subject to any control or discipline.[18] And its control, even refraining from any thoughts about it, is indispensable for an atmosphere of *kedushah* or holiness. So that the very fact of mixed company, despite our very best intentions, gives rise to the kind of milieu which makes holiness impossible. "Know before Whom you stand," we were commanded, and not "know next to whom you are sitting." "It requires a great effort *to realize before Whom we stand,* for such realization is more than having a thought in one's mind. It is a knowledge in which the whole person is involved; the mind, the heart, body, and soul. To know it is to forget everything else, including the self." [19] That is why halakhic authorities have ruled that a synagogue with mixed pews loses its status as a holy place in the judgment of Halakhah.

BASHFULNESS

In addition to distraction and frivolousness, there is yet another aspect of mixed seating which makes it undesirable for an authentically Jewish synagogue. That is the matter of bashfulness.

Few of us are really "ourselves" at all times. We "change personalities" for different occasions. The man who at home does nothing but grumble and complain is full of charm when talking to a customer. The harried housewife who shouts at her children all day speaks in a dignified whisper when the doctor comes to visit. Especially when we are in mixed company we like to "put up a front," we take special care to talk in a certain way, smile a certain way, we become more careful of posture, of looks, of expression, of our sense of humor. These things are not necessarily done consciously—they just happen as part of our natural psychological reaction.

Now prayer, real Jewish prayer, the kind we should strive for at all times though we achieve it rarely, demands full concentration on our part. It must monopolize our attention. We must be unconcerned with our outer appearance at that time. And full and undiminished concentration on the holy words of the Siddur can sometimes result in unusual physical expression. Sometimes it can move us to tears. Sometimes the spiritual climate of a particular passage makes us want to smile with happiness. At other times we feel inclined to concentrate strongly and shut out all interference from the outer world, so that our foreheads become wrinkled and our eyes shut and our fists clenched—the physical symptoms of intense thought. Sometimes we feel like reciting a verse aloud, of giving full vocal expression to our innermost feelings. "All my bones shall say, O my Lord who is like Thee?" [20]

Can this ever be done in a mixed group? When we are so concerned with our appearances, can we ever abandon ourselves so freely to prayer? When we tend to be self-conscious, can we become fully God-conscious? Are we not much too bashful, in mixed company, to give such expression to our prayer? In congregations maintaining separate seating, it is usual to *hear* the worshippers worshipping, each addressing God at his own rate and in his own intonation and with his whole individual being (except, of course, for the silent *Amidah*). Do we ordinarily hear such *davenning* at the Temples? Is the mechanical reading-in-unison and the slightly bored responsive reading and the deadly-silent silent-meditations —is this *davenning*, the rapturous flight of the worshipper's soul to God? Have not the mixed pews and the attendant bashfulness thoroughly frustrated the expression of prayer?

An English poet, James Montgomery, once wrote that prayer is

> The motion of a hidden fire
> That trembles in the breast.
> Prayer is the burden of a sigh,
> The falling of a tear,
> The upward glancing of an eye
> When none but God is near.

Note that the inner experience of prayer results in an outward physical expression as well. And in the mixed company of a family-pew-Temple, who is not going to be bashful? Who will tremble just a bit, and give vent to a sigh, and shed a tear, and glance upward with a pleading eye? Who is brave enough and unbashful enough to risk looking ludicrous by becoming absorbed in prayer and letting the innermost thoughts and feelings show outwardly, without any inhibition? Bashfulness presents enough of a problem as is, without the added complication of mixed seating which takes *kavvanah* out of the level of the difficult and into the realm of the highly improbable.

THE SENSE OF INSECURITY

To understand the next point in favor of *mechitzah*, we must mention yet one other argument in favor of family pews that merits our serious attention—the desire of a wife to sit next to her husband because of the feeling of strength and protection and security that his presence gives her. (The old and oft-repeated desire for mixed pews because "he has to show me the page in the Siddur" is no longer relevant. In most synagogues there are regular announcements of the page from the pulpit if necessary to serve this purpose.) That such feeling exists we cannot doubt—and it is a genuine one too.

What is the verdict of our Tradition on this issue? First, it should be clear that when we pray, we must do so for *all* Israel and for all humanity, not just each for his own little family. Only occasionally is there a special prayer for the members of one's family or one's self; usually our prayers are phrased in the plural, indicating our concern for all the community. Praying in public *only* for the family is a relic from ancient days when the family worshipped as a tribal unit. And Judaism has from the beginning rejected the pagan institution of the household idol and all its trappings.

Second, as Rabbi J. B. Soloveitchik has pointed out,[21] this reliance upon a husband or a wife is precisely the opposite of the Jewish concept of prayer. As was mentioned before, the approach of the Jew to God must be out of a sense of isolation, of insecurity, of defenselessness. There must be a recognition that without God none of us has any security at all, that my husband's life is dependent on God's will, his strength on God's favor, his health on God's goodness. Standing before God there is no other source of safety. It is only when we do not have that feeling of reliance on others that we can achieve faith in God. When we leave His presence—then we may feel a sense of security and safety in life.

Third, and finally, when Orthodoxy tells the modern woman not to worship at the side of her husband in whom she so trusts, it reveals an appreciation of her spiritual competence much greater that that of the Reformers and half-Reformers who offer mixed pews for this very reason. Torah tells her that she need not rely upon a strong, superior male. It tells her that she is his spiritual equal and is as worthy of approaching God by herself as he is. It reminds her that women are the daughters of God no less than men are His sons, and that our Father is no less disposed to the company of His daughters than of His sons. It tells her to address God by herself; that she both cannot and need not rely on anyone else.

MIMICRY

The final reason we offer in favor of the age-old system of separate seating at all religious services is that of religious mimicry, of copying from other faiths. The principle of Jewish separateness is fundamental to our people and our religion. We are different and we are unique. There is no other people about whom no one can agree whether they are nation, race, or religion, because they are all three, and more. There is no other people that has lived in exile for two thousand years and then returned to its homeland. We are different in the way we pray, in the food we eat, in the holidays we observe, in the strange hopes we have always entertained for the future. It is this separateness, this anti-assimiliation principle, which has kept us alive and distinct throughout the ages in all lands and societies and civilizations.

The source of this principle in the Bible is the verse "Neither shall ye walk in their ordinances," [22] and similar verses, such as "And ye shall not walk in the customs of the nations." [23] Our Tradition understood this prohibition against imitating others to refer especially to the borrowing from gentile cults and forms of worship. Our ritual was to be completely Jewish and in no way were we to assimilate any gentile religious practices. This is more than a mere verse. According to Maimonides, this principle is so fundamental that it is responsible for a major part of the Torah's legislation. Many a *mitzvah* was given, he says, to prevent our mimicking pagan rituals. Most of Part III of the *Guide for the Perplexed* is an elaboration of this principle.

We can now see why from this point of view the whole idea of mixed seating in the synagogue is thoroughly objectionable. It is an unambiguous case of religious mimicry. The alien model in this case is Christianity; worse yet, the specifically *pagan* root of Christianity.

In its very earliest history, while still under the influence of classical Judaism, Christianity maintained a traditional Jewish attitude towards women's participation in religious services, and already found a strong pagan undercurrent making itself felt in opposition. It was Paul who found it necessary to admonish the Corinthian Christians to prevent their women from preaching in the church.[24] The position of the early church was against allowing its women to take part audibly in public worship, and included a prohibition on praying in mixed company. [25] The Pauline position was clearly "a rule taken over from the synagogue and maintained in the primitive church." [26] The Corinthian Church proved, however, to be a channel for the introduction of pagan elements into Christianity, foreign elements which later were to become organic parts of that religion. Corinth itself was a city of pleasure, noted for its immorality which usually had religious sanction. It was full of prostitutes, thousands of courtesans attached to the temple of Aphrodite. This pagan environment, with its moral laxity, had a profound effect upon the Corinthian Church.[27] The effort to introduce mixed seating and women's preaching is thus part of the pagan heritage of Christianity, just as Paul's initial efforts to resist these reforms were part of Christianity's Jewish heritage. The pagan influence ultimately dominated, and today mixed seating is a typically Christian institution.

When Jews agitate for mixed pews they are guilty, therefore, of religious mimicry. In this case, as stated, it is a borrowing from paganism [28] transmitted to the modern world by way of Christianity. In the more immediate sense, it is a borrowing from Christianity itself—for who of us stop to consider the historical antecedents of a particular ritual or institution which attracts us?

Mixed seating thus represents a desire by Jews to Christianize their synagogues by imitating the practices of contemporary Christian churches. And this kind of mimicry is, as we pointed out, a violation not only of a specific law of the Torah, but an offense against the whole spirit of Torah.

Lest the reader still remain skeptical of our thesis that mixed seating represents a pagan-Christianization of the synagogue, he ought to consider the origin of mixed pews in the synagogue itself. Reform in Europe did not know of mixed seating. It was first introduced in America by Isaac Mayer Wise, in about 1850, when he borrowed a Baptist Church for his Reform services in Albany, N.Y., and found the mixed pews of the church so to his liking that he decided to retain this feature for his temple! [29]

Those who have favored family pews have unwittingly advanced the cause of the paganization and Christianization of our synagogues. Understanding that it is wrong to assimilate *Jews*, we are now witnessing the attempt to assimilate *Judaism*. When a congregation finds itself wondering whether to submit to the pressure for mixed pews, it must consider this among other things: Are we to remain a Jewish synagogue—or a semi-pagan house of worship? Are we to incorporate the *ezrat nashim* of the Holy Temple—or the family pew of the Baptist Church? Are we to carry on in the spirit of Jerusalem—or of Corinth? Are we to follow the teachings of Hillel and R. Akiba and Maimonides—or of Isaac Mayer Wise and his ministerial colleagues?

CONCLUSION

In conclusion, we do not mean to imply that the rationale elaborated in this essay should be the primary motive for the observance by moderns of *kedushat beit ha-kenesset*, the sanctity of the synagogue, which requires the separate seating of men and women in its confines. The Halakhah is essentially independent of the reasons the Jews of every succeeding age discover in and ascribe to it, and its sacred origin is enough to commend its acceptance by faithful Jews. What we did want to accomplish—and if we have failed it is the fault of the author, not of Orthodox Judaism—is to

show that even without the specific and clear judgment of the
Halakhah, separate seating ought to be the only arrangement
acceptable to serious-minded modern Jews; for it is consistent not
only with the whole tradition of Jewish morality and the philosophy of Jewish prayer, but also with the enlightened self-interest
of modern Jewish men *and* women—and children—from a social
and psychological point of view.

NOTES

1 The terms "mixed pews," "separate seating," and *mechitzah* are used
interchangeably in this essay. While there are important halakhic differences
between some of these terms, the fundamental principles upon which they
are based, and with which this essay is concerned, remain the same.

2 *Sukkah,* 51b.

3 *Megillah,* 29a; *Tur* and *Sh. Arukh, Or. Ch.,* 151; *Sefer Yereim,* 324.

4 *Philo De Vita Contemplativa* 32–34; Josephus, *Wars of the Jews,* v. 5.2.

5 The following is only a random sample from the halakhic literature
confirming the absolute necessity for separate pews: *Chatam Sofer, Ch. M.,*
190, and *Or. Ch.,* 28; *Maharam Shick, Or. Ch.,* 77; *Teshuvot Bet Hillel,* 50;
Divrey Chayyim, Or. Ch., 18. For a more elaborate treatment of the text of
the Talmud in *Sukkah,* 51b, and for other halakhic references, see Rabbi
Samuel Gerstenfeld, "The Segregation of the Sexes," *Eidenu,* Memorial
Publication in Honor of Rabbi Dr. Bernard Revel (New York: 1942), 67–74.
Additional historical references may be found in: J. T. *Sukkah,* 5:1; Tos.
Sukkah, 4:6; *Terumat Ha-deshen,* 353; *Mordekhai* quoted in *Turey Zahav,
Or. Ch.,* 351:1; cf. Cecil Roth's introduction to George Loukomski, *Jewish
Art in European Synagogues,* p. 21.

6 *United Synagogue Review* (Winter, 1958), p. 10. Italics are mine.

7 Jacob B. Agus, *Guideposts in Modern Judaism,* p. 133 f., and in *Conservative Judaism,* Vol. XI, No. 1 (1956), 11.

8 It is true that there are Orthodox rabbis who minister to family pew congregations. Yet there is a vast difference between the Conservative who at best
"condones" a mixed pews situation, without regrets, and the Orthodox rabbi
who accepts such a pulpit with the unambiguous knowledge that mixed pews
are a denial of the Halakhah and hence an offense against his own highest
principles. An Orthodox rabbi accepts such a post—*if* he should decide to do
so—*only* with the prior approval of *his* rabbi or school, *only* on a temporary
basis, and *only* with the intention of eliminating its objectionable features by
any or all of the time-tested techniques of Jewish spiritual leadership. The
difference, then, is not only philosophical but also psychological. This spiritual
discomfort of the authentic Orthodox rabbi in the non-conforming pulpit
constantly serves to remind him of his sacred duty to effect a change for the

better in the community he serves. Any reconciliation with the permanence of the anti-halakhic character of a synagogue does undeniable violence to the most sacred principles of Judaism and is hence indefensible.

9 Also cf. *Maharil, Laws of Tzitzit; Mordekhai, Laws of Tzitzit* and on *Pes.,* 108; Tosafot *R.H.,* 33a (s.v. *Ha*) and *Eruvin,* 96a (s.v. *Mikhal*).

10 The blessing recited as part of the morning service, ". . . Who hast not made me a woman," is to be understood in the light of what we have written. This is not a value-judgment, not an assertion of woman's inferiority, any more than the accompanying blessing ". . . Who hast not made me a heathen" imputes racial inferiority to the non-Jew. Both blessings refer to the comparative *roles* of Jew and non-Jew, male and female, in the religious universe of Torah, in which a greater number of religious duties are declared obligatory upon males than females and Jews than gentiles. The worshipper thanks God for the opportunity to perform a larger number of command-ments. The woman, who in general is excused by the Halakhah from positive commandments the observance of which is restricted to specific times, there-fore recites a blessing referring to *value* instead of *function* or *role:* ". . . Who has made me according to His will." The latter blessing is, if anything, more profoundly spiritual—gratitude to God for having created me a woman who, despite a more passive role, is, as a daughter of God, created in His image no less than man.

11 "The Triumph and Tragedy of the American Woman," *Saturday Review* September 27, 1958, p. 14, and cf. Margaret Mead, *N. Y. Times Magazine* February 10, 1957.

12 *Life,* December 31, 1956.

13 Ashley Montagu, "The American woman," *Chicago Jewish Forum,* Vol. XVII, No. 1 (1958), p. 8.

14 Stanley R. Brav, *Marriage and the Jewish Tradition,* p. 98.

15 Theodore Frankel, "Suburban Jewish Sunday School," *Commentary* (June, 1958) p. 486.

16 This argument has often been objected to on the grounds that it takes an unrealistic and exaggerated view of man's erotic responsiveness and that certainly devout Jews who come to pray should not be suspected of romantic daydreaming. That such objections can be raised seriously in our present post-Freudian culture and society is unthinkable. Evidently, our Sages, who lived in a society of much greater moral restraint, had a keener and more realistic insight into psychology than many of us moderns in our sophisticated society where the most grievous moral offense is no longer regarded as par-ticularly shocking.

The late Dr. Kinsey's works prove that the intuitive insights of the Jewish sages are confirmed by modern statistics and sexological theory. In his first book (Kinsey, Pomeroy, and Martin, *Sexual Behavior in the Human Male* [Phila. & London: W. B. Saunders Co., 1948] p. 363), Kinsey and his associates inform us of an inverse relationship between full sexual expression and erotic responsiveness to visual stimulation. Upper-level males have much lower frequency of full sexual outlet than lower-level males; they are therefore far more responsive to external sexual stimuli, such as the very presence of women, than the lower level males. In addition, "the higher degree of eroticism in the upper level male may also be consequent on his greater capacity to visualize situations which are not immediately at hand."

Thus, greater erotic responsiveness is experienced by higher class men, both because of their greater restraint from full sexual outlet and because of their greater capacity for imagining erotic situations. It is well-known that, with the economic growth of the Jewish community, the great majority of American Jews fall into this category of "upper-level males." Certainly the more advanced education of so many American Jews needs no documentation here. Add to this the fact that, according to Kinsey's statistics, the more pious have a lower rate of sexual activity than the less pious, (*ibid.*, 469–472) and it is fairly evident that if erotic thoughts are to be prevented during worship, as indeed they must be, then the synagogue-going Jew needs the safeguard of separate seating certainly no less than anyone else.

This Jewish insight into the human mind, upon which is based the institution of separate pews, is thus neither exaggerated nor insulting; it is merely realistic. We might add that women find it more difficult to accept this thesis than men. This is a quite understandable phenomenon. Women have greater purity of mind than do men. According to Prof. Kinsey, they are half as responsive to visual stimulation as are men. (Kinsey, Pomeroy, Martin, & Gebhard, *Sexual Behavior in the Human Female* [Phila. & London, W. B. Saunders Co., 1953], p. 651). No wonder that Orthodox Rabbis often find it harder to convince women than men of the propriety of separate pews!

17 See my *A Hedge of Roses: Jewish Insights into Marriage and Married Life* (New York: Ph. Feldheim, 1966).

18 We are indebted to Dr. Kinsey for recording the intriguing paradox of, on the one hand, the openness and frankness of Jews in talking about sex and, on the other hand, their relatively greater restraint in its full biological (and especially illict) expression (*Sexual Behavior in the Human Male*, p. 486). *Perishah me-arayot* is a matter of principled self- discipline, not prudishness. And this and other such Jewish attitudes color the lives even of those non-observant Jews who have had very little contact with Judaism. "The influence of several thousand years of Jewish sexual philosophy is not to be ignored in the search for any final explanation of these data."

19 Abraham J. Heschel, *God in Search of Man* (New York: Farrar, Straus & Cudahy, 1955), 407.

20 Psalms 35:10.

21 *The Day-Morning Journal*, November 22, 1954, p. 5.

22 Lev. 18:3.

23 *Ibid.*, 20:23.

24 I Corinthians 14:34, 35.

25 Charles C. Ryrie, *The Place of Women in the Church* (New York: Macmillan Co., 1958) pp. 78–80.

26 F. Godet, *First Epistle to the Corinthians* (Edinburgh: T. & T. Clark, 1887) II, pp. 324, 325.

27 *Ibid.*, pp. 7, 60, 62, 140.

28 This point was conceded by the late Prof. Louis Ginzberg, the Talmud expert of the Conservative movement, in a letter quoted in *Conservative Judaism*, Vol. XI (Fall, 1956), p. 39.

29 Samuel S. Cohen, "Reform Judaism," in *Jewish Life in America* (ed. Freedman and Gordis) p. 86.

ZVI ZINGER

*

Public Services on the Sabbath

IN THE gray area of religion-and-state relationships in Israel that have received close attention lately, one aspect that needs further illumination is public and official observance of the Sabbath. On the face of it, anomalous and contradictory practices seem to pervade. For example, offices of the electrical company are closed, but the power stations operate as usual; post offices are shut down, but telephone exchanges are in operation; the Ministry of Foreign Affairs is closed, but the coded messages come in ceaselessly; police, water pumping stations, and so on are all caught up in routine work.

On the other hand, the Sabbath remains the official day of rest and every Jew who wants to observe the Sabbath usually has no difficulty in doing so. The religious Jew is not obligated to join the police or another government service, or work in a power station. At the same time, religious Jews are part of a Jewish State that is kept going by public services and utilities which are run on the Sabbath. They make use on the Sabbath of running water and electric light, while being aware that both water and electric light are supplied by the Sabbath work of Jews. And religious Jews who reside in Israel are affected by the work of the police and the up-to-date alertness of the army and the diplomatic service. Were it not for the many non-religious Jews who are willing to work on the Sabbath the problem of State services would be far more acute. Indeed, it is the non-observant majority which is enabling the observant minority to benefit from the State services on the Sabbath. The depth of the issue would become apparent if we were to imagine what would occur should the population of Israel one day become overwhelmingly religious.

Soon after the establishment of the State of Israel the late Chief Rabbi I. H. Herzog wrote: "Even if the Jewish State had been established fifty years ago or earlier, when the majority of the

Jewish people was observant of Torah and *mitzvot*, there would have arisen those problems which confront us now as a result of the establishment of the State, although perhaps they would have not have assumed the contemporary dimensions." Actually, the late Chief Rabbi foresaw this problem some years before the establishment of the State. Rabbi Jacob Goldman, secretary to Rabbi Herzog for many years, told me that before the outbreak of the Second World War, Rabbi Herzog set up a secret committee which dealt with halakhic problems arising out of the work of the Haganah, the secret Jewish defense force operating in Palestine. Rabbi Meir Berlin (Bar-Ilan) acted as a liaison with the Haganah, and he brought the questions to the rabbinical committee which consisted of the two Chief Rabbis, Herzog and Uziel, Rabbi Pesach Frank, and, occasionally, Rabbi Issar Zalman Meltzer. Later this committee broadened its scope to include activities other than Haganah.

The way the committee worked set a pattern for similar methods of arriving at contemporary responsa. When a technical problem confronted the rabbis, they appointed as a consultant a rabbi who was an expert in the special field of the Halakhah in question. The job of the expert was not only to advise the rabbinical committee, but also to search for technical ways and means to avoid a violation of the Sabbath. One incident that occurred during the war will illustrate: When the Nazi general Rommel reached El-Alamein, there was serious danger that he would succeed in overrunning the whole of the Middle East. The British army was laboring under a shortage of tires, a situation that threatened to paralyze military communications. An Australian Jew had set up in Palestine a factory for repairing tires, and the question then arose whether it was permissible to keep this factory at work on the Sabbath during the military crisis. The rabbinical committee asked Rabbi Meir Karelitz, a brother of the famed *Chazon Ish*, to deal with this halakhic question. With the advice of technicians Rabbi Karelitz found a method of doing the essential work on Sabbath, without infringing upon a prohibition of Biblical authority (*melakhah de'oraita*).

When in 1948 the national leaders were preparing for the establishment of the Jewish State, Rabbi Herzog took the initiative and set up a *Va'adah Toranit* as the successor to the pre-war committee. It consisted of Rabbis Shelomoh Zalman Auerbach, Joseph Shalom Elyashiv, Mordechai Leib Sachs, Shelomoh Goren, Aharon Bilistotzky, Ephraim Gerboz, Gershon Lapidoth, Joseph Babliki, Shlomo Katzin and Ezra Hadaya. The first meeting took place on the 29th of Adar I, 5708 (1948), and Rabbi Herzog defined the tasks of the committee thus: "The men of the Torah have to deal with various topical problems. There have arisen a series of important and momentous questions with which we have not grappled, except in theory, for almost two thousand years. Now we have to deal with them in actual practice. One of the main and most important questions is the Sabbath in the State. There exist many difficulties, and we introduce great Torah scholars into this work, and with the help of God we shall succeed . . ."

The areas of concern were four: 1) Government services (administration, police, post, ports). 2) Public utilities (water, electricity). 3) Defense (army). 4) Industry (oil refineries, cement, glass).

At first the committee met three times a week, and its members visited factories to familiarize themselves at first-hand with the technical problems. At some meetings experts were on hand to impart technical information. Thus a large amount of source material was collected by the committee, including both technical information and halakhic material. On the 10th of Teveth, 5709 (1949), a report was presented to the Chief Rabbinate, which included recommendations on questions of telephone, radio, and electricity. This is the last date on which the committee still functioned officially. It appears that the committee was never formally dissolved, but in the winter of 1949 it simply ceased to exist.

To this day no attempt has been made to re-establish such a committee, and there exists in Israel neither an institution nor even a rabbinical department to deal systematically with the problems of Halakhah and State. But life has an impetus of its own, and its problems cannot be ignored. Religious Jews keep thinking and inquiring about these questions, rabbis publish halakhic dissertations in rabbinical journals, public lectures are held on these topics, and in recent years a few Israeli rabbis have published halakhic responsa on these problems. But except for halakhic directives issued by the Chaplaincy of the Israeli army, we have not had any authoritative discussions and decisions on the Halakhah of State services on the Sabbath.

It is obvious, therefore, that it is not yet possible to summarize halakhic decisions dealing with the problems of a modern State. What can be done usefully at this time is to single out some of the underlying problems and to analyze the various tentative solutions which have been suggested. Such an analysis may help to clarify the basic issues involved.

ELECTRIC POWER

What lies at the heart of the contemporary problem of Sabbath observance is the production of electricity. The use of electricity cuts across all lines: it is used by official bodies, institutions, individuals; it is used by the religious and non-religious. It is true that Rabbi Avraham Isaiah Karelitz, the *Chazon Ish*, did not use electricity in his home in Bnei-Brak on the Sabbath and he also published his view as a halakhic decision. Yet, although the *Chazon Ish* was venerated as an authority on Halakhah, this decision was not accepted in practice. There are not many people in Israel who abstain on the Sabbath from using electricity or water from the tap. Among public institutions only the Shaarei Zedek Hospital in Jerusalem has a special electric generator for use on the Sabbath, which works automatically throughout the Sabbath.

Why do most religious Jews use electricity on the Sabbath? It cannot be argued that the reason is that the electric power stations are working on the Sabbath regardless of whether religious Jews are making use of the electricity produced. The Halakhah does not acknowledge this justification, for the rule is that if a Jew works knowingly on the Sabbath it is forbidden to benefit from his work during the Sabbath. It is possible to rely on the automation of the power stations, but automation is not yet complete and in Israel the power stations still require a certain amount of manual interference. So far the engineers have not found a method of running a power station automatically for twenty-four hours.

What then, should be the view of the Halakhah on the question of operating electric power stations on the Sabbath? No one has suggested that the power stations should be closed on the Sabbath. But opinions differ with regard to the necessity for generating electricity on the Sabbath. Some rabbis explain that the decisive argument is *Pikuach Nefesh* (saving a human life), for electricity is needed in hospitals. Others point to the example of the Shaarei Zedek Hospital with its own generating plant, and argue that the need of a number of hospitals cannot justify the *Chillul Shabbat* (desecration of the Sabbath) for the whole country. They go on to explain that electricity is needed not only for hospitals but for the very existence and security of the modern State. Left without electricity for a whole day the machinery of the State cannot function.

HALAKHAH AND THE STATE

Can this argument justify the desecration of the Sabbath in the power stations? The only observant Jew in Israel to answer this question in the affirmative is Professor Isaiah Leibowitz, who maintains that a State requires its own Halakhah, or does not need any Halakhah of Sabbath observance, because it cannot exist at all if the Halakhah were applied to it. He suggests that religious Jews who want a Jewish State must *ipso facto* accept the elimination of Sabbath observance from the public utilities and the State services. Leibowitz is not interested to find any support in the traditional Halakhah, because in his view the State should be exempted from the Halakhah.

This view has not been accepted by the religious community. On the contrary, in the debate about the role of the Halakhah in the State, all emphasize that the problems must be solved within the framework of the Halakhah. One of the most discussed suggestions is the argument that "vital services" fall under the exception to Shabbat prohibitions, *Pikuach Nefesh* (saving of human life).

PIKUACH NEFESH

The rule of *Pikuach Nefesh* is usually applied to the case of dangerously ill persons. This means that as an argument for permitting work on the Sabbath it is limited to exceptional circumstances. Moreover, it is used in relation to an individual person or to many persons when *each one of them* is in a state of danger. But does the argument of *Pikuach Nefesh* have any validity in connection with the needs of a State?

The nature of this question may be clarified if we take up the one example in which *Pikuach Nefesh* may concern a whole nation: fighting a war, which is permissible on the Sabbath. In the discussion in Tractate *Yoma* (85) references are made to various Biblical sources, the most famous of which is the verse in Leviticus 18:5: "Ye shall therefore keep My statutes, and Mine ordinances, which if a man do, he shall live by them; I am the Lord." The Talmudic interpretation emphasizes the phrase "he shall live by them"—an individual shall live by keeping the *mitzvot* and not endanger his life through them. On the other hand, in the tractate *Shabbat* (19a), an exception for waging war is based on Deuteronomy 20:19–20: "When thou shalt besiege a city . . . until it fall." The last phrase is interpreted to mean that it is permissible to wage war even on the Sabbath until the enemy is entirely conquered.

The fact that the Talmud has separate biblical sources for the two types of *Pikuach Nefesh* suggests the possibility that the Halakhah treats the law of war as an independent law which is not related to the law of *Pikuach Nefesh*. Consequently, it might mean that war on the Sabbath is not a matter of *Pikuach Nefesh* at all, but a separate Halakhah dealing only with the needs of security and defence of the Jewish nation.

This implication has been dealt with in recent years by three Israeli rabbis of the younger generation. Rabbi Mosheh Neriah, in *Milchemet Shabbat* (5719), takes the extreme position that there exists only one halakhic principle, the one of *Pikuach Nefesh*. When a person is in physical danger the threat to his life is fairly clear, but in a war it is not clear at any given moment whether there is a real danger. It is therefore necessary to add a corollary that in time of war there exists *Pikuach Nefesh* for the whole community; hence there is no need to discover in each person's case to what extent he is directly involved in the national danger. Thus, *Pikuach Nefesh* applies both to individuals in time of peace and to a whole community in time of war.

Rabbi Saul Yisraeli approaches the question in an entirely different manner. In his book *Eretz Chemdah—Halakhot of Eretz Yisrael* (5717), he points out a contradiction between *Pikuach Nefesh* and the duty to wage war. If it is a duty to preserve life, how can there be an obligation to endanger life (of the Jewish soldier) by waging war? The answer is, concludes Rabbi Yisraeli, that when the nation is involved, the national interest overrides the needs of the individuals. He interprets the duty to fight a war as a national task, and this task is carried out not by a multitude of individuals but by a nation *per se*. The implication is that the Halakhah recognizes two distinct categories: 1), the individual; 2), the nation as an entity.

The Chief Chaplain of the Israeli Army, Rabbi Shelomoh Goren, is of the opinion (see *Sinai,* 5718) that matters of war and security stand in no relationship to the Halakhah of *Pikuach Nefesh.* Unlike Rabbi Yisraeli, who differentiates between the individual and the nation, Rabbi Goren distinguishes between civil and military needs. Though military precautions do not always correspond to an immediate threat to the lives of the population, the Halakhah allows any work on the Sabbath which is necessary for the security of the State even if there is no clear and present danger to life.

Both Rabbi Goren and Rabbi Yisraeli interpret the law of *ad ridetah* ("until it fall") as a Halakhah of the nation and the State, differentiating it from the law of *Pikuach Nefesh.* This introduces a separate category in the Halakhah, but it still remains a law affecting military matters alone. Neither of the two rabbis, however, finds a basis in Halakhah for applying the principle of "security" (according to Rabbi Goren) or "nation" (Rabbi Yisraeli) to the problem of public utilities.

STATISTICAL PROBABILITY

Eliezer Goldman, a graduate of Yeshiva University and one of the leading thinkers in the religious *kibbutz* movement, suggests an entirely different approach in his booklet entitled *Ha'halakhah Ve-ha-medinah* (1954). He proposes that the principle of *Pikuach Nefesh* be used for the administration of all vital services of the

State. Any work which will prevent danger to life should be permitted even if this danger is not clear and present, but only statistically probable. The normal running of a modern State includes many activities which prevent such dangers from materializing. Goldman suggests that this principle should serve as the basis for an overall Halakhah of the State.

Goldman's approach has met with approval neither in rabbinic circles nor among the religious intelligentsia. The feeling generally persists that *Pikuach Nefesh* is intended for exceptional and personal cases, that it is an emergency law and is not meant to cover the ramified routine of running a modern State. The doctrine is not acceptable as a rationale for normal, routine behavior and activities on each and every Sabbath.

VITAL SERVICES

But the term "vital services" (*Sherutim Chiyuniim*) covers a good deal more than State services. To the Israeli, little is being done in his nascent state that is not "vital" to its existence and development. Indeed, there is on record an instance of a glue factory that considered itself vital to the State and therefore found nothing wrong in maintaining a seven-day operation. In the early years of this industry's growth in the new nation, the Israeli Ministry of Trade and Industry invited a British expert, Mr. Israel Chait, to advise the new Israeli glue industry. He spent some time investigating productivity and the general running of one of the more important factories, and his conclusions were rather critical of both management and methods of work. A meeting was called during which the expert presented his findings to the managers of the factory. At this point, one of the managers solicited the expert's help in trying to convince the Rabbis that operation on the Sabbath was vital. Mr. Chait pointed out that no glue factory in the world operated seven days a week, that it was unnecessary and unprofitable.

A similar case involved the papermill of Haderah, which did no actual manufacturing on the Sabbath, but used the off-day for overhauling machinery. The Chief Rabbinate interfered and threatened to ban the use of Haderah paper for sacred books if the papermill continued its policy. A compromise eventually was worked out and the Chief Rabbinate granted special permission to employ non-Jews on the Sabbath. However, the implications of this decision were disturbing. The papermill was not a "vital service" to the public or the State; on the contrary it kept losing money and was a burden to the State's balance of payments. There was absolutely no economic need to increase its unprofitable production by adding another working day, and to look for a halakhic *hetter* to permit operation on the Sabbath. It was further argued that such special halakhic treatment, though conforming with the provisions of the Sabbath Halakhah, posed a serious threat to Sabbath observance in industry. The conclusion of the matter may be described in terms of divine humor. A change of management took place in an attempt to eliminate financial losses, and the new manager immediately suspended Sabbath operations.

One of the avenues of serious investigation for the solution of the Sabbath problem is the extent to which automation can be used. There are, however, lamentably few cases where preplanning took into account a pause in operation every seventh day. But what a few have done may be predictive of what can be done.

SHIPS

Yet automation cannot solve all Sabbath problems. A well-known example is the running of ships on the Sabbath. When the Chief Rabbinate dealt with this problem, the Israeli shipping company officially announced that the ships were running automatically on the Sabbath. But automation means one thing to an engineer and quite another to the rabbinate. From the point of view of the Halakhah the question is whether human beings have to interfere with the engines and thus perform work which is considered a *Chillul Shabbat*. Besides, the work on a ship involves far more than running engines. There are international laws and insurance company requirements which necessitate writing in the ship's log. The ship must also maintain continuous radio communications. These questions were dealt with in great detail by Rabbi Menahem Mendel Schneirsohn, the Lubavitcher Rebbe, in several responsa which revealed both halakhic erudition and an astonishing grasp of ship engineering.

The Lubavitcher Rebbe decided that according to the Halakhah Jewish ships are not allowed to run on the Sabbath. Hence observant Jews may not travel on a Jewish ship which desecrates the Sabbath. The Chief Rabbinate did not agree with the Lubavitcher Rebbe's view, and tried instead to find ways and means to overcome the problem of *Chillul Shabbat* (one suggestion was to employ non-Jews for the work on the Sabbath). Here, too, there is general agreement that the Jewish State cannot exist securely without its own merchant navy. At the same time, it is held that this necessity in itself does not justify *Chillul Shabbat*. As in the case of electricity, the tendency is to search for technical solutions.

There is no dearth of scientific and rabbinic talent in the United States and Israel that could conceivably solve many of the Sabbath problems, but there is no coordination of this talent. Only one institution devotes itself to these problems, and then only to agronomy, "The Institute of Agricultural Research According to the Torah." * Whatever improvements the future may hold, the present-day problems re-occur with the regularity of the arrival of Sabbath. In the absence of technical solutions, Rabbis have turned to other means of dealing with the difficulties. One of the suggestions is the use of the non-Jew, "*the Shabbos Goy*," and to the controversy on this concept we now turn.

* Planning for Sabbath observance was initiated by the members of Kibbutz Chafetz Chayyim of Poalei Agudath Israel some twenty years ago when they developed a milking machine in accordance with halakhic specifications, and thus solved the problem of milking cows on the Sabbath. A few years ago they enlarged this idea of technical planning for requirements of the Halakhah, and established an "Institute for Agricultural Research According to the Torah." This Institute employs agronomists who work closely with the Government Agricultural Research Station, and at the same time receive their directives from a panel of rabbis who reside in agricultural settlements. This Institute has worked out a detailed schedule of agricultural work for the year of the *Shemittah*. Experimental work is now being carried out on hydroponics, growing plants without soil in a manner which is permissible in the *Shemittah* year. Perhaps the most interesting experiment is the attempt to grow some plants in a two-year cycle, with the view of sowing in the year preceding the *Shemittah* and harvesting two years running.

THE "SHABBOS GOY"

The idea of using non-Jewish labor on the Sabbath has evoked a different kind of discussion from that on the concept of *Pikuach Nefesh*. That legal exception could be argued purely on halakhic grounds; the proposition of the *Shabbos Goy* has a wider context that deals not only with Halakhah, but with the recent history and sociology of the Jewish community.

Halakhically, the *Shabbos Goy* is first mentioned as a prohibition. It is usually called *amirah lenokhri* (requesting a non-Jew to perform work for a Jew on the Sabbath), and it is laid down in principle as a prohibition. It is not a biblical prohibition but the rabbinical injunction is based on a biblical verse (Exodus 12:16). *Mishnah Berurah* (*Shabbat* 243) summarizes briefly the variant readings in the Mekhilta and Yalkut Shimoni on this verse, and concludes that most authorities regard it as a rabbinical prohibition.

But while halakhic literature permits in certain instances work by the *Shabbos Goy*, these cases are exceptions to the rule. When Jews lived in exile, these exceptional circumstances were considered "normal," because Jews were not in a position to change the conditions of life and work. Now that we have an independent Jewish State, the argument concludes, we must observe the Sabbath without recourse to "exceptional circumstances," because a truly normal life demands the application of a normal Halakhah. The guiding rule of Halakhah in Israel, then, ought to be the observance of the Sabbath without help of the *Shabbos Goy*.

The halakhic argument against the *Shabbos Goy* is supplemented with a theological proposition that rests on the assumption that Zionism and the Jewish State are pregnant with religious significance. By normalizing the Jewish pattern of living, Zionism widens the scope of Jewish work and life. Jews are entering occupations from which they were hitherto excluded. The inevitable corollary is that the normalization of Jewish life leads to a normalization of halakhic problems. In terms of Sabbath legislation the change can be expressed in the following manner. In the Diaspora we asked: "How can we use certain services on the Sabbath?" In Israel we must ask: "How can we *produce and use* these services on the Sabbath?" Now that the Jew can again lead an independent Jewish life, he must strive for independence also in religious life. The *Shabbos Goy* is not an essential part of Judaism. Surely it could not be the intention of the Torah that we should be able to observe the *mitzvot* only with the aid of people who deny the truth of the Torah. In the State of Israel there are unfortunately many non-religious Jews, but, the argument continues, the Halakhah must be predicated on the assumption that a whole nation is involved. Both questions and answers have to be formulated from the point of view, not of the individual religious Jew, but of the State. The question is no longer, "How can I observe the Sabbath in a non-Jewish society?" but "How can the Jewish nation and State observe the Sabbath?" Once the question is put in this manner, concludes the argument, there can remain little doubt that there is no room for the *Shabbos Goy* as a solution to the running of public services on the Sabbath.

Both the halakhic and theological arguments have met with considerable opposition. One serious objection is based on the fundamental premise that the objections to the *Shabbos Goy* are not really halakhic, that they represent an attempt to introduce extraneous considerations into a discussion which should be concerned purely with Halakhah. The Torah itself is addressed to a society which includes non-Israelite elements and there are consequently, in the Bible, many laws dealing with the strangers dwelling amongst the people of Israel. The Halakhah also alludes to various types of strangers who lived amongst Jews. It is further suggested that even the Messianic vision includes a description of non-Jews working for a Jewish society. This idea derived from a verse in Isaiah (61:5): "And strangers shall stand and feed your flocks, and aliens shall be your plowmen and your vinedressers."

In Israel, the opposition to the *Shabbos Goy* concept is usually associated with the *Kibbutz Dati*, the organization of the religious Kibbutzim. The *Kibbutz Dati* is supported in these views by a large number of people who may be loosely described as the Israeli "religious intelligentsia." This is a social stratum which is an outgrowth of the rabbinical situation in Israel. In a country where the average religious intelligent young man attends university, only a handful of rabbis, however, are university graduates.

The result is that the type of *Torah-im-Derekh-Eretz* rabbi (as he is known in the Western World) and Yeshiva University graduate has not made its mark in the Israeli rabbinate. But this does not mean that this kind of religious intellectual Jew does not exist in Israel. In fact he is to be found in large—and growing—numbers in the professions, at the universities, and in the civil service. Many of them have acquired *semikhah* after having studied at one of the Israeli yeshivot; most of them were members of a religious Zionist youth movement and have served in the Israeli army.

Although this religious intelligentsia is largely unorganized and has not even a publication to voice its views, it has found an able spokesman on the issue of the *Shabbos Goy* in the person of Rabbi Goren. "The utilization of the non-Jew for doing work (on the Sabbath)," he wrote, "is a dangerous development, which occurred in the conditions of the Jews in exile, and this utilization is explictly opposed to what is laid down in the Talmud. On the contrary, our sages have decreed against the utilization of non-Jews on the Sabbath and putting them to work for the purpose of achieving things that cannot be done by Jews. The purpose of those decrees was: a) complete elimination of any dependence upon non-Jews in our country and our environment; b) opposition to the possibilty of evading the laws of the Torah with the aid of non-Jews; c) faith and confidence in the possibility of basing the independent life of the nation upon the laws of the Torah."

ARMY AND POLICE

So far we have discussed problems of the Sabbath in industry and the production of vital means of communication. These facets of life in Israel do not include, however, work done in the army and police force on Sabbath.

Since the establishment of the State the old secret Haganah became the official Israeli army, and the halakhic problems could no longer be tackled sporadically. There was need for continuous and systematic halakhic decisions, not only in cases that come up occasionally but for the purpose of planning the routine work of the army. This task fell to the Chief Chaplain, Rabbi Goren, who has worked out a kind of Shulchan Arukh for the individual soldier as for the army. His halakhic rulings have in most cases been incorporated in the official army regulations, and are therefore binding upon all soldiers. Other rulings have provided halakhic responsa for religious Israelis serving in the army.

The rabbinical authorities base their new Halakhah for the Israeli army upon the traditional laws of warfare on the Sabbath. The concept of national security is interpreted as defense against an enemy, and it is further enlarged to take into account the need of having the Israeli army in a permanent state of alertness against a potential attack. In the Israeli army the Chaplaincy ruled that what is prohibited to a religious soldier is prohibited also to the non-religious soldier and what is permissible, is similarly permissible to all. All Jews are equal before the Halakhah, whether they accept its discipline or not. If there is a job essential for security, then there is no *Chillul Shabbat* and the religious soldier should do it himself and not attempt to find a non-religious comrade who "does not mind" working on the Sabbath.

On the other hand, the Sabbath work of the police is predicated on the willingness of the majority of policemen to work on the Sabbath. Needless to say that from the point of view of the Halakhah this is an intolerable situation. The solution of the problem must be a solution in principle, and it must be applicable to all policemen. However, there is nothing in the halakhic sources about police activity that involves work on the Sabbath. Although we do find a rule for special police work on the festivals, it is clearly not the kind of work that is carried out by modern police, and it certainly does not involve work which is otherwise prohibited on a *Yom Tov*. This ruling is laid down by Maimonides (*Hilkhot Yom Tov* 6:21) and is based on the Talmud in *Kiddushin* (81a.) Its purpose is to send out police to prevent immoral behavior that may result from the levity induced by the festival; the task of this special "morals squad" was mainly to see to it that men and women should not celebrate in mixed company.

This Halakhah provides no precedent for the kind of work that modern police carry out. In the police station there is the uninterrupted work of the telephone and radio, and a police officer on duty writes notations of all incoming reports. Patrol cars are continually cruising over the town and countryside. All this involves work which is forbidden on the Sabbath.

Only a few isolated dissertations have been published on the subject, the Chief Rabbinate has issued no authoritative decision, and there exists no Chaplaincy for the police force other than a rabbi to supervise Kashrut of police canteens and prison kitchens.

Religious policemen avoid these duties on the Sabbath because they enjoy special dispensation which enables them to observe the Sabbath. Paragraph 21 (b) of the Standing Orders of the Israeli Police Headquarters reads as follows: "On the Sabbaths and the festivals everything possible is to be done to put observant policemen on such tasks as will not compel them to desecrate the Sabbath, on the distinct condition that this arrangement will not interfere with the work of the police and its efficiency." This is the only instance in the State of Israel in which there is an official ruling with special provisions for religious Jews. The Sabbath ruling is generally adhered to in the police force, and observant policemen are given every opportunity on the Sabbath either to be free from duty or to carry out duties which do not involve them in prohibited work.

This special dispensation has an inherent weakness: it can work only so long as there are few religious policemen. There are no official statistics, but highranking officers estimate that *less than two percent* of the Israeli police are observant. The implication is that religious Jews do not join the Israeli police force, and the few that have joined are given "tolerant consideration." But there is a serious halakhic corollary to this method, for it means that religious policemen can observe the Sabbath because there are plenty of non-religious policemen who are prepared to work on the Sabbath. There may be an argument about the *Shabbos Goy*, but there can be no argument about Jews acting as *Shabbos Goyim*.

To begin with, the Halakhah would question whether all the police activities are really necessary on the Sabbath. This question was taken up in the Israeli journal *Ha-Torah ve-ha-Medinah*. The late Chief Rabbi Herzog wrote a dissertation on the subject in which he proposed that *Pikuach Nefesh* be the criterion for the permissibility of police work on the Sabbath. Accordingly, he analyzed the various activities of the police to ascertain which of them could be classified as preventing a threat to life. Though it may be argued that dealing with a thief is a matter of *Pikuach Nefesh*, what reason can there be for permitting routine patrolling in police cars, and why should it be necessary to write out reports? Rabbi Herzog questioned the necessity of all these routine police activities, and therefore would not invoke the principle of *Pikuach Nefesh* to permit them. Instead, he suggested that ways be found to carry out police work in a manner that would not involve a biblical prohibition (e.g., writing in an unconvential manner, or that some of the work should be done by two persons together).

Police experts have an entirely different view. They argue that the importance of police work cannot be appreciated if each activity is looked at separately. It is police work in its totality which forestalls dangerous situations. Patrol cars must cruise in the streets, even before they have an inkling where—and if at all—they will be needed. Each report must be written because one never knows what may turn out to be important. Police work is necessary not only after the event or when the danger is obvious, but also for instilling into the population the knowledge and the feeling that the police are ever-ready. The very existence of an active police is a guarantee of internal security, and the security is really a matter of life and death.

The argument of the police experts is supported by Rabbi Saul Yisraeli (in *Ha-Torah ve-ha-Medinah*) from the point of view of the Halakhah. Rabbi Yisraeli does not accept Goldman's statistical concept of *Pikuach Nefesh*, but he contends that without the police there would be real danger to lives. Each time a patrol car goes out on a routine tour it may be a matter of *Pikuach Nefesh*. Hence the Halakhah should permit all routine patrols. Rabbi Yisraeli brings further evidence for permitting police work on the Sabbath. He quotes the Talmud (*Shabbat* 42a) that one may extinguish a burning coal which is lying in a public place in order to prevent the public from getting hurt. True, there is a difference of opinion whether this exception applies even to cases when the act of extinguishing involves a biblical prohibition. But Rabbi Yisraeli contends that even those rabbinic authorities who refuse to sanction it when the violation of a Biblical law is involved do so only because, in their opinion, burning coal does not really represent a danger to the public, since people can notice and avoid it. All authorities would agree that in the case of unquestionable public danger, the Halakhah would look upon such a situation like a regular case of *Pikuach Nefesh* of an individual. Where the public is involved it is not necessary to show that *Pikuach Nefesh* is imminent. It is sufficient to show that the case involves damage to the public, even if this damage will not necessarily cause danger to life, as in the case of the burning coal in a public place which may be extinguished although there is only a danger of damage, not death. According to Rabbi Yisraeli, the general danger of damage to the public inevitably includes a certain amount of *Pikuach Nefesh* to some persons. The Halakhah decrees, therefore, that a danger of damage to the public equals a *Pikuach Nefesh* of an individual. Accordingly, the principle of "public danger" can be used to permit the essential routine work of the police on the Sabbath.

The problems of work on Sabbath in the State of Israel are certainly not exhausted by this survey. The intentions of this paper were not to set down major responsa, but to outline the questions, explore the implications, delineate the lines of solutions, and, mainly, to encourage further discussion.

IMMANUEL JAKOBOVITS

*

The Dissection of the Dead in Jewish Law

A COMPARATIVE AND HISTORICAL STUDY [1]

M ORAL autonomy or moral automation—that is the most fateful choice confronting mankind today. As long as the moral law reigns supreme, the spectacular advances in science and technology will be effectively controlled by the overriding claims of human life and dignity. Man will be safe from the menace of his own productions. But when the quest for knowledge and power is unhemmed by moral considerations, and the fundamental rights of man are swept aside in the blind march to mechanical perfection, the ramparts protecting mankind from self-destruction are bound to crumble. Today the struggle between science and religion is no longer a competitive search for the truth as in former times. It is a battle between excesses and controls, between the supremacy of man's creations and the supremacy of man himself.

In the past, the human inventive genius served mainly to aid nature in the amelioration of life. Now it bids fair to supplant nature, replacing it by an artificial, synthetic existence in which the deepest mysteries of creation are not only laid bare but subjected to the arbitrary whims of mechanized man. The push of one button can now exterminate life by the millions; psychologically waged advertising campaigns can determine the eating habits of whole nations; chemical drugs can curb or release human emotions at will, and break down the most determined will-power to extract confessions. The control over man's conscience, over procreation and extinction, over human existence itself is being wrested from nature and surrendered to scientists and technicians.

In this new dispensation the physician, too, is playing an ever more vital rôle. Human life, which he can artificially generate out of a test-tube and terminate out of a syringe-needle, is now at his bidding. Psychiatry may soon bring even human behavior under his sway, almost like a robot plane guided by a remote radio operator. But who will control the physician and the growing army of other scientists? That is the crux of the moral dilemma of our times.

There can be little doubt that, of all practical sciences, it is pre-eminently medicine with which Judaism, historically and intellectually, enjoys a natural kinship, and to which Jewish law is best qualified to address its reasoned, pragmatic rules of morality. For many centuries rabbis and physicians, often merging their professions into one, were intimate partners in a common effort for the betterment of life. The perplexities of our age challenge them to renew their association in the service of human life, health, and dignity. Indeed, they challenge Judaism itself to reassert its place as a potent force in the moral leadership of humanity.

I

Jewish law has insisted from the beginning that the physician may practise his art only by virtue of an express sanction granted to him by God.[2] The control over health, life, and death is essentially a Divine prerogative.[3] It cannot be exercised by man except in so far as he is delegated by the Creator to do so. Even the setting aside of religious precepts for the preservation of life is not a natural right but a scriptural mandate.[4] For in the Jewish view man's claim to any inalienable rights, whether in life or in death,[5] derives primarily from his creation "in the image of God."[6] In other words, man is the recipient of rights and God the giver; He alone can confer and define those rights.

In accordance with these basic principles, Jewish legislation has always asserted its right to intrude into the domain of the physician (no less than of the rabbi[7]). Its provisions include precise regulations on the doctor's duty to heal, his professional charges, his legal responsibilities, and his title to ignore certain religious laws in his medical work. But above all it sets out to define and circumscribe his rights in cases where human life and dignity may be at stake. Hence the detailed laws on such operations as artificial insemination, sterilization, contraception, abortion, and euthanasia.

Since the biblically assigned rights of a person, as we have mentioned, extend beyond death, Jewish law must obviously also concern itself with the problem of dissection. The subject occupies considerable and constantly growing space in current rabbinic literature. The final verdict is still a matter of debate. We shall here attempt to trace the origins and development of that debate in its historical and comparative context, from antiquity to the present day.

I I

In the Talmud, the ultimate source of Jewish law, the dissection of human corpses *for medical ends* is not mentioned. This is not surprising. At the time of the Talmud, anatomical experiments on humans were entirely unknown. There had been some occasional excursions into this field in ancient times, but all these early steps into human anatomy were soon abandoned, usually because of religious restraints in one form or another. The first dissections in China are ascribed to the legendary physician Pien Ch'ioa many centuries before the Alexandrian exploits in this branch.[8] But these operations came to be regarded as incompatible with religious piety and were, with rare exceptions, discontinued until modern times.[9] In ancient India, where medicine and surgery had developed to a high standard, the dissection of the human body was opposed on religious grounds,[10] even if some non-surgical methods for exposing the internal organs were very occasionally tolerated.[11] The Syriac *Book of Medicines* has a few references to human dissection,[12] due no doubt to the impact of the Alexandrian school where the author had studied in the 2nd century B.C.E.[13] In Greece, the classical home of medicine, the study of anatomy may go back to Aristotle[14] or even earlier savants.[15] But any sustained advances were rendered impossible not

only by the failure to appreciate its importance for medical purposes, but also by social and religious prejudices,[16] particularly the
insistence on immediate burial.[17] Even in Egypt, where it had
long been customary to disembowel and embalm the dead, anatomical science failed to gain from the experience because of
religious scruples. Although the Bible expressly states that Jacob's
body was embalmed by "the physicians" in Egypt,[18] the belief
that it was an act of gross impiety gradually militated against the
employment of doctors. Consequently, the operation was left to
special functionaries, the "Paraschite," who became an object of
popular execration.[19]

The only real break in this deep-rooted antagonism to dissection
in antiquity occurred at Alexandria in the 3rd century B.C.E. At
that Egyptian outpost of Hellenistic culture the new anatomical
science flourished for a time virtually unhampered. But even that
interlude was of short duration. By the time Galen commenced
his medical education in 146 C.E. the practice of human dissection had already ceased everywhere for half a century.[20] From
that time even the faintest scientific research into the human
body was not initiated again until over twelve centuries later.

The earliest Jewish reference to the practice is a remarkable
statement, generally overlooked by medical historians, by the
Alexandrian philosopher Philo. He speaks of ". . . physicians of
the highest repute who have made researches into the construction of man and examined in detail what is visible and also, by
careful use of anatomy, what is hidden from sight in order that,
if medical treatment is required, nothing which could cause serious
danger should be neglected through ignorance." [21] This passage
may, of course, reflect local influences rather than Jewish teachings, but its unqualified endorsement of anatomical dissection is
nonetheless notable.

III

In talmudic times, then, the whole problem was no longer
acute, since dissection for medical research had fallen completely
into disuse. There is no foundation for the allegation [22] that the
Babylonian Talmudist Rab of the 3rd century "bought cadavers

and dissected them," [23] nor do any facts justify the claim by the medical historian Baas that "dissection in the interests of science was permitted by the Talmud." [24] Yet there is some evidence to support the assertion by some historians [25] that dissections and autopsies on humans were carried out by the authors of the Talmud, albeit only very occasionally and never for medical purposes. In fact, the Talmud records several significant references to the subject, all of them of importance to our problem.

In one passage [26] the Palestinian teacher of the 1st century, Rabbi Yishmael, relates that the Ptolemaic Queen Cleopatra once delivered her female slaves, following their execution for treason, to the king for anatomical investigations; he opened their bodies and studied the stages in foetal development.[27] In a more important statement,[28] the Babylonian sage-physician Samuel records that the disciples of the same Rabbi Yishmael [29] once boiled [30] the body of a condemned prostitute to ascertain the exact number of bones in human beings.[31] Practical researches must also be presupposed for the detailed list of human bones given in the Mishnah,[32] particularly since the figure given is at variance with the less accurate number listed by the Greek physicians.[33] In other places the Talmud speaks of "hands soiled through [handling] blood, foetal growths and placentas" for ritual enquiries; [34] of one sage who had kept the skull of King Jehoiakim in his home; [35] of another who had held up a bone of his tenth son to comfort mourners; [36] and of a third who admitted that "he used to bury the dead and to observe their bones," whereby he studied the osteological effects of alcoholism.[37]

None of these statements deals specifically with anatomical experiments for purely medical ends.[38] They therefore hardly imply an unconditional sanction of human dissection. But it is noteworthy that no voice of protest was raised against these practices, a fact all the more remarkable since Jewish law in general rigorously upholds the inviolability of the human body in death as in life. It condemns any undue interference with the corpse as an execrable offence against the dead. Though never explicitly set forth in the Talmud, the prohibition to disgrace or disfigure the dead was always assumed as a logical extension of the biblical ban [39] on allowing even a criminal's body to remain unburied overnight.[40] The prohibition itself, and the question whether it can be waived for legal purposes, is mentioned in two discussions on the right to defile the dead for procuring evidence in court proceedings—the one criminal and the other civil. The outcome of both discussions is not altogether conclusive. The circumstances in the first case (a murder charge) were such as would in any event render the findings of an autopsy, had it been permitted, irrelevant to the conviction of the suspected offender and insufficient for his complete acquittal.[41] But the trend of the argument suggests that the Talmud would not rule out post-mortem examinations for forensic purposes if the results might yield crucial information to the court.[42] In the other case permission for an exhumation to ascertain the age of the deceased (in support of legal claims by his relations) was refused as an unwarranted sacrilege, but only on the additional grounds that the features might have changed after death; moreover, it is argued that the obligation to accept financial loss rather than disturb the dead may apply to the relations only.[43] Altogether, the Talmud rules "whatever is done in honour of the living does not constitute a disgrace to the dead," [44] but the context in which this occurs deals merely with delays in carrying out the burial.

To the extent, then, to which these talmudic sources are relevant to our problem, Jewish law became heir to a rather tolerant attitude to dissection. But it must be emphasised, before applying these arguments to medical needs, that the cases in the Talmud just mentioned deal only with very minor infringements of the peace of the dead. Furthermore, there was generally a sharp distinction between legal autopsies and scientific dissections. The anatomical experiments at Alexandria, and later at Bologna and elsewhere, were quite independent of medico-legal dissections which developed as a separate discipline and not as a branch of scientific anatomy.[45]

We may here digress for a while to look at the corresponding development within Christianity. While the decline of anatomy in the 1st century of the Common Era can hardly be ascribed to the as yet quite insignificant influence of the new faith,[46] the Christian tradition of disapprobation was set quite early. Already in about 400, St. Augustine had declared: "With a cruel zeal for science, some medical men who are called anatomists have dissected the bodies of the dead, and sometimes even of sick persons who have died under their knives,[47] and have inhumanly pried into the secrets of the human body in order to learn the nature of the disease and its exact seat and how it might be cured." [48] Tertullian, two centuries later, is said to have "hated dissection." [49] Although the early Church never issued a formal ban on anatomy, the idea of dissection must have outraged Christian sentiment.[50] It was regarded as a violation of man's dignity and as incompatible with the belief in bodily resurrection. Even the dissection of animals was not always possible, since the student was in danger of being taken as a magician.[51]

IV

As we enter the second millennium, we find little change in this outlook. The progress of anatomy was slow and tortuous. At the School of Salerno in the 11th century, often described as the first university, the ape used by Galen was replaced by the pig,[52] because it was thought to resemble man internally—a belief already found in the Talmud.[53] But human corpses were still excluded, probably because of the opposition of the Church.[54] Scientific interest in the human cadaver did not begin to revive until the 13th century. In 1238 Frederick II ordered that a corpse should be dissected every five years for study purposes [55]—the first mention of dissection as an established practice,[56] even if the instruction was purely nominal.[57] At Bologna dissections were introduced later in the same century.[58] The first clear reference to a postmortem examination dates from 1286, when a physician at Cremona investigated the cause of a pestilence then raging in Italy, and the first "modern" work on anatomy was published by Mondino de' Luzzi in 1316, following dissections at Bologna University.[59]

Thenceforth, the renewed interest in dissection spread only in small stages. It was officially sanctioned—with certain safeguards which usually restricted the subjects to criminals—at Venice in 1368, at Montpellier in 1375, and at Lerida in 1391.[60] These experiments, still of little scientific value, generally served to illustrate ancient medical texts rather than foster independent research. The public displays of "anatomies" often turned into academic feasts, to which the civil and ecclesiastical authorities were invited.[61] Anatomical demonstrations did not commence in Paris, Vienna, and Prague until the 15th century,[62] while at Padua the study of anatomy was not included in the elaborate medical curriculum in the middle of that century.[63] Even in the 16th century dissections were not common.[64] Paracelsus still "despised anatomy and failed to see how any knowledge could be gained from the dead body." [65] Only some years later was the entire outlook changed by the great pioneer in anatomy, Vesalius.[66] In Italy, Holland, and France dissection as a means of teaching anatomy began to be quite frequent only in the 17th century; in Germany and England it was introduced later still.[67] At most European universities regular anatomical instruction on cadavers was not initiated until the beginning of the 18th century.[68]

Throughout this tedious progress of the new science, the religious prejudice against dissection faded only very gradually and then often reappeared. By an extraordinary coincidence, it happened twice—in 1300 and in 1737—that the Christian and Jewish authorities made pronouncements, quite independently of each other and yet on strikingly similar subjects, with an important bearing on dissection; in both cases the two religions adopted opposing viewpoints. In 1300 Pope Boniface VIII issued a Bull which banned the practice of boiling human corpses (presumably of crusaders who had died far from their homes) to facilitate their removal to consecrated burial grounds.[69] Medical and social historians are about equally divided in their views on the Bull's relevance to anatomical studies. While some discount the influence of the Bull,[70] many others aver that, even if the edict was not specifically directed against anatomists, it certainly fortified the public abhorrence of dissection and was, in fact, largely responsible for delaying the progress of anatomy.[71] It is certain that some pioneers in anatomy were hindered in their work by theological considerations [72] or opposition,[73] that religious prejudice was mainly responsible for the objections to dissection until its introduction at the various universities,[74] and that the practice often required ecclesistical sanction,[75] sometimes to be obtained from the popes as an indulgence.[76] Gradually the resistance eased. In 1556 Charles V received the following reply to an enquiry from the theological faculty at the University of Salamanca: "The dissection of human cadavers serves a useful purpose and is therefore permissible to Christians." [77] But the undercurrent of theological misgivings did not finally disappear until Prospero Lambertini, later Pope Benedict XIV, expressed the official attitude of the Catholic Church as favouring the practice for the advancement of the arts [78] and sciences in unequivocal terms in 1737.[79] Since then the Church has raised no objection to medical dissection.[80]

The stagnation of medieval anatomy and surgery has also been attributed to the "superstitious horror of mutilating a corpse" among Jews and Arabs,[81] and to "the Jewish tenets, adopted by the Mohammedans, [which] compelled students to be satisfied with making their observations on the carcasses of brutes." [82] Among the Arabs religious opposition to dissection was certainly explicit and sustained.[83] The Koran itself expressly forbids the opening of a corpse, even if the person should have swallowed the most valuable pearl which did not belong to him. [84] This was always applied in support of the ban on anatomical dissection at Turkish,[85] Persian, and other Mohammedan universities.[86] In 1838 the law was amended to permit the dissection of Christian and Jewish bodies, though not of Moslems.[87] But in practice the religious prohibition of dissection was usually upheld even in very recent times.[88]

It is clear from our records that the Jews, too, did not actually make any significant contributions to the advancement of anatomy in the Middle Ages. But it is highly questionable whether this was due to any religious inhibitions, as has been claimed by even so knowledgeable a master of Jewish medical history as Harry Friedenwald.[89] There is absolutely no substance in the charge, first made by Jean Astruc[90] early in the 18th century and later often repeated,[91] that the laws of ritual defilement militated against the dissection of human bodies. These laws do not prohibit the touching of a dead body (except to Jews of priestly descent); they merely lay down the conditions of impurity resulting from such contact and the procedure to be adopted to regain ritual cleanliness.[92] True, the duty to inter all human remains is reinforced by the fear lest some unburied parts might cause a priest to be unwittingly defiled.[93] But this consideration would hardly prove a greater obstacle to autopsies than the biblical law of immediate burial itself.

The evolution of the Jewish attitude almost exactly reversed the chronological pattern of the development within the Church. As we shall now discover, the papal edict *against* reducing a corpse to its bones coincided with a rabbinic ruling *sanctioning* a similar operation. As long as Christian theologians occasionally *condemned* the dissection of the dead, the Jewish authorities remained *silent*; and at the moment when the Church finally *ended* the argument by a clear statement in favour of the practice, the Jewish discussion was *opened* by a decision against dissection. We may now review these stages in some detail.

In about the same year as Boniface VIII promulgated his Bull against the mutilation of corpses to facilitate the transportation of the remains, the Jewish savant R. Solomon Aderet gave a ruling permitting placing quick-lime on dead bodies to hasten their decomposition in order to ease their removal elsewhere in accordance with the wishes of the departed [94]—a decision also codified in the *Shulchan Arukh* [94] and later occasionally mentioned as an argument in favour of post-mortem operations [96] (just as the Bull was mentioned to support the opposition). A similar practice was sanctioned by the 16th century scholar R. David ibn Zimra for speeding the admission of the soul to Heaven (which, according to early sources,[97] must await the body's decomposition), but he nevertheless advised against such interference with the ordinary course of nature.[98] By a curious reversal of effects, Aderet's ruling (used by some to promote anatomy) was utilised by R. Isaac Elchanan Spector, a leading scholar of the 19th century, to foil the anatomists; he counselled a questioner from America concerned with the pilfering of cemeteries to bury the remains with lime in order to render them unfit for anatomical dissection.[99]

During the time when Christian protests against dissection were occasionally heard, there is no record of any Jewish objections to the practice. Indeed, there is some evidence to the opposite effect. While the claim that Maimonides himself made practical tests in anatomy [100] can probably be dismissed as conjectural, clear proof exists of the participation in dissections by Jewish or Marrano doctors. Thus the celebrated physician Amatus Lusitanus—in whom his parents had "implanted . . . an attachment to Jewish religion, tradition and customs" [101]—performed twelve dissections at Ferrara to confirm his discovery of the valves in the azygos veins in 1547.[102] Again, it is said of Abraham Zacutus, the Marrano who joined the Jewish Congregation at Amsterdam in 1625,[103] that he "deserves special praise for the frequency with which he made autopsies at a time when they were rare . . . As a result he published post-mortem findings in the plague, in affections of the heart, malignant tumours, renal and vesical calculi, etc." [104] The famous rabbi-physician of the 17th century, Jacob Zahalon, also appears to have at least condoned autopsies; he refers with evident approval to a post-mortem examination carried out by a Gentile doctor on a Jewish victim of the plague in 1656 to discover if death was due to a bubo or an intestinal hernia.[105] Interesting, too, is an anatomical illustration in Tobias Cohn's *Ma'asei Tubiah*, a popular medico-religious work first published in Venice in 1707; it depicts the body of (what appears to be) a Jew opened to expose the internal organs and compares them to the divisions of a house.[106]

These few instances are obviously far too isolated to admit of any general conclusions on the Jewish religious attitude at the time. More significant may be the complete absence of rabbinic protests prior to the 18th century. Jewish leaders can scarcely have been unaware of the problem. Practical studies in anatomy, as we have shown, began to be well established at many European universities in the 17th century or even earlier, and the many Jewish physicians and medical students of that age are bound to have been confronted with the need from time to time to witness, or even to participate in, autopsies and the "anatomies" regularly performed at the medical schools. In fact, Jews were particularly concerned with this problem for another reason. Their corpses

were often especially favoured by the anatomists. An anonymous
tract of 1829 informs us that, "as the Jews bury early, their ceme-
tery formerly produced the best and freshest subjects, equal in
freshness to the body sent to the venal undertaker . . ." [107] The
problem distressed the Jewish community in Padua already in
1680, when the students at the famous university demanded all
Jewish corpses for their anatomical institute.[108] Jews certainly
objected to this wretched "body-snatching" no less bitterly than
their neighbours, but there is no record of any condemnation of
dissection itself in the prolific rabbinic literature of those centuries.

V

It was not until 1737—the very year when the Christian debate
finally concluded in favour of dissection—that the Jewish arguments against the practice first began. In that year a medical student at the University of Goettingen asked R. Jacob Emden
whether he could participate on the Sabbath in the dissection of
dogs used in the absence of human material. The rabbi, one of
the leading authorities of his age, replied that such operations on
the Sabbath involved many prohibitions, whether they were performed on humans or animals. Moreover, in the case of human
corpses, whether of Jews or not, it was in any case forbidden to
derive any benefit from them.[109] Within the same century the
question was treated again by R. Ezekiel Landau, the renowned
scholar who died in Prague in 1793. He was asked on behalf of
the rabbinical authorities in London whether they might accede
to a request for an autopsy on a Jew—who had died after an operation for calculus in the bladder—to ascertain the proper treatment
for similar cases in the future. The reply, while not adverting to
the ban on benefiting from a human corpse, stated that such a
post-mortem examination was an act of gross indignity to the dead,
strictly prohibited in Jewish law. This consideration could be set
aside only if there was a reasonable and immediate prospect of
thereby saving a human life. But with no patient at hand to gain
from the experience of the autopsy, its object was too remote to
warrant the act. Moreover, "even non-Jewish doctors do not make

anatomical experiments on any corpses except those of executed criminals or of people who gave their consent whilst alive; and if we were—Heaven forfend!—to be lenient in this matter, they would dissect all our dead in order to study the arrangement of the internal organs and their function so as to determine the medical treatment of the living." [110]

Since the beginning of the 19th century, the problem has engaged the attention of almost all leading rabbis in numerous responsa. As the practice became more widespread and the religious difficulties it created more pressing, a number of new elements were introduced into the discussion. The great respondent R. Moses Schreiber, in a judgment dated 1836, accepted the position taken up by Emden and Landau; only he thought the ban on benefiting from the dead might not apply to the bodies of non-Jews in accordance with their own views and their religious teachings. But he emphatically agreed that the remote possibility of saving life could not override the certainty of desecrating the dead; by the same token all work involved in medical studies would suspend the Sabbath laws on the assumption that a human life might thereby be preserved at some future date. Hence he regarded it as reprehensible for a Jew to bequeath his body for anatomical research.[111] In 1852, R. Jacob Ettlinger, a famous German rabbi, further argued that the duty to save life could obligate only the living, not the dead who were free from this as from any other religious obligation.[112] Also, as the saving of life at the expense of one's neighbour's possessions or dignity was in any case questionable,[113] one would not be justified in disturbing the dead even for the immediate cure of a patient with a similar complaint. But he sanctioned the operation if the deceased had sold or allotted his body for that purpose in his lifetime.[114] Both opinions were later opposed by R. Moses Schick, an eminent Hungarian rabbi. He concluded from the Talmud [115] that no-one could renounce the respect due to his body. On the other hand, he held that the talmudic rule whereby all laws (except idolatry, bloodshed, and incest) must give way to the saving of life [116] also applied to the prohibition of disgracing the dead; hence autopsies were warranted if the lives of other existing patients might thereby be preserved.[117] Two leading German rabbis at the time also expressed this view.[118]

In the present century opinions have varied widely. With the growing and direct benefits accruing to medical science from studies on human corpses, some rabbis strongly favoured permitting the practice. The British Chief Rabbi Dr. Hermann Adler, in a memorial address in 1905, lauded the late Frederic David Mocatta for having directed that, if he died from an obscure disease, a post-mortem examination be performed at the expense of his estate "for the advancement of medical science." [119] Rabbi Benzion Uziel, a Chief Rabbi of the Holy Land, saw no objection to the dissection of Jewish bodies, provided it was carried out with due care and respect; but he disapproved of persons selling their bodies before death.[120] Another rabbi even suggested a popular campaign to persuade people to grant their written consent for the dissection of their bodies after death.[121] In favour of the sanction it was argued that to study anatomy by observation did not constitute a forbidden "benefit" from the dead; [122] that any intrinsically prohibited act performed for study purposes was altogether exempt from the original prohibition; [123] that there was no disgrace to the dead when the welfare of the living was at stake; [124] that a ban on anatomical studies would "close the door to medical science"; [125] and that, with hospitals everywhere full of patients actually awaiting the findings of anatomical research and with the speed of modern communications, the objections raised by Ezekiel Landau no longer applied.[126]

Nevertheless, many rabbinic authorities remained implacably opposed to any general sanction of dissection, particularly on Jewish bodies. The American scholar Rabbi Yekuthiel Greenwald has listed an impressive array of rabbis who were adamant in their refusal to countenance autopsies, let alone anatomical experiments, on human bodies. He himself caustically suggested that those desiring their sons to study anatomy or advocating the use of Jewish bodies should bequeath their own bodies for dissection. He would not allow even Jewish suicides and criminals to be delivered to the anatomists, since the Bible stressed the respect due to the dead specifically in regard to executed persons.[127]

Exceptions might be made only in cases of people afflicted by some hereditary disease if an autopsy could help in the proper diagnosis and thus benefit the descendants.[128] A London rabbi, too, advised relatives not to give permission for post-mortem inquests, though they need not resist the demand for autopsies required by law.[129] Even a scholar as modern in outlook and secular learning as Dr. David Hoffmann, the late Rector of the *Rabbiner Seminar* in Berlin, was not prepared to go beyond the restrictive position taken up by Ezekiel Landau nearly two centuries earlier.[130]

The opposition became especially bitter when rabbinical authorities were faced with the problem on a communal scale. For instance, when the "Prosectorium" in Warsaw demanded the supply of Jewish bodies for anatomical studies in 1924, the local rabbinate fiercely resisted the demand.[131] Many rabbis insisted on the ban even if it meant the exclusion of Jews from medical schools or their estrangement from the Jewish faith, unless that attitude might provoke measures against the Jewish community in general.[132] The actual delivery by the Warsaw Burial Society of a Jewish woman's corpse for dissection led to a great upheaval at the time.[133] When the question was raised by a tuberculosis hospital in Denver, U.S.A., the leading American rabbis likewise maintained an uncompromising stand against the supply of Jewish bodies for dissection.[134]

Among the arguments to justify these objections—widely upheld right up to the present—were that dissections involved a proper "benefit" from the dead since they included acts and not merely observation,[135] and since they directly promoted the doctors' material interests; [136] that the motive for disgracing the dead was not the honour of the living but their physical advantage; [137] that all concessions on those grounds were in any case limited to keeping the dead unburied for a maximum of twenty-four hours; [138] that in Jewish law all parts of the body required burial which could not be assured after its dissection; [139] that the indiscriminate renunciation of Jewish bodies would publicly shame the Jewish name; [140] and that any general sanction would lend itself to many abuses which could not be controlled. [141]

The problem became really pressing with the foundation of the Hebrew University at Jerusalem and the planned establishment of a medical school there. Already in 1924 the difficulties were widely discussed in rabbinical circles.[142] But for two decades religious objections to dissection remained an insuperable obstacle to the realization of the project. The University simply had to carry on without a medical school, just as had been the case at several Moslem universities and as was still the case in the State of New Jersey, where anatomical experiments continued to be banned until recently.[143] But with the rise of Israel as an independent state the pressure became so great that an adequate compromise between religious and medical claims had to be found.

Negotiations ensued between Chief Rabbi Dr. Isaac Herzog, acting on behalf of the Chief Rabbinate of Israel, and Dr. Yaski of the "Hadassah" University Hospital at Jerusalem, leading to an agreement whereby post-mortem examinations were sanctioned when (i) they are legally required, (ii) the cause of death cannot otherwise be ascertained, on condition this is formally attested by three physicians (as designated in the agreement), (iii) they may help to save the lives of other existing patients, on condition a similar certification is produced, and (iv) they are required in cases of hereditary diseases to safeguard the health of the surviving relations; provided always, among other stipulations, that the hospital authorities will carry out the autopsies with due reverence for the dead, and that they will deliver the corpses and all parts removed therefrom to the burial society for interment after use.[144] Regarding the use of bodies for medical teaching purposes, Dr. Herzog further issued the following statement: "The Plenary Council of the Chief Rabbinate of Israel . . . do not object to the use of bodies of persons who gave their consent in writing of their own free will during their life-time for anatomical dissections as required for medical studies, provided the dissected parts are carefully preserved so as to be eventually buried with due respect according to Jewish law." [145] In 1953 similar provisions were embodied in the Anatomy and Pathology Law passed by the Israeli Parliament.

In the discussions which led to these decisions, it was emphasized that there could be no distinction in Jewish law whereby "the body of an honoured or rich person must not be dissected, whereas that of a poor or forsaken person could be so used; the sole foundation of a sanction could only be the saving of human life, and in that consideration no difference could be made between one or another." [146] This attitude, as has been observed,[147] is in direct contrast with, for example, the English Warburton Anatomy Act of 1832 which released for anatomical study all bodies which were unclaimed and which civil law therefore regarded as res nullius.[148] In Jewish law it is, on the contrary, the body of a person left without relatives whose burial imposes a special obligation upon the whole community; even the High Priest—otherwise forbidden to defile himself even for his closest next-of-kin— must ignore his sanctity by personally attending to the immediate burial of such a person! [149]

With the concordat reached and in operation between the highest religious and medical authorities in Israel the problem was by no means finally resolved. The argument over those who can no longer speak for themselves continues unabated. The traditionalists charge that the official agreement, itself of doubtful merit, is being abused: far more bodies are subjected to indignity than is really essential, and the dissected parts are not always treated and eventually interred as required by law. The agreement, it is alleged, is being used as a subterfuge to allow the anatomists to lay their hands and knives on the dead with utter disregard to the rights of the deceased and the feelings of their relations.[150] Indeed, the agreement itself is attacked as an excessive surrender to the profanation of Jewish values.[151] The devotees of anatomy, again, complain that popular prejudice and religious opposition still hinder the proper scientific exploitation of the secrets revealed by every dead body for the advancement of medical science.

Lately several religious doctors have also joined in the rabbinical debate, though often in a spirit of polemics rather than of sober enquiry. Friedenwald has listed five medical articles on "Post-mortem Examinations among the Jews" written between 1914 and 1939.[152] To this list a few further contributions could be added.[153] More recently the extreme views of the two camps have been zealously defended by Dr. Sussman Muntner and Dr. Jacob Levy, both of Jerusalem. The two doctors claim that the main debate is now only of academic interest: the former because he believes the rabbinical opposition to be at an end, and the latter because he considers the medical need of bodies at an end. To Dr. Muntner it appears that, in regard to autopsies, "all arguments have already ceased and everyone has now been reconciled to the sanction even from the religious point of view." [154] Virtually all talmudic and rabbinic sources he has collected lead him to the conclusion that there never existed any objection to anatomical dissection; if some Jewish scholars did express a contrary opinion, it was only "because they wished to introduce the heathen concept of the honour of the dead and the ban on dissection into our literature." [155] For Dr. Levy, on the other hand, "the star of anatomy is now sinking." The present tendency is for the science of anatomy—the important findings of which are already known—to be replaced by various physical methods in the diagnosis and treatment of disease. Thus, three most recent and revolutionary advances in medicine—the discovery of penicillin and other antibiotics, heart operations and polio vaccinations—owe their development to biological, chemical, and X-ray research, not to dissection.[156]

In respect of medical training, Dr. Levy admits, some facilities may have to be sacrificed in order to maintain the highest moral and religious standards in the Holy Land. But he suggests that practical anatomy can now be studied on drawings and plastic models, on tissues removed in live operations or imported from abroad, and—if necessary—by a short course at a foreign university.[157] For, in practice, the conditions under which even the more lenient authorities approved of dissection simply cannot be carried out: there can be no respect for the dead in the anatomy room (often there is levity instead!), and it is impossible to ensure that all parts of the corpse are ultimately buried.[158] Dr. Levy denounces the Anatomy and Pathology Law—which permits the dissection of any corpse on medical certification without regard to the wishes of the deceased or his family—as an affront to the freedom of conscience, unparalleled in any other civilized country.

In Israel, he protests, 90% of all who die in hospitals are subjected to autopsies, as against only 30% at the famous Columbia University! Even with this wholesale violation of the dead, he argues, no commensurate advantages either in prestige or in scientific discoveries have accrued to medicine in Israel which would vindicate the disregard for the sanctities of Jewish law.[159]

VI

And so the debate continues. There are no doubt weighty considerations on both sides. The many complex technical arguments advanced in the different rabbinic rulings must not obscure from our view the profound moral issues behind, and embedded in, these discussions. Let us summarize the main principles involved. Were it simply a matter of choosing between life and law, Judaism would require the latter to give way without question. But the issue is not so simple. The conflicting interests are really between those of life and those of the dead. The living are free agents, and as such charged with the supreme duty to preserve life at all costs. Not so the dead. Their bodies are not our property, and *their title to undisturbed rest may be as great as the claim of the living to life.*

The subjective element, too, is of paramount importance. To reduce the human corpse to the utilitarian function of a text-book from which the pages are torn out one by one, and to ransack the body by wanton raids on its scientific treasures is as irreverent to the dead as it is degrading and spiritually hebetating to the living. Those training to bring succour to the sick and the suffering may themselves lose their regard for the dignity of man—the first prerequisite in the practice of the healing art. That loss may well outweigh the gain in medical knowledge. One is reminded of Johnson's scathing attack on animal vivisection two hundred years ago, when he castigated "the anatomical novice . . . [who] prepares himself by familiar cruelty for the profession which he is to exercise upon the tender and the helpless . . . ," and condemned "these horrid operations, which tend to harden the heart, extinguish those sensations which give man confidence in man, and make the physician more dreadful than the gout or stone." [160]

As against these considerations, it seems clear that some of mankind's worst scourges, such as cancer and coronary thrombosis, will not be conquered without the most painstaking studies on thousands of victims from these dread diseases. Modern communications have made the world shrink into a single parish, so that we may consider the revelations of an autopsy in America to be potentially of immediate benefit to a sufferer in Asia. It must also be accepted that a certain amount of experimentation in anatomy is indispensable in the training of competent doctors.

How can these clashing interests be reconciled in conformity with Jewish law? All Jewish religious authorities agree that any sanction of dissection can be contemplated solely on the grounds of its immediate, if only potential, contribution to the saving of life; that the number and extent of autopsies must be limited to an irreducible minimum; that a sense of reverence must be preserved during and after the operation; and that all the remains must be buried as soon as possible with due respect. Prior consent for every autopsy should also be obtained from the subject during his life-time or his family. Ideally all operators should themselves be God-fearing and fully conscious of the dignity with which every human body is endowed as a creation "in the image of God." In their absence, the proposal by Dr. A. H. Merzbach of Israel to establish a council of three religious doctors at every major [Jewish] hospital to determine the necessity of post-mortem examinations [161] is worthy of consideration. Alternatively, hospital chaplains or visiting rabbis might be appointed to sanction and supervise all autopsies in compliance with Jewish law.

Far more perplexing is the problem of dissection for teaching purposes. Happily the aids produced by modern science are often such as help to solve the very problems it creates. It ought now to be possible gradually to replace normal anatomy by the use of artificial models, combined with the experience gained from animal dissections and attendances at surgical operations.

The Mishnah concludes with the significant words: "The Holy One, blessed be He, found no vessel holding greater good for

Israel than peace." [162] Every major prayer in the Jewish liturgy concludes with the craving for peace. Life itself concludes with peace, "for the latter end of man is peace." [163] Life may be worthless if sustained by means of disturbing that peace.

NOTES

1 We have generally retained the British spelling and usage in Dr. Jakobovits' article—Ed.

2 Cf. ' "He shall cause him to be thoroughly healed" (Ex. xxi. 19)—from here [it is deduced] that permission is given to the physician to heal' (*Berakhot* 60a; *Bava Kamma* 85a).

3 Cf. "I kill, and I make alive; I wound and I heal; and there is none that can deliver out of My hand" (Deut. xxxii. 39). See also commentaries of Rashi and Tosaphot, on *Bava Kamma* 85a; Abraham ibn Ezra, on Ex. xxi. 19 and xv. 26; and Nachmanides, on Lev. xxvi. 11.

4 "Ye shall therefore kep My statutes . . ., which if a man do, he shall live by them" (Lev. xviii.5)—"that *he shall live by them*, and not that he shall die by them" (*Yoma* 85b). See also Maimonides, *Yad, Hil. Shabbat*, ii. 3.

5 Cf. "And if a man have committed a sin worthy of death, and he be put to death, and thou hang him on a tree; his body shall not remain all night upon the tree, but thou shalt surely bury him the same day; for he that is hanged is a reproach unto God. . . ." (Deut. xxi. 22–23).

6 Gen. i. 26, 27.

7 Rabbis and physicians are often governed by identical rules of professional conduct; for several examples, see *Tur* and *Bet Yoseph, Yoreh De'ah*, cccxxxvi.

8 See D. Campbell, *Arabian Medicine and its Influence on the Middle Ages*, 1926, vol. i, p. 8.

9 See M. Neuburger, *History of Medicine*, 1910, vol. i, p. 62 f.; and A. Castiglioni, A *History of Medicine*, 1947, p. 102.

10 See Th. Puschmann, A *History of Medical Education*, 1891, p. 14.

11 See Neuburger, *op. cit.*, p. 48; and Castiglioni, *op. cit.*, p. 88.

12 See E. A.W. Budge, *Syrian Anatomy, Pathology and Therapeutics; or "the Book of Medicines"*, 1913, vol. i, p. clxii f.; and vol. ii, pp. 107 and 129.

13 See Budge, *op. cit.*, vol. i, p. xlvii.

14 See Puschmann, *op. cit.*, p. 57.

15 See Th. C. Allbutt, *Greek Medicine in Rome*, 1921, p. 98.

16 See G. Wolff, "Leichenbesichtigung und Untersuchung bis zur Carolina als Vorstufe gerichtlicher Sektion," in *Janus*, vol. xliii (1938), p 228 f.

17 See Neuburger, *op cit.*, p. 150.

18 Gen. l. 2.

19 See G. Maspero, *The Dawn of Civilisation: Egypt and Chaldea*, ed.

A. H. Sayce, 1910, p. 216; Puschmann, *op. cit.*, p. 23; and Castiglioni, *op. cit.*, p. 59.

20 See C. Singer, "Galen as a Modern," in *Proceedings of the Royal Society of Medicine*, vol. vlii (1949), p. 565.

21 Philo, *De special. leg.*, iii. 117; see translation by F. H. Colson, *Loeb Classical Series*, vol. vii, p. 549 f.

22 First made by E. Carmoly (*Histoire des médecins juifs*, 1844, p. 12) and later endorsed by R. Landau (*Geschichte der jeudischen Aerzte*, 1895, p. 15).

23 The allegation is based on a passage in the Talmud (*Sanhedrin* 47b) in which the use of earth from Rab's grave is justified for curing a fever; ostensibly that indicated the people's desire to avenge Rab's (alleged) dissection of the dead by destroying his grave. In fact, the passage evidently describes some form of homage to a saint; see J. Preuss, *Biblisch-Talmudische Medizin*, 1911, pp. 45 and 184.

24 H. Baas, *Outlines of the History of Medicine*, 1889, pp. 37 and 295 (note 2).

25 A. H. Israels, *Collectanes gynaecologica ex Talmude Babylonico*, 1845; cited by H. H. Ploss and M. Bartels, *Woman*, ed. E. J. Dingwall, 1935, vol. i, p. 380 f.; and Puschmann, *op. cit.*, p. 30.

26 *Tosephta, Niddah*, iv. 17; cf. *Niddah* 30b, where the account is slightly varied.

27 A similar report is mentioned by the Roman historian Pliny (*Nat. Hist.*, xix. 27); see Preuss, *op. cit.*, p. 44. Cf. J. Needham, *A History of Embryology* 1934, p. 47.

28 *Bekhorot* 45a.

29 Rabbi Yishmael, though also a physician, probably did not carry out the operation himself because he was of priestly descent; see Preuss, *op. cit.*, p. 46.

30 Hebrew: "*Shalak.*" This is translated as "slit," "anatomised," or "dissected" by J. Levy (*Neuhebraeisches und Chaldaeisches Woerterbuch*, vol. iv, p. 566), A. Kohut (*Aruch Completum*, 1926, vol. viii, p. 90) and M. Jastrow (*A Dictionary of the Targumim*, etc., 1926, p. 1588). But Preuss (*op. cit.*, p. 48), supported in a note by Immanuel Loew, maintains that the word should here, as usual, be rendered "cooked" or "boiled hard." Preuss therefore believes that this may be the only mention of boiling as a method of dissection in antiquity, a method otherwise unknown until Vesalius introduced it.

31 I. L. Katzenelsohn (*Ha-talmud vechokhmat ha-refu'ah*, 1928, p. 237 f.) regards this experiment as the first return to human anatomy since Herophilus and Erasistratos of Alexandria.

32 *Oholot*, i. 8. See Katzenelsohn, *loc. cit.*

33 Thus I. M. Rabinowitch (*Post-Mortem Examinations and Jewish Law*, 1945, p. 25 [note]) argues that the Talmudic figure—at 248 to 252 bones —approximates more closely the findings of modren anatomy (assigning 270

to the new-born, 350 at the age of 14 years and 206 after middle life) than the number given by Hippocrates (111) or Galen (over 200).

34 In a statement ascribed to King David (*Berakhot* 4a).

35 *Sanhedrin* 82a.

36 *Bava Batra* 116a.

37 *Niddah* 24b.

38 With the exception of the last three statements, which have no bearing on medicine, all the preceding accounts deal with observations for ritual purposes. The formation of the foetus affects the laws of uncleanliness in cases of miscarriages. The number of bones in the body determines the defilement caused by touching an incomplete skeleton. The examination of blood and other discharges is necessary to decide whether a woman is ritually pure or not.

39 See note 5, above.

40 See *Sanhedrin* 46b.

41 *Chullin* 11b.

42 See Rabinowitch, *op. cit.*, p. 28; and Preuss, *op. cit.*, p. 46.

43 *Bava Batra* 154a and b; see R. Gershom, *a.l.*

44 *Sanhedrin* 47a.

45 See Wolff, *op. cit.*, pp. 226 and 285.

46 Vesalius himself attributed the decline of dissection since ancient times to the practice of entrusting manual operations to barbers "who were too ignorant to read the writings of the teachers of anatomy"; see translation by B. Farrington, in *Proceedings of the Royal Society of Medicine*, vol. xxv (1932), p. 1357; cited by B. J. Stern, *Society and Medical Progress*, 1941, p. 13.

47 The charge of human vivisection, repeated by Augustine elsewhere (*De anima, iv.* 3 and 6), was already levelled by the 1st century writer Celsus (*Proem*) against the Alexandrian anatomists; it was also sustained by Tertullian (*De anima*, x). It is probably quite unjustified; see C. Singer, *The Evolution of Anatomy*, 1925, p. 34 f.

48 Augustine, *The City of God*, lib. xxii, cap. xxiv (*A Select Library of the Nicene and Post-Nicene Fathers of the Christian Church*, ed. Ph. Schaff, 1903, vol. ii, p. 503); see Stern, *op. cit.*, p. 179 f.

49 Singer, "Galen as a Modern," *op. cit.*, p. 570.

50 H. E. Sigerist, "Die Geburt der abendlaendischen Medizin," in *Essays on the History of Medicine, presented to K. Sudhoff*, ed. Singer and Sigerist, 1924, p. 196.

51 See Puschmann, *op. cit.*, p. 144.

52 *Ibid.*, p. 202.

53 *Ta'anit* 21b. The belief survived to modern times, though Tyson had dismissed it as a "vulgar error"; see F. J. Cole, *A History of Comparative Anatomy*, 1944, p. 48.

54 See D. Riesman, *Medicine in Modern Society*, 1939, p. 94.

55 See Puschmann, *op. cit.*, p. 244.

56 See Mary N. Alston, "Attitude of the Church to Dissection before 1500," in *Bulletin of the History of Medicine*, vol. xvi (1944), p. 225 f.

57 See W. Osler, *The Evolution of Modern Medicine*, 1921, p. 146.

58 See C. Singer, *The Evolution of Anatomy*, 1925, p. 71.

59 *Ibid.*, p. 73; and Puschmann, *op. cit.*, p. 244 f.

60 See Puschmann, *op. cit.*, p. 247.

61 See Sigerist, *op. cit.*, p. 196 f.; and Castiglioni, *op. cit.*, p. 375.

62 See Puschmann, *op. cit.*, p. 249 f.

63 See Osler, *op. cit.*, p. 116.

64 *Ibid.*, p. 148; and H. Rashdall, *The Universities of Europe in the Middle Ages*, 1936, vol. i, p. 148.

65 D. J. Guthrie, *A History of Medicine*, 1945, p. 159.

66 *Ibid.*

67 See F. H. Garrison, *An Introduction to the History of Medicine*, 1929, p. 282.

68 *Ibid.*, p. 398.

69 For the text of this Bull, see J. J. Walsch, *The Popes and Science*, 1912, p. 32 ff.

70 So H. Haeser (see *Catholic Encyclopedia*, vol. i, p. 458), J. L. Pagel (*ibid.*), M. Neuburger (*Geschichte der Medizin*, 1906, vol. ii, p. 432), Walsch (*op. cit.*, p. 28 ff.), Garrison (*op. cit.*, p. 161), Rashdall (*op. cit.*, vol. i, p. 244 f.), and Castiglioni (who omits the reference to the Bull altogether).

71 S. R. Virchow ("Morgagni and the Anatomical Concept," in *Bulletin of the History of Medicine*, vol. vii [1939], p. 981), R. Park (*An Epitome of the History of Medicine*, 1903, p. 93), Baas (*op. cit.*, p. 295), Puschmann (*op. cit.*, p. 245), Allbutt (*op. cit.*, p. 476), Stern (*op. cit.*, p. 177 ff.) and Singer (*op. cit.*, p. 85 f.).

72 Thus Mondino declared: "The bones which are below the 'os basilare' cannot well be seen unless they are removed and boiled, but owing to the sin involved in this I pass them by" (*From the Fasciculo di Medicina*, Venice, 1493; ed. C. Singer, 1925, p. 96).

73 Around 1340 the famous physician Guido de Vigevano expressly stated (in his *Anatomy*) that the Church forbade dissection; see Alston, *op. cit.*, p. 225 f. In 1519 Pope Leo X denied Leonardo da Vinci admission to the hospital at Rome, where he wished to study anatomy, because he had engaged in dissection; see J. P. McMurrick, "Leonardo da Vinci and Vesalius," in *Medical Library and Historical Journal*, vol. ix (1906), p. 344; cited by Stern, *op. cit.*, p. 177. A little later Vesalius complained that "the ecclesiastical caucus would not countenance the vivisection of the brain" (see Cole, *op. cit.*, p. 57) and that in Madrid he could not lay his hands on as much as a dried skull; see M. Forster, *History of Physiology*, 1901, p. 17.

74 See Rashdall, *loc. cit.*; Puschmann, *op. cit.*, p. 327; and Sigerist, *op. cit.*, p. 197.

75 In 1482 Pope Sixtus IV authorised dissections provided ecclesiastical

sanction was first obtained, a practice again confirmed by Pope Clement VII in 1524; see Singer, *The Evolution of Anatomy*, p. 85 f.; and Castiglioni, *op. cit.*, p. 368.

76 See G. Sarton, *Introduction to the History of Science*, 1927, vol. ii, pp. 783 and 1081; and Stern, *loc. cit.*

77 See A. H. Buck, *The Growth of Medicine from the Earliest Times to about 1500*, 1917, p. 346.

78 From the 15th century onwards, experimental anatomy was greatly stimulated by the desire of artists to portray the human body realistically. Among those who engaged in dissection were Verrocchio, Andrea Manegno, Lucio Signorelli, Pollajuolo, Donatello, Leonardo da Vinci, Albrecht Duerer, Michelangelo, and Raphael; see Stern, *op. cit.*, p. 49; and Guthrie, *op. cit.*, p. 135.

79 See Alston, *op. cit.*, p. 221 ff. For the full text of the reply, see Th. Puschmann, *Handbuch der Geschichte der Medizin*, 1902, vol. ii, p. 227; and Walsch, *op. cit.*, p. 58 f.

80 The present-day Code of Canon Law only regards the "dishonouring of the bodies of the dead by theft or other crimes committed on the bodies or graves of the deceased" as a penal offence, but not dissection for medical ends; see S. Woywood, *A Practical Commentary on the Code of Canon Law*, 1926, vol. i, p. 526; and vol. ii, p. 479.

81 Rashdall, *op. cit.*, vol. ii, p. 136.

82 P. L. Burshell, *Ancient History of Medicine*, 1878, p. 18.

83 See Puschmann, *Medical Education*, p. 163; Osler, *op. cit.*, p. 102; Garrison, *op. cit.*, p. 135; E. G. Brown, *Arabian Medicine*, 1921, p. 36 f.; and M. Meyerhof, "Science and Medicine," in *Legacy of Islam*, ed. T. Arnold and A. Guillaume, 1931, p. 344.

84 See Ploss and Bartels, *op. cit.*, vol. iii, p. 8.

85 See B. Stern, *Medizin, Aberglaube und Geschlechtsleben in der Tuerkei*, 1903, vol. i, p. 53.

86 See S. Muntner, "Persian Medicine and Its Relation to Jewish and Other Medical Science," in *The Hebrew Medical Journal*, vol. xxv (1952), p. 202.

87 See Stern, *op. cit.*, p. 54.

88 See Castiglioni, *op. cit.*, p. 284.

89 H. Friedenwald, *The Jews and Medicine*, 1944, vol. i, p. 192.

90 *Ibid.*, p. 251. Astruc (1684–1766) was himself of Jewish descent.

91 The charge occurs, for instance, in *The Healing Art the Right Hand of the Church*, 1859, p. 111 f.; and in *A General Exposition of the General State of the Medical Profession*, by "Alexipharmacus," 1829, p. 12.

92 See Preuss, *op. cit.*, p. 45; and Rabinowitch, *op. cit.*, p. 23 f.

93 For that reason graves should be marked; see *Mo'ed Katan* 5a. Following this law, Jacob Ettlinger (responsa *Shomer Tziyon*, no. 213) ruled that one must not preserve in spirit even a foetus for anatomical studies; see also Moses Schick, responsa *MaHaRaM Shik, Yoreh De'ah*, no. 344.

94 Aderet, responsa *RaSHBA*, no. 369; see H. J. Zimmels, *Magicians, Theologians and Doctors*, 1952, p. 58.

95 *Yoreh De'ah*, ccclxiii. 2, gloss.

96 So first the questioner in R. Ezekiel Landau's famous responsum (*Noda Bi-yehudah*, part ii, no. 210). See also A. A. Price, *Mishnat Abraham* on *Sefer Chasidim*, 1955, p. 179.

97 Cf. *Shabbat* 152b. Hence also the rule to bury the dead in direct contact with the earth; see *Yer. Kilayim*, ix. 3; and *Yoreh De'ah*, ccclxii. 1.

98 Ibn Zimra, responsa *RaDBaZ*, part i, no. 484; see Zimmels, *op. cit.*, p. 58.

99 Isaac Elchanan of Kovno, responsa *Eyn Yitzchak*, *Yoreh De'ah*, no. 33; see Zimmels, *loc. cit.*

100 So D. Z. Katzburg (in *Tel Talpiyot*, vol. xxxi [1924], p. 123), based on the assertion by C. J. D. Azulai (*Debash Lefi*, Livorno, 1801, no. 20) that "Maimonides was familiar with all sciences . . . including anatomy." A similar view was already expressed by Isaac ben Sheshet Barfat (responsa *RIBaSH*, no. 447) in the 15th century. Benzion Uziel (responsa *Mishpetei Uziel*, no. 4), too, maintained that "without doubt all our early rabbis who were also competent doctors must have examined dead bodies for study purposes" (quoted by S. Muntner, *Ba'ayat ha-nitu'ach vechokhmat ha-bittur be-yisrael*, 1955, p. 9).

101 Friendenwald, *op. cit.*, vol. i, p. 334; see also pp. 339 (note), 342, and 381 ff.

102 Amatus, *Centuria* i, cur. 52; see I. Muenz, *Die juedischen Aerzte im Mittelalter*, 1922, p. 112 f.; and Friedenwald, *op. cit.*, pp. 338 and 354.

103 See C. Singer, "Science and Judaism," in *The Jews: Their History; Culture and Religion*, ed. L. Finkelstein, 1949, vol. iii, p. 1069.

104 Friedenwald, *op. cit.*, p. 312.

105 J. Zahalon, *Otzar Ha-chayyim*, Venice, 1683; see J. Leibowitz, "On the Plague in the Ghetto at Rome," in reprint from *Dappim Rephu'im*, 1943, p. 3.

106 The illustration is reproduced in *Jewish Encyclopedia*, vol. iii, p. 162; and in *Encyclopedia Hebraica*, vol. iv, p. 406.

107 *Address to the Public, Drawn from Nature and Religion, against the Unlimited Dissection of Human Bodies*, London, 1829, p. 7.

108 See S. W. Baron, *The Jewish Community*, 1942, vol. ii, p. 151; citing Antonio Ciscato, *Gli Ebrei in Padova*, Padua, 1901; see also *Jewish Encyclopedia*, vol. ix, p. 459. Complaints of "body-snatching" from Jewish cemeteries were also made in London in the 18th century (see *The Jewish Chronicle* [London], March 25, 1955) and in America in the 19th century (see note 99 above).

109 J. Emden, responsa *She'ilat Ya'abetz*, part i, no. 41. As this decision is dated Shevat 15, 5497 (corresponding to January 17, 1737), the enquiry leading to it can hardly have been prompted by the similar question answered in Rome in the same year.

110 E. Landau, responsa *Noda Bi-yehudah*, part ii, no. 210; see Rabinowitch, *op. cit.*, p. 28 f.

111 M. Schreiber, responsa *Chatam Sofer, Yoreh De'ah*, no. 336.

112 Hence, for example, the dead may be clothed in shrouds made of materials Jews must not otherwise wear (*Yoreh De'ah*, cccli. 1).

113 The question is already raised in the Talmud (*Baba Kamma* 60b). For further sources on the subject, see *Talmudic Encyclopedia*, vol. v, p. 457.

114 J. Ettlinger, responsa *Binyan Tziyon*, no. 170.

115 The Talmud assumes that burial is required to prevent disgrace; hence a person's expressed desire not to be buried must not be fulfilled (*Sanhedrin* 46b).

116 *Pesachim* 25b; cf. *Sanhedrin* 74a.

117 M. Schick, responsa *MaHaRaM Shik, Yoreh De'ah*, no. 347.

118 B. H. Auerbach (*Nachal Eshkol*, 1868, part ii, p. 117 ff.); and S. Bamberger (responsa *Zekher Simchah*, no. 158).

119 H. Adler, *Anglo-Jewish Memories*, 1909, p. 137.

120 B. Uziel, responsa *Mishpetei Uziel, Yoreh De'ah*, nos. 28 and 29.

121 Hillel Posek, in *Ha-posek* (Tel Aviv), vol. vi (1949), no. 111 (Ab 5709).

122 See Joseph Zweig, responsa *Porat Yosef*, no. 17; and Price, *Mishnat Abraham, op. cit.*, p. 180. See also Simon Gruenfeld, in *Tel Talpiyot*, vol. xxxi (1924), pp. 117 and 122.

123 Eliezer Duenner, *Zikhron Abraham Mosheh*, 1945, p. 82 ff.; based on the permission to engage in sorcery for study purposes, though otherwise biblically forbidden (*Sanhedrin* 68a).

124 So Bamberger, *loc. cit.*; D. Z. Katzburg, in *Tel Talpiyot, op. cit.*, p. 130; Hillel Posek, *loc. cit.*; Uziel, *loc. cit.*; and Zweig, *loc. cit.*

125 J. L. Lewin, in *Yagdil Torah*, vol. viii, no. 31; cited by J. D. Eisenstein, *Otzar Dinim Uminhagim*, 1917, p. 453. See also Uziel, *loc. cit.*

126 See Hillel Posek, *loc. cit.*; Duenner, *loc. cit.*; and Price, *op. cit.*, p. 184. Cf. also Rabinowitch, *op. cit.*, p. 29.

127 Y. J. Greenwald, *Kol Bo*, 1947, vol. i, p. 40 f.

128 *Ibid.* p. 44 f.

129 Asher Gronis, *Peri Asher*, 1936, no. 3.

130 D. Hoffmann, responsa *Melamed Le-ho'il, Yoreh De'ah*, no. 109.

131 See Yehuda Meir Schapira, responsa *Or Ha-me'ir*, part i, no. 74.

132 *Ibid.*; see also David Menahem Babad, responsa *Chabatzelet Hasharon, Yoreh De'ah*, no. 95; and authorities cited by Greenwald, *loc. cit.*

133 See Elazar Hayim Schapira, responsa *Minchat Elazar*, part iv, no. 25; cited by Greenwald, *loc. cit.*

134 See *Yagdil Tovah*, vol. vii, p. 17; and vol. viii; cited by Greenwald, *loc. cit.*

135 See Moses Jonah Zweig, responsa *Ohel Mosheh*, part i, no. 4. See also Jacob Levy, "Nituchei Metim Be-yisrael," in *Ha-ma'yon*, vol. iii. (1956), p. 26.

136 *Ibid.*, and Babad, *loc. cit.*

137 See M. J. Zweig, *loc. cit.*

138 *Ibid.*, based on Malkiel Tzevi Halevy of Lomza, responsa *Divrei Malkiel*, part ii, no. 95.

139 See Y. M. Schapira, in *Or Ha-me'ir, loc. cit.* See also Levy, *op. cit.*, p. 29.

140 See M. J. Zweig, *loc. cit.*

141 See following pages.

142 See Katzburg, in *Tel Talpiyot, loc. cit.*; quoting Hayim Hirschson, *Malki Ba-kodesh.*

143 See Ch. LaWall, *Four Thousand Years of Pharmacy*, 1927, p. 133.

144 See M. D. Silberstein, "Ba'ayat Nitu'ach Ha-metim Upitronah," in *Yavneh* (Jerusalem), 1949, p. 214 ff. (Nisan 5709); and in *Dat Yisrael Umedinat Yisrael*, 1951, p. 159 ff.

145 *Ibid.*, p. 161. The terms of the agreement are also given and fully discussed by Eliezer Judah Waldenberg (a member of the Chief Rabbinate), responsa *Tzitz Eliezer*, part iv, no. 14.

146 Silberstein, *loc. cit.*

147 *Ibid.*

148 The Act still governs the law in England.

149 See Lev. xxi. 11, and Rashi, *a.l.* This point is emphasized by Levy, *op. cit.*, p. 25.

150 See Levy, *op. cit.*, p. 28 f.

151 *Ibid.*, and *The Jewish Chronicle, loc. cit.*

152 Friedenwald, *op. cit.*, vol. i, p. 126. The articles listed are: C. D. Spivak, "Post-Mortem Examinations Among the Jews," in *New York Medical Journal*, June 13, 1914, p. 11; N. Mosessohn, "Post-Mortem Examinations Among the Jews," in *Jewish Tribune*, December 18, 1914; J. Z. Lauterback, "The Jewish Attitude Toward Autopsy," in *The Jewish Indicator*, October 30, 1925; M. Robinson, "The Advancement of Science through Autopsy," in *The Synagogue Light*, Brooklyn, February 1938; and O. Saphir, "Autopsies Among Jews," in *Medical Leaves*, 1939.

153 Apart from the monographs and articles by Rabinowitch, Silberstein, Muntner, and Levy already noted, the following could be added: H. L. Gordon, "Bedikat Metei Yisrael al pin Dinei Yisrael," in *The Hebrew Medical Journal*, 1937, part i, p. 141 ff.; M. Greiber, *Nituach Ha-metim Le-tzorkhei Limmud Vachakirah*, Jerusalem, 1943; and A. Kottler, "The Jewish Attitude on Autopsy," in *New York State Journal of Medicine*, 1957, p. 1649 ff.

154 Muntner, *op. cit.*, p. 3.

155 *Ibid.*, p. 6.

156 Levy, *op. cit.*, p. 30. This trend was also confirmed by Professor H. Baruk of the Sorbonne (as reported in *Ha-aretz*, Elul 7, 1955); see Levy, *loc. cit.* (note 25).

157 *Ibid.*, p. 31. In fact, Prof. Baruk offered to supply Jerusalem with all materials required for a model anatomical institute to dispense with dissection; see Levy, *loc. cit.*

158 *Ibid.*, p. 28 f.
159 *Ibid.*, pp. 21 and 30 (note 23).
160 Johnson, in *Idler*, no. 17 (August 5, 1758).
161 A. H. Merzbach, in *Dat Yisrael Umedinat Yisrael*, 1951, p. 150.
162 *Uktzin*, iii. 12.
163 Ps. xxxvii. 37.

BIBLICAL STUDIES

DAVID S. SHAPIRO

*

The Rationalism of
Ancient Jewish Thought

I

UNLIKE Greek philosophy, the Old Testament never indulges in
any speculation about the *arche*, the origin of the world which is
inherent in it so long as it endures, and which makes the continuance
of the world and the events staged within it rationally intelligible as
a unity. Certainly, God is the Creator, the source of all life from
of old and for all time. But He is the Creator of the world. The
doctrine of creation is not a speculative cosmogony, but a confession
of faith, of faith in God as Lord. The world belongs to Him, and
He upholds it by His power. He sustains human life, and man owes
Him obedience. It is symptomatic that Hebrew monotheism did not
originate in theoretical reflection. It was implicit in the Israelite belief
in God from the outset, and it was only gradually clarified in the
course of historical experience.[1]

THIS quotation from the writings of a modern theologian and
historian is typical of the prevailing view regarding the origin
of Israel's religious outlook. The Hebrews are regarded as essentially a simple, naive folk, unencumbered by sophistication and
speculative propensities. Were this a judgment of ingenuous believers who accept the faith of Israel as the product of divine revelation handed down full-blown from heaven to men walking in
darkness, we would be hardly surprised. But that historians for
whom the religion of Israel is a product of an evolutionary process
should maintain that ratiocination and philosophizing had nothing to do with this process is rather bizarre. Speculative thinking
has undoubtedly been going on from the very dawn of history.
Man has always been asking questions and devising answers. That

things were different in Israel, that questions were not asked and answers not propounded in that culture, is not only incredible; it is contrary to the testimony of the Bible itself which quotes opinions of a heretical character and the musings of questioning minds.[2] It includes numerous reflections on the character of human life, and its heroes have the temerity to hurl challenging questions at the Almighty Himself.[3] The Scriptures attempt to counter the arguments of the "foolish" and "brutish" men by appealing to reason [4] just as they expose idolatry for its immorality and even more ludicrous unreasonableness.[5]

It should prove rather difficult to account for the absence of reflective thinking in the development of a religious system which, in the long run, turned out to be the most rational of all faiths. The claim that Israel's faith is grounded in a divine revelation does not in any way negate the speculative character of its origins. A divine answer can confirm the rational deductions of human beings as well as their hopes. There are many roads that lead to God. Many a man of faith has travelled the pathway of reason. That a prophet of God may also be a philosopher need not be rejected *a priori*.[6] In Jewish tradition, Abraham is conceived of as a profound thinker who arrived at religious truth by means of speculation only to have his rational certainties verified by a direct communication from God.[7]

The Holy Writings picture monotheism not as having arisen in a vacuum, but as having been preserved within a select circle through which the teachings concerning the sovereignty of God, His unity, and His spiritual character were handed down from one generation to the other. Our tradition speaks of the schools presided over by Shem and Ever.[8] The doctrines of these schools very likely found their way into various cultures of antiquity and left their vestiges in many, if not all, codes and moralistic writings.[9] Moreover, Abraham was said to have attained a full knowledge of the will of God by the sheer power of his own reasoning.[10] This was never regarded by tradition as inconsonant with either the need or the fact of the Sinaitic revelation. Discovery of truth by speculation and its authentication by divine disclosure were never regarded in Judaism as mutually exclusive.[11]

II

Philosophic speculation revolves basically around the problem of unity—the search for a unifying principle or abiding reality within a world of constant flux. The major achievement of the faith of Israel—the doctrine of monotheism—represents not merely a triumph of faith, but also the triumph of reason. Man's constitution makes it impossible for him to find sane and rational contentment without positing a unitary ground of harmony. Pagan man undoubtedly suffered from the schizophrenic character of his world-outlook. There was no tranquility in his soul because he had failed to find the *principium rationis* which a human being needs as much as bread. The quest for unity within diversity could not but have occupied the minds of thoughtful men every-where—even prior to the intense search for this unity in Ionia and Hellas or on the banks of the Indus and the Ganges. Witness the monistic tendencies in pagan religions which not only reflect a primeval revelation but also the deep-seated need of human beings for a rational *Weltanschauung*. Israel's religious strivings and achievements can no less than others' mirror man's urgent concern for the discovery of rational meaning in the labyrinthine maze of existence.

The Greek philosopher Anaxagoras posited *Nous* or mind as the ultimate ground of all existence.[12] In Israel, this conclusion had already been arrived at a long time before. That the Hebrews pondered over the problems of permanence and transience which led Anaxagoras to his discovery of *Nous* is evident from biblical sources. Like others, before and after them, they observed that ours is a world of change. There is a constant flux, genesis and degeneration, alteration and transformation, birth and death. Is there anything permanent in this fluid world? It is transparently clear that the ephemeral character of reality troubled them considerably:

All flesh is grass,
And all the goodliness thereof is as the flower of the field;
The grass withereth, the flower fadeth . . .
Surely the people is grass (Isaiah 40:6–7).

In the morning they are like grass which groweth up.
In the morning it flourisheth, and groweth up;
In the evening it is cut down, and withereth (Psalm 90:5–6).

And the everlasting mountains are dashed to pieces,
The ancient hills do bow (Habakkuk 3:6).

Plants, animals, men, and empires are all subject to this everlasting law of change. "Behold, the nations are like a drop from
a bucket, and are accounted as the dust on the scales; behold, he
taketh up the isles like fine dust" (Is. 40:15). Is there an abiding
and permanent existence within the world of evanescence? The
human mind cannot be at rest until it discovers this enduring
reality which transcends all forms of change and transiency. The
Hebrews found this permanent reality not in any aspect of the
phenomenal world. They were not seeking for this permanence,
like Thales and Anaximander, within the protean world itself.
They could find nothing in it that *per se* was of enduring character. They sought this reality outside the phenomenal world. They
discovered God, the continuously abiding and everlastingly existent
Reality Who alone persists when everything else has perished.
The very name by which God makes Himself known to the Hebrews is expressive of the eternal and changeless character of the
reality for which they had been searching. The Tetragrammaton,
God's proper name, is expressive of being, because He is being in
the true sense of the word and the source of all secondary, derivative forms of being. To Moses He reveals His full name as EHYEH
ASHER EHYEH or simply EHYEH which describes His un-
changing character as seen by Himself. His name in the mouth
of human beings is the Tetragrammaton in third person,[13] "This
is My name forever, this is My memorial for all generations"
(Exodus 3:15). This is the eternal name of God, because it expresses the eternal character of God, the only enduring Reality in
the universe. The conception of God as eternal Reality could be
intelligible only to a people capable of reflective thinking.
    Hebrew thought, to be consistent, and consistent it was, realized
that the universe which manifests its evanescent character in all
its aspects, could not have been eternally existent. But there is an
eternal God. The conclusion could be only that God has created

this universe. Actually, this reasoning turns out to be none other than the cosmological proof for the existence of God, a proof which is based on the contingent nature of the world. The contrast of the transiency of the world and the eternity of God is vividly emphasized in biblical writing:

> Of old Thou didst lay the foundation of the earth;
> And the heavens are the work of Thy hands.
> They shall perish but Thou shalt endure;
> Yea, all of them shall wax old like a garment;
> As a vesture shalt Thou change them, and they shall pass away;
> But Thou art the selfsame,
> And Thy years shall have no end (Ps. 102:26–28).

> Know ye not? hear ye not?
> Hath it not been told you from the beginning?
> Have ye not *understood* the foundations of the earth?
> It is He that sitteth above the circle of the earth,
> And the inhabitants thereof are as grasshoppers;
> That stretcheth out the heavens as a curtain,
> And spreadeth them out as a tent to dwell in;
> That bringeth princes to nothing;
> He maketh the judges of the earth as a thing of nought.
> Scarce are they planted, scarce are they sown,
> Scarce hath their stock taken root in the earth;
> When he bloweth upon them they wither,
> And the whirlwind taketh them away as stubble . . .
> Lift up your eyes on high,
> And see: who hath created these? (Is. 40:21 ff.).

God is thus proclaimed as the one who created heaven and earth in the beginning.

I I I

Ernst Cassirer [14] makes the following assertion: "To mythical and religious feeling nature becomes one great society, the society of life. Man is not endowed with outstanding rank in this society. He is a part of it but he is in no respect higher than any other member. Life possesses the same religious dignity in its humblest and in its highest forms. Men and animals, animals and plants are all on the same level." It might be assumed by implication that inanimate creation is also included in this fellowship of life. Perhaps it should be posited that in the higher religions all existence consists of a fellowship, a fellowship of gods. All existence is equally divine. The whole world is full of gods, as Thales put it.[15]

In biblical thought there is no vestige of this fellowship in which all that exists is of the same significance. The basic postulate of the biblical writers is that the sensual world is, by and of itself, lifeless. Matter is not a god, nor is it full of gods. Alone, it is completely inanimate, and that which is dead cannot produce life. But there is life within nature. Everything alive lives because of a spirit (*ruach*) which informs it. And whatever possesses the spirit of life is born and dies. The spirit is a separable aspect of living things. "Thou withdrawest their spirit (*ruach*), they perish, and return to their dust; Thou sendest forth Thy spirit (*ruach*), they are created; and Thou renewest the face of the earth" (Ps. 104:29–30). Plants, animals, and men are all mortal. They are kindred to inanimate matter, from which they are distinguished only by the spirit of life. But the spirit comes and goes, appears and evanesces, and is no more divine than matter. What then is the source of this spirit in the animal and vegetable kingdoms? How does motion originate in the inanimate world? The answer given by the biblical thinkers is: God Whose Spirit is, of course, not to be taken as a distinct entity, but as His creative will expressing itself. This infinite Will or *Ruach* is the source of the manifold finite spirits through whose mediacy life is transmitted to created beings.

This writer has suggested elsewhere [16] that the first chapter of Genesis contains more than a record of the order of creation. It presents its outlook on the nature of contingent reality and what it finds to be the Permanent and Abiding Reality in all of existence. It presents an implicit demonstration, at the same time, of the existence of God, the Creator and the Fashioner, based on this new conception of the nature of matter. We are presented with a picture of the earth at the initial stages of creation: "Now the earth was *tohu va-vohu* and darkness was on the face of the deep" (Gen. 1:2). The phrase *tohu-vohu*, which is found in two other passages in the Bible (Jer. 4:23; Is. 34:11), appears to mean waste, desolate, lifeless. Matter as such, the writer seems to emphasize, is completely devoid of life. Light itself, through which life becomes possible, is lifeless. It is the creation of God. Since all matter, as such, is inanimate, it must, like light, be the product of God's creative word. All life originates in the spirit of God which hovered over the face of the waters and endowed them with the power of motion. The Scriptures do not speak of God as hovering over the face of the waters—this expression would have been too anthropomorphic (the Bible permits anthropomorphisms only in reference to God's relationship with man)—but of His *Ruach* through which life and motion are imparted to all beings.

I V

The conception of a constantly changing and inanimate nature, by itself devoid of the spirit of life, leads to the conception of a Reality of a permanent and eternal nature that is empowered to endow existence with a spirit of life. While it is generally accepted that the concept of God is the primary datum of the Bible, this is true insofar as the awareness of God in the Bible is the product of immediate intuition or direct communication with God, the possibility of which is accepted as axiomatic by the biblical writers. However, in the reflective thinking of the Bible, God is the product of logical necessity. This is evident from the fact that reason is invoked to testify to the truth of God's being. Thus we read in Isaiah (40:26):

> Lift up your eyes on high, and see who hath created these.
> He that bringeth out their host by number,
> He calleth them all by name;
> By the greatness of His might,
> And for that He is strong in power, not one faileth.

The question raised is more than rhetorical. Some verses previously, the prophet asked: "Know ye not? Hear ye not? . . . Have ye not *understood* the foundations of the earth?" The *lifting of one's eyes* can imply an attitude of arrogance (Is. 37:23). One can *lift up his eyes on high* and be drawn away to worship the motley host of heaven (Deut. 4:19). Isaiah exhorts his listeners to lift their eyes heavenward and see for themselves that God has created the heavenly bodies. The argument of the prophet appears to be that since the heavenly hosts make their appearance regularly without fail, they must have been created by God. Were they divine beings or independent powers they could not be under the absolute and complete sway of God. There would be havoc and disorder in heaven alone. Only God can establish peace in His high places.[17]

The biblical writers know that there are regularities which characterize the universe that we know. They speak of the "ordinances" of heaven and earth (chukkim):

Thus saith the Lord: If My covenant be not with day and night, if I have not appointed the ordinances of heaven and earth . . . (Jer. 33:25).

Thus saith the Lord: Who giveth the sun for a light by day, and the ordinances of the moon and of the stars for a light by night . . . if these ordinances depart from before Me . . . (Ibid., 31:35–36).

Fear ye not Me? saith the Lord; will ye not tremble at My presence? Who have placed the sand for the bound of the sea, an everlasting ordinance which it cannot pass . . . (Ibid., 5:22).

He hath established them for ever and ever; He hath made a decree which shall not be transgressed (Ps. 148:6).

Knowest thou the ordinances of the heavens? (Job 38:33).

While this concept of the "ordinance" (chok) is also found elsewhere in the Bible in reference to the bounds and regularities set upon nature,[18] it is not found in the Pentateuch. Here the regular order of the physical world is spoken of as the "covenant" between God and the earth (Gen. 9:13), so that the world will persevere at all times, and "while the earth remaineth, seedtime and harvest, and cold and heat, and summer and winter, and day and night shall not cease" (Ibid., 8:22). Whatever permanence obtains in the world of flux is not inherent in its structure as such. It originates in the Will of the only abiding Reality.

The existence of these ordinances is evidence to the biblical

writers that there is one Harmony that informs the entire universe.
Although not explicated in the Scriptures, the sense of the argument might be taken as similar to that presented by the medi-
evals,[19] that the uniformity of nature makes the hypothesis of a
multiplicity of divine powers either impossible, if they were to be
in conflict among themselves, or totally superfluous, if there were
cooperative endeavor among them. Perhaps this is the sense of the
words of Isaiah:

> Who hath meted out the spirit of the Lord?
> And who was His counsellor that he might instruct Him?
> With whom took He counsel and who instructed Him,
> And taught Him in the path of right,
> And taught Him knowledge,
> And made Him to know the way of discernment?

Could God possibly need a teacher to guide Him? If there are
others who are wiser, then He is not God. If He is wisest, He
has no need of others.[20]

Since the doctrine of the multiplicity of powers finds fertile
ground where the unity of the cosmos is not accepted, the recognition of an all-encompassing harmony renders polytheism
totally impossible:

> I form the light and create darkness;
> I make peace and create evil;
> I am the Lord that doeth all these things (Is. 45:7).

I V

The wisdom apparent in the universe not only filled the biblical writers with wonderment; it proved to them the existence
of a Creator and a beneficent Providence. The infinite variety of
creatures in the world is evidence of a divine wisdom. "How
manifold are Thy works, O Lord! In wisdom hast Thou made
them all; the earth is full of Thy creatures" (Ps. 104:24).[21] There
is not a mere mechanical unity that permeates all existence, but
there is a diversity within this unity which evinces the creative
powers of a divine Artisan. The human artist is filled "with the

spirit of God to work in all manner of workmanship, to devise skillful works, to work in gold, silver, brass, and in cutting of stones, and in carving of wood" (Ex. 31:3–5). All this varied ability, the gift of God, constitutes man's wisdom, understanding, and knowledge, and is but a pale reflection of the divine wisdom which operates with all sorts of materials to fashion its manifold works.

However, not only in the diversity of the physical properties of the various creatures is this wisdom manifest. The provisions that every creature finds ready-made for its sustenance, the amazing adaptation of creatures to their environment, the perpetuation of species, are all evidence to the Scriptures not of a chance relationship, but of the purposeful activity of a super-human Providence that watches over and cares for all creatures, with wisdom and compassion:

Who sendeth forth springs into the valleys;
They run between the mountains;
They give drink to every beast of the field,
The wild asses quench their thirst . . .
All of them wait for Thee,
That Thou mayest give them their food in due season.
Thou givest it to them, they gather it;
Thou openest Thy hand, they are satisfied with good (Ps. 104:10 ff.).

The eyes of all wait for Thee,
And Thou givest them their food in due season.
Thou openest Thy hand,
And satisfiest every living thing with favour (Ps. 145:15–16).

When his young ones cry unto God,
And wander for lack of food? (Job 38:41).

The miracle of birth and maturation of animals,[22] the passion of certain animals for freedom and their refusal to submit to the domination of man, in contrast to the readiness, on the other hand, of other creatures to allow their domestication,[23] the success of creatures who have seemingly been deprived of wisdom by their Creator to perpetuate themselves and thrive,[24] the martial glory of the horse,[25] the majestic soaring of the mighty birds and their distance-conquering vision,[26] the monsters with whom man struggles, and those whom he cannot even approach [27]—all these facts of nature cannot be the product of blind forces in a meaningless world. So the Scriptures reason.

Even greater evidence for a wise and beneficent Creator are the wonders of the human body, and its development from the embryo into a full-grown person.

For Thou hast made my reins;
Thou hast knit me together in my mother's womb.
I will give thanks unto Thee, for I am fearfully and wonderfully made;
Wonderful are Thy works;
And that my soul knoweth right well (Ps. 139:13–14).

Hast Thou not poured me out as milk,
And curdled me like cheese?
Thou hast clothed me with skin and flesh,
And knit me together with bones and sinews.
Thou hast granted me love and favour,
And Thy Providence hath preserved my spirit (Job 10:10–12).

The regularity of the processes of nature, the wisdom manifested in the variety and unique qualities of the innumerable creatures, the mercy evident in adaptation of all forms of life to the world, in addition to the wondrous beauty and magnificence of the heaven and earth, make the Psalmist break forth in song:

O Lord, our Lord, how glorious is Thy name in all the earth! Whose majesty is rehearsed above the heavens (Ps. 8:82).

The heavens declare the glory of God,
And the firmament showeth His handiwork (*Ibid.*, 19:2).

V

Man finds joy when he contemplates God's creation in heaven above and upon the earth beneath:

For Thou, Lord, hast made me glad through Thy work;
I will exult in the work if Thy hands (*Ibid.*, 92:5).

Why is man's heart gladdened when he lifts his eyes to the heaven?
Man can look up to the sky and also be persuaded to turn away
from God and worship the heavenly host.[28] When men envisage
the heavenly bodies as living beings they can recognize in them a
source of delight. When thoughtful human beings have concluded
that the host of heaven is an aggregate of beings lifeless in themselves, the delight as well as the awe they experience in the con-
templation of the vast expanses above are attributed to the living
God, Whose presence endows the heavens with ineffable glory.

Man experiences joy and he experiences hope. What are the
sources of man's joy, and whence does he draw his hope?

> To declare Thy loving-kindness in the morning,
> And Thy faithfulness in the night seasons (*Ibid.*, 92:3).

The joy is not a sensuous delight. It is the joy of contempla-
tion, the fruit of the awareness that a divine love radiates forth
in the day, and the starry night beckons man to hope. When
exaltation and hope speak to man from the breast of nature there
must be a heart that causes nature to speak for it, and enables joy
and hope to spring forth in the heart of man. That which is dead
cannot speak to man's heart.

Not merely the noble sentiments that man experiences are the
product of God's loving-kindness and faithfulness. The development of the minds of little children and the halting but certain
growth of their powers of articulation are, to the Psalmist, evidence of God's presence, as much as the heavens and the earth
which rehearse His majesty:

Out of the mouth of babes and sucklings hast Thou founded strength
Because of Thine adversaries;
That Thou mightest still the enemy and the avenger (Ps. 8:3).

The very ability of man to know and see bespeak the creative
powers of God:

> And they say: "The Lord will not see,
> Neither will the God of Jacob give heed."
> Consider, ye brutish among the people;

And ye fools, when will ye understand?
He that planteth the ear, shall He not hear?
He that formeth the eye, shall he not see? . . .
The Lord knoweth the thoughts of man . . . (Ps. 94:7 ff.).

While we must not assume that God eats because he created stomachs, we cannot preclude from Him consciousness and knowledge. When the source of life brings forth creatures who possess minds, and whose lives are guided by purpose and value, we can hardly assume that the source is blind, unaware of purpose, and unresponsive to value.[30] The biblical writers would recoil at the thought that knowledge and value had their origin in man. Like life itself, they could not possibly emerge out of a lifeless existence. Life originates in life, wisdom in wisdom, and love in love.

"He that chastiseth the nations, shall He not correct?" (Ib., 94:10). The Scriptures see the hand of God in history. They see mighty nations rise, grow, prosper, and fail. They see empires established, only to be crushed by others. The powers of iniquity flourish in the history of nations but temporarily. There is judgment in history. If there is judgment, there must be a Judge. If there is a Judge, there must be a Lawgiver Who teaches man what is right and what is wrong. That God is a God of Providence, that He is the Judge and the Lawgiver—these are not blind articles of faith to Israel's ancient teachers. They are reasoned-out truths which the God of the Bible has Himself affirmed.

VI

This reasoned-out universe, of course, has its major hurdle to overcome when it is confronted by the problem of evil. The God Who makes man leap with joy and Who fills his heart with hope, He Who teaches, guides, and inspires must be a God of justice and love, for it is from the existence of these principles that His existence is deduced. How about the evil and injustice in this world? No one is aware of this overwhelming problem more than the biblical writers themselves. Is not the presence of evil, suffering, and iniquity a breach in the harmonious structure that they have erected?

To the Bible good and evil are principles of value that apply
only to man's life and have meaning only insofar as they affect
him. The explanation of the presence of evil must be sought in
its relationship to the life of man. Since there are two poles of
reality, God and the material world, man serves as the bridge between the two. God is life.[31] The material world as such is lifeless.
The life that resides within it and that it produces has its source
in God. The closer one reaches to God the fuller and completer
is that life.

> But as for me, the nearness of God is my good (Ps. 72:28).

The more distant a man is from God, the closer he is to the
earth which by itself is lifeless.

> For dust thou art and unto dust thou shalt return (Gen. 3:19).

All evil is the absence of life and is the product of the separation from the source of life.

> For, lo, they that go far from Thee shall perish (Ps. 72:77).

The poles of good and evil are the poles of life and death
(Deut. 30:15). Man who is the liaison between the living God
and the lifeless earth is attracted by both. It is up to him to choose
life. When man will choose to lift himself to God, the whole com-
plexion of existence will change. The heavens will rejoice and the
earth, the sea, and all that are in it.

> The beasts of the field shall honour Me,
> The jackals and the ostriches (Is. 43:20).

The biblical writers were not blind to the disharmonies in
nature, to the destruction and the brutalities that prevail in it.
"Thou hast made man like the fishes of the sea, as the creeping
things that have no ruler over them" (Habakuk 1:14). That the
fish swallow one another and that animals consume each other is
in itself out of harmony with the basic adaptive design of life to
environment. That the biblical thinkers were deeply troubled by

this unruly situation is evidenced by their conception of a primeval harmony prevailing in the animal kingdom [32] which is destined to be restored in the future.

> The wolf shall dwell with the lamb
> And the leopard shall lie down with the kid;
> And the calf and the young lion and the fatling together;
> And a little child shall lead them . . .
> They shall not hurt nor destroy
> In all My holy mountain;
> For the earth shall be full of the knowledge of the Lord
> As the waters cover the sea (Is. 11:6–9).

The disharmonies that obtain in nature at present reflect the lifelessness that is the basic characteristic of nature before it is vitalized by God. The presence of death or suffering, which is a diminution of life and an approximation of death, constitutes, for the Scriptures, a moral, not an intellectual, problem. Death is an ultimate characteristic of the world of phenomena, and because of this fact, life rather than death is the mystery whose reality can be explained only by reference to God. The immorality of death and its ramifications which constitute so grave a difficulty are biblically resolved by squarely throwing the blame for their presence on man who can either increase or diminish life in the universe by his choice of good or evil. And yet, God has not been unjust to man by granting him a gift whose consequences are so dubious and often so disastrous, in full knowledge of what man's choice would be, for He is omniscient.[33] He has pointed out to man a way to reconstruct his life out of the very embers of his shattered self,[34] and has cleared a highway leading from the ruins of his life back to Him.[35] God knows beforehand what man will do, but His thoughts are not man's thoughts,[36] and He transforms all evil into good, as will become clear in the end of days.[37] In the meantime man has been given his opportunity to participate in the process of world-building like God Himself.

The fate of righteous individuals who suffer and of the wicked who prosper is a phase of the comprehensive problem of evil. The innocent sufferer and the prosperous evil-doer apparently do not fit into the picture of the concomitant variation of lifelessness and distance from God. However, in the biblical doctrine the righteous man has the power to convert death into life because of his closeness to God, and by his faith in God he achieves a greater life in suffering than the evil-doer in his well-being. In trouble God is with him as he is with his God (Ps. 91:15).

NOTES

1 Rudolf Bultman, *Primitive Christianity* (New York: Living Books, 1956), p. 15.

2 Ps. 10:11; 14:1; Is. 29:15; Jer. 5:12; Job, *passim*. Cf. also Psalms 39 and 73, *et passim*.

3 Gen. 18:25; Jer. 12:1; Job, *passim*; Ps. *passim*. Cf. my paper on *"The Problem of Evil and the Book of Job"* in *Judaism*, Vol. V, No. 1, p. 49.

4 Ps. 92:7 ff.; *ibid.* 94:8 ff.

5 Deut. 4:28; I Kings 18:27; Is. 37:19; 44:9 ff. In Is. 41:1 the nations are called to present their arguments before the Lord. See also *ibid.* v. 21: "Produce your cause, saith the Lord; bring forth your reasons, saith the King of Jacob." The nine chapters of Is. 40–48 are largely built around the disputation that the God of Israel is holding with the idolatrous world, in which the claims of the Lord are based on the empirical evidence of verified prophecy. Much of the meaningfulness of this section of Isaiah is vitiated by the hypothesis of multiple authorship of the book of Isaiah. However, this question, as well as a discussion of the nature of the argument employed here by the prophet lie beyond the scope of this paper.

6 Cf. *Nedarim* 38a; Maim. *Mishneh Torah, Yesodei Ha-Torah*, VIII, 1; *et passim*.

7 Maim. *Avodah Zarah* I, 3; *Gen. Rabbah* 38:13, 39:1, 61:1; cf. Louis Ginzberg, *Legends of the Jews* (Philadelphia: The Jewish Publication Society, 5715–1955), Vol. V, p. 210, n. 16.

8 *Gen. Rabbah* 63:10; cf. L. Ginzberg, *op. cit.*, p. 192, note 63.

9 Zeev Jawitz, *Toledot Yisrael* (Tel Aviv: Achiever, 5694), III, Appendix, p. 22, note 1. See also Philip Biberfeld, *Universal Jewish History* (New York: The Spero Foundation, 1948), Vol. I, pp. 121 ff.

10 *Gen. Rabbah* 61:1; cf. *Yoma* 28b.

11 See Saadia *Emunot ve-Deot*, Introduction, 6; Maim. *Guide* I, 32. Cf. *Baba Metzia* 85b (R. Chanina's statement).

12 See Theodor Gomperz, *Greek Thinkers*, Eng. tr. by Laurie Magnus (London: John Murray, 1949), I, 215; Edward Zeller, *Outlines of the History of Greek Philosophy*, Eng. tr. by Sarah Frances Alleyne and Evelyn Abbott (New York: Henry Holt and Company, 1890) p. 85; Wilhelm Windelband, *A History of Philosophy*, Eng. tr. by James H. Tufts (New York:

Harper Torchbooks, 1958), pp. 41 ff.; John Burnett, *Early Greek Philosophy* (New York: Meridian Books, 1960), p. 267.

13 I have since found this explanation of the change from EHYEH to the Tetragrammaton in Elie Munk's *The World of Prayer* (New York: Philip Feldheim, 5714–1954) Eng. tr. by Henry Biberfeld and Leonard Oschry, p. 61, in the name of RSBM. However, the statement in RSBM is very enigmatic, and I'm not sure it yields this particular meaning. Strangely enough, David Hoffman in *Leviticus* (Berlin: Verlag Von M. Poppelauer, 1905), I, 98, rejects the metaphysical meaning of the passage in Exodus as unintelligible to a slavefolk. See, however, Etienne Gilson, *The Spirit of Mediaeval Philosophy*, Eng. tr. by A. H. C. Downes (New York: Charles Scribner's Sons, 1940), p. 51, and p. 433, note 9. The rabbinic interpretation of this name as applied to history (*Berakhoth* 9b and elsewhere) does not negate its basic metaphysical character. Martin Buber, however, in his *Moses* (New York: Harper Torchbooks, 1958) p. 52, does not accept the ontological interpretation of the name.

14 *Essay On Man* (New York: Doubleday Anchor Books, 1953), p. 110.

15 Aristotle, *De Anima*, 411A.

16 See my paper on *The Existence of God in Judaism*, Vol. IV, No. 4.

17 Job 25:2. The biblical concept of *differentiation* entails divergency of goals and essential dissimilarity. The idea expressed in *Berakhot* 58a and *Sanhedrin* 37a as to the uniqueness of every human personality is inherent in biblical doctrine. Unity in human life can be obtained only by suppression of differences and submission to a unifying principle. Similarly, were the deities to be identical in their essential character and purposes they would merge into unity. Cf. a similar application to the disembodied intelligences in Maim., *Guide*, II, Prop. XVI, and *Yesodei Ha-Torah*, I, 7, and II, 5. In the light of the above, the biblical thinkers might have answered the strictures of Hume to this proof of the unity of God (David Hume, *Dialogues Concerning Natural Religion*, Part V, in *The English Philosophers From Bacon to Mill* [New York: The Modern Library, 1939]). Needless to say a general discussion of the biblical arguments for the existence and the unity of God is outside the purview of this paper. On this subject, see Harry A. Wolfson, *Religious Philosophy* (Cambridge: Harvard University Press, 1961), Chap. 1.

18 Cf. Prov. 8:29.

19 Cf. Bachya, *Chovot Ha-Levavot* 1, 7.

20 Cf. Job 21:22.

21 The manifoldness of creation, in biblical thinking, never leads to the principle of plenitude, i.e., that God has created all possibles. See Arthur O. Lovejoy, *The Great Chain Of Being* (New York: Harper Torchbooks, 1960), pp. 50 ff., *et passim*. However, the diversity of existence as an intrinsic value as affirmed by Plato (*op cit.*, pp. 50 ff.), Aquinas (pp. 76 ff.), and others, was already anticipated in the Bible.

22 Job 39:1–4.

23 *Ibid.* 5–12.

24 *Ibid.* 13–17.

25 *Ibid.* 19–25.

26 *Ibid.* 26–30.

27 *Ibid.* 40:15–41:26. The detailed description of God's creatures was obviously meant not only to overwhelm Job.

28 Deut. 4:19.

29 It seems to me that this is the correct meaning of Psalm 8:3, as is evidenced by the parallel argument in Ps. 94:7 ff. Joseph Albo in the *Ikkarim* IV, 10, sees in this passage a reference to the innate ideas and axiomatic truths implanted in the human soul. Samson Raphael Hirsch in *Die Psalmen* (Frankfort: J. Kaufmann, 1898) p. 34, interprets the argument as based on the essential purity of the uncorrupted human soul and its awareness of God's Being. See also *Interpreter's Bible* (New York: Abingdon Press, 1955), Vol. IV, pp. 49–50, for a similar construction. The comments of Ibn Ezra and Malbim are close to the one suggested in the text. The emendations of Hirsch P. Chajes in *Beur Madai* (Kiev: A. Kahana, 1908) and Heinrich Graetz in his *Kritischer Commentar zu den Psalmen* (Breslau: S. Schottaender, 1882) are gratuitous and totally unsupported by readings in the Targum, the Septuagint, and the Vulgate. The "enemy and avenger" of Ps. 8:3 are the "taunter and blasphemer" of Ps. 44:17.

30 Cf. Maim. *Guide* III, 19.

31 Cf. Maim. *Mishneh Torah, Yesodei Ha-Torah*, II, 10; see also Is. 37: 4, 17; Jer. 10:10; *et passim*.

32 Gen. 1:29–30.

33 Cf. the critique of the traditional doctrine of freedom by Nicholas Berdyaev, *The Destiny of Man* (New York: Harper Torchbooks, 1960) pp. 18–19.

34 Ps. 25:8.

35 While Ps. 90:2: "Thou turnest man to contrition, and sayest: 'Return, ye children of men'" may not literally refer to repentance (Cf. *Midrash Tehillim, ad locum*), the concept developed in that chapter, it appears to me, can be understood properly only on the basis of Malbim's interpretation. The call to return can hardly be a call to man to return to the dust. This Psalm contrasts not only the eternity of God with the transiency of man's life, but the ephemeral and sorry existence of man on earth with the eternity of the soul's life in the presence of God. The Psalmist pleads with God to lighten man's burden during his brief sojourn in this world where God's anger, rather than His grace, seems to prevail. But God is the dwelling-place of the human soul in all generations (v. 1), and before the physical world was formed, God was Lord of the human soul. The term "E–L" used in v. 2, appears to me to have this meaning, and so removes the difficulty raised by the commentators: of course, He is God before He created the mountains; otherwise, He couldn't create them (see H. P. Chajes, *op. cit., ad locum*). An examination of the term "E–L" in the Bible will reveal, it appears to me, the Lord as the God Who stands in personal relationship to His creatures, not as the Creator of the world. The concept of the eternity of the soul in the presence of God

hardly seems biblical, but all the Psalmist means is that the soul was created before the physical world. While this doctrine itself does not appear anywhere else in the Bible (at least, so it seems without further investigation), a rethinking of this subject is a desideratum.

36 Gen. 50:20; Is. 55:8–9.

37 Jer. 23:20; 29:11. Some of these ideas were developed more fully in later ages, but they are already found in a germinal state in the Scriptures.

SIDNEY B. HOENIG

*

Notes on the New Translation
of the Torah

A PRELIMINARY INQUIRY

THE APPEARANCE of a new translation of the Torah has always been an occasion for rejoicing. Philo thus relates: "Therefore, even to the present day, there is held every year a feast and general assembly in the island of Pharos, whither not only Jews but multitudes of others cross the water, both to do honor to the place in which the light of that version first shone out, and also to thank God for the good gift so old, yet ever young." [1] The joy perhaps is due to the inner feeling that by means of a translation one comes closer to God's word and understanding of the meaning of Holy Writ, thereby "serving Him with joy."

The publication of a new translation in any age also reveals historically the growth of Jewish communities, their achievements and affluence. It points to Jewish life reaching such a status which demands a new translation or perhaps even new interpretation for a new generation. Thus we see the affluent ancient community of Alexandria, the growth in medieval Moslem countries, and the advanced structure of Jewish life in our own modern day. On the other hand, a translation also betokens factors of assimilation which seep into a Jewish community where many persons are unable to read the Bible in the original and are lacking the knowledge of Hebrew and Judaism.

Translations further augur new epochs in Jewish life and world civilization. The Septuagint aided in blending Greek and Jewish thought into Hellenism, giving rise to Christianity. Saadia's translation ushered in the glorious Spanish-Arabic period where Jews became the mediators between the Orient and Occident, and Mendelssohn's German translation strengthened and encouraged the Haskalah Movement.

With this historic background and precedent, the publication of a new translation of the Torah * in our own day naturally becomes the concern of all—clergy and laity, scholar and general reader. One begins to reflect: What will the new translation mean, or set forth for American Jewry?

The present translation issued by the Jewish Publication Society (JPS) seems to have taken Rav Saadia Gaon as its guide; in fact the Preface notes on one point ". . . the present translation is merely following the example of Saadia." This is commendable, for Saadia's chief thought was to present the Bible in a rational, intelligible form as a book accessible to all, to Muhammedans as well as to Jews who had not sufficient learning to understand the original. He aimed at the greatest possible clarity and consistency and did not hesitate to insert words and phrases, or to divide and connect verses and sentences in his own way, when necessary to convey to the reader the intended sense. Hence he did not always bind himself to the rules of the Masorah, to grammar, or to common usage.[2]

All of the above is also true of the present new translation: "We are the first authorized publicly sponsored translation of the Bible that has broken with the past, with unimaginative and courageless conformity to the past. We have rejected the age-old convention of translating the Hebrew word for word, even letter for letter sometimes, mechanically into English."[3] Thus the present translation is in response to a need "to make it more easily understood, substituting modern terms for words and expressions that have become archaic or unfamiliar . . ."[4]

It is known that scholars earnestly seeking the truth have spent close to ten years in their research and painstaking writing of the translation. Every word or phrase was carefully weighed over the academic table. There must have been many a battle until the final word was written down. In the files, the editor and his

* The Torah, The Five Books of Moses, A new translation of The Holy Scriptures according to the Masoretic text, First Section (Philadelphia: The Jewish Publication Society of America, 1962).

assistants no doubt possess all of their notes explaining their disagreement, vote, and final decision.

It is self-evident that difficulties in translation always persist. There has never been any translation that was not attacked and derided. One must only remember the rabbinic comments on the Septuagint (LXX) translation, where the event is compared to the day of the Worship of the Golden Calf.[5] Yet tradition and history recognize that despite the difficulty, one cannot ignore the need for translation. Thus Ben Sira notes in his prologue . . . "You are urged therefore to read with good will and attention, and to be indulgent in cases where, despite our diligent labor in translating, we may seem to have rendered some phrases imperfectly. For what was originally expressed in Hebrew does not have exactly the same sense when translated into another language. Not only this work, but even the law itself, the prophecies, and the rest of the books differ not a little as originally expressed." [6]

So, also, when Jerome composed his translation he wrote: "This is a labor of piety, but at the same time one of dangerous presumption; for in judging others I will myself be judged by all; and how dare I change the language of the world's old age and carry it back to the days of its childhood? Who is there, whether learned or unlearned, who, when he takes up the volume in his hands and discovers that what he reads does not agree with what he is accustomed to, will not break out at once in a loud voice and call me a sacrilegious forger, for daring to add something to the ancient books, to make changes and corrections in them?" [7] Such outcry, unfortunately, has already come.

Today the imprecations and bans have been heaped upon the translators and aspersions cast upon their religiosity.[8] This is regrettable, for surely, it is predicated, translators act and serve with integrity, seeking the truth as they see it, in their scholarly judgment; striving, thus, to produce a commendable translation on the basis of their research.

But attack of the "new" is a human frailty. Even in ancient days there must have been some uproar which many sought to curb, for we read in the Letter of Aristeas:

When the rolls had been read the priests and the elders of the translators and some of the corporate body and the leaders of the people rose up and said, "Inasmuch as the translation has been well and piously made and is in every respect accurate, it is right that it should remain in its present form and that no revision of any sort take place." When all had assented to what had been said, they bade that an imprecation be pronounced, according to their custom, upon any who should revise the text by adding or transposing anything whatever in what had been written down, or by making any exclusion; and in this they did well, so that the work might be preserved imperishable and always.[9]

Our present purpose is to see whether a full consent (*haskamah*) can be given the 1963 New Text or whether revision is necessary. Above all, a spirit of fairness ought to prevail, even when there is sharp disagreement. Scoffing from any corner, becoming emotional over, or vindictive about, the translation, can hardly be considered gentlemanly or in keeping with that objective, dispassionate attitude that is the hallmark of genuine scholarship.

The present translation has been commissioned by JPS; it has not been "authorized" by the Jewish community, nor by any Jewish denomination like the Revised Standard Version (RSV) which "was authorized by vote of the National Council of Churches in the U.S.A. in 1951" (See Preface, RSV, p. v). Perhaps in years to come this NT (New Translation) may be accepted in Jewish homes and Synagogues even as the old JPS Bible had been, with all of its inaccuracies and deviation from rabbinic norm and despite the *issur* of the *Agudat ha-Rabonim* then, as recorded by J. D. Eisenstein:

The magnate Jacob H. Schiff of New York had contributed fifty thousand dollars to the Jewish Publication Society of Philadelphia for the purpose of an English translation of the Bible in accordance with the spirit of Israel. However, the two volumes which have already appeared, Psalms by Dr. Kohut and Micah by Dr. M. L. Margolis —were not satisfying. The writer of these lines (namely J. D. Eisenstein) in his reviews has demonstrated the deficiencies of this translation in the light of the Masorah and the spirit of Judaism. No doubt

the other volumes will not be much better. This is because the scholarly members of the Committee designated by the Society to supervise this translation are Reform Rabbis and others known as Liberal
Orthodox, young and old. The majority of them does not understand
the nature of the Hebrew language and the whole spirit of true Judaism is foreign to them; hence they are not fit at all for this work.

As a result of a motion by Rabbi Hayim Hershensohn before the
Orthodox *Agudath ha-Rabonim* on the 26th of Sivan 5673 (1913)
it was decided to protest against this English translation. In this protest, the Rabbis aim not to argue about the mode of the translation,
—to find therein deficiencies. Even if the work were perfect, it
would not be acceptable since they (i.e., these Rabbis) are specifically
opposed to the translation: *It shall not be considered an authorized*
(official) *translation of the people of Israel* as the Luther translation
is for Germans, or the King James for Englishmen. This project,
the members of the Agudah held, is in opposition to the spirit of
Israel which disregards translations in general; as even concerning
the Septuagint, did the Sages assert, that darkness descended upon
the earth for three days. The Rabbis therefore announce that the
Translation and the commentaries of these translators are their own
undertakings. All Israel has no responsibility to them, in any manner.
For the people of Israel the only official or authorized translations
are Targum Onkelos and the Commentaries on the Bible as based
on the Talmud.[10]

In the *Jewish Forum* volumes of 1928, a series of three articles
(plus an additional note), called "The Conservative Halacha"[11]
was written by the late Rabbi Samuel Gerstenfeld, one of the
Roshei-ha-Yeshiva of Rabbi Isaac Elchanan Theological Seminary.

Rabbi Gerstenfeld focused his attention on the legal parts of
the five Books of Moses:

I must say that in this translation is found material sufficient to construct a new sect and germs enough to breed many a change in the
religious life of Israel . . . Besides the objections to the detailed
variations from the oral law, the act of differing in itself is to be
objected to as a gross error.

Rabbi Gerstenfeld listed many passages to which Orthodox
Judaism objects. He shows "many flaws in the rendition of the

Divine Name . . . and grave deviations from Halacha." He sums up:

These are the variations from the oral law which I detected during my cursory reading . . . May these notes offend no one but may they serve a useful purpose . . . May He in His Goodness open the eyes of His erring children to see the truth of the oral part of the Divine Torah so that no schism be created in Israel . . .[12]

The fact that the criticism of 1917 has been forgotten, or that many observant rabbinic scholars of that decade refrained from retorting, or because of lack of knowledge of English they ignored that rendition in their houses of worship does in no wise mean that, due to its popular acceptance in the course of years, one cannot today still inveigh against it. The silence over the 1917 translation with its errors cannot serve as an argument for further silence or for full acceptance of the new translation which is generally believed to be superior to the old one.

At present, the criticism is given with the viewpoint of *tik-kun*, betterment for the future. We come not to condemn, but also not to commend. Moreover, objection should never be raised without also suggestion; one should not destroy if he cannot build. It is in this mood that these Preliminary Notes are collated.

Analysis and evaluation of the New Bible Translation of the Torah fall into seven different categories which are discussed in the pages which follow: 1) Language 2) Scholarly research 3) Masorah 4) Tetragrammaton (Lord) 5) Rabbinic tradition 6) Comparison with recent translations and 7) Procedure in preparation of the Text. The conclusions reached are presented with the sincere and fervent thought of maintaining the Bible as the Eternal Book of Israel and humanity, for "the Torah which Moses had commanded us, is the heritage of the Congregation of Jacob" (Deut. 33:4).

I

The general reader will be concerned first with understandability, clarity and intelligibility of the translation. Numerous examples of such excellent passages with easy flow of expression, will be found, such as Gen. 6:2: "divine beings" instead of "sons of God"; Numbers 6:26: "The Lord deal kindly and graciously with you" instead of "The Lord make His face to shine upon thee and be gracious unto thee." [13]

Most commendable are the many fine, concise, clear statements which follow traditional interpretation and do not befuddle the reader as to exact meaning. As examples we have:

Ex. 10:10: "Clearly, you are bent on mischief," [14] which follows the Targum.[15]

Ex. 12:41: "to the very day," [16] following Rashi.[17]

Ex. 13:8: "and you shall *explain* to your son" [18] as interpreted by *Mekhilta.*

Ex. 13:14: "and when *in time to come,* your son asks," [19] as explained by Rashi.[20]

Ex. 12:11: "Passover offering" [21] (or the note, "protective offering") follows Rashi, Targum, and Jonathan ben Uziel.[22]

Other examples of such fine understanding of the text are: Ex. 19:12–13: "Whoever touches the mountain shall be put to death; no hand shall touch him, but he shall be either stoned or pierced through." [23] This means that no one shall touch the person. He shall be stoned or pierced through (from afar), as explained by Ibn Ezra and Rashbam. Ex. 19:10: Warn them to "stay pure," [24] as explained by Nachmanides,[25] is better than the old rendition of the JPS: "sanctify them." Further samples of interpretation may be also seen in Gen. 49:21: [26]

JPS: Naphthali is a hind let loose. He giveth goodly words.
AT (American Translation): Naphthali is a free ranging deer that bears fawns.
RSV: Naphthali is a hind let loose that bears comely fawns (note: or *who gives beautiful words*).
NT: Naphthali is a hind let loose which yields lovely fawns.

The usage of the Aramaic *a-m-r* as "lamb" (doe) instead of the Hebrew homonym "word" is very fitting to the context.

Translations derived from Ugaritic affinities also enhance the meaning of the biblical text. Thus Ex. 15:2: "The Lord is my strength and might," stems from the Ugaritic *d-m-r,* "strength" and not the Hebrew z-m-r, "song." [27] Further examples of "reading ease" are:

Ex. 2:6: "when she opened it, she saw that it was a child, a boy crying." [28]

Ex. 8:5: Moses said to Pharaoh, "you may have this triumph over me: for what time shall I plead." [29]

Ex. 9:34: "Pharaoh reverted to his guilty ways, as did his courtiers." [30]

Other evidences of modern improvement based upon meaning of words may be commended, as in the case of Deut. 2:13: "Up now! Cross the *wadi Zered*" [31] or Gen. 49:14: "Issachar is a strong boned ass, crouching between the *saddle bags*." [32] Though the Targum renders *mishpetaaim* as "boundaries," [33] it is Seforno who hints at "saddlebags," [34] which the NT translators may have used, though the usage of the same *mishpetaaim* in the Song of Deborah may mean *sheep folds*.

Simplicity in using English words may likewise be seen in Gen. 25:27; but, one may inquire: was Jacob a *mild* [35] man (as rendered in NT) or a sincere, perfect individual? The *tam* of Jacob or *tamim* of Noah [36] (correctly rendered as "righteousness") surely cannot be mildness; such usage of *tam* may be considered a colloquialism, a popular folk usage, as in the Yiddish.

The multitude of gratifying renditions with clarity, which naturally one cannot list in an appraisal, are however marred at times by puzzling phrases. Such, for example, is Ex. 19:19: NT: "God answered him in thunder" [37] So also is the translation by RSV. However, JPS has "answered him by a *voice*." The Commentaries remark—"in the sound of the Shofar." Rashbam explains *"in a loud voice* to overcome the sound of the Shofar," a rendition which Moses Mendelssohn adopts in his *Biur* and translates as "Gott antwortete ihm mit lauter Stimme." Joseph Hertz, too, explains "God answered with a voice loud enough to surpass the ever increasing sound of the horn." One may therefore ask, what is the source for the translation "in thunder?"

Nevertheless no criticism can or should be made of any usage by the translators till one sees whether a text which at the surface seems peculiar in its rendition has as its basis some medieval commentary. The translators have truly displayed their erudition in their consultation and probing into the medieval commentators. Alas, that the Notes and Sources were not given together with the translated text! The question arises—if a medieval commentator, like Ibn Ezra, Kimchi, or Rashbam, has a strange interpretation, are we to ignore the *usual*, if it is still intelligible and also supported in other sources such as Talmud or Midrash? Choosing the *rare* (or *chiddush*) is not always the desideratum.

Comparison of these translated passages or of the poetic selections, as the Song at the Red (elongated e) Sea,[38] with the renditions in the old JPS or King James version will reveal superiority in the present simplicity of language, though one may disagree about "poetic elegance." The attempt is commendable, but this is not the "final word." English stylists and those concerned with conveying "understandability" may find many passages confusing and unacceptable. One may ask: is it modern English to say: "Adam   *knew* (or "experienced") his wife and she conceived." Why not say "cohabited" or "had conjugal relations with," if intelligibility and modernity are the criteria. The *American Translation*, seeking all of the same purposes, was bold enough to translate "had intercourse with." On the other hand, if we seek elevating, lofty speech, is it spiritually uplifting to say in Balaam's speech (Numbers 23:8): "How can I damn whom God has not damned." [39]

Moreover, it is apparent that just as in ancient translations the attempt was to do away with anthropomorphisms, so here one notes an attempt to do away with a sense of harshness. The following passages show the trend in Ex. 20:5: Instead of "hate" we read *reject*; "sin"—*guilt*; "jealous"—*impassioned*; [40] in Ex. 18:16,22: "judge"—*arbitrate, exercise authority*; [41] The word "hate" is even deleted in the new translation of Genesis 50:15: [42]

JPS: It may be that Joseph will *hate* us and requite us all the evil.
RSV: It may be that Joseph will *hate* us and pay us back for all evil.
But NT: What if Joseph seeks to pay us back for all the wrong.

The following examples of *changes* of words will also show the modern trend, as compared with the other translations:

Gen. 4:10: AT and NT—Hark, your brother's blood cries. RSV—the voice of your brother's blood is crying.

One may ask: Is *Kol, voice* or *hark?* Likewise, Ex. 21:1: "These are the *norms*." [43] Are norms laws?

Sometimes to give intelligibility, Hebrew words are dropped or others not found in the text are inserted: Thus, Gen. 44:19: My Lord asked his servants, 'Have you a father or *another* brother.' [44]

At times there is even a reversal in expression from the Hebrew idiom: Gen. 44:26 [45] RSV, "for we cannot see the man's face." So also 43:3. But in NT we read "for we may not show our faces to the man." "Do not let me see your faces." (Note: lit. "Do not see my face."). Similarly in Gen. 27:18: [46] "Which of my sons are you" is the translation, instead of the Hebrew, "who are you, my son."

Especially interesting, as one of the peculiarities of translation, is the *different* usage of a similar word, e.g., *k-l-l* (curse) in the various passages.

Exodus 22:27: [47] You shall not *offend* God.

Lev. 19:14: You shall not *insult* the deaf; RSV: you shall not *curse* the deaf.

Lev. 20:9: "If any man *repudiates* his father or mother."

The word *k-l-l* basically means "to make light, dishonor"; *k-b-d*, "to give weight, honor"; hence, rabbinic law (*Sanhedrin* 85a) notes that even after death there may be "no dishonor of a parent." This rule is aimed as a continuity of respect from son to father, back to early generations, thus preserving the weightiness and respect of ancient tradition. The phrase "repudiate" perhaps bears this connotation, especially in its meaning "to refuse to acknowledge, disclaim, disavow, refuse to have dealings with, reject; to put away, abandon, renounce, to refuse to accept as authentic, such as to repudiate authority." But the word *curse* has ever stronger implications for those who break tradition. As Ibn Ezra notes: the repetition in the verse of "he has *cursed* his father and mother" means he has done a most "abhorrent act." [48] "Repudiate" does not imply such bloodguilt; "curse" does.[49]

One can go through every page of the New Translation with a fine comb and point out lack of clarity, or inconsistency in many passages, despite its superior simplicity. But no journal is the place for such detailed study. Moreover, reactions to various translations are in the realm of *de gustibus non est disputandum*.

The question still unanswered is: Should the Bible be in a lofty, inspiring language that one is accustomed to find in the Bible, or should it be presented in the vulgar, profane language, the *lingua franca*. (These terms are used not in derision but as in Vulgate, *chol.*) [50] One is struck by the fact that the AT and RSV retained "Thee" and "Thy" when they occur in language addressed to God since they convey a more reverent feeling than the blunt *you* (cf. AT, preface VI). Thus Gen. 3:11 RSV: I heard the sound of *Thee* in the garden and I was afraid. NT, however has a similar reading to the AT rendition: I heard the sound of *You* in the garden and I was afraid.[51] Besides the awkwardness of the phrase "sound of You," it seems that *Thee* should be used when addressing God and *you* for man, as accepted even by modern Christians. We know that "the Torah speaks in the language of man." [52] Hence, are we to translate both *you* and You for Hebrew *atah?* [53] Is this modicum to be applied only to the ancient Hebrew or does it also refer to translations in the common language of our contemporaries who seek "intelligibility" when reading a rendition?

Perhaps the scholars who did the spade work, knowing the reason chosen for every word, after the many revisions they made, would have gained immeasureably by submitting this *magnum opus* to a stylist,—to one who appreciates English style and has a feeling for elegance in poetry. Dry scholarship must be whetted with the flavor and flow of literary style. Though Jewish literature abounds in many scholarly descriptions of historic occurrences of our people, *only* a Yehudah Halevi could write the Zionides in an *elegant* style. The question then is, does this new Jewish version also possess elegance, loftiness and sanctity in phrase?

The answer must await the verdict of the *vox populi*.

II

A major item of interest in this new translation is the scholarly research and accuracy. It displays aptly evidences of the new Near East, Akkadian, and Ugaritic studies. Thus the translation of

Genesis 34:10: "You will dwell among us and the land will be open before you; settle, *move about*,⁵⁴ and acquire holdings in it" is based upon the Aramaic and Akkadian *s-h-r*. The new translation, "move about," based on knowledge of Near East etymology and customs is better than the word *trade* used in the older translations. It is interesting, however, that the Aramaic *Targum Onkelos* renders *s-h-r* as "trade." One may then well ask: is the Aramaic-Akkadian source preferable to the Aramaic-Targumic rendition? Moreover, can one *trade* without *moving about freely?* Does such rendition truly change our perspective and yield a better understanding of the text?

Another instance of translation for modern understanding is in Numbers 34:3: "Great Sea" is in a note: Mediterranean; "Sea of Chinnereth" is in a note "Sea (or Lake) of Galilee"; but *Yam ha-melach* ⁵⁵ (in a note, Gen. 14:3 "Salt Sea") is translated "Dead Sea" in the text. Jews never called it *Dead Sea*, *Yam ha-ma-vet* (?); it was always *yam-ha-melach*, as used by Josephus and others: The Asphalt Sea. Calling the Salt Sea—*Dead Sea* in the Bible Text is a modernity,⁵⁶ influenced no doubt by the finding of the Scrolls. A consistency should have been adopted by noting the correct name in the text, and below it the modern name, for the purpose of identification today.

Similarly, in the translations of Numbers 23:10: "Who can count the dust of Jacob; number the *dust-clouds of Israel*." ⁵⁷ Old JPS renders: "Who hath counted the dust of Jacob or numbered the *stock* of Israel." RSV: "Who can count the dust of Jacob or number the fourth part of Israel (in note—or *dust clouds*)." AT: "Who can count Jacob's masses or number Israel's *myriads*."

In comparison we see that the NT is close to the RSV, except that what is in the note in the RSV is in the text of NT. (Other examples of this practice are given below). No doubt the rendition "dust clouds" is based on scholarly research. The question is, does an academic suggestion in a scholarly paper that *r-b-a* is a "dust cloud" outweigh *r-b-a-* as seed, stock, or quarter? Moreover, "counting the dust of Jacob" is a biblical idiom: "counting clouds" is not.

There are similar puzzling phrases, as in Ex. 22:17: ⁵⁸

AT: "you must not let a sorceress live."
RSV: "you shall not permit a sorceress to live."
NT: "you shall not *tolerate* a sorceress." (note, lit., "let live").

The NT text apparently ignores the incident of Saul and the witch of Endor, where the woman said (I Samuel 28:9): "Surely you know what Saul had done, how he has cut off the mediums and the wizards from the land, to bring about my death." The Talmud, (*Sanhedrin* 67a), notes that the punishment was "stoning." Rashi likewise remarks that there was a death penalty administered by the court.[59] As such, one may ask: Should not objective truth, pertaining to an ancient practice, be adhered to without "whitewashing by tolerance?" However, if indeed the translators aimed at "whitewashing" or moderating unseemly instances in the Bible, one is puzzled why, Genesis 4:70 [60] is translated, "Sin is a demon at the door," emphasizing demonology in the Bible. Surely the Jews after Ezra, studying the Bible, did not know of the Akkadian *rabisu*. The term *rovetz*, "crouch," is already commonly used in the Bible, as in Gen. 49:14 [61] and may also stem from a Ugaritic root referring to the lying down or "enclosure" of animals, or, if truth is the main objective in the translation, why read in Ex. 21:6: "His master shall take him before God," if basically it means "before the judges.[63]

In general, the use of basic language roots or new knowledge of the Near East may improve "neglected insights" through understanding the mode of living and thinking of the ancient Israelites, but it cannot always be a criterion for exact translation. One wonders why in Ex. 7:1 Aaron is a "spokeman" (*navi*) while in Ex. 15:20 his sister Miriam is recorded as a "prophetess" (*neviah*) and in Num. 11:26, Eldad and Medad "spoke in ecstasy" (*va-yit-nabu*)?

The root *k-n-h* is used in Gen. 4:1 (re: birth of Cain) to read, "I have *gained*"; [64] in Gen. 14:19 (re: Abraham and Melkhizedek) as *Creator* [65] and in Ex. 15:16 (re: Song at the Sea "whom you have *ransomed*.[66] Apparently the Hebrew connotation of *k-n-h* "possession" could not easily be conveyed throughout by the translators.

Similarly, the root *r-r* is taken as the basis for the translation in

Gen. 3:14: "Banned shall you be from all cattle" [67] and is also applied to Ex. 14:20 "it cast a spell upon the night"; [68] only in a note do we see: "others 'and it lit up.'" Such freedom of translation, changing *light* to *ban*, may lead one to wonder whether Numbers 6:25, traditionally translated as "light up, or shine (His countenance)" [69] should be rendered instead as "ban" bringing it in conformity with Exodus 33:23, "But my face must not be seen."

Another puzzling usage is Lev. 24:16: "But if he *pronounce* the name Lord he shall be put to death." [70] It is true that the context refers to blaspheming and the Targum uses the term *yefaresh*, "pronounce." But the Talmud (*Sanh.* 56a) [71] and such commentators as Rashi (*ad loc.*) expound upon it and stress that the meaning is *curse*. [72] Moreover it is awkward to translate "if he pronounce the name Lord, he shall be put to death." The NT reader is doing this very thing as he reads the text, which is replete with references to the name Lord. Likewise, the translators could have used, as suggested by Rashi, the root *k-b-h* instead of *n-k-b*) as in Numbers 23:8 in the utterance of Balaam. [73] It is known that only the High Priest was permitted to pronounce the Ineffable Name on the Day of Atonement; hence the present NT reading is hazy when it renders as a separate phrase: "but if he pronounces the name Lord, he shall be put to death." Rather, verses 15 and 16 are one and should for clarity be thus connected: "Anyone who blasphemes his God shall bear his guilt if he pronounces the name Lord: he shall be put to death."

Moreover, the present rendition of this verse brings to mind Karaitic tendencies as revealed by J. Mann [74] in "An Early Karaitic Tract": "There follows in our work a long discourse about the pronounciation of the Tetragrammaton. The writer's chief contention is that *n-k-b* in Lev. 24:16 does not mean cursing, as many explain the word, but uttering, pronouncing. Thus the pronounciation of the divine name involves capital punishment." One surely would not want to regard this NT as Karaitic!

The Preface notes, "In accuracy alone we believe this translation has improved on the first JPS translation in literally hundreds of passages." To read Gen. 49:22 "Joseph is a wild ass" [75] (from *pera*) as in AT: "Joseph is a young bull, a young bull at a spring, a wild-ass at Shur," instead of RSV, or old JPS: "Joseph is a fruitful bough," may be open to question as to "improvement." Not every son of Jacob in this blessing is compared to an animal; reference is also made in the blessing to ships and bread; could not *vine* also be appropriate in the context when one seeks "accuracy?" Deut. 33:17 is not the criterion since Joseph is called there *shor* [76] (bull), not *pera* (ass).

One of the questions of accuracy that has already aroused controversy pertains to the use of the word *ruach* in the opening passage of Genesis; AT renders: "a tempestuous wind raging over the surface" but NT is milder, "a wind from God sweeping over the water." What prompted the usage of *wind* instead of *spirit* was Gen. 8:1 describing the flood: "God caused a wind to blow across the earth and the waters subsided." It is true that the Targum renders "a wind before God," but Rashi makes reference to "the heavenly throne or word of God," implying the Spirit—and this cannot at all be considered a Christian notion. Interestingly, all other passages in the Pentateuch mentioning *ruach e-lohim* (Gen. 41:38; Ex. 31:3; Ex. 35:31, Numbers, 24:2) refer to Spirit and not *wind*. On the other hand, in the instances of the locust plague (Ex. 10:13) [77] or the quail (Numbers 11:13)[78] we do not find the phrase *ruach e-lohim*, but "God *drove* an east wind" or "a wind *went forth* from God."

Objection to *spirit* in the first verse of Genesis is noted in the JPS publicity on the ground that "it is 'Christian' and implies a secondary, or intermediary power participating in the Creation, . . . an implication totally unacceptable to Judaism." One wonders whether *ruach* in the prophetic "Not by might or power by My spirit"[79] is also a non-Jewish *spirit*. Surely the theological argument against the implication of an "intermediary" is not valid since the Targum already mentions the notion of *Memra*. Moreover, the notion of Beginning, i.e., *Maaseh Bereshit* [80] has become a religious concept which tradition enunciates constantly. It is stressed in Mishnah *Chagigah*. Could not it be maintained in this new translation? Following Rashi's suggestion, we could easily read: "In the beginning of God's creation of heaven and earth . . . ," without tampering with tradition and thus retaining *Bereshit*, In the beginning, as the opening of our Bible.

Another puzzling element in scholarly accuracy, among the many difficult to list here, is Gen. 48:6–7,[81] pertaining to Jacob's blessings of his grandchildren. Old JPS: Ephraim and Manasseh, even as Reuben and Simeon shall be mine. And thy issue, that thou begettest after them, shall be thine; they shall be called *after the name* of their brethren in their inheritance. AT: . . . upon receiving their heritage they shall be called *by the names* of their brothers.

RSV . . . They shall be called by *the name* of their brothers in their inheritance. But NT . . . they shall be recorded *instead* [a] of their brothers in their inheritance (Note— [a] lit., by the name).

The usage of the phrase "instead of" in lieu of "by the name of" implies that the younger brothers of Ephraim and Manasseh are not to be included (or listed) in the older brothers' record; rather, their inheritance supplants that of the older brothers; they are to be substitutes. This is not at all so; their *inclusion* is definitely the meaning of the verse, even as Rashi notes "they are included within Ephraim and Manasseh.[82] Hence the translation of the NT is wrong here, unless the reading implied is *"in the stead"* (dialect, place) meaning 'within the province of," i.e., "inclusion." All this, however, would be contrary to the intent expressed in the Preface. "A translation which is stilted where the original is natural . . . is the very opposite of faithful."

III

A further point of investigation in this translation is the *Masorah.* In the Preface, the Editors note that they have followed Saadia Gaon who "joined separate verses of the masoretic text (whose authority he did not question) into single sentences when the sense required it."

The adoption of Saadia's method in this translation may be of commendable value when it applies to joining parts of sentences together. But does it also apply to paragraph division, i.e., taking a sentence from one paragraph and inserting it into the next or beginning a paragraph with the middle of a Hebrew verse? There are traditional rules of *open (petuchah)* and *closed (setumah)* in the Torah which refer to the mode of paragraph beginnings.

This traditional rule was disregarded by the Editors, though
Maimonides (*Yad, Hilkhot Sefer Torah,* 8:3) notes that any
Torah which is not in accordance with the list he gives is not a
valid one.[83]

Thus *petuchah* is ignored: Genesis 2:4–5.[84]

"4 such is the story of heaven and earth as they were created.
*"When the Lord God made earth and heaven—5 no shrub, etc.

Thus NT breaks up the Hebrew sentence, contradictory to the
Masorah.

Another example of ignoring the traditional *petuchah* is Ex.
40:34: (p. 175 bottom) where NT joins two Hebrew sentences
from two separate paragraphs: [85]

"When Moses had finished the work [34] the cloud covered the tent,
etc." [85]

An example of ignoring *setumah* is in Num. 16:20: (p. 278)
where again the NT makes a combination from two adjoining
paragraphs:

Then the presence of the Lord appeared to the whole community, [20]
and the Lord spoke to Moses . . ." [86]

It is known that in the State of Israel today every effort is being
made by Koren Publishers (Jerusalem) to produce a Hebrew
Bible following the mode of the Scribes in the Torah. Should not
a Jewish version, which is now aimed to give accuracy, also follow
such a mode, even in translation for the Jews in the Diaspora?

The translators have followed the consonantal Masorah, apparently at times ignoring vocalization. To their credit, it should
be emphasized, caution was followed, as in Gen. 10:10 a note
to "Calneh" (a place) [87] reads "better vocalized *we-kh'ullanah,*
'all of them being' " in the land of Shinar. The suggested rendition was not inserted in the text. The attempt to refrain from
changing the text is therefore to their merit. But a change of a
letter *d* to *r* may be noted in Gen. 22:13: a *ram;* [88] and an instance

* NT begins a new paragraph with "when . . .

of changed vocalization is seen when one studies a comparison of Lev. 8:31 with 8:35.[89]

We also find often in translation that the Hebrew passive voice is used instead of the active, such as Gen. 50:8: "their herds were left" or Gen. 50:20 "he (Joseph) was embalmed" or Ex. 18:5: "Jethro . . . brought Moses' sons and wife to him." Though this seemingly is a minor point it may cause much difficulty if ultimately, as planned, the Hebrew text is printed by the side of this new translation.

I V

Another matter of concern is the usage of the word *Lord* as the translation of the Tetragrammaton. Though this mode of rendition is the common translation of *Ado-nai*, as the *Shem ha-va-yah* is pronounced today, stressing *adnut*—Lordship, one feels that the Jewish Publication Society had the opportunity here of making this Bible (The Torah) truly a version in the full Jewish spirit. In the State of Israel it is the practice today with rabbinic sanction, to print the Divine Name in Hebrew texts, by breaking the combination of letters. Instead of utilizing the common usage: *Lord*, why could not the translators have used *Ado-nai* throughout for the Tetragrammaton? It is singularly printed in Hebrew characters in Exodus 6:3 (p. 107) and in English, Exodus 17:5. Instead of the common terminology: *God*, for the translation of *E-lohim*, its basic meaning, *Almighty*, could have been now introduced. As such, we would have "*Ado-nai*, our Almighty,"—"your Almighty." "*Ado-nai* is the Almighty." Such rendition would definitely be more in the Jewish spirit than any other present usage.

Similarly, the phrase (Lev. 22:2) "Mine the Lord's" [90] is puzzling because the sentence deals with profaning "My holy name." In the entire context of Leviticus (chapter 22) there is a constant declarative emphasis "I am the Lord." This is no doubt more majestic in meaning, and better for conveying the thought that the Law emanates as a directive from *Ado-nai*.

A further perplexity is the omission of the word *Israel* in Deut. 22:22.[91] It may be an inadvertent error, because the context

(Deut. 22:20–23) in a number of repetitions has the phrase "sweep away evil from your midst." [92] Nevertheless, the middle verse, containing the word *Israel*, should have been carefully checked before publication, and *Israel* not deleted.

V

One of the major concerns to the traditional Jew is the rendition of the Bible in accordance with Halakhah and rabbinic tradition. Otherwise its spirit is Sadduceean or Karaitic. The late Rabbi Samuel Gerstenfeld has already pointed this out in his articles on "The Conservative Halacha." [93] Moreover, in the posthumous volume *Eisenstein's Commentary on the Torah* [94] four "examples" of *faulty translation* in the Jewish Publication Society text are listed:

1—Ex. 21:19: "on his *staff*." [95]
2—Lev. 23:15: "morrow after the *Sabbath*." [96]
3—Deut. 18:3: "from them that offer a *sacrifice*." [97]
4—Deut. 25:9: "spit *in* his face." [98]

Other examples of such questionable renditions may be noted here, leaving a full listing for some future occasion.

Ex. 12:15: "only what *every person is to eat*," [99] AT reads "only what every person has to eat" . . . Halakhically this refers even to food for animals, as Rashi indicates. The reading should therefore be "only what every *being* is to eat . . ." RSV has "what every one must eat" which seems to be better, for even the old JPS had the error "save that which every man must eat."

Ex. 12:17: "you shall observe the (feast of) Unleavened Bread." [100] So also JPS and RSV. The text traditionally refers to the *matzah*, not to the festival. Rabbinically it indicates careful preparation (the watch-over or the vigil) that the *matzah* does not become susceptible to leavening. The Targum reads *petira*. Interestingly AT reads "You must observe this command," touching upon the rabbinic concept of *mitzvot*, as a play on *matzot*.

Ex. 12.45: "a resident hireling." [101] Is it a reference to one person or to two? Rabbinic commentaries set it as *two*. RSV has "sojourner or a native." JPS: "sojourner and hired servant." AT: "serf or laborer."

Ex. 13.4: "you go free on this day in the month of Abib," [102] so also RSV. A note below reads: "on the new moon." So also AT reads: "on the moon of Abib." This note is perplexing for the day definitely refers to the 15th of the month. See *Targum Jonathan, ad loc.*[103]

Ex. 13:16: "and as a *symbol* on your forehead." [104] The usage of "forehead" instead of "between your eyes" demonstrates an attempt at a traditional rendition, since the phylacteries are placed exactly midway between the eyes on the forehead where the hair begins to grow. But, one may ask, why not use (in a Jewish Bible) the word *Tephillin* and read "These shall be a sign upon your hand and *Tephillin* on your forehead that with a mighty hand *Ado-nai* freed us from Egypt." Even the (Protestant) Interpreter's Bible [105] speaking of *Totafot*, notes: "The etymology is uncertain but it is this word which is rendered by *tephillin* in the Targum . . ." If in Lev. 23:40 [106] because of uncertainty of the original meaning, the translation is rendered product of *hadar* trees" (which we believe to be *etrog*), why could not this new Jewish version write *totafot* (*tephillin*), as well? Moreover, where uncertainty abounds, as in many instances, recourse to traditional usage and rabbinic interpretation should have been taken with good reason.

The perplexity of translation in halakhic elements is apparent in other cases too:

Ex. 12:15: "*on the very first day* you shall remove leaven."[107] It is well known that this verse refers to the removal of leaven before the commencement of the festival. Rashi has, "before the holiday." [108] The reading should be traditionally: "*By* the first day you shall remove . . ." Even Moses Mendelssohn did not alter the rabbinic tradition, for he translated "jedoch am ersten Tage muesst Ihr schon den Sauerteig aus Euren Häusern geraumt haben." [109] The RSV ignores the Hebrew *ach*, but NT translates it "the very." Indeed, where laws are involved, like those of Passover, those should be explained, at least in a note. Translators generally may be free to render the sense of the Bible as they see it, but they are not free to upset rabbinic authority in rendition of verses pertaining to actual practice of Judaism.

Very interesting also is the following comparison of the different renditions of the biblical section dealing with "support of the poor" (Lev. 25:35–36):

JPS	RSV
And if thy brother be waxen poor, and his means fail with thee; then thou shalt uphold him: as a stranger and a settler shall he live with thee. Take thou no interest of him or increase; but fear thy God; that thy brother may live with thee.	And if your brother becomes poor, and cannot maintain himself with you, you shall maintain him; as a stranger and as sojourner he shall live with you. Take no interest from him or increase, but fear your God; that your brother may live beside you.

AT	NT
If a fellow-countryman of yours becomes poor, so that his ability to meet his obligation with you fails, *and you force on him the status of a resident alien or a serf,* and he lives under you, take no interest from him in money or in kind, but stand in awe of your God, while your countryman lives under you.	If your brother, being in straits, comes under your authority, *and you hold him as* though a resident alien, so that he remains under you, do not exact from him advance or accrued interest,[f] but fear your God. Let him stay under you as your brother.[110]
	[f] I.e., interest deducted in advance, or interest added at the time of repayment.

By translating "and you hold him as though a resident alien" the NT like AT (unlike JPS and RSV) sets aside the *mitzvah* of "maintenance," which is so emphatically stressed by Rashi [111] and Seforno.[112] Morover, the whole rabbinic concept "let thy brother live with thee" [113] is ignored here.[114]

A further interesting rendition, perplexing to the talmudic student, is the beginning of Exodus 23. It reads: You must not carry false rumors; you shall not join hands with the guilty to act as an unjust witness. Do not side with the mighty to do wrong,[115] and do not give perverse testimony in a dispute by leaning toward the mighty; nor must you show deference to a poor man in his dispute.

AT and RSV translate *rasha* as *wicked* person, not a *guilty* one: *rabim* is *multitude*, not *mighty* ("multitude" is mentioned in a note). To read "Do not side with the *mighty* to do wrong" and not "Do not follow a multitude to do evil" (AT: "you must not follow a majority by doing wrong") upsets the whole rabbinic notion of *rabim*, majority rule. What prompted the choice of *rabim* as "mighty"? Moreover, to translate "carry false rumors" is contrary to Targum and Rashi, as based on the *Mekhilta*. The text means "not to *accept* or tolerate false rumors." "Carrying false rumors" is in the realm of "talebearing" recorded in Lev. 19:16, which is here translated, "Do not deal basely with your fellows." [116] This phrase, too, is followed by the strange reading, "Do not profit by the blood of your neighbor," when its precise meaning, talmudically, and in accordance with the commentators, is, "Do not stand by the side if your neighbor's life (blood) is in danger."

To argue that to follow rabbinic notion one would have to translate such passages as "eye for eye" as "money indemnity for an eye" is not convincing. It is already widely recognized that "eye for eye" is not to be taken literally; *lex talionis* is to be interpreted only as meaning *compensation*. Hence, there is no fear of miscomprehension here as in the case of the many other mistranslations which may cause confusion as to the manner of Jewish teaching and tradition unless one follows the traditional rabbinic interpretation.

Another instance involving rabbinics is Deut. 25:9 translated as "spit in his face," [117] the same as the old JPS and other renditions. One wonders, in this new attempt, being "not a revision but a new translation," why not use "*before* their face" or "in his presence" even as *be-fanav* [118] is rendered in Deut. 4:37. Would such rendition in accordance with rabbinic tradition have spoiled the present rendering or understanding of the text?

Another important halakhic point is in Deut. 25:5: "When brothers dwell together and one of them dies and *leaves no son*." [119] The old JPS reads "*and has no child*" which is halakhically correct. But NT ignored the tradition.

Though one may argue that a Bible translation need not defer to rabbinic interpretation, we must recognize that a Jewish version implies not merely search for truth as scholars see it, but especially adherence to the Jewish mode of explanation. If it is only "scholarly research," Jewish funds may encourage it but such does not fulfill the main aim: to guide Jewish life therewith. Gentiles seek inspiration in their christological notions; should not a Bible for Jews, on the other hand, be in the spirit of full rabbinic teachings? Judaism is rabbinic in perspective and mode of conduct, not biblical. A "New Translation" therefore should be in the full spirit of rabbinic *Torah* (Instruction).

Two other examples of basic concern to Jewish tradition must also be considered:

Gen. 2:2: "He ceased on the seventh day from all the work which He had done." Utilization in the text of the words "He *rested* on the seventh day" (as given in the note) would have better conveyed the spirit of tradition pertaining to Sabbath, even as interpreted in *Megillah* 9a concerning the Septuagint rendition. Similarly, one fears the misunderstanding of the prohibition of labor on the festivals, when reading, for instance, Leviticus 23:8: "you shall not work at *your* (italics mine) occupations." Does it imply that other activities are permitted?

In Exodus, Chapter 20, verses 2 and 3 of the Decalague are given as part of *one* commandment, separated by a colon (:), thus, "I the Lord am your God . . . : You shall have no other gods beside Me." Then verse 4, beginning a new paragraph, is "you shall not make for yourself a sculptured image . . . ," thus apparently considering it the *Second* Commandment. Though a note delineates that "Tradition varies as to the division of the Commandments" it is to be remembered that "I the Lord am . . ." is the *First* and "You shall not have . . ." is the *Second* Commandment, even according to Rabbi Ishmael's view in *Sifre* Numbers 15:31 and *Sanhedrin* 98b. Jewish tradition has so recognized it also in the listing inscribed on tablets placed over the Ark of the Law in the Synagogue or on the *Parochet* (curtain). Non-Jewish works, however, seem to reckon verse 2 and 3 together as the first Commandment about Unity, and "the second Commandment prohibits all forms of Idolatry. No image of the deity is to be made." (See Ten Commandments, *Interpreter's Dictionary of the Bible*, Vol. IV, p. 570). The old JPS correctly begins the second Commandment (verse 3) as a separate paragraph, including therein verses 4 ff., thus making us question where "this translation has improved on the first JPS translation" (see Preface to NT).

VI

A comparison of the recent translations of the past decades is in order for the purpose of determining modernity of language, as well as the accomplishments of the NT above all others, as the "last word" in translation.

Below is the first paragraph of Genesis as rendered in

AT
(AMERICAN TRANSLATION, 1927)

When God began to create the heavens and the earth, the earth was a desolate waste, with darkness covering the abyss and a tempestuous wind raging over the surface of the waters. Then God said, "Let there be light!" And there was light; and God saw that the light was good. God then separated the light from the darkness. God called the light day, and the darkness night. Evening came, and morning, the first day.

RSV
(REVISED STANDARD VERSION, 1952)

In the beginning God created [a] the heavens and the earth. The earth was without form and void, and darkness was upon the face of the deep; and the Spirit [b] of God was moving over the face of the waters. And God said, "Let there be light"; and there was light. And God saw that the light was good; and God separated the light from the darkness. God called the light Day, and the darkness he called Night. And there was evening and there was morning one day.

[a] Or when God began to create
[b] Or wind

NT
(NEW TRANSLATION, 1963)

When God began to create [a] the heaven and the earth—the earth being unformed and void, with darkness over the surface of

[a] Or "in the beginning God created"

NT

the deep and a wind from [b] God
sweeping over the water—God
said, "Let there be light"; and
there was light. God saw how
good the light was, and God separated the light from the darkness. God called the light Day,
and the darkness He called Night.
And there was evening and there
was morning, a first day.[c]

[b] Others "the spirit of"
[c] Or "one day"

The comparison reveals that greater freedom in both approach
and style is found in AT,—that which NT certainly could not
have wisely permitted itself. But the "beginnings" of the text are
similar, nevertheless.

When, however, one sets RSV by the side of NT, it appears
that RSV was conservative in its approach, putting its "revisions"
into the notes. NT, conversely, was bolder—putting that which
the RSV has in its text into the notes at the bottom of the NT
page, and the suggestions of the RSV Notes into the actual body
of the text in the Jewish rendition.

Further comparison of the *Shema* (Deut. 6:4 ff.) in the new
translations demonstrates the modern trend.

AT

Listen, O Israel; the LORD is
our God, the LORD alone; so
you must love the LORD your
God with all your mind and all
your heart and all your strength.
These instructions that I am
giving you today are to be fixed
in your mind; you must impress
them on your children, and talk
about them when you are sitting
at home, and when you go off on
a journey, when you lie down and
when you get up; you must bind

NT

Hear, O Israel! The LORD is
our God, the LORD alone. You
must love the LORD your God
with all your heart and with all
your soul and with all your might.
Take to heart these words with
which I charge you this day. Impress them upon your children.
Recite them when you stay at
home and when you are away,
when you lie down and when you
get up. Bind them as a sign on
your hand and let them serve as

AT	NT
them on your hand as a sign, and they must be worn on your forehead as a mark; you must inscribe them on the door-posts of your house and on your gates.	a symbol on your forehead; inscribe them on the doorposts of your house and on your gates.

These differences and similarities of the recent translations may be multiplied, and the wisdom of the choice is debatable. Thus, does *alone* mean "He, alone is our God, none other," i.e., "excluding all others" or "unparalleled," "only" "solely"; where then is the teaching of monotheism? [120] Where is the concept of the uniqueness, the Oneness of God, His Unity, which Maimonides stresses so emphatically in his creeds, in his Introduction to *Chelek* (Chapter X, *Sanhedrin*)? Tradition teaches: God is one, there is none besides Him.

Using the best of other translations is commendable. But NT sought often to introduce a "modernity" far beyond the actual biblical practice. Such, for instance, is the rendition of the law of interest, Deut. 23:20:

AT	NT
You must not exact interest on loans to a fellow-countryman of yours, interest in money, food, or anything else that might be exacted as interest. On loans to the foreigner you may exact interest, but on loans to a fellow-countryman you must not, that the LORD your God may bless you in all your undertakings in the land which you are invading for conquest.	You shall not deduct interest from loans to your countryman, whether in money or food or anything else that can be deducted as interest. You may deduct interest from loans to foreigners, but not from loans to your countryman—so that the LORD your God may bless you in all your undertakings in the land which you are about to invade and occupy.

Does the phrase "deduct interest," at the time of taking a loan, reveal an old practice or a "modern banking process" derived from the *discount* of medieval Italian bankers? [121] Traditionally it means here that the *borrower* should not give or add interest.

See Rashi *ad loc.*, and compare also the translation in Lev. 25:37: "Do not lend him money at advance interest," referring to the *lender*.

It is to be remembered, as noted in the Preface, "While the committee profited much from the work of previous translators, the present rendering is not a revision, but essentially a new translation," citing briefly the obvious differences. A detailed comparative study therefore would have to be made to see the influence of the previous translations and in what manner this NT excels.

VII

One of the most distressing of features in the NT is the mode of its preparation and the procedure followed. The working members of the Committee "arrived at decisions by majority vote" (Preface). Are decisions in matter of "principle" to be reached on basis of *vote?* Can *democratic procedure* be applied to the meaning of the Bible? The Septuagint procedure, it seems, displayed practical action: Though each translator was closeted in his own room making his translation, there was finally unanimous opinion and agreement. It was not on the basis of a *vote*, which certainly may vary with circumstances; especially if, for instance, one of the traditionalists or liberals was away from a particular meeting at the discussion table. The absence of a member of the committee might influence the "decisive" truth. The procedure of deciding the truth for the Bible, hence, is a matter of great concern. It was already called to the attention of the Jewish Publication Society more than half-century ago. In the *American Hebrew*, Oct. 27, 1905, J. D. Eisenstein suggested a plan of action and considered the method adapted by the Society then as inadequate.[122]

Another matter of concern to the reader who wishes to abide by the traditional Hebrew Masoretic text is the mode of reference in the notes to "uncertainties," "other ancient versions" and "other readings." These are not the traditional *Kri* and *Ketiv* which are given, for instance on page 53. Rather, these notes are suggestions of readings different from the accepted Masorah.

Thus, *Samaritan*, pp. 105, 296, 350: *Greek Septuagint*, pp. 288, 381. To the general reader this may suggest an emendation process for the Bible, though the translators have conscientiously and traditionally refrained from it. It is believed that such suggestions have no place in the NT for the general reader. Such should be contained in Full Notes or in a Scholarly Appendix. One may also be disturbed by reading "traditionally, but incorrectly Red Sea." This jars the ears; there was no need of joining "traditionally" with "incorrectly." Were the text to contain simply the words "Traditionally, the Red Sea" it would have sufficed to convey the translator's new rendition.

Finally, it is noteworthy that in both the case of the Septuagint and the *Targum Onkelos*, reference is made to *approval* of the translation: The reference to the Septuagint approval is in the *Letter of Aristeas*,[123] and that pertaining to Onkelos is in the Talmud (*Megillah* 3a), stating that the Targum was "with the approval of Rabbi Elazar and Rabbi Joshua.[124] One wonders, what is or will be the nature of approval for this New Translation of the Torah?

One of the beneficial results of the New Translation and its publicity is the stimulus it has given to Bible study. Jewish laymen are now devoting attention to the Bible; adult classes and lectures on the subject have been well attended. It is even expected that in the Fall, with the renewal of Adult Education Institutes, the study of the Bible, as a result of this edition, will advance immensely. The battle of the Torah (*milchamta shel torah*), with pro and con, attack and defense, is before us. As students of the Torah we welcome this, for even from the criticisms much will be learned, to sharpen the minds and pencils for the future.

The present writer concludes that while the new JPS translation represents an improvement in many respects, which is commendable, it still falls short, as delineated above, and needs *tikkun* —further revision. In many aspects the work is to be recognized more as a *paraphrase*, "sense for sense" than a literal *translation*, "word for word." As such, the "paraphrased text" cannot be utilized by the side of a proposed Hebrew edition for it may bring confusion into the minds of students, studying the Hebrew text grammatically and etymologically in a classroom. For the general reader, who wishes to know the contents of the Pentateuch from a free and cursory reading, to read it like a novel, gracefully and meaningfully, without careful study and comparisons, this rendition may serve admirably. But a concept of the traditional interpretation will be inadequate, and cannot be gained therefrom. Its utilization for inspirational purposes in school and synagogue is also questionable. The RSV was prepared "for use in public and private worship, not merely for reading and instruction." [125] Does the New JPS Torah Translation also make that assertion?

Moreover, a perplexing question remains: should the *Bible translated for Jews* be interpreted *archaeologically*, as scholars objectively see it, or shall it be definitely set in a Jewish traditional manner? Our view is: Judaism is a rabbinic product and discipline, not a biblical way of life. Hence, for the message today, not only for objective truth, the Bible must be interpreted according to rabbinic standards.

To assert, as has already been done by some rabbinic organizations, that a new translation should and will presently be prepared, because of the alleged *Apikursos* in this new JPS rendition, is alarming. Scholarly study of the text, weighing all phases of commentaries in the line of tradition, and suggestion of revision in accordance with rabbinic, scholarly approach should be undertaken. It is unrealistic to ban, to condemn, and to begin producing newer, competitive translations. The finished, basic work is here; with the experience of careful research it can and should be revised with the honest intention of making it valuable and useful. The efforts of the present translators, who are recognized scholars, cannot and should not be invalidated, resulting in disunity in the Jewish community. A waste of Jewish funds will ensue if a "second" new translation is undertaken by a rabbinic body. Cooperation by sending in suggestions and comments, and a re-evaluation of the NT for full acceptance by all groups, leading to united recognition, should be the process. At present the work is a scholarly research, but bears no distinct official Jewish imprimatur. However, the inclusion of rabbinic interpretation into the text as well as following carefully the Masorah in all its details, together with the usage of *Ado-nai* for the Tetragrammaton, will give this work "the Jewish flavor" not found in previous translations.

Moreover, a translation cannot be published without full annotations to explain the reasons and details of choice and to forestall criticism. Hence a new edition should include full notes and comments. One recalls Saadia's medieval *Tafsir*—translation and commentary—which was directed to such a purpose. A modern translation, therefore, must especially utilize that approach—"comments for better comprehension."

The Jewish Publication Society, surely, in a cooperative manner with rabbinic organizations, can accomplish this, not relying merely upon individual "commissioned" scholars. One therefore looks forward in time to the betterment of the text, remembering on the one hand *Avot* 2:16, "we are not to free ourselves from the task,[126] and on the other, *Soferim* 1:5 that "the Torah cannot be perfectly translated." [127] It is hoped that in the very near future this new publication of the Torah translation will be carefully revised so that it may become a valued contribution to expanding Jewish life in America.

NOTES

1 Philo Judaeus, *On Moses*, p. 42 ff.

2 Cf. H. Malter, *Saadia Gaon*, p. 143.

3 Response by Dr. H. M. Orlinsky at the JPS Dinner of Dedication of New Torah Translation, Feb. 10, 1963.

4 Publicity of JPS, *The Eternal Book*.

5 *Soferim*, I, 5. See also *Megillat Taanit* (8th day of *Tevet*): "When darkness descended on the world for three days."

6 Ecclesiasticus, Prologue.

7 Jerome (c. 384) to Pope Damasus (Cf. F. C. Grant, *Translating the Bible*, p. 38).

8 גיטין מה : ספר תורה שכתבו מין ישרף ; רש"י — מין האדוק בעו"כ כיון כומר ;
רצ"ה חיות : מין, היינו שאין מאמין בדברי חז"ל (רמב"ם, הלכות ספר תורה יא :
... אפיקורוס ושאר פסולין). ט: ייזפזפ—

To quote *Gittin* 45b,—Rashi's view and the discrepancy noted by R. Zevi Chayes or compare this with Maimonides' notation—and then include *translations* into this category of *Sefer Torah*, giving *translations* the *dignity* of a *Sefer Torah*, may be a *guzmah*—farfetched.

The views of Rabbenu Hananel and Rashi in *Shabbat* 116a are also to be regarded, with reference to this problem.

רש״י ספרי מינין משרתים לע״ז וכתבו להן תורה נביאים וכתובים כתב אשורית ולשון הקדש. רבנו חנגאל : ספרי דבי אבידן ... ויש בהם ספרי תורה ... כתובים בלשה״ק.

Apparently "the *Sefer Torah* in the Hebrew tongue" and "translations" cannot be put into the same class for purposes of imprecation or evaluation of sanctity.

9 *Letter of Aristeas*, 308. Dropsie College Ed.

10 *Otzar Yisrael*, X, 309.

11 *Jewish Forum*, Sept. 1928, p. 439; Oct. 1928, etc.

12 *Ibid.*, Nov. 1928, p. 576.

13 "Shalom" (peace) in the Priestly benediction is rendered in a note as "friendship."

14 .ראו כי רעה נגד פניכם

15 .בישא דאתון סבירין למעבד

16 .ויהי בעצם היום הזה

17 .לא עכבן כהרף עין

18 ... והגדת לבנך

19 ... כי ישאלך בנך מחר

20 .ויש מחר שהוא לאחר זמן

21 .פסח הוא

22 .חמל, חס, חייסא

23 .לא תגע בו יד כי סקל יסקל או ירה יירה

24 .וקדשתם היום ומחר

25 .הנשמר מן הטומאה נקרא מקודש

26 .נפתלי אילה שלוחה הנותן אמרי שפר

27 Cf. S. Rin, "Ugaritic-OT Affinities," *Biblische Zeitschrift*, Jan. 1963, p. 241.

28 .ותראהו את הילד והנה נער בוכה

29 .התפאר עלי למתי אעתיר לך

30 .ויכבד לבו הוא ועבדיו

31 .נחל זרד

32 .בין המשפתים

33 .תחומיא

34 .רובץ בין החבילות הנתונות למשא

35 .יעקב איש תם

36 .נח איש צדיק תמים היה

37 .יעננו בקול

38 שמות יג, יח, רש״י : וסוף הוא שגדלים בו קנים. אבן עזרא : וסוף הוא שם מקום. י״א : ים אוקינוס.

39 .מה אקב לא קבה א-ל

40 .א-ל קנא פוקד עון ... לשונאי

41 .ושפטתי

42 .לו ישטמנו

43 .ואלה המשפטים

44. היש לכם אב או אח.

45. לא נוכל לראות פני האיש.

46. מי אתה בני.

47. לא תקלל.

48. וטעם אביו ואמו קלל כאומר תועבה גדולה עשה.

49 If the usage of *k-l-l*, having other meanings besides "curse," is based on Akkadian Code Laws, it is absolutely wrong and inconsistent with Jewish tradition to prefer such interpretations to the rabbinic interpretations—when preparing a Bible edition for Jews.

50. לשון הדיוט, חול.

51. את קולך שמעתי בגן.

52. דברה תורה כלשון בני אדם.

53. אתה.

54. שבו וסחרוה.

55. ים המלח.

56 Cf. S. Zeitlin, "Some Reflections on the Text of the Pentateuch," *JQR*, April 1961, p. 330.

57. ומספר את רבע ישראל.

58. מכשפה לא תחיה.

59. אלא תמות בב״ד.

60. לפתח חטאת רבץ.

61. רבץ בין המשפתים.

62 See above, note 27.

63. והגישו אדניו אל האלהים [דיניא]

64. קניתי איש.

65. קונה שמים וארץ.

66. עם זו קנית.

67. ארור אתה מכל הבהמה.

68. ויאר את הלילה.

69. יאר ה׳.

70. ונקב שם.

71. ...ממאי דהאי נוקב לישנא דברוכי הוא דכתיב מה אקב

72. אינו חייב עד שיפרש את השם. ולא המקלל בכינוי. ונקב לשון קללה כמו מה אקב.

73. מה אקב לא קבה.

74 *JQR*, XII (Jan. 1922), p. 263.

75. בן פורת יוסף.

76. בכור שורו.

77. וה׳ נהג רוח קדים.

78. ורוח נסע מאת ה׳.

79. לא בחיל ולא בכח כי אם ברוחי.

80 Cf. *Chagigah* 11b. See also Husik, *A History of Medieval Jewish Philosophy*, p. XVI.

81. על שם אחיהם יקראו בנחלתם.

82. אלא בתוך שבטי אפרים ומנשה יהיו נכללים.

83 See also Soferim 1–14: פתוחה שעשה סתומה, סתומה שעשאה פתוחה הרי זה יגנז, איזהו פתוחה כל שהתחיל בראש השיטה [הג׳ הגר״א].

84. אלה תולדות השמים... ביום עשות.

85. ויכל משה את המלאכה: פ. ויכס הענן את האהל.

86. וירא כבוד ה׳ אל כל העדה. ס. וידבר ה׳ אל משה.

87. ואכד וכלנה בארץ שנער.

88. איל (אחר) [אחר] [אחד] נאחז. See note *a* on page 36 of NT.

89. צויתי.

90. אני ה׳.

91. ובערת הרע מישראל.

92. ובערת הרע מקרבך.

93. See above, notes 11, 12.

94. Subtitled: A defense of the Traditional Jewish Viewpoint, 1960, p. 19.

95. והמתהלך בחוץ על משענתו [על בוריה].

96. ממחרת השבת [ממחרת יו״ט].

97. מאת זבחי הזבח.

98. וירקה בפניו.

99. אשר יאכל לכל נפש.

100. ושמרתם את המצות.

101. תושב ושכיר לא יאכל בו. רש״י: תושב זה גר תושב ושכיר זה הנכרי.

102. היום אתם יוצאים בחדש האביב.

103. בחמיסר בניסן הוא ירחא דאביבא.

104. ולטוטפת בין עיניך.

105. Vol. IV, 808, *s.v.* Phylacteries.

106. פרי עץ הדר.

107. אך ביום הראשון.

108. מערב יו״ט וקרוי ראשון.

109. באור תשביתו: העניין כאשר יכנס היום הראשון כבר יהי׳ השאור נשבת
מהבתים והוא זמן מורכב מעתיד ועבר כמו שמתורגם בל״א.

110. והחזקת בו ...

111.   והחזקת בו. אל תניחהו שירד ויפול ויהא קשה להקימו אלא חזקהו משעת
מוטת ידו.

112. והחזקת בו להקימו.

113. וחי אחיך עמך.

114 See Ramban *ad loc.* Cf. S. Belkin, *In His Image*, p. 98 (The Sacred-
ness of Human Life).

115. אל תשת ידך עם רשע ... לא תהיה אחרי רבים להטות.

116. לא תלך רכיל בעמך.

117. וירקה בפניו.

118. ויצאך בפניו בכחו.

119. ובן אין לו.

120 See Rashi's explanation of first verse of *Shema.* Cf. also Ibn Ezra,
Rashbam and Malbim: הוא אחד ואין זולתו.

121 See Woodward & Rose, *A Primer of Money*, p. 35; Graham & Seaver,
Money, pp. 147–148: "Italians began to advance large sums . . . and receive
interest until the money advanced was repaid." Cf. also *Encyclopedia of Banking and Finance*, 1924, p. 159: *Bank Discount:* Interest paid in advance

. . . ; p. 314 *Interest:* The excess payment made when the borrowed dollar is returned . . .

122 See also his *Critical Notes on Psalms,* 1906.

123 See quotations above, *Aristeas to Philocrates,* 308 ff.

124 תרגום של תורה אונקלוס הגר אמרו מפי ר׳ אלעזר ור׳ יהושע.

125 See Preface, RSV, IV.

126 לא עליך המלאכה לגמור. ולא אתה בן חורין ליבטל ממנה.

127 שלא היתה התורה יכולה להתרגם כל צרכה.

LEON D. STITSKIN

*

Ralbag's Introduction to the Book of Job

INTRODUCTION

LEVI BEN GERSON, *Ralbag* (commonly called Gersonides or Gershuni, in Hebrew) was born at Bagnols, Southern France, in 1288. He was a philosopher, exegete, physician, and mathematician. As a philosopher, his chief philosophical work, *Milchamot Hashem*, occupies a distinguished place alongside of the *Guide* of Maimonides. As a commentator of the Bible, he depicted the philosophical essences of biblical thought and brought them into harmony with Aristotelianism. This was especially true of the Book of Job which he, like Maimoindes, regarded as purely a philosophical work dealing with the problems of good and evil and God's providence.

Though a distinguished Talmudist, Levi ben Gerson never held a rabbinical post. He earned a livelihood most probably by the practice of medicine. He was a descendant of a family of scholars. His father was Gershon b. Solomon, the author of *Shaar ha-Shamayim*, and Nachmanides was his maternal grandfather.[1] He was only in his late twenties when he began writing his magnum opus, *Milchamot Hashem*. In addition to his commentaries on the Bible and Talmud, he wrote treatises on logic,[2] mathematics,[3] physics,[4] medicine,[5] and a résumé on Averroes.

The Book of Job offered for Gersonides, as well as for Maimonides before him, an excellent opportunity to project the representative opinions held by philosophers on the nature of providence and theodicy. There is first of all the Aristotelian view that God's providence extends only to species and not to individuals. Then there is the notion held by the majority of our people that God provides for every individual of the human race—*hashgachah peratit*. The third view maintains that some individuals are specially provided for but others are under the protection only of "general" providence.

Essentially the problem resolved itself into a consideration as to whether God's omnipotence is so central that we can circumscribe His goodness or vice versa. Now if we assume as some traditionalists do that it is inadmissible that evil proceed from God, we are confronted by the shocking dilemma: why are the righteous oppressed by miseries while the wicked are triumphant? What is even more paradoxical is the question why evil exists altogether in a universe which is apparently orderly and purposefully-directed.

Classical and medieval philosophers (unlike some modern thinkers who, geared as they are to a scientific view of reality, assert that we must learn to live with our dilemmas and not waste our energy attempting to resolve them in a rational manner, inasmuch as paradoxes abound in all fields of natural research) worked over in massive theological schemes the contradictions and aberrations posed by the problem of evil. Their doctrines ranged from the Platonic view (adopted by Philo) that evil, being simply the absence of good, is not anything positive or absolute, to the notion that good and evil are distributed in this world according to the law of justice and that in the sublunar world God's omnipotence limits His goodness.

Abraham bar Chiyya, Maimonides, and Gersonides, in the tradition of a philosophy of personalism, maintain that moral evil befalling man is due to the defect of the recipient rather than the dispenser. When man fails to realize his potentialities and rational faculties, he is subject to the immutable, determining laws of nature. He can only escape the rigor of the iron laws of the physical environment by developing his intellectual excellence. The higher he stands in the scale of creation, the greater solicitude and protection is bestowed upon him. The degree of divine protection is proportional to the degree of development through man's free choice. Thus those who strive to develop the faculties of the soul enjoy the care of a special, individual providence, while those who grope in ignorance are guarded only by "general" providence.

What follows is my translation of a major portion of Ralbag's introduction to Job which contains in essence his notions on theodicy and providence, expanded upon in his *Milchamot Hashem*.

L.D.S.

L EVI BEN GERSON said: it is appropriate to interpret this book, the book of Job, in a broad perspective, and to delve deeply into its content in accordance with the dictates of our wisdom, considering especially the great value derived from this work for man's political and intellectual well-being. In fact, the Torah generally is conceived on the principle elucidated in this book.

For this reason, our sages ascribed the authorship of this work to Moses our teacher and observed: "Moses authored his book as well as the portion of Balaam and Job." To be sure, there were differences of opinion among them whether the episode of Job was an allegory or an actual event.

The central problem we shall investigate in this book is whether God's special providence is extended to each person individually, in keeping with basic biblical doctrine, and whether the Almighty watches over all human activities or not. Accordingly, if we establish the premise that God's providence is over all his creatures individually in consonance with the doctrines of the Torah, it follows inevitably that we ascribe an injustice to the Almighty on account of the apparent evil order in the world pertaining to good and evil that befalls particular individuals. For, invariably, we can find a righteous person who suffers and a wicked one who is prosperous. This paradox led philosophers to believe that the Almighty does not apprehend particular things in the sublunar world, as we indicated before.

Doubts about the doctrine of divine providence continued to receive renewed impetus among ancient and later thinkers and even among the prophets and revered sages. Our sages maintained that even Moses, our teacher, already made reference to this cosmic paradox when he beseeched the Almighty: ". . . Do make me know Thy way that I may know Thee" (*Exodus* 33:13). From the very response by the Almighty to this supplication, it is apparent that this was the problem agitating Moses. For the Almighty proclaimed: "The Lord is the immutable, eternal Being, merciful and gracious" (*Ibid* 34:6).

The prophet Habakkuk likewise was concerned about this doctrine when he queried: "Wherefore wilt Thou look upon those that deal treacherously, be silent when the wicked swalloweth up him that is more righteous than he?" (Hab. 1:13).

The Psalmist David similarly was troubled when he stated: "For I was envious of the arrogant, when I saw the prosperity of the wicked. For there are no pangs at their death but their strength is firm . . . Behold, such are the wicked, and they that are always at ease increase riches. Surely in vain have I cleansed my heart and washed my hands in innocence . . . And when I pondered how I might know this, it was wearisome in mine eyes" (Ps. 73:3, 4, 12, 13, 16).

Before we commence the interpretation of this book we shall preface one postulate that is all-embracing in this work. It is our contention that the evils that befall men are generally due to human potentialities that have not been actualized, or to pure accident. This is because tragic incidents basically originate either with the recipient of the misfortune himself or with an object external to him. As regards the former, the roots of evil occurrences in the recipient are to be found either in human temperament, one's character, or psychological disposition. If it is due to human temperament, then it must surely be ascribed to one's potential faculty. For the cause of the disorder here is the submergence of the passive powers to the active ones as demonstrated in the fourth proof. The same explanation holds true for the other factors of man's character or psychological disposition as the cause of evil. For in those instances as well, danger strikes when man does not channel his potentialities in the proper direction, that is, when they are not guided by his rational mind. For alas, it is only one's rational spirit that leads man in the right direction in everything that has to do with human needs.

By the same token, tragedies originating outside of man, which have their roots in human temperament or man's free choice, as is the case with wars, may be explained in the same manner as previously and ascribed to man's potentialities not developed.

Misfortunes, however, that do not have their genesis in human temperament or in man's free-will, such as earthquakes, violent storms, lightnings, and similar disorders are the result of pure accidents. For what is involved in this instance are destructive forces whose very nature is to destroy by design. It is necessary to assume, therefore, that in some cases there are celestial causes determining and guiding them so that at one time one malevolent force prevails over the other and vice versa. This takes place according to a determined rhythmic design and a permanent plan as has been indicated by our physical sciences. For this reason, too, we find at one time the element of fire predominant; at another time air, or water, on earth in accordance with the relation that exists between the active and the passive forces. In this way it is possible to maintain the sublunar forms of existence whose survival depends upon the uniform elements found in the substances that compose them. The cause for the unity in sublunar nature is the impact upon the substances from heavenly bodies.

From this standpoint, then, we deduce that such calamities strike us as pure chance. Consider for instance the case of one individual struck down by a conflagration or a group of people, who by chance dwell in a certain area, suddenly overtaken by a calamitous earthquake. Surely in those instances only a chance element is involved. In general, then, it is inadmissable that evil can proceed directly from God. That is why we often hear the expression that no tragedy ever descends from on High.

NOTES

1 *Yuchasin*, Abraham Zacuto (ed. Fillipowski, p. 224).
2 *Sefer ha-Hekkesh ha-Yashar*—a treatise on syllogism.
3 *Sefer ha-Mispar*—a treatise on algebra and *Melo Chofnayim* on Euclid.
4 *Dillugim*—a treatise on the seven constellations.
5 *Meshichah*—a remedy for gout.

CRITICISM

ELIEZER BERKOVITS

✳

Reconstructionist Theology

A CRITICAL EVALUATION

I. THE THEOLOGY OF RECONSTRUCTIONISM

THERE can be little doubt that wide sections of modern Jewry are engulfed by a deep spiritual crisis which is due to the conflict between traditional Judaism and the secular civilization of the age. On the American Jewish scene Reconstructionism represents the school of thought whose chief preoccupation has been the interpretation of the meaning of this conflict and that has devoted its intellectual energies almost exclusively to its resolution. The movement, led vigorously by its founder, Mordecai M. Kaplan,* has now achieved sufficient self-assurance to claim to offer "the only alternative to Orthodoxy and Secularism." [1]

Is this claim justified? Does Reconstructionism indeed offer a way out of the present predicament of our destiny? This study has been undertaken for the sole purpose of finding the answer to this question. We shall have to consider the main teachings of Reconstructionist religious philosophy and then inquire into their objective validity.

Rejection of Supernaturalism—Transnaturalism

Reconstructionism links the cause of the spiritual crisis of our time to the supernatural element in traditional religion. The modern mind is unable to accept supernaturalism. As long as religion is associated with the supernatural, modern civilization will remain secular. According to Reconstructionist thought, supernaturalism is "gone with the wind" never to return again. If religion is to be saved at all, it will have to be "wedded to naturalism." [2] Therein

---

* Dr. Mordecai M. Kaplan's works, *The Meaning of God in Modern Jewish Religion* and *Judaism Without Supernaturalism*, are referred to as *M. of G.* and *J. W. Sn.* from the 1958 ed.

lies the solution to the problem. Reconstructionism undertakes the task of purifying Judaism from its admixture of supernaturalism.

Occasionally the attempt is made to use the term "supernaturalism" in a specific way: as the belief that God may at will suspend the laws of nature in order to reward those whom He loves and punish those who have earned His wrath.[3] However, it is obvious that the inherent logic of Reconstructionism does not allow it to stop at the negation of the supernatural in this limited sense only. The stumbling block is not just the concept of "God as miracle worker" or "as a reservoir of magic power to be tapped whenever they (the believers) are aware of their physical limitations." [4] The idea of the supernatural as such is objectionable. According to Dr. Kaplan, modern science has invalidated "the distinction between natural and supernatural." [5] For the Reconstructionist the idea of God as a transcendental, omnipotent, all-kind and all-wise Supreme Being that confronts the world and man as their Creator has no meaning. Modern man, so he maintains, is able to conceive the godhead only as immanent in the world; modern man is incapable of entering into relationship with the supernatural.[6] His concern is with life on this earth exclusively; there is no other. His goal is self-fulfillment, which may also be called salvation—not, of course, in its traditional other-worldly meaning, but as this-worldly self-transcendence through the realization of man's inherent potentialities. Religion must help man "to live and to get the most out of life." This it can do only if it teaches him "to identify as divine and holy whatever in human life or in the world about him enhances human life." [7] The forces in us and around us which make "for health, happiness and progress" [8] are the manifestations of the divine. The God idea may be seen as the sum total of the process which in man and in nature contributes to human salvation. Reconstructionism asserts that this new concept may rightly be considered a re-interpretation of the traditional one, for it "can function in our day exactly as the belief in God has always functioned; it can function as an affirmation that life has value."[9]

At this point, however, the question might be asked: since the supernatural is rejected, what need is there for religion at all? In view of the fact that man's purpose in life is this-worldly self-fulfillment, could he not strive for it without having to identify as divine those forces which assist him in his endeavor? Why should we not be satisfied with a purely secular form of self-realization? In answer to such and similar questions the concept of man's striving for salvation is elaborated. Man is inspired to transcend the inheritance of his evolutionary origin from the brute by certain ideals and values which are of the spirit. Even though they are not part of the world of objective facts, they are no less real than the world of the senses. However, naturalistic science cannot account for values and meanings. It is for this reason that "secularism is not enough." [10] Human salvation depends on the realization of man's ethical aspirations. As man yearns to transcend his "sub-human tendencies," he is really raising himself above the dominion of the natural laws of the scientist. On account of that he is in need of "a transnatural religion." Transnaturalism is then the "alternative" that Reconstructionism submits as the union between religion and scientific naturalism.

Transnaturalism is defined as "that extension of naturalism which takes into account much that mechanistic or positivistic science is incapable of dealing with. Transnaturalism reaches out into the dominion where mind, personality, purpose, ideals, values and meanings dwell. It treats of the good and the true." [11] The distinction between fact and value is, of course, a very old and valid one. Our question, however, has still not been answered. If one so pleases, one may call the reaching out into the realm of meanings and values by the term "transnaturalism." But why transnaturalist *religion?* What is gained by it? May this recognition of a realm of ends and purposes as an aspect of reality not be adequately expressed within the scope of some secular humanism or ethical culture movement? However, Reconstructionism avers that "a godless humanism" [12] is an inadequate interpretation of life, because "it fails to express and to foster the feeling that man's ethical aspirations are part of a cosmic urge, by obeying which man makes himself at home in the universe." [13] Man needs the awareness that something in the very nature of the universe answers to his desire for self-fulfillment. This applies not only to man's individual happiness, but also to his endeavor for "maximum social cooperation," which is inseparable from salvation. It is maintained that "a religionless humanism fails to provide. . . . a motive for 'dedication to mankind.' That motive can come only from seeing in mankind potentialities which are in rapport with the creative principle in the cosmos—with God." [14] Without being able to see that his efforts at self-realization are indeed in keeping with the inherent nature of reality, man could not maintain himself in defiance of the endless temptations, failures, and disappointments which forever beset his path.

Godhood as a Cosmic Process

Reconstructionism does not find it difficult to show how "the inner drives of man" are a manifestation of cosmic reality. As is well known, man is not a self-sufficient being, independent of the rest of the world. "Human nature is part of the larger world of nature." [15] Whatever constitutes his being reflects powers outside him in the universe, the source whence he derives his existence. His very will for self-fulfillment is part of the cosmic will to live and is characteristic of all living things. Ethical inclinations and purposeful aspirations reveal aspects of reality because human nature itself has its place in the universal scheme. We have to learn to view the drives and urges of man for self-transcendence "as no less an integral part of the cosmic structure of reality than the life-drive and the sex-drive . . ." [16] In the very choice of goals, as we strive for salvation, we are impelled by the cosmic powers that have formed us and that sustain us. These powers we identify as divine, because they alone make life meaningful and valuable. The divine reveals itself in us in our own urge for self-realization. The very purpose of speaking of God as "the Power that makes for salvation" is "to identify the particular human experiences which enable us to feel the impact of that process in the environment and in ourselves which impels us to grow physically, mentally, morally and spiritually. That process is godhood. It reveals itself in those particular experiences." [17]

Needless to say that if godhood is the cosmic process that impels man to grow, the "cosmic urges that are manifested in him also represent the will and the law of God for him. A deity that is immanent in nature and in man cannot communicate his will or law in a specific act of personal revelation." The law of God is revealed to man in man's "own best vision of his capacity for rendering service to the cause of humanity." [18] It follows from the Reconstructionist premise that "we cannot see the will of God in any one specific code of laws. Only in the spiritual life of man as a whole, only in the complex of forces which impel man to think in terms of ideals and seek to implement their ideals through laws as well as through social institutions can we discover the will of God."[19] This is a new interpretation of the old adage, *vox populi vox dei*. From the Reconstructionist point of view one might say that while the Torah is of course not *min ha-shamayim*, as tradition understands the term, all law that aims at cooperation represents a form of divine self-revelation, brought about through the instrumentality of man's "best vision." By relating man's higher aspirations to cosmic nature and bestowing the name of God on "the totality of all those forces in life that render human life worthwhile," religion becomes the source of values and meanings, whereas science "describes objective reality." [20]

It would of course matter little by what name we called the cosmic forces whose self-revelation we discern in man's idealistic impulses. Name-calling is often a mere game of semantics. The religious significance of identifying those forces as the process of godhood lies in the fact that by doing so we affirm our confidence in the validity of the meanings and purposes for which they are responsible. By recognizing godhood in everything that impels man "to grow," we express our confidence that indeed he will grow. The "process of godhood" assures the Reconstructionist of the possibility of the realization of man's yearning for salvation. He calls this process "God" because he defines the term as the Power, inherent in the universe, that—by the very fact of its activity in the human soul—"endorses what we believe ought to be and that endorses that it will be." [21] The word "God" is for Reconstructionism a symbol that expresses "the highest ideals for which men strive and, at the same time, points to the objective fact that the world is so constituted as to make for the realization of those ideals." [22] This may be called the faith of Reconstructionism. To argue from man's position as part of nature for the recognition of the cosmic roots of his strivings is one thing; to conclude that, because of their being rooted in cosmic forces, they are bound to

382]   A TREASURY OF "TRADITION"

find fulfillment is quite another. It implies an act of faith in the cosmos.

The Faith of Reconstructionism

Let us see what must be assumed in such an act of faith. Not only does the Reconstructionist believer reason from man, placed in the context of "a larger nature," to his relatedness to universal life, but he assumes—on account of this relatedness—a kind of "pre-established harmony" between his impulses and the cosmic urge. He must further assume some form of built-in harmony between the order of nature, as described by science, and the powers that are responsible for the human drives that manifest values and purposes. Unless the realm of nature and that of the spirit are coordinated, there can be little hope that the material conditions in the universe will ever allow the realization of man's aspirations. Reconstructionism is aware of what is implied in its belief in the possibilities of human salvation. It interprets faith in the sovereignty of God as "faith that in mankind there is manifest a power which, in full harmony with the nature of the physical universe, operates for the regeneration of human society." [23] Underlying this assumption is the concept of unity among all the cosmic forces. Unless they are purposefully interrelated, no purpose can prosper in the universe. The cosmic drives, active in man and society, in nature as well as in the realm of the spirit, must be related to each other in an all-embracing universal harmony; otherwise the fulfillment of man's striving for self-realization is left to mere chance. Only on the basis of a concept of universal oneness does it make sense to affirm that the world is so constituted that what the human mind recognizes as valuable will indeed come to be for the sole reason that it ought to be. Reconstructionism perceives God "as the apotheosis of the interrelated unity of all reality; for it is only such unity that is compatible with life's worthwhileness." [24] Only by virtue of its purposefulness can life have meaning.

No doubt, man does have some experience of life's unity. Personality itself may be looked upon as the result of the unifying process in the world. Man's own creative urge as well as his appreciation of value are manifestations of life's general trend towards unity.

Meaning achieved in an act of creativity is always a deed of unification. However, such experiences testify mainly to a *tendency* toward unity, to an effort in life "to achieve and express unity, harmony and integrity." [25] There is, however, a long way from such tendencies to the affirmation of actual harmony between man and the universe, and among all the cosmic powers themselves. How is such affirmation justified? The father of Reconstructionism assures us repeatedly that the concept of "the interrelated unity of all reality," which alone "spells God" for him, is based on an intuition—on the intuition "that human life is supremely worthwhile and significant." [26] The belief in God, accordingly, means to subscribe to "the certain assumption" that the nature of cosmic reality endorses and guarantees "the realization in man of that which is of greatest value to him." "It is an assumption that is not susceptible to proof," says Dr. Kaplan, but if we believe in it, we believe in God.[27] Thus, the basic Reconstructionist concept of life's worthwhileness, to affirm which is "the function" of the idea of God, becomes a matter of intuitive assumption. This implies also that it cannot be "demonstrated" that self-fulfillment, the goal of Reconstructionist religion, will ever be attained. What alone may be said concerning it is that "faith must assume it as the objective of human behavior, if we are not to succumb to the cynical acceptance of evil, which is the only other alternative." [28] One should, however, not be misled by this quotation into believing that the faith that is meant here is only the result of a tragic choice between itself and the despair of cynicism. Such a faith would indeed be nothing but a mere opiate. In one of the finest passages of Reconstructionist literature, part of which has already been quoted in connection with Dr. Kaplan's rejection of secular humanism, one reads: "Without the emotional intuition of an inner harmony between human nature and universal nature, without the conviction, born of the heart rather than of the mind, that the world contains all that is necessary for human salvation, the assumptions necessary for ethical living remain cold hypothesis lacking all dynamic power. . . . It is only this emotional reaction to life that can make humanity itself mean more to us than 'the disease of the agglutinated dust.' " [29] Notwithstanding the recurring echo of the alternative of despair, there is no doubt that the intuition of Reconstructionist faith is presented as an actual experience of deep emotional intensity.

Chaos and Cosmos

Having followed thus far the analysis of the Reconstructionist thesis, the question may no longer be put off: What is the status and the meaning of evil in the Reconstructionist world view? Since the emergence of values and purposes in man and society are attributed to the interrelated complex of helping cosmic powers which we identify as divine, shall we be justified in identifying evil in the world as the self-revelation of some diabolical cosmic forces that "unmake" man's striving for salvation and unity? In view of human experience with nature as well as in history, it would not seem to be an unwarranted conclusion. Shall we then assume a Manichean "universe" in which the two principles of good and evil are locked in struggle with each other? Reconstructionist thinking does not countenance such a solution. It does not agree to the spelling of the word evil as Evil. According to it, evil must not be granted status side by side with "the goodness of life which is its godliness." Evil does not exist in a positive way, so Reconstructionism avers. Evil is a mere negation, a chance, an accident. It is "inevitable only in the logical and passive sense that darkness is the inevitable concomitant of light." Evil is mere unshaped and unformed *Tohu va-Vohu*, that phase of the universe which has not yet been invaded by the creative energy, not yet conquered by will and intelligence, not yet completely penetrated by godhood. The creative energy, which is the element of godhood in the universe, is all the time at work, in man and in nature, forming cosmos out of chaos.[30]

Such an interpretation of evil must be paralleled by an appropriate interpretation of life's worthwhileness. Life is worthwhile in spite of all that mars it. It is worthwhile not so much because of the actually realized good in it, but mainly owing "to the infinite potentialities that are still latent and that will in time come to fruition." [31] Latent potentialities can, of course, never be demonstrated. It is again a matter of intuitive faith, a knowledge of the heart rather than of the mind.

Whatever the value of this interpretation of evil may be, it is obvious that the Reconstructionist credo has been badly jolted. Even if one is not prepared to grant evil positive status, the mere existence of chaos beside the process of godhood necessitates a new definition of the concept of the deity. A god that, "like an artist" struggling with the passive resistance of a block of marble, step by step forms cosmos out of the meaninglessness of chaos is obviously lacking the attributes of infinity or perfection. As long as there is evil, there is chaos; and chaos exists because godhood has "not yet penetrated it." But a deity that needs time to do his job is of necessity limited in his capacity. This, indeed, is recognized to be one of the consequences of the Reconstructionist position. The Reconstructionist interpretation of evil involves "a radical change in the traditional concept of God. It conflicts with that conception of God as infinite and perfect in His omniscience and omnipotence." [32] However, we are assured that there is really no need for such an idea of the godhead. A concept which symbolizes "the sum of the animating, organizing forces and relationships which are forever making a cosmos out of chaos" is quite sufficient. It is such a concept that the Reconstructionist has in mind when he speaks of "God as the creative life of the universe." [33]

This, of course, gives us an entirely new idea of the deity. As our awareness of the divine aspect of reality is derived from the meaningful and purposeful contents of the universe, divinity must manifest itself in the cosmos. The cosmos, however, is continually growing. As the cosmos expands, so does its divine quality develop with it. We ought, therefore, to conclude: the more cosmos, the richer the potency of the creative life of the universe that is identified as God. We have actually netted a god that is neither perfect nor infinite; one that, though finite in his effectiveness, is infinite in possibilities of further development; one that grows more and more perfect as it forces cosmos upon the face of chaos.

Enthusiasm for Living

The extremely original idea of the Reconstructionist godhead illustrates dramatically how much the Reconstructionist intuition must accomplish in order to establish the worthwhileness of life. We see now that the belief in the unity of all reality, which alone could guarantee the realization of man's nobler aspirations, in-

volves belief in cosmic powers that are finite in potency as well as
in wisdom. No one is, of course, in a position to evaluate the vastness of universal chaos as compared with the finite amount of creative life which at any moment may be immanent in the cosmos.
Whether the potency of a finite godhead may not be after all
exhausted in its struggle with the passive resistance of the "Tohu
and Bohu"; or whether the process of cosmic godhead may not
occasionally lead to a blunder of universal magnitude and thus
allow chaos to regain its lost terrain—such questions receive no
adequate attention. Apparently, it is felt that the emotional reaction of faith in life is convincing enough to silence such problems. On of the strongest statements of Reconstructionist faith
seems to be directed against such and similar carpings of the
intellect. Toward the end of one of Dr. Kaplan's major works on
Reconstructionist theology once again the question is asked:
"Whence do we derive this faith in a Power that endorses what
ought to be?" And the answer is given in the following words:
"Not from that aspect of the mind which has to do only with
mathematically and logically demonstrated knowledge. Such faith
stems from that aspect of the mind which finds expression in the
enthusiasm for living, in the passion to surmount limitation. . . .
The fact that many lack this enthusiasm does not invalidate the
truth (of the faith), any more than the fact that it took the genius
of an Einstein to discover the principle of relativity should lead
us to cast a doubt upon its truth. This enthusiasm is man's will
to live the maximum life. Just as the will to live testifies—in an
intuitive, not a logical sense—to the reality of life, the will to live
the maximum life testifies to the realizable character of such
life." [34] We must confess that we are not quite able to see how
"the enthusiasm for living" may be considered an "expression" of
an "aspect of the mind," since this enthusiasm is also equated
with "man's will to live the maximum life." Be that as it may, the
passage quoted indicates that "the enthusiasm for living" is the
cornerstone of the Reconstructionist philosophy of religion. Without it there can be no faith in the power that endorses what ought
to be and guarantees that it is also realizable. This enthusiasm
must therefore be the source of the conviction, "born of the heart
and not of the mind," of the harmony between individual striv-

ings and cosmic urges, and finally, the origin of the intuition of the unity of all reality. As one realizes that the entire scheme of Reconstructionist salvation depends on "the enthusiasm for living," one can hardly suppress the thought that the far-reaching cosmic conclusions of the Reconstructionist heart represent no less a bold "leap of faith" than the boldest ever performed by Karl Barth and his disciples.

At this point, one is induced to recall the way the founder and leader of Reconstructionism pokes fun at an author who has stated that a sense of sureness, "a sense of overmastering certainty which grips the spirit," is the characteristic mark of supernatural revelation. After the summary dismissal of the illogicality of such notions, one would be entitled to look forward to something more tangible than "emotional reaction," "intuitive affirmation," and "enthusiasm for living" to form the foundation of Reconstructionist religious faith. Should one, perhaps, use Dr. Kaplan's own words with which he contemptuously rejects the sense of sureness and overmastering certainty of supernatural revelation and say regarding the intuitive convictions of Reconstructionism that "one takes exception, as a modernist must, to the folly of making sureness a criterion of truth, since stupidity is almost invariably sure of its own wisdom?" [35] We shall not follow Dr. Kaplan's example. We believe that a sense of sureness need not always be wrong, only because at times even fools seem to possess it; just as we hold quite confidently that the value of the most enthusiastic enthusiasm will not be proved by the argument that it took the genius of an Einstein to conceive the theory of relativity. Suffice it unto us to have traced the place of intuition and enthusiasm in the structure of Reconstructionist thought.

In bringing to a conclusion this presentation of Reconstructionist theology, we may point out that its characteristic feature is a mood of optimism, of "trust in life and in man." The optimism is intuitively derived from "the quality of universal being," which is called divine and is identified with godhood. One may say that Reconstructionist thought is a variation on the religious theme of the seventeenth and eighteenth centuries; it is a form of Natural Religion. The very title of Dr. Kaplan's latest work, *Judaism Without*

Supernaturalism, reminds one of that classic of eighteenth century deism, *Christianity Not Mysterious,* authored by John Toland and published in 1696. The "natural light" by which the deists were guided was, of course, reason, which possessed the dignity of logical necessity and universal validity. Reconstructionism, however, is familiar with the intellectual climate of the twentieth century. Its "natural light" is provided by the insights of experimental science and psychology. Reconstructionism is, therefore, guided by human experience, by aspirations, urges, yearnings, drives. Universality is acquired by granting these manifestations of human nature cosmic status as the expressions of a cosmic vitality. In such an atmosphere reliance on intuition and on an enthusiasm for living is, perhaps, understandable. At the same time, one is also reminded of certain specific forms of Natural Religion which were in vogue in the seventeenth and eighteenth centuries. In particular, one is induced to recall the English philosopher, Shaftesbury, who in his writings, published in 1711, placed at the center of his thought the principle of enthusiasm for life and living. He, too, derived the meaning and worthwhileness of life from a universal harmony. Not unlike Reconstructionism, Shaftesbury, too, saw the meaning of religion in the enhancement of personality, which may be achieved because man knows himself at one with the interrelated unity of all reality. For Shaftesbury, too, the interrelated unity of reality is the divine aspect of reality. It follows logically from such a position that, like Dr. Kaplan, the Englishman, too, is compelled to deny the reality of evil. If evil existed positively and actively, and on the world-wide scale in which it does seem to exist from the point of view of common sense observation, what would become of the enthusiasm for living?!

It should also be noted that in Reconstructionism we are confronted with a form of pantheism. By identifying certain processes in man and the world as divine, we identify the divinity with the world and, indeed, with man. In a striking passage it is stated: ". . . we must not identify the sovereignty of God with the expression of the will of a superhuman, immortal and infallible individual personality, but with that Power on which we rely for regeneration of society and which operates through individual human beings and social institutions." [36] In untold other passages we are assured that God is a cosmic vitality, the creative urge in the universe; that man is in God and God is in man. Godhead is immanent in nature and in humanity; its sovereignty is exercised through man and society.[37]

We should then say that Transnaturalism, the religion of Reconstructionism, is a pantheistic faith of optimism, conceived in a twentieth-century setting, in the traditions of eighteenth century Natural Religion. According to its own testimony, its reasoning is not conclusive; but it feels very strongly that its tenets are securely anchored in convictions "born of the heart rather than of the mind," in a number of intuitions, and—ultimately—in an enthusiasm for living.

II. CRITICISM

One should, perhaps, not attempt to reason with intuitions and enthusiasms. In themselves they are matters of purely personal concern and those who say that they have them may well be trusted to speak the truth. However, Transnaturalism is presented to us as a re-interpretation of Judaism and we are asked to accept it as "the only alternative to Orthodoxy and Secularism." For one who is not a Reconstructionist the way to take the Reconstructionist solution of our spiritual dilemma seriously is to investigate its philosophical and theological validity. In this attempt we shall at first turn our attention to the self-consistency of Reconstructionist religious philosophy. We shall do this under three headings: the problem of evil, the problem of freedom, and the problem of unity.

The Problem of Evil

The interpretation of evil as chaos and of good as the purposive urge that forms cosmos from chaos is a thought for which one is not prepared by the premises of Reconstructionism. Among these premises we find the idea that modern science, in revising our picture of the universe, has abolished the distinction between the natural and supernatural as well as the dichotomy between the physical and the metaphysical.[38] This would seem to be one of the main reasons why Reconstructionism is so impatient with the supernatural in religion, which is—usually—so strongly supported by metaphysical speculations. Having thrown out the supernatural, Reconstructionism is forced to establish a new distinction, that between cosmos and chaos or, as one might also say, between nature and sub-nature. The relationship between the two is not altogether unlike that which—according to Reconstructionist interpretation—existed in traditional religions between the natural and supernatural: cosmos forces its will and its intentions on chaos. There is, of course, a difference. Chaos is mere resistance, absence of meaning. Its only weapon of self-defense against being penetrated by the cosmic urge is its inertia. Chaos can be overcome and conquered, but not so nature. Nature has laws and order; it has positive existence. But why should it not be mastered by a more powerful supernature? The answer is, of course, that supernature does not exist. No one has ever seen it. We know for a certainty that science has "invalidated the distinction between natural and supernatural." But does science approve of the distinction between natural and sub-natural? Has anyone ever encountered the "Tohu and Bohu" of Dr. Kaplan, the neutral, negative inertia of the unformed "resistant?" What people know from actual experience, the only witness admitted in the Reconstructionist court, is evil and wickedness, sorrow and suffering, failure and sin, prevalent in history and nature on a far more impressive scale than the goodness of life that, according to Reconstructionism, is godliness. It is possible to interpret evil as mere chaos, the mere absence of goodness; but to do so is good old-fashioned metaphysics. The Reconstructionist distinction between chaos and cosmos, or—as we may say—between sub-nature and nature, is no less a metaphysical supposition than that between natural and supernatural. He who rejects the one cannot cling to the other.

The idea itself that evil is a mere absence of goodness "as darkness is the inevitable concomitant of light" has, of course, a long and glorious history. It originated in neo-Platonism in the third century and ever since it has been made use of in numberless philosophical systems. (In the history of Jewish philosophy Saadia Gaon, in the tenth century, was its most distinguished spokesman.) But neo-Platonism is purest metaphysics. It denies the very existence of nature, in the sense in which Reconstructionism uses the term. According to Plotinus, there is only the One and everything else is emanation of its substance. In this context evil represents a logical inconsistency. How can it exist, if everything is an emanation of the divine substance of the Infinite? And so its existence is denied. It is only in this way that the idea of evil as the mere absence of the good may be used and has been used. It is always the logical requirement of an originally purely metaphysical interpretation of reality. Only the power of metaphysical thought has ever dared to deny the reality of evil in defiance of overwhelming human experience. Such defiance, however, makes little sense if one starts out with naturalism, as Reconstructionism does, and acknowledges experience, with the framework of nature, as the only arbiter of truth. In actual life we find some goodness and a great deal of disgustingly positive and sickeningly real evil. This is the material the Reconstructionist has with which to work and with it he has to justify his intuitive affirmation of the worthwhileness of life and his enthusiasm for living. He dare not deny experience, since his entire *raison d'être* is derived from experience.

When ideas are made to serve in contexts for which they were originally not intended, they often take revenge on their despoilers by involving them in the most absurd illogicalities. The consequences of the denial of the positive nature of evil are an interesting example in case. It is not easy to define exactly the area of the Reconstructionist "chaos." Fortunately, there are a few passages in the classical Reconstructionist writings which are quite explicit. We read, for instance, that earthquakes and volcanic eruptions, devastating storms and floods, famines and plagues, noxious plants and animals "are simply that phase of the universe which has not yet been completely penetrated by godhood.[39] In another context again we are told that the divine quality of life is not to be seen in tempests, conflagrations and earthquakes, but "in 'the still small voice' in which the patiently creative and constructive forces of life find expression." [40] These statements make it quite clear that if evil was denied positive status, it meant that the destructive powers in the universe were neutral towards concepts of value; they were mere resistance to, and not active opponents of, meaning. However, the intention was not to deny its status as nature. No doubt, Reconstructionism cannot be blind to the fact that tempests and earthquakes, obnoxious plants and animals, belong to the dominion of nature and are subject to its laws and orderliness no less than its more pleasing and constructive manifestations. From the scientific point of view, the existence of toadstools, cobras, and man-eating tigers is no less natural than that of strawberries, kittens, and babies. We now realize that the distinction between chaos and cosmos is not between sub-nature and nature, but between two manifestations of nature itself: nature that makes for human survival and salvation—we call it cosmos because it is penetrated by the purpose of the constructive life forces; and nature, as exemplified in tornadoes, cobras, and man-eating tigers, not so conducive to human survival and salvation—we call it "Tohu and Bohu" because it has not yet been "conquered by will and intelligence."

This is meant to be taken seriously. Not only do the two forms of nature follow logically from the Reconstructionist concepts of chaos and cosmos; we find the idea so stated explicitly. Reconstructionism identifies "as divine the forces in the physical environment that make for physical survival and well being." [41] This is clear enough. Forces in the physical environment that do not make for man's survival and well-being are not divine; they are not yet invaded by purpose; they are not of the cosmos, but of chaos. It is also emphasized that "the creative powers in the physical world" alone are the manifestations of godhood. Needless to say there are others too which are not creative and, therefore, not divine. But that which is not divine is not purposive, not directed toward a goal which is worthwhile—it is chaotic. Chaos, too, is nature, no less than cosmos. Chaos is the merciless order of casual connections, utterly indifferent to the outcome of its own processes; whereas cosmos is the condition of the natural order, after having been compelled to admit purpose and meaning. The one is blind, the other, guided nature. It is, of course, unlikely that naturalism could consider such a distinction anything but mere foolishness. To us it would seem to be the most bizarre product of an extremely fertile metaphysical imagination or—shall we perhaps say —intuition.

The Problem of Freedom

The most serious objection to the distinction between chaos and cosmos, between the blind order of natural law and the one guided by purpose and plan, comes from another quarter.

One of the premises of Reconstructionist thinking is that one "cannot believe that God performs miracles and at the same time believe in the uniformities of natural law demanded by scientific theory." [42] The uniformities of natural law cannot be suspended or disturbed. However, one cannot help wondering what happens to these uniformities when "the creative urge" of the universe breaks into their domain with purpose and plan. What an infinite, omnipotent God could not be believed to be capable of accomplishing is now assumed to be successfully performed by a creative impulse in the cosmos that, as we have seen, must be thought as finite and imperfect. It is true that the creative urge is conceived as being immanent in the world, whereas the omnipotent and omniscient Supreme Being is transcendental to it. In both cases, however, the problem is the same: How can the lawful orderliness of nature be made to obey a purposeful will without interfering with the "uniformities" of natural law? It makes no difference whether the purpose emanates from an immanent cosmic urge or a transcendental divine will; its origin in each case is seen in something that is external to the dominion of "the immutable laws of cause and effect." In each case we are confronted with the conflict between the order of nature, held together by the unbreakable bonds of its laws, and the order of the spirit guided by the chosen goals of an intelligent will. The order of nature is the realm of necessity; that of the spirit, the realm of freedom. No matter how one imagines the power of the spirit, immanent or transcendent, the problem is unchanged: How can purpose, conceived and pursued in freedom, penetrate the unconquerable fortress of necessity?

Reconstructionism fully appreciates the fact that the conquest of chaos by purposeful intelligence is an act of freedom. It is, however, doubtful that it realizes the magnitude of the problem of the possibility of freedom as it arises on the basis of its own naturalistic premises. We are assured that there is a principle of creativity in the universe. This principle is responsible for "the continuous emergence of aspects of life not prepared for or determined by the past." Needless to say that a principle that is active independently of what is prepared for or determined by the past is free from the iron yoke of the law of causality that dominates nature. It is a principle of cosmic freedom that is said "to constitute the most divine phase of reality." [43] The same creative urge that is forming cosmos from chaos in the universe is also at work within man as he is struggling with the "Tohu and Bohu" within himself. The ethical life of man is itself a manifestation of creativity.[44] In fact, in accordance with the Reconstructionist deduction of the divine from human experience, it is foremostly man's awareness of alternative courses of possible action, and his power to choose between them, that grant us the knowledge of a creative principle which is free from what has been "prepared for or determined by the past." It is because of this creative impulse, experienced by us, that we are entitled to speak of its cosmic correlate —since man himself is "part of a larger nature"—as the divine power that makes for freedom. The creative urge within man, which reflects corresponding cosmic powers, is the freedom that is "at the root of man's spiritual life, and is the prime condition of his self-fulfillment, or salvation.[45] This is nobly said. Undoubtedly, freedom is to the life of the spirit what air is to our bodily existence. The question, however, is, how is freedom possible in the context of a reality that is dominated by the determinism of irrepressible laws.

Reconstructionism does make a number of bold affirmations in favor of freedom. The attitude of naturalistic determinism that "looks upon everything as the effect of everything else" is derided as an obsession.[46] The idea that the realm of natural law is not amenable to the influence of freedom and responsibility is likened to "a resurgence" of the old belief in fate of Greek antiquity. According to such an idea the realm of nature is the modern concept of fate. This is said in the best tradition of A. N. Whitehead's *Science in the Modern World*. But how does Reconstructionism meet the power of the sinister empire of nature-fate? The most significant passage on this issue that we are able to discern runs as follows: "But no more fatal error can be committed than that of overlooking the element of personality. There is in every human being something irreducible which renders him a monad, a world in himself, a mirocosmos. . . . the individual is a center of reference, an end in himself and fully responsible for what he does with his life." [47] This is indeed edifying. Unfortunately, one cannot solve the decisive problems of human existence by homiletics. Having started out with the premise of "the immutable laws of cause and effect," the Reconstructionist road points clearly to determinism and the denial of freedom. If Reconstructionism nevertheless wishes to affirm freedom, it must show how freedom and necessity may be accommodated in the same system. When Whitehead drew our attention to the idea that in modern thought the concept of the natural law has taken the place of the old Greek concept of fate, he also showed how to cope with the resulting problem by giving us one of the imposing metaphysical systems in the history of philosophy. But he who, because of "the uniformities of natural law," rejects the belief that God may perform miracles, cannot logically assert the creative principle of freedom merely by affirming its existence very firmly. It is fine to hear that the human personality is a monad, a world in itself, a center of reference. However, we should like to know how this monad may be responsible for its life in the context of "the uniformities of natural law." Reconstructionism overlooks the point that in relationship to the uniformities of nature every ethical deed of freedom is, indeed, a miracle; and perhaps an even greater "miracle" than the suspension of a natural law by the intervention of the will of a Supreme Being. As Kant has already shown, freedom is transcendental to the order of nature.[48] It is essentially supernatural. We may say, then, that the Reconstructionist distinction between chaos and cosmos is not, as we first thought, a distinction between sub-nature and nature, nor one between two types of nature, as it appeared to us on second consideration; but the good old "dichotomy" between natural and supernatural, the rejection of which is one of the premises of Reconstructionism.

We are led to the same conclusion about the implied supernaturalism of Reconstructionist thought, if we consider that cosmos-forming creative urge which is "the element of godhood in the world." [49] It is the urge that is responsible for the intelligence and the will that forever seeks to invade the chaos. It introduces meaning and plan into the world. It is "the divine process" which brings into being "personalities, men and women, with souls," liberating them "from Tohu and Bohu, the void of meaningless-ness and purposelessness." [50] As we have noted already, the Re-constructionist theologian prefers to talk of "the divine process," "the creative urge" which is godhood, of God as the power in the universe that makes for one thing or another, in order to em-phasize that what he understands by the deity is not transcendent-ally apart from the world but immanent in reality as its "con-structive" and meaningful aspect. It would seem to us that all this terminology is mere semantic juggling with words which have become empty because the ideas which they are supposed to convey are not properly understood. The founder of Reconstruc-tionism does not realize that intelligence and will, purpose and plan, meaning and value, are not the manifestations of urges and processes, nor of impulsions or powers, however universal and cosmic they may be imagined to be. Intelligence and will are not conceivable without intellect and soul; purposes and plans are conceived by minds; and meaning and value are meaningless and valueless unless they are related to some individual being. There-fore, to speak of cosmic powers as being responsible for cosmic intelligence, will, and purpose implies a cosmic intellect, a uni-versal mind. Since such cosmic intellect, according to the theory, faces chaos with the intention of penetrating it by the imposition of a purpose of its own, the cosmic intellect must be transcen-dental and prior to both chaos and cosmos. It is supernatural; and as a mind, associated with a will and purpose, it must be imagined in some terms of personal existence.

Of "freedom and responsibility of which human nature is cap-able" Reconstructionism maintains that they are the natural manifestation, on a self-conscious level, of the cosmic principle of polarity; freedom standing for selfhood and responsibility, for cooperation. However, neither selfhood nor cooperation have any meaning without selves.[51] If freedom and responsibility should indeed be the manifestation of a cosmic principle, then it must be the principle of cosmic selfhood cooperating with other selves; or—paraphrasing what we heard Reconstructionism call the human personality—a cosmic monad or, perhaps, even Leibniz' "monad of monads." No doubt this would still not be the God of traditional religion. Reconstructionism's "divine aspect of reality," which we have now unmasked as a cosmic personality is, as we recall, neither infinite nor perfect. We may, therefore, say that implied in the Reconstructionist concept of godhood is a finite, Platonic demiurge, which is apart from the cosmos it forms. We have landed again in supernaturalism, so much despised by the Reconstructionist.

In order to avoid a possible misunderstanding, we shall take another glance at the statement that freedom and responsibility "are the natural manifestation, on a self-conscious level," of a cosmic principle. The phrase, "natural manifestation on a self-conscious level" suggests ideas borrowed from the evolutionary theory of ethics. Evolutionists speak of levels of evolution, among which self-consciousness is the latest and highest. They would see in freedom and responsibility the manifestation of evolutionary progress on the level of self-consciousness. However, no evolutionist of rank will today look for correlates to human freedom and responsibility in the cosmos. He knows that in order to do so he would have to assume one of two alternatives. Either the cosmic correlate produces all the levels of evolutionary development, including consciousness, freedom, responsibility, and purpose, by consciously directed activity, or else by some unselfconscious, purposeful drive. In either case one would have to conclude that all ethical values are latently present in the evolving cosmic powers just as all the qualities of a plant are dormant in the seed. If ethical values are evolved by some conscious cosmic power, they must be forever present in a transcendental cosmic mind. If, on the other hand, they are brought into being by some unself-conscious cosmic drive from a condition of immanent possibility into a state of actuality, one would still have to posit the potentiality of the ethical life in the cosmos as "pre-formed" by a transcendental cosmic consciousness. This was indeed the meaning of evolution in the pre-Darwinian days. Evolution was seen as the unfolding of latent possibilities, which were originally planted in the cosmos by the Creator.

This position has been abandoned by the post-Darwinian evolutionary theory, especially by its latest representatives. From the scientific point of view, the evolution of latent possibilities which are inherently present in the universe is mere metaphysical speculation with suspiciously theological implications. Modern evolutionary theory, even though it recognizes the evolutionary validity of ethical concepts, will not acknowledge any cosmic correlates to ethical values, no "powers that make for freedom and human salvation." The evolutionary principle is able to explain the rise of ethics by means of adaptive functions which work automatically within the context of causation. As one of its ablest present-day representatives writes: ". . . . We have the glorious paradox that this purposeless mechanism (of evolution), after a thousand million years of its blind and automatic operations, has finally generated purpose—as one of the attributes of our own species." [52]

All the Reconstructionist affirmations of a universal urge that forms cosmos from chaos with will and intelligence are a relapse into pre-Darwinian concepts of a metaphysical evolutionary theory. One might, however, say in defense of Reconstructionism that it does not understand the supernaturalist implications of such metaphysics. In order to save its affirmation of the harmony between individual strivings and cosmic urges, Reconstructionism may attempt to take refuge in some mysterious *élan vital* or *evolution créatrice*. If so, Reconstructionist teachers will be well advised to make peace with some metaphysical and supernaturalist philosophy, for neither of these Bergsonian principles have any status outside metaphysics and the supernatural.

Freedom and Reconstructionist Pantheism

As freedom and responsibility, purpose and plan, related to a cosmic canvas, lead back into entanglements with the metaphysical and the supernatural, so does Reconstructionist pantheistic immanence, in its turn, undermine the foundations of all purposeful human endeavor undertaken in a spirit of responsibility and as an act of free commitment to a worthwhile goal. We have noted that Reconstructionism regards the powers which within man make for ethical action as the extension of cosmic reality. From this point of view, the ethical life of man is intensely impulsive. We heard it described as "no less integral a part of the cosmic structure of reality than the life-drive and sex-drive." [53] Wisdom, co-operation, and creativity are presented as the natural offsprings of universal urges. They "too are hungers" which are "irrepressible until they are satisfied." The idea of right is really "a form of might, an overpowering impulse" to do the right. Man's ethical aspirations are viewed as "part of a cosmic urge." Social ethics must conform to "certain fundamental laws that are as intrinsic to human nature as the law of gravitation is to matter." [54]

The entire ethical life of man is thus conceived in terms of urges and drives, impulsions and compulsions, which on the level of self-consciousness reflect corresponding cosmic activities. This, of course, is inherent in the logic of Reconstructionism. No Reconstructionist ever encountered cosmic powers which make for life's worthwhileness. His experience is only with the worthwhileness of individual lives. The ethical aspirations of man might be sufficient material to base on them a religionless humanism; they were, however, turned into the foundations of transnaturalist religion by looking on them as manifestations of cosmic powers, representing the divine aspect of universal reality. We saw how this was accomplished. It is, therefore, necessary for Reconstructionism to interpret man's ethical life as rooted in drives, urges, irresistible impulses, and hungers which give man no rest until they are satisfied. It is an almost biologically determined ethics. Unfortunately, ethical drives built into the cosmic structure are the blight of all personal ethics. The ethical deed is the fruit of freedom. Actions that are prompted by irrepressible impulses and hungers which cannot be denied are not performed in free commitment to an ideal. The teachers of the Talmud were bold enough to state that "everything is in the power of Heaven except the fear of Heaven." [55] The closer the bond between man's ethical aspirations and the cosmic powers in which they originate, and which become manifest in them, the less free the human deed which results from such aspirations; and the less free the deed, the less ethical will it be adjudged. Yet, Reconstructionism cannot sever the bond and dissolve the identification. For unless we see the ethical strivings of man as the activity of the cosmic reality of which he is part, we know nothing of "the divine aspect of universal being," the belief in which is the essence of Reconstruc-

A TREASURY OF "TRADITION"

tionist religion. Reconstructionism is faced here with a dilemma. Either freedom is taken seriously as being at "the root of man's spiritual life," [56] in which case his ethical strivings are not the manifestations of the activity of any cosmic powers and Reconstructionism cannot identify the divine aspect of reality; or else, the strivings are the activity of the cosmic process of godhood in man, then freedom has become an empty phrase, and ethics a nobler aspect of biology.

Reconstructionism does not seem to be aware of the problem and affirms enthusiastically both freedom and the immanent ethics of a cosmic mechanism which works with the forcefulness of hungers and other natural drives for the realization of the good. It would seem that whenever man performs an ethical deed, he acts in freedom as well as under the pressure of some cosmic compulsion. He himself desires this-worldly salvation and sets his goal accordingly, "but neither the quest for salvation nor the choice of goods is entirely man-determined." [57] As we have already learned, "human nature is a part of the larger world of nature. . . ." Such ideas render the extent of personal responsibility extremely vague. Obviously, man cannot be made responsible for what is not "man-determined" within him but is the action of a cosmic urge through him. If as "moral agents we are *inwardly impelled* to consider the consequences from the standpoint of their destroying or enhancing the value of life," it will be difficult to censor an agent who does not act morally. The very fact that he does not consider consequences may be an indication that he is not sufficiently impelled by the powers that make for responsible behavior. His very action proves that "the consciousness of the power and the responsibility to choose the right in the face of temptation" [58] were not really "irrepressible" within him, as they were supposed to be accoridng to the Reconstructionist affirmation.

The nature of the problem may perhaps be best illustrated by the Reconstructionist re-interpretation of the concept of sin. Man's failure to live up to the best that is in him is sin because "it means that our souls are not attuned to the divine, that we have betrayed God." The best that is in man is the divine in him, the function of cosmic forces in the soul of man. We "identify" it as God because it is identical with "that aspect of reality which confers meaning and value on life and elicits from us those ideals that determine the course of human progress." [59] If this is indeed true, one cannot help wondering how it is possible ever to know that a person has failed to live up to the best that is in him. Whenever a person does not come up to our expectations, may it not be due to the fact that what we consider the best in man has not been "elicited" in this man with sufficient forcefulness so as not to let him fail? Instead of accusing him of "betraying God," may it not be that the poor soul was let down by the "divine aspect of reality," a supposition all the more within the realm of possibility since the Reconstructionist process of godhood is itself finite and imperfect? In vain is it maintained that the fact that the same man often does not fail proves that he is responsible for his failures. Since "the best in man" is due to the activity of cosmic powers, the extent of their presence and effectiveness may only be gauged by the strength of the ideals that they "elicit." Occasional successes and repeated failures will allow us the one conclusion that the cosmic forces which make for salvation are indeed extremely limited and not very consistent. Such a conclusion would not be unjustified, especially if one recalls that the creative powers are all the time locked in struggle in every human being, no less than in the universe, with the resistance of the chaos that "invades his soul." Every failure may be due to the finitude of the creative urge that, momentarily, may be lacking in power or wisdom to overcome the "Tohu and Bohu" which is "not of man but in man."

It is mere running around in a circle to say that our task is to cultivate the sense of responsibility and "not one of calling into being something that does not exist." [60] Every task is a responsibility. The responsibility of cultivating a sense of responsibility is itself part of our sense of responsibility. Since, however, responsibility is among those "certain fundamental laws that are as intrinsic to human nature as the law of gravitation is to matter," the fundamental law of cultivating the sense of responsibility will either function, as any decent law should, or it will not function. No matter what happens, it will have as much bearing on ethics as has the law of gravitation.

The issue at hand may also be stated by saying that Reconstructionism became entangled with the implications of the pantheistic element of its teachings. Every form of pantheism is destructive of individuality. Individuality is a mere sham or shadow, as in Hinduism, or a mode of the infinite substance, as for instance in Spinozism. In either case, it has no reality or value of its own. Pantheism is inherently deterministic. There is no "Ought", only an "Is." All reality is a manifestation of divine nature, which is what it is of intrinsic necessity and could not be anything else. From this point of view, freedom is a mere illusion as is also all personal ethics. Notwithstanding the title of his *chef d'oeuvre*, i.e., Ethics, Spinoza had to regard human actions and desires "exactly" as if he were dealing "with lines, planes, and bodies." [61] Such is the inescapable logic of pantheism. Human aspirations and actions are "part of the larger world of nature." They are manifestations of cosmic reality which cannot be affected by the illusions of the sham that we like to call personality. Since there is neither freedom nor personal existence in reality, good and evil "indicate nothing positive in things considered in themselves." [62] All these implications of pantheism also apply to Reconstructionism. If God is in man and man is in God, the human personality cannot be an irreducible monad, a world in itself, an independent center of reference, as Reconstructionism also teaches. If human strivings are the "revelation" in man of the activities of cosmic urges, if they reflect the cosmic structure of reality, if they are irrepressible hungers, impulses, and fundamental laws, as Reconstructionism has to assert, freedom cannot be "at the root of the soul," which Reconstructionism also affirms, so that it may make room for ethics within the scope of its world view. Reconstructionism is not aware of its inconsistencies. It has no appreciation of the logical implications of its own position.

The Problem of Unity

We have discussed above the problem of the possibility of freedom in a world which is ruled, according to the premise, by the flawless "uniformities" of the causal nexus in nature. The problem is greatly aggravated by the assumption that freedom is not only possible but that its aspirations will ultimately be realized. We have heard the *Ani Maamin* of Reconstructionism that the world is so constituted that its "divine aspect" not only endorses what ought to be, but also guarantees that what ought to be will indeed be realized. We noted that such a belief implies a strong faith in a universal harmony between the order of physical nature and the realm of values and ideals. It is the idea of the "interrelated unity of all reality," which we had occasion to analyze earlier in our presentation. Without such universal harmony, man's striving for self-fulfillment or salvation would be a hopeless undertaking. It would seem, then, that not only does Reconstructionism affirm a faith that freedom is possible, notwithstanding the uniformities of natural law, but that freedom and necessity are in harmony with each other; that physical nature and the moral order are somehow attuned to each other; that they represent the "interrelated unity of all reality." Judged by the premises of Reconstructionism, such an affirmation—with all due respect to the "heart of which it is born"—sounds rather fantastic. From all our experience we know that the laws of nature are indifferent to the considerations of right and wrong, that the causal nexus is the deadly enemy of freedom and teleological guidance. This indeed is the Reconstructionist position on naturalism. Ideals and values are recognized to point to a phase of reality of which "natural law does not take account." How then, is it possible to conceive of the natural and the moral order as being in harmony with each other? According to Hermann Cohen, the agreement between the causal order of nature and the teleological nature of ethics is *das Urproblem*, the fundamental problem of all systematic philosophy.[63] Spinoza, having identified nature with God, had to eliminate the concept of freedom and purpose from his system and to reduce the distinction between good and evil to a mere subjective illusion. Fichte, on the other hand, who saw God in an active moral order, beheld the universe exclusively as the manifestation of that order. Kant was the outstanding personality in the history of philosophy who made it his major task to reconcile the order of nature with that of ethics. He was struggling with the problem in his three *Critiques*. His philosophy of "practical reason" demanded that what ought to be may be possible of realization, or else human salvation was inconceivable. It is a concept which is often used

by Reconstructionism itself. As long as the order of nature and
the realm of ethics remain alien to each other, such a concept will
make no sense. Kant, of course, realized that the principle of their
harmonization or unity could not be found in either of them but
had to be sought outside them. In this manner he was led to the
major "postulate of practical reason," the existence of an omnipotent, omniscient, and perfect Being, who alone—as the Supreme
Lord of the universe— would have the power to make the uniformities of the causal order submit to guidance by the purposefulness
of the "categorical imperative." The need for the "practical postulate" of a Supreme Being, transcendental to both the order of
nature and that of ethics, is all the more significant, since Kant
himself insists that "theoretical reason" is unable to prove the
existence of God and can acknowledge the idea only as a "regulative principle" of reasoning.[64]

Reconstructionism, of course, need not accept either Spinoza's
or Fichte's or Kant's solution of the problem. However, it must
offer some solution if it desires to be taken seriously. It is not
enough to affirm intuitively that the realm of causal necessity is
in harmony with purposeful ethical aspirations. On the basis of
the Reconstructionist premise of identifying godhood with cosmic
processes, the affirmation contains a logical contradiction.

In one important passage the founder of Reconstructionism
quotes Thomas H. Huxley as having said: "Ethical nature may
count upon having to reckon with a tenacious and powerful enemy
as long as the world lasts." The quotation is taken from Huxley's
famous Romanes Lecture of 1893. One might say that in it the
speaker was discussing the Kantian problem of the discrepancy
between natural and moral order from the point of view of the
evolutionary naturalist. Huxley's conclusions, right or wrong, deserve serious treatment. Not so, however, in the opinion of Dr.
Kaplan. Having practically stumbled on the problem, he orders it
out of court by one of his many edifying affirmations. After berat-
ing one of the fathers of evolutionary theory for treating cosmic
nature as if it were "a new name for the old Satan," he continues:
"In reality, however, it is incorrect to assume that cosmic nature is
'red in tooth and claw,' and that the ethical strivings of men lie
outside nature and constitute as it were a world by themselves. If

there is any metaphysical significance to the doctrine of the unity of God, it is that the ethical and spiritual strivings should be considered as belonging to the same cosmos as the one in which there is so much that is evil and destructive of the good." [65] These are noble words which, however, Reconstructionism is not entitled to use. Reconstructionism has no right to take recourse to the doctrine of the unity of God in order to prove the unity of the cosmos. Only the supernaturalist can do that. For him, God is the Supreme Being that transcends the world, confronting it as its Creator and Sovereign. Indeed, the significance of such a doctrine of the unity of God has always been that from it followed the unity of all created reality. The world is one as the creation of the One God. With such a faith, the supernaturalist may confront all the disharmony in the cosmos. But the Reconstructionist rejects the concept of the One God, the Creator of the universe. For him, God is an immanent aspect of reality; it is identical with the cosmic processes themselves. As we have seen, the Reconstructionist recognizes the "interrelated unity of all reality" as "the divine aspect of reality" or, as we have also heard it put, godhood is "the sum of the animating, organizing forces and relationships which are forever making a cosmos out of chaos." The Reconstructionist cannot, therefore, argue from "the doctrine of the unity of God" in order to prove the unity of reality. He has to move in the opposite direction. He can only affirm the unity of God by establishing first the "interrelated unity of all reality." Dr. Kaplan's argument runs in a circle. First it affirms intuitively the unity of all reality. Identifying, then, such unity with the "divine aspect of reality," it concludes from the affirmation the unity of God. When, now, anyone should point to the wide areas of disharmony in reality, the answer is given rather indignantly: "But you are wrong! Haven't we proved the unity of God? Everyone knows that the unity of God signifies the interrelated unity of all reality." Since, however, on the Reconstructionist assumption the immanent godhood of the world is "identified" as the "interrelated unity of all reality," Dr. Kaplan has logically proved only that the intuition of the interrelated unity of all reality signifies the interrelated unity of all reality.

The truth is that relying completely on naturalistic experience,

as Reconstructionism does, one has no possibility of discovering
the unity of all reality. In experience we encounter multiplicity,
diversity, and disharmony. There are small areas in which a unifying tendency may perhaps be discerned, as there are others of
chaos and conflict. We are aware of ethical strivings in man and
we also know the nature "red in tooth and claw." If they belong
to the one cosmos, even though their respective orders of freedom
and necessity are exclusive of each other, who dare affirm it on
the basis of naturalism?! The very idea of a cosmos is a metaphysical concept. It is either the fruit of a monistic and deterministic pantheism or of a supernatural ethical monotheism. The
logic of the Reconstructionist position, however, leads to a modern polytheism. The polytheist of old, too, was an empiricist. He
observed and encountered the plurality of powers in nature and
in himself. By personifying these powers, he came to know them
as gods. Reconstructionism too starts out with man's naturalistic
experience of strivings, drives, impulsions, within himself and in
society. In trying to understand them, it searches for their "cosmic
correlates." The Reconstructionist is, of course, not a primitive
polytheist; his feet are firmly planted in the world of modern
science. He does not "personify" these powers; he identifies them
as divine. Since, however, the interrelated unity of all reality is
unsupported by naturalistic experience, the Reconstructionist is
left with a plurality of powers that, if not gods, ought to be properly referred to as *processes* of godhood and divine—and occasionally with greater justification, chaotic—*aspects* of reality. "Process
of godhood" and "divine aspect of reality," in the singular, have
no logical justification in the Reconstructionist context.

The attempt to re-interpret Judaism comes to grief on the failure
of Reconstructionism to establish meaningfully the unity of reality.
Reconstructionism maintains that only by "dissociating Jewish
religion from supernaturalism can the universal significance of its
ideals and values be made apparent and the Jewish contribution
to the world order take effect." [66] It is exactly such dissociation
which cannot be brought about. Jewish universalism is essentially
anchored in the supernaturalist concept of the unity of God. As
has been made clear by Hermann Cohen in his *Die Religion der
Vernunft*—"The Religion of Reason"—the world of experience

is not one. The idea of the One God constitutes the world as a unity, a universe. And what is true of the world is even more so of human beings. In actual experience we find only tribes, races, and nations. The very concept of the unity of the human race, the idea of mankind, has its origin in ethical monotheism. The concept of the One God, the originator of the one universe as well as the source of the moral law, alone makes known to us the multitude of people as the brotherhood of men. [67] We can do no better than to quote the observations of Max Scheler on the same subject. In his work, *Vom Ewigen im Menschen,* he writes: ". . . Actually as well as logically it is correct to say that the assumption of the unity . . . of the world is only to be derived from the assumption of an only God its Creator. . . . The world is world (and not chaos) and only one world, when, and because, it is God's world —when, and because, the same infinite spirit and will is powerfully active in all Being. Just as the unity of human nature is ultimately not based on the proven natural characteristic of man, but on the image of God which he shows; and just as mankind as a whole is mankind when all individuals and all groups are united with each other, legally as well as morally, by means of their bond with God, so is the world one world only because of the unity of God." [68] The Rabbis in the Talmud were expressing the same thoughts in the Midrashic style when they remarked: "Why was man created alone?" (Or, as we may paraphrase the question: Why does, according to the Torah, only one Adam stand at the beginning of human history?) And the answer is given: "So that no man may say to his fellow: My father was greater than your father (and therefore, being of nobler descent, I am superior to you)." [69] The equality of the human race is established by its issuance from the one act of creation by the One God.

In vain does Reconstructionism declare that it is "one of the main functions of religion in the modern world to curb aggressive nationalism, by insistence on the essential unity of human society." [70] Aggressive nationalism is certainly bad and Reconstructionism is always well-meaning. However, having rejected the traditional concept of God as the transcendental Supreme Being and Creator, Reconstructionism has failed to provide a valid foundation for the essential unity of human society. Such essential unity has never been a matter of experience. On the contrary, the whole of history testifies to the actual inequality of men and the disunity of the human race. To quote a Reconstructionist text, "mankind is not all of one piece. It is divided among peoples, communities and families." [71] In this respect too the implied logic of the Reconstructionist position is a modern version of the old polytheistic one. Neither the concept of one humanity nor the ideal of equality could emerge in a polytheistic world in which people and nations claimed their descent from the various gods. Mankind was as much divided as its gods were many. The gods, have, of course, departed; the division and the disunity have remained. The Reconstructionist is confronted with a multiplicity of races which he explains as having developed from an animal ancestry as a result of the activity of "cosmic powers." Search as one may, one will not find unity and equality on such a basis. The different races may indeed represent different evolutionary trends. The Cro-Magnards and Grimaldis, as well as their latterday children, may be the offspring of cosmic forces acting in a pluralistic world. The actually experienced inequality of men may logically reflect the nature of a multiple cosmic reality. Any other conclusion is not justified on the basis of the Reconstructionist world view. The attempt of Reconstructionism to re-interpret Judaism by dissociating the universal significance of Jewish ideals from their source in the One God, the Creator, must be considered a complete failure. Having rejected Jewish monotheism, Reconstructionism has not provided a convincing foundation for Jewish universalism. It does not understand the age-old truth, which represents "the Jewish contribution to the world order," that before one may speak of the brotherhood of man one must acknowledge the fatherhood of God. Without it, all ethics is mere utilitarianism and politics.

III. EVALUATION

Having analyzed the logical implications of the main concepts of Reconstructionist theology and religion from the angle of their own consistency, we shall now attempt to offer a general evaluation of both Reconstructionist transnaturalism and its starting point in what Reconstructionism considers present-day naturalism.

From the Ego to the Cosmos

The method of transnaturalism is, as we saw, a simple one. We know of the existence of personality, of human ideals and ethical strivings. They are no less real than the material aspects of life, yet naturalism cannot account for them. Transnaturalism is able to explain them by viewing them as the manifestations of cosmic powers that are responsible for their existence. These powers are identified as "the divine aspect of reality," since they tend to render human life worthwhile. It is the function of the idea of God to assure the worthwhileness of human existence. From the striving of man for self-transcendence transnaturalism concludes not only the existence of certain cosmic powers but also the nature of cosmic reality, which is seen to be such as to guarantee the ultimate fulfillment of man's aspirations.

It would seem to us that, notwithstanding the fact that man is seen as "part of a larger nature," any conclusions drawn from his own aspirations for self-fulfillment or salvation to the nature of cosmic reality is not logic but a form of megalomania. A contemporary astro-physicist, in trying to convey an idea of the proportion which exists between our earth and the rest of the universe, uses the following comparison. If the major railway terminal of a large metropolis represented the size of the cosmos, then one particle of dust floating around in its atmosphere would represent the earth. In relationship to the world man is the inhabitant of such a particle of cosmic dust. What conclusions may be drawn from his aspirations to the structure of reality? The founder of Reconstructionism does attempt to answer this question in a very few words: "But does not the very ability to think in cosmic terms render physical measurements and proportions irrelevant . . ." [72] We cannot agree that he has met the objection. Though the idea was already voiced by Saadia Gaon, and, in addition, has also a Kantian ring about it, we do not know what is meant by "the ability to think in cosmic terms." Man, we would say, is able to think only in human terms; in terms of the human intellect he is even able to think of cosmic extension and structure. Be that as it may, we are in hearty agreement with the insight that physical measurements and proportions are irrelevant. Value and meaning of the smallest order are superior to mere physical bigness of the largest size. Mere physical bigness is nonsensical. All this is, however, beside the point. The objection that Reconstructionism has to meet, but does not, is as follows: Is the universe empty of meaning and does its vastness, surpassing all human imagination, represent nothing but bigness?—then the little sense and purpose which are noticeable in the human inhabitant of the particle of cosmic dust, our earth, is indeed the greatest conceivable miracle. However, it would be a miracle illogically set in an ocean of cosmic meaninglessness, completely out of harmony with the structure of reality. Or else, beside its physical brilliance, the universe does incorporate significance in true cosmic terms, then all conclusions from the nature of human strivings as to how reality is constituted are bound to be fallacious.

It is of little use to say, as if anticipating such objection: "We do not need to pretend to any knowledge of the ultimate purpose of the universe as a whole. . . . But it is an undeniable fact that there is something in the nature of life which expresses itself in human personality, which evokes ideals, which sends men on the quest of personal and social salvation.[73] As so much of Reconstructionist reasoning, this is begging the question. For the question is: what is the status of this "something in the nature of life" in the context of cosmic reality? May it not be that this something is a cosmic flaw, that from the point of view of the structure of all reality "the evoking of ideals which send men on the quest of personal and social salvation" was a regrettable oversight? Personal and social salvation are of great human importance. Reconstructionism, however, has not proved that there exists a correlate to them in the nature of reality which has positive significance in terms of that reality.

Reconstructionism regards life as the supreme value: for "if life itself is worthless, no object on earth can have any value." [74] This would not be illogical, if the meaning of it were that life had supreme value for most men. Unfortunately, what is meant is "the life of the universe of which our lives are but a part." The supreme value is supposed to be objective, cosmic value, "from which all others are derived." Since our lives "are but part of universal life," Reconstructionism expects human life "to yield cosmic meaning." To speak of the life of the universe and human life as if both belong in the same category and were one and the same phenomenon is not justified. On the contrary, all our scientific knowledge suggests that life, as we know it on this globe, is completely out of step with the life of the universe. The Second Law of Thermodynamics is one of the concepts of science in which the human mind has revealed its ability "to think in cosmic terms." According to it, the life of the universe consists in an irreversible process of cosmic dying. Like a wound-up clock, the universe is "running down" by the inevitable increase of Entropy. Evolution, which—scientifically speaking—is responsible for life on earth, is a process running in the opposite direction. Entropy implies, as it were, the continuous degradation of the universe from higher forms of organization to lower ones, until—by the equal distribution of heat—all activity is brought to a standstill and universal *rigor mortis* ensues. Evolution, on the other hand, works from lower forms of organization to higher ones; from death to life, as it were. We are certainly not competent to pass judgment on the significance of the relationship between global evolution and the universal law of Entropy. From the writings of scientists, however, one is able to gather that, in cosmic terms, life as we know it is an insignificant side-show, enacted in a tiny corner of the universe. It was rendered possible, so it would appear, by the mere accidental coincidence of a certain state of Entropy in the universe and the mechanically determined, no less accidental, conditions on that cosmic particle of dust, our earth.[75] One of the great astrophysicists of this century, Sir Arthur S. Eddington, has occasion to describe the rise of human life in the following manner: "Nature seems to have been intent on a vast evolution of fiery worlds . . . As for Man—it seems unfair to be always raking up against Nature her one little inadvertence. By a trifling hitch of machinery—not of any serious consequence in the development of the universe—some lumps of matter of the wrong size have occasionally been formed. These lack the purifying protection of intense heat or the equally efficacious absolute cold of space. Man is one of the gruesome results of this occasional failure of antiseptic precautions." [76]

This is how man looks when considered in "cosmic terms." It is foolish to draw any conclusions from his own strivings as to the structure of cosmic reality. Notwithstanding the fact that human nature is part of a larger nature, it is preposterous to discern in human nature a manifestation of the structure of cosmic reality. Reconstructionist religion is far from being "the triumphant exorcism of Bertrand Russell's dismal credo 'Brief and powerless is man's life. On him and all his race the slow sure doom falls pitiless and dark,'" as it maintains. [77] However dismal, from the scientific point of view, Russell's credo makes more sense than Reconstructionist transnaturalism. We agree that the idea of God implies "the absolute negation and antithesis of all evaluations of human life which assume that consciousness is a disease, civilization a transient sickness, and all our efforts to life ourselves above the brute only a vain pretense. [78] The traditional Jewish belief in God does mean all that, but not the Reconstructionist "intuition of God." We are familiar with this intuition by now. It begins with our experience of human strivings for self-fulfillment and ends with "the assumption" of a cosmic reality so "constituted as to endorse them and to guarantee their realization." The Reconstructionist intuition of God is the conclusion from man to the structure of reality which is identified as divine. The intuition has as much significance as the conclusion makes sense. Man cannot derive status from his position in the cosmos, but from his relationship to the Lord of the cosmos. The idea was poetically expressed by the Psalmist, when he exclaimed:

> When I behold Thy heavens, the work of Thy fingers,
> The moon and the stars, which Thou hast established;
> What is man, that Thou art mindful of him?
> Yet Thou hast made him but little lower than the angels,
> And hast crowned him with glory and honor. [79]

This makes sense. The Psalmist recognizes the insignificance of man when judged as "part of a larger world nature," an evaluation borne out by modern science, and sees that the only source of human dignity may be found in the fact that the son of man is the child of God. Reconstructionism, however, which knows only man and a larger world of which he is a part, but not a universe that "Thou hast established," has but one way to ascertain the glory and honor of man, i.e. to derive it from his place in the cosmos. As we have seen, judged by its cosmic position, human life certainly does not yield any "cosmic meaning." The question that in such a case may it not be "the course of wisdom to pursue a policy of 'eat and drink and make merry, for tomorrow we die?' " [80] proves nothing to the contrary. Such a course of wisdom may indeed follow from the inherent logic of the Reconstructionist world view.

Reconstructionist Pan-Anthropoism

The Reconstructionist method of drawing conclusions from the higher aspirations of man to the structure of universal reality is tantamount to fashioning the cosmos in the image of human aspirations and values. The cosmic "correlates" are nothing else but the projection of man's wishes and desires into the cosmos. This is the origin of the distinction between cosmos and chaos. From the point of view of nature there is no distinction between "tempests, obnoxious plants and animals" and the, for man, more agreeable manifestations of nature. When Reconstructionism calls the constructive powers of nature "the creative urge" and identifies as chaos that aspect of reality which may doom human aspirations, it introduces purely human value concepts in the determination of the nature of reality. Outside human consciousness and strivings we find only facts and not values. The life of the universe of which we are part and which is "the supreme value because from it all other values are derived" is the projection of the Reconstructionist "enthusiasm for living" onto the cosmic canvas.

By learning to view man's nobler desires as an "integral part of the cosmic structure of reality," Reconstructionism attempts to give human values universal objectivity; however, all it accomplishes is the view of a world seen through the rose-colored glasses of human ambitions. When it "identifies" the powers that make for those nobler impulses in man as the divine aspect of reality, far from discovering God, it has merely defined certain aspects of the human personality. Ludwig Feuerbach was not right in generalizing that the idea of God represented nothing but the deification of human nature; nevertheless, the Reconstructionist inflation of human aspirations into cosmic proportions, their projection into the universe where they are discovered as divine, proves that his theory is not always wrong.

When Reconstructionism speaks about God, it is really moving in a circle, starting with man and concluding with him. This is nowhere more amusingly illustrated than when it attempts to offer a "reinterpretation" of the biblical idea of man's having been created in the image of God. We have already discussed the quotation in which reference is made to "the something in the nature of life" which becomes manifest in the existence of human personality, evolving in man ideals and the quest for salvation. It is maintained that by identifying that "something" with God, "we are carrying out in modern times the implications of the conception that man is created in God's image. For such an identification implies that there is something divine in human personality, in that it is the instrument through which the creative life of the world affects the evolution of the human race." [81] The truth is, of course, that the aspect of reality which is responsible for the emergence of human personality is referred to as "the creative life of the world" only because man attaches value to personality. The "something in the nature of life" which is responsible for the "evoking" of ideals and for sending man in quest of self-fulfillment is identified as God only because man approves of his own ideals and of the quest. This is the deification of human values. No wonder Reconstructionism discovers something divine in the human personality. It starts out with the projection of human personality into the universe as "the something in the nature of life" which is responsible for it. In this state, human personality is deified. It is then re-discovered in man as "something divine," which it is because we call it so right from the beginning. Such semantic juggling, however, has nothing in common with the conception of man's creation in God's image. It is its very opposite; it is God's creation in man's image. This is the essence of the Reconstructionist "intuition of God."

Whenever Reconstructionism speaks about God, it is in reality speaking about man. When man sins he betrays that which is "best in him." On Rosh Hashanah the Reconstructionist, standing before the bar of judgment, judges himself "in the light of whatever truth experience has revealed to him." [82] The true meaning of the acceptance of God's kingship is to attain faith in man. [83] To serve God is to strive for self-fulfillment.[84] By the holiness of God religion means to convey the idea that life is the supreme value.[85] The "main problem of Jewish religion" is defined as the task to discover "a common purpose, which makes for the enhancement of human life" and to which Jews as a people are willing to be committed so passionately "as to see in it a manifestation or revelation of God." [86] This is quite logical. The divine is in man because man deifies "the best in him." When, then, he is passionately devoted to a cause which enhances life, such commitment and devotion is divine revelation for it represents the best in him. All the while man is gyrating around himself; or better still, around his best potentialities. He serves and worships his noblest aspirations. In practicing transnaturalism, he is forever engaged in an intellectually incestuous mystical communion with his deified super-ego.

In our presentation of Reconstructionist theology, we pointed out that transnaturalism was a form of pantheism. In the light of our analysis and evaluation, we now have to qualify this appellation. In the history of philosophy we distinguish between acosmic and atheistic pantheism. Acosmic pantheism is, for instance, that of Spinoza. Its origin is a metaphysical vision of the Infinite God whose very infinity leaves no room for a cosmos. Identifying nature with God, Spinoza denied not God but nature. It is for this reason that he was called the God-intoxicated philosopher. (The philosophy is, of course, contrary to Judaism because it eliminates creation and the Creator.) It is obvious that Reconstructionism has nothing in common with this type of pantheism. The other form of pantheism beholds, again in a metaphysical inspiration, the wholeness of nature and identifies God with it. Not such is the Reconstructionist position, which is based on the naturalistic rejection of metaphysics. The Reconstructionist starting point is not a vision of the wholeness of nature but man, his aspirations, drives, and values. Insofar as

A TREASURY OF "TRADITION"

man approves of his goals and impulsions, they are projected into the cosmos and become inflated into cosmic urges, revealing the structure of reality. The viewing of these aspects of reality as divine does identify God with the cosmos, but with a cosmos shaped in the image of human aspirations and interests. Reconstructionist transnaturalism should, therefore, not be called pantheism. It is the most radical manifestation of anthropomorphism. It should properly be known as pan-anthropoism. It is much too original a religious philosophy to be considered a mere "revaluation" of traditional Jewish concepts. If one should use Dr. Kaplan's own criterion for what constitutes re-valuation one would have to say that transnaturalism shows not the least trace of a "psychological kinship with what the ancients did articulate." [87] Christianity as well as Islam are by far closer to Judaism than Reconstructionist religion.

"Wedding Religion to Science"

As indicated in the opening sentences of this study, the task of harmonizing the valid results of scientific theory with the truth of religion is indeed of vital religious importance. All the more is it to be regretted that the Reconstructionist endeavor "to wed religion to science" has to be considered such a dismal failure. It should be obvious that it has not been our intention in this paper to offer another solution to the problem of the conflict between naturalism and traditional Judaism, one—perhaps—from a supernaturalistic viewpoint. Nor did we make any attempt to defend supernaturalism against Reconstructionist criticism. We investigated Reconstructionist theology and religion on its own philosophical and theological merits and found it very much wanting. At the same time, it is rather a pity that Dr. Kaplan should have been so impatient with, and intolerant toward, the supernaturalist element in Judaism and treated it with utter intellectual contempt. Impatience, intolerance, and contempt are, of course, the historic privileges of all prophets of new religions in their attitude to the old one that they "re-valuate." Yet, had he possessed only a small suspicion that the believers in a supernaturalist religion need not all be intellectualy incompetent, he might have felt induced to take another good look at his own naturalism. Such a second look, we believe, might have prevented him from failing so wretchedly in his transnaturalist "re-interpretation" of Judaism.

We shall, therefore, attempt to review those principles of "the new scientific world view" which seems to be mainly responsible for the Reconstructionist rejection of supernaturalism. These are essentially: "the uniformities of natural law demanded by scientific theory," also referred to as the scientific thought or insight of "the assumption of the universality of natural law"; "the immutable laws of cause of effect"; and "that inner necessity which compels things to be what they are." [88] Anyone can see that these principles are completely in "gear with the thinking of the average intelligent person at the present time." [89] This is as it should be from the Reconstructionist ponit of view. The "average intelligent person at the present time" is the supreme authority to whose thinking Professor Kaplan bows in the spirit of childlike faith. It is, however, surprising that these concepts of the uniformity of nature are also claimed as being "in keeping with the most advanced ideas of reality." [90] The facts are quite to the contrary, as any average intelligent person may easily find out for himself by doing some elementary reading in present-time scientific method and philosophy.

In the light of modern scientific theory, the reference to "that inner necessity which compels things to be what they are" must be considered the vestigial remnant of some obscure mysticism. The statement could have been made meaningfully—as indeed it was, though perhaps not exactly in those words—by Spinoza. However, it is fair to say that the spectacular development of modern science began when scientists stopped explaining natural events by inner necessities that compel things to be what they are. We shall not go wrong in stating that the ghost of inner necessity as a principle of scientific explanation has not shown itself in any responsible quarter for at least the last one hundred years. As for the uniformities and the universality of natural laws, it is now realized that there is no foundation for them either in experimental or theoretic science. The quantum theory, Heisenberg's principle of indeterminacy, the incalculable "jumps" of the electrons from orbit to orbit, prove that the good old principle of *natura non facit saltus* was a mere illusion. Natural laws of today show no such uniformity. Quantum mechanics and wave mechanics, the indeterminism of events in the atomic structure, and the statistical laws of micro-physics made an end to the assumption of the universality of natural laws. In the wake of all these new developments, the concept of "the immutable laws of cause and effect" governing nature is gone.

An outstanding scientist draws a number of fundamental conclusions "from the mere fact of the atomicity of radiation, coupled with those well-established facts of the undulatory theory of light." Among them we find, for example, these:

'So far as the phenomena are concerned, the uniformity of nature disappears.

"So far as our knowledge is concerned, causality becomes meaningless.

"If we still wish to think of the happenings in the phenomenal world as governed by a causal law, we must suppose that these happenings are determined in some substratum of the world which lies beyond the world of phenomena and so also beyond our access." [91]

We fully realize that there are many who do wish to think of the happenings in the phenomenal world as governed by a causal law. However, following the discussion between eminent scientists on the subject of the principle of causality, on which uniformity and universality depend, it is safe to say that it is not really possible to disagree with the factual statement made by the late Professor Eddington that "the law of causality does not exist in science today—in that body of systematic knowledge and hypothesis which has been experimentally confirmed." Eddington is careful to point out that this does not mean that modern science has proved that the law of causality is not true of the physical universe, but that "present-day science is simply indifferent" to the law of causality. "We might believe in it today and disbelieve in it tomorrow; not a symbol in the modern textbooks of physics would be altered." [92]

We do not pretend to be able to settle the issue as between the scientists. However, one thing is certain: the uniformities and the universality of the laws of nature are not only not demanded by scientific theory but they are not even used in "the body of systematic knowledge which has been experimentally confirmed." The division between determinists and indeterminists among scientists is not a matter of science, but one of philosophy; it is based essentially on theoretical speculation. In our days, the principle of causation itself has become a metaphysical concept. He who affirms it as an explanation of universal order can adduce no proof that may be experimentally secured. As Jeans says, he *supposes* that the happenings in the phenomenal world "are determined in some substratum of the world which lies beyond the world of phenomena and so also beyond our access." But he who deals with substrata of the world which lie beyond the world phenomena is dangerously close to the border of the supernatural. The truth is that modern science excludes as little the Will of God "of the ancients," as a possible substratum to the world of observable phenomena, as it confirms the principle of causation as such a determining metaphysical background. The worst one may say about the Will of God as being responsible for the world of phenomena is that science is no more indifferent toward it as it is toward Dr. Kaplan's immutable laws of cause and effect.

These new insights, which were only more recently gained by the scientists, corroborated what was accepted by critical philosophy ever since the days of Hume. Independently of any particular advances in actual scientific knowledge, critical philosophy since Hume has shown that experience can never serve as the foundation of the principles of causation and the universality of natural law. In his *Science and the Modern World*, A. N. Whitehead has maintained that Hume's criticism of these principles have never been answered by experimental science. If science nevertheless proceeded to treat causation and universality as if they were validated principles of experience, this was based "on a widespread instinctive conviction" of the existence of an order of nature. Hume was right, "but scientific faith has risen to the occasion and has tacitly removed the philosophic mountain." [93] We shall be in a better position to evaluate the significance of the Reconstructionist ideas about the order of nature, if we recall the source of "the scientific faith" in that order. Says Professor Whitehead: "My explanation is that the faith in the possibility of science, generated antecedently to the development of modern scientific theory, is an unconscious derivative from medieval theology." [94] This, of course, needs some elaboration. The true meaning of Hume's criticism consisted in the rejection of the theory of induction. Since the days of Bacon, induction had been the main tool of scientific logic. Unfortunately, the theory of induction presupposes the existence of an order with a uniform system of organization. Only on the a priori assumption of such a uniform cosmos was it logical to conclude that events belonging to the cosmos would be controlled by the same laws. The task was to discover the laws. However, without the a priori assumption of a uniform cosmic order, induction would prove nothing. As Whitehead puts it, "induction presupposes metaphysics." [95] Medieval theology did have a theistic metaphysics from which the concept of a uniform order of nature was derived; modern experimental science, however, rejected any a priori assumptions of a natural order and based itself on the observation of "brute facts." The reliance on the principle of induction, which is valueless without the corresponding metaphysical assumptions, was indeed an act of faith in the orderliness of nature which was "an unconscious derivative from medieval theology." The point worth noting is that the principles of causation and universality never had any scientific validity; they were affirmed as a matter of faith, unconsciously borrowed from the system of a supernatural theism. (When some scientists realized the intellectual implications of such a situation, scientific positivism was born.)

We can do no better than quote here an illuminating passage from J. W. N. Sullivan's *The Bases of Modern Science*:

"The general medieval outlook made the assumption that Nature was rational a reasonable one. Since both Nature and man had the same author, and Nature was designed to foward man's destiny, it was not unreasonable to suppose that the workings of nature should proceed in a manner intelligible to the human mind. Later, when science gave up this basis for the rationality of Nature, there was nothing to replace it but a pure act of faith. Science replaced the medieval scheme by a different one, but the new scheme did not contain within itself any grounds for supposing that it must be successful. Science itself provides no ground, beyond the pragmatic one of success, for supposing that Nature forms an orderly and coherent whole. Science, therefore, rests not upon a rational basis but upon an act of faith. The scientific belief in the rationality of Nature is seen to be, historically, an inheritance from a system of thought of which the other terms have been discarded." [96]

The inevitable conclusion is that modern science cannot scientifically explain its own spectacular success, which pragmatically confirms a faith that has its origin in a scientifically rejected metaphysical and theistic system.

It is the irony of the Reconstructionist declamation about the immutable laws of cause and effect and the universality of natural law that these laws are purest metaphysical principles, historically and logically derived from supernaturalist religion. At a moment when experimental science, for the first time in its history, may be intellectually true to its nature and be "indifferent" to the principles of causation and universality, Reconstructionism still blindly believes that they are "demanded by scientific theory." Because of its faith in their scientific rationality, Reconstructionism rejects supernaturalist theism. In reality, the laws of universality and causation made sense only in the context of a supernaturalist religion, whence they were unconsciously lifted by an irrational scientific faith. Truly, the Reconstructionist insight into the modern world view is the acme of scientific-philosophic innocence.

Since the Reconstructionist view of naturalism is so extremely naive and outdated, nothing but failure was to be expected from its "wedding of religion to naturalism." Any one who undertakes the task will have to attempt to harmonize a mature naturalism with a mature supernaturalism (and not the old-wives' tale of supernaturalism with which Dr. Kaplan is bickering all the time). The moment is not at all inpropitious. With the brilliant progress made by scientists in describing phenomena with mathematical exactitude has come a continually deepening realization that the more exact our description, the more mystified our understanding of what is being described. Matter has been equated with energy; the notion of substance has been replaced by behavior. And energy is that something that behaves in a certain way, of whose

existence we know because it so behaves. No one, of course, has
the slightest notion what it is that behaves. Discussing such concepts of Newtonian physics as mass, force, weight, J. W. N. Sullivan, whom we quoted earlier, says that whereas Newton considered them "objectively existing entities," we know now "that
these terms are not names of entities, but are concise descriptions
of behavior. They tell us nothing about what is behaving. This
is true of all terms used in physics." [97] Needless to say, neither
do they tell us why the unknown It behaves as it does. "Our most
advanced ideas of reality," on which Reconstructionism imagined
it could build its own structure, are not unlike the theology of
the medieval philosopher. As to reality, we know that it is, but
we do not know what it is. We do not know it by its essence, but
only by its actions. We know what it does, but we do not know
why it does it.

Furthermore, it appears that it would be even more correct to
say that science does not even describe the behavior of the unknown reality, but only the pattern which results from such
behavior; the relationship that exists in a field between unknown
events performed by unknown actors. Modern science deals with
group structure, which can be described without specifying the
material used or the operations by which it was composed.[98]

Eddington sums up the resulting situation in the following
words:

"Our present concept of the physical world is hollow enough
to hold almost anything. . . . What we are dragging to light as
a basis of all phenomena is a scheme of symbols connected by
mathematical equations. That is what physical reality boils down
to when probed by the methods which a physicist can apply. A
skeleton scheme of symbols proclaims its own hollowness. It can
be—nay it cries out to be—filled with something that shall transform it from skeleton into substance. . . . from symbols into an
interpretation of the symbols."[99]

Reconstructionism can make no contribution to the task indicated in the above words. Whereas its conception of the physical
world filled as it is to the brim with the deadwood of outdated
ideas, is not hollow enough to hold anything meaningful, its conception of the spiritual world is much too hollow to provide it.

Only from the fullness of the spirit will the cold skeleton of physical experience be clothed with life and saving dignity.

NOTES

1 Cf. subtitle of *J.W.Sn.*
2 *J.W. Sn*, p. 18.
3 *Ib.*, p. 16.
4 *J.W. Sn.*, p. 98 and *M. of G., P.* 25.
5 *M. of G.*, p. 26.
6 *Ib.*, pp. 25–26.
7 *Ib.*
8 *Ib.*, p. 294.
9 *Ib.*, p. 29.
10 *J.W. Sn.*, pp. 10, 111.
11 *Ib.*, p. 10.
12 *M. of G.*, p. 325.
13 *Ib.*, p. 244–5.
14 *J.W. Sn.*, p. 120.
15 *Ib.*, p. 119.
16 *Ib.*, p. 101–2.
17 *Ib.*, p. 110.
18 *M. of G.*, p. 118.
19 *Ib.*, p. 160–1.
20 *J.W. Sn.*, pp. 48, 52.
21 *M. of G.*, p.323.
22 *Ib.*, p. 295.
23 *Ib.*, p. 110.
24 *Ib.*, p. 226.
25 *Ib.*, p. 167.
26 *Ib.*, p. 27.
27 *Ib.*, p. 29.
28 *Ib.*, p. 54.
29 *Ib.*, p. 245.
30 *Ib.*, pp. 64, 73, 76.
31 *Ib.*, p. 272.
32 *Ib.*, p. 76.
33 *Ib.*
34 *Ib.*, p. 327.
35 *Ib.*, pp. 12–13.
36 *Ib.*, p. 110.
37 Cf. *Ib.*, pp. 26, 113, 120, 161, 245, etc.
38 *M. of G.*, pp. 26, 88.
39 *Ib.*, p. 76.
40 *Ib.*, p. 137.

41 *Ib.*, p. 269.
42 *Ib.*, p. 20.
43 *Ib.*, p. 62.
44 *Ib.*, p. 282.
45 *Ib.*, p. 270–1.
46 *Ib.*, p. 273.
47 *Ib.*, p. 274.
48 Cf. Kant's discussion of the problem, f.i., in *Kritik der reinen Vernunft, Elementarlehre,* II Teil, II Abt., II Buch, II Hauptstueck, III.
49 *M. of G.*, p. 62.
50 *Ib.*, p. 281–2.
51 *J.W. Sn.*, p. 27.
52 *Evolution and Ethics,* 1893–1943, by T. H. Huxley and Julian Huxley, (London, 1947) p. 175.
53 See above I, Note 16.
54 *J.W. Sn.*, p. 101–2; *M. of G.*, 177, 213, 244–5, 316.
55 *Berakhot* 33b.
56 *M. of G.*, p. 270–1.
57 *J.W. Sn.*, p. 119.
58 *M. of G.*, p. 173.
59 *Ib.*, p. 165.
60 *Ib.*, p. 177.
61 Spinoza, *Ethics,* III, Pref.
62 *Ib.*, IV, Pref.
63 Cf. *Die Religion der Vernunft* etc., p. 484.
64 See the discussion of this subject by W. R. Sorley in his Gifford Lectures. *Moral Values and the Idea of God,* p. 387; cf. also the position of Hermann Cohen in his *Ethik des reinen Willens* and *Der Begriff der Religion im System der Philosophie.*
65 *M. of G.*, p. 75.
66 *J.W. Sn.*, p. 77.
67 H. Cohen, *Die Religion der Vernunft* etc., pp. 278, 471, 517.
68 P. 107–8 of the IV. ed.
69 *Sanhedrin* 38a.
70 *J.W. Sn.*, p. 221.
71 *Ib.*, p. 120.
72 *M. of G.*, p. 176.
73 *Ib.*, p. 89.
74 *Ib.*, p. 83.
75 Cf. the discussion of the subject by Joseph Needham in his *TIME The Refreshing River;* The chapter, Evolution and Thermodynamics.
76 *New Pathways in Science* (Cambridge, 1935), p. 309.
77 *M. of G.*, p. 27.
78 *Ib.*
79 Psalms 8: 4–6.
80 *M. of G.* p. 29.

81 *Ib.*, p. 89.
82 *Ib.*, p. 148.
83 *Ib.*, p. 135.
84 *J.W. Sn.*, p. 33.
85 *M. of G.*, p. 83.
86 *J.W. Sn.*, p. 216.
87 *M. of G.* p. 7.
88 *Ib.*, pp. 30, 335; *J.W.Sn.*, pp. 110–11.
89 *J.W. Sn.*, pp. 110–11.
90 *Ib.*, p. 68.
91 Sir James Jeans, *Physics and Philosophy* (Cambridge, 1943), p. 145.
92 See the discussion in *New Pathways of Science*, pp. 300–2.
93 *Ib.*, pp. 4–5.
94 *Ib.*, p. 16.
95 *Ib.*, p. 56.
96 *Ib.*, p. 11.
97 *Ib.*, p. 186.
98 Cf. A. S. Eddington, *New Pathways in Science*, p. 262.
99 *Ib.*, pp. 313–14.

MARVIN FOX

*

Heschel, Intuition, and the Halakhah

IN THE drabness of the landscape of Jewish thought in America the writings of Professor Abraham Joshua Heschel stand out brilliantly. His works are fresh and vital, casting light where it is sorely needed, and helping us to achieve a renewed understanding of what it means to be a Jew. While we can learn much from Heschel, there are some points in his philosophy of religion and of Judaism which require revision or, at least, a different emphasis. This brief essay proposes to examine several of these points in order to see whether Heschel's position is sound and whether it is in accord with the main body of Jewish teaching.[1]

I

Philosophy of religion, according to Heschel, is concerned, among other things, with clarifying and validating the claims of particular religions. If we want to validate religious insights we must have a method, and the only method which Dr. Heschel offers us is intuition. He explicitly rejects the claim that religious truth can be established by some kind of empirical technique or by discursive reason. The existence of God, revelation, God's working in history, the uniqueness of human nature—none of these can be established either by observation or demonstration. Our certainties about these matters are ultimately dependent on direct intuition.

The most common objection to any theory based on intuition is that we have no reliable way to distinguish between those experiences which are genuine perceptions of a higher reality and experiences which are mere delusions or hallucinations. How can we be certain whether a given intuition is a prophetic vision or the aberration of a madman? Dr. Heschel has taken note of this difficulty and has tried to deal with it. His answer consists of the assertion that the man who has had a true experience of the divine is so completely in the power of that vision that he is absolutely incapable of doubt or uncertainty. Obviously this is not a solution of the problem, but merely an avoidance of it, since we are given no criterion by which we can distinguish between genuine and delusory experiences.

There are some other aspects of this same problem which Professor Heschel has not dealt with in his book, but which require some comment. Must we not admit the equal validity of every religious doctrine which bases itself on intuition? Can we reject all but our own? Surely we, as Jews, are bound to insist on the truth of our own position and to reject any religious view that contradicts our teachings. Presumably, devout Christians will find themselves in precisely the same position with regard to the articles of their faith. But on what ground do we make such a selection? Is there any element in the intuitive experience that should lead us to believe that *our* intuitions alone are correct and that all others are false? Can any persuasive arguments be formulated in favor of one given set of intuitions as *the true set?* In the market-place of competing and often contradictory religious ideas the appeal to intuition seems to be a self-defeating weapon. If it is used to justify one doctrine it can be used with equal success to justify every other doctrine. The net result, it would appear, is an intolerable theological chaos, which offers a fertile field for the saccharine inanities of the "good-will" movement.

Furthermore, a religion which depends on intuition as its primary method restricts itself to a very small segment of mankind. Great spiritual sensitivity is not very widespread. What are we to do about the largest proportion of mankind, those who are neither prophets nor the sons of prophets? According to Rabbinic tradition, during the revelation at Sinai even the untutored hand-maidens had greater prophetic visions than Ezekiel was to experience at a later time. But we, the Jews of this age, do not have this rare prophetic gift. Flashes of insight, moments of spiritual exaltation, soul-shattering visions are available to very few of us. A conception of religion which is rooted in such experiences automatically restricts the realm of faith to a small group of the spiritually elite.

Professor Heschel believes that "the supreme problem in any philosophy of Judaism [and, presumably, in the other major religions as well] is: what are the grounds for believing in the realness of the living God?" and he asks whether man is capable of discovering such grounds. According to his analysis there are three ways that lead man to God, three ways of reliable intuition. Man can come to a knowledge of God by sensing His "presence in the world, in things, . . . sensing His presence in the Bible, . . . sensing His presence in sacred deeds." But each of these three ways, it can be argued, is open only to the man who is already responsive to the reality of God; they will be of little help to others.

If one looks at the world with the eyes of the spirit closed, he is likely to see nothing at all of religious significance. It is true that a man who already conceives of the world as a divine creation can see evidence of divinity throughout the realms of nature and history. However, the mind that finds in nature nothing but matter and motion and that sees man as only one more animal in the natural order is not likely to achieve religious insight through this route. To see the sublime, and the more than sublime, in the world one must look with the eyes of faith. There is no evidence that men can achieve that faith by inspecting the world.

The proposal that men can find God in the Bible involves us in a similar difficulty. The reader who approaches the Bible in the conviction that it is a divine book will have his religious awareness deepened and intensified by study of the sacred text. What reason have we to hope that the reader who denies the divinity of the Bible will also be able to find his way to God through the instrumentality of that great work? All that Professor Heschel has to say about the divine character of the Bible will be convincing only to those who already agree with him. There is perhaps a tacit recognition of this fact in his almost too vigorous defense of the Bible. Each of his arguments begs the question,

since it presupposes what is to be proved. A typical example may
be seen in his basic argument which states that failure to respond to the Bible is testimony of the limitations of the reader
and not the book. "No sadder proof can be given by a man of his
own spiritual opacity than his insensitiveness to the Bible." "We
accept it because in approaching it our own splendid ideas turn
pale, because even indisputable proofs appear vulgar at the sound
of prophetic words . . . Ultimately, then, we do not accept the
Bible because of reasons, but because if the Bible is a lie all reasons are a fake."

True as we believe these claims to be, they are not an argument. Men who stand outside the world of the Bible will only be
perplexed or enraged by such strong demands. Having examined
the very same pages, they often discover nothing more than a
collection of superstitions and errors, which seem to be the work
of relatively undeveloped primitive minds. To these men belief
in the Bible is evidence of a shallow intelligence and a weak character. Exchanging epithets will not solve the problem, nor will
vociferous reassertions of our counter-claims. We, who have
found light and inspiration in the Bible, must acknowledge that
we are dependent on intuition. By way of this intuition we sense
the presence of God in even the most ordinary words of sacred
Scripture. But how can the Bible serve as a pathway to God for
those who approach it without religious faith and without any
sense of the spiritual impoverishment of their humdrum lives?

The third of Professor Heschel's ways to God seems also to
suffer from essentially the same difficulty. At first glance it appears that even men who stand outside the world of faith may
be able to discover God through the performance of sacred deeds.
Presumably this is a way which is open to men whose intellectual
orientation has closed their eyes to the presence of God in nature,
in history, in the Bible. For no matter what they think or believe,
they can act as if they believed: מתוך שלא לשמה בא לשמה.
As Professor Heschel himself puts it, "A Jew is asked to take a
leap of action rather than a *leap of thought*. He is asked to surpass his needs, to do more than he understands in order to understand more than he does . . . Through the ecstasy of deeds

he learns to be certain of the hereness of God. Right living is a way to right thinking."

This, too, is a road which can lead to religious conviction only if it presupposes some measure of such conviction. If a man performs deeds without any sense of their spiritual significance whatsoever how can they be effective in leading him to God? In his later exposition of the *mitzvot*, Dr. Heschel himself argues impressively against mere mechanical observances which reduce the religious life to a kind of "sacred physics." A "leap of action" must be religiously motivated if it is to lead a man to awareness of the reality of God. As Dr. Heschel puts it, "At the beginning is the *commitment, the supreme acquiescence.*" Without the commitment of faith a man is most unlikely to undertake the performance of "sacred deeds," and if he should they will be mere posturings without any spiritual effect.

This very point, I believe, is the one that should be stressed most of all. We cannot depend on direct intuition. Perhaps this is what Rabbi Yochanan meant when he taught that since the destruction of the Holy Temple prophecy was taken away from the prophets and given to madmen and children. Sober men know how utterly unreliable intuitions can be. Those who envision themselves as having direct insight into ultimate truth too often turn out to be either mad or infantile. Professor Heschel's position would be far sounder if he consistently put the main emphasis on the initial act of faith, on "the supreme acquiescence."

Contemporary Jews can come to live a life of Torah-loyalty in one of two ways. Some simply accept the entire tradition as valid because they received it from parents and teachers. For them there are no very serious personal or intellectual obstacles to a Torah-true life, and it is not to them that Professor Heschel has addressed his writings. Their faith is firm.

The Jew who is perplexed and searching is our special concern. He will never be persuaded to live as a Jew by an appeal to religious intuitions which he does not have and cannot understand. Instead of being asked to look for evidences of God in nature or in the Bible, he must be confronted with the greatest of all challenges—the challenge to find meaning in his own life.

He must be forced to see that without God and His Torah men are reduced to being animals and automata. Our faith does not derive from personal prophetic visions or from moments of personal revelation. It is forced upon us as the only alternative to forfeiting our very humanity. Only when we recognize the depth of our own need are we ready, in faith, to pass beyond the limits of our discursive knowledge. We then affirm that "In the beginning God created," because we recognize that to deny God means to destroy ourselves. With this faith we are endowed with heightened awareness so that the evidence of God's presence in nature and history is apparent to us. With this faith we are able to discover something of the divine truth hidden in each letter of sacred scripture. Not in vain did Maimonides set down as the first principle in his Code the obligation to know that God exists and that He is the source of all being. Without this conviction there can be no religious thought, no religious intuition, and no religious action.

In summary, our difference with Professor Heschel on this point is one of direction. He seems to suggest in many places that intuition is the way to faith. We are arguing that faith must precede intuition. This view seems more consistent with post-exilic Jewish tradition which saw the age of prophecy as ended, and a more realistic approach to the religious dilemma of the contemporary Jew.

I I

Dr. Heschel's philosophy of Judaism reflects his general philosophy of religion. The Judaism which he sets forth is a religion of deep spiritual craving, of an insatiable thirst for God. While he acknowledges and even stresses the absolute importance of Halakhah it is quite clear that he demands something beyond Halakhah. "The meaningfulness of the mitzvot," he says, "consists in their being vehicles by which we advance on the road to spiritual ends." The implication is that the *mitzvot* themselves are insufficient for the elevation of man's spirit, that they are a means to a higher end. In fact, very early in his book Dr. Heschel affirms that "Religion is, indeed, little more than a desiccated remnant of a once living reality when reduced to terms and definitions, to codes and catechisms."

There can be little quarrel with the ideal representation of Judaism which Professor Heschel has formulated. Any fair examination of the authentic Jewish tradition will recognize, with Dr. Heschel, that it seeks a disciplined life whose pattern is set by Halakhah with the aim of bringing man as close as possible to God. But even among faithful and pious Jews the exalted spiritual moments are infrequent. One has the feeling that Professor Heschel has over-emphasized this dimension of the religious life, that he places too little value on the ordinary routine of piety and demands far too much spiritual fire of the ordinary Jew.

Is it necessary to go as far as Dr. Heschel does in his absolute requirement of spontaneity, burning religious feeling, and inner devotion? Must we, in effect, scorn the piety of the vast numbers of meticulously observant Jews because it is often routine and mechanical? Does not such a view of Judaism grant (without intending to do so) the old (and probably malicious) charge that the letter kills while the spirit gives life? With all of Dr. Heschel's repeated affirmations of the fundamental need for Halakhah in the religious life, his qualifications and restrictions of the place of Halakhah undermine the effectiveness of his stand. Jewish tradition devoted its major efforts to the development of Halakhah without qualifications or apology. Judaism recognized (in Heschel's own words) that "man may be commanded to act in a certain way, but not to feel in a certain way; that the actions of man may be regulated, but not his thoughts or emotions." A Jew who lives in accordance with Halakhah has done all that can be asked of him. Whenever he acts in response to the *mitzvah*, he draws close to God, even if he never has a mystical experience, even if he never knows the anguish of craving for the divine presence and the transcendant joy of breaking through the barriers. Professor Heschel seems to underestimate the worth of the most prosaic fulfillment of the divine commandments.

While we applaud the skill with which he has explicated and defended the often neglected Aggadah we must note that this enthusiasm seems to have blinded him somewhat to the special place of Halakhah in Judaism. For, according to Dr. Heschel,

"Halakhah does not deal with the ultimate level of existence." He believes that "The law does not create in us the motivation to love and to fear God, nor is it capable of endowing us with the power to overcome evil and to resist its temptations, nor with the loyalty to fulfill its precepts. It supplies the weapons; it points the way; the fighting is left to the soul of man."

The greatest Jewish sages were, of course, cognizant of the importance of Aggadah and many of them made brilliant contributions to aggadic literature. Nevertheless, they consistently centered the bulk of their study and concern on Halakhah. Their preference for Halakhah indicates that they found in it far more than Professor Heschel does. They were convinced that Halakhah *does* deal with the ultimate level of existence. They understood that Halakhah is more than a dry legal code and that halakhic study is more than intricate mental gymnastics. By way of Halakhah Judaism grasped in a clear and communicable form the profoundest religious insights. Dr. Heschel fails to see this when he attacks "pan-halakhic theology" as "a view which exalts the Torah only because it discloses the law, not because it discloses a way of finding God in life." Jewish tradition has always taught that Halakhah is the only reliable way of finding God in life. In Halakhah Judaism bridges the gap between the man of rare spiritual genius and the rest of the people. The great religious insights, which are ordinarily restricted to men of prophetic sensitivity, are made available and real through Halakhah to every Jew in all the ordinary circumstances of his every-day life.

"Insights are not a secure possession; they are vague and sporadic; they are like divine sparks, flashing up before us and becoming obscure again, and we fall back into a darkness 'almost as black as that in which we were before.'" Because he sees very clearly that we cannot rest with such insights, Professor Heschel goes on to ask the most earnest questions. "The problem," he says, "is: How to communicate those rare moments of insight to all the hours of our life? How to commit intuition to concepts, the ineffable to words, insight to rational understanding? How to convey our insights to others and to unite in a fellowship of faith?" Surely Dr. Heschel must admit that the historic Jewish answer to his questions has always been a reliance on Halakhah.

Given the vagueness and insecurity of our moments of insight
they must be translated into terms that are related to man's life
in order to be effective. This is precisely what Halakhah does. It
is an objectification of Israel's collective religious experience, a
concrete expression, in human terms, of those elusive truths
granted us through divine revelation and grasped in especially
sensitive moments by our choicest spirits. The entire structure
of Halakhah is the Jewish way of committing "intuition to concepts, the ineffable to words, insight to rational understanding."
This is neither a rejection of religious thinking, nor a derogation
of theology. It is not a condemnation of the restless craving of
men for spiritual exaltation and overpowering insight. What we
are insisting upon is that all of these are present in Halakhah.

In spite of his strictures Dr. Heschel will surely grant that
the talmudic discourse concerning "the ox which gored the cow"
is not merely an arid discussion of certain technical problems
in the law of damages. It is the Jewish way of concretizing the
presence of God in the most mundane aspects of daily life. Rabbi
Elazar ben Chisma made this point eminently clear when he laid
down the principle קנין ופתחי נדה הן הן גופי הלכות.   This is
the view of the world of Halakhah as an ideal world in which
we met God face to face. What seems impractical and irrelevant
is shown in that world to be especially meaningful. What seems
ugly and indelicate is transformed in that world to the highest
level of beauty and refinement. In his life and in his study, the
halakhic Jew renews continually the essence of his own being.
Though he may have no great moments of mystical insight he is,
nevertheless, always very close to God, for it is the objectification
of divine reality in Halakhah that stands at the center of the
halakhic life. It is only in Halakhah that moments of genuine
religious awareness are given a stable, intelligible, and communicable form.

This explains the consistent priority which rabbinic tradition
gave to halakhic literature as a subject of study. How revealing
is the rabbinic observation that the study of sacred Scripture is
only a partially satisfactory activity, while the most desirable
of all study is the study of Gemara: "They who occupy themselves with the Bible (alone) are but of indifferent merit; with

Mishnah, are indeed meritorious . . . ; with *Gemara*—there can be nothing more meritorious" (*B. M.*, 33a). This teaches us that the apparently dry legalisms of halakhic debate encompass all of the divine beauty and wisdom of the Bible. Even more than this—divine revelation receives its most specifically concrete and crystallized form in halakhic discourse and halakhic decision. However lovely and moving the flights of aggadic imagination may be, they lack the stability and clarity of Halakhah. Aggadah may inspire us, but only Halakhah can give direction to our actions. The need for aggadic inspiration is granted without question, but Aggadah is effective only with halakhic discipline and direction. God and man can find each other only by way of the bridge of halakhic study and action, for we have been taught that "Since the day that the Temple was destroyed the Holy One blessed be He has nothing in this world but the four cubits of Halakhah alone" (*Berakhot* 8a). The world of Halakhah is the distillation of all our authentic efforts to encounter the divine. It is in that world that man elevates himself so that he can be with God.

Repeatedly, in his writings, Professor Heschel affirms this very same point, only then to back away from it because of a fear of "pan-halakhism." It is this hesitation about the full power of Halakhah that is inconsistent with the normative Jewish tradition. At his best, Dr. Heschel offers us a superb exposition of the ultimate significance and the ultimate claim of Halakhah. His philosophy of Judaism would be immeasurably strengthened if he held to his own insights with complete consistency.

NOTES

1 This essay is based on Heschel's book, *God in Search of Man* (Philadelphia: Jewish Publication Society, 1956). All quotations, unless otherwise noted, are from this volume.

WALTER S. WURZBURGER

*

The Oral Law and the
Conservative Dilemma

Law and tradition in Judaism [1] represents a collection of scintillating studies which are offered by its erudite author as a contribution towards a "philosophy of Jewish religious law from the point of view of Historical-Traditional Judaism."

To this task Professor Boaz Cohen brings not merely the learning and perspective of an eminent scholar of Jewish and Roman law. His many years of service to the Rabbinical Assembly as chairman of its "Committee on Law" provided him with ample opportunity to step outside the cloistered walls of the academic ivory tower and to gain the vantage point of one who has grappled with the vexing and perplexing problems of religious observance in the modern Jewish world.

The author's deep reverence for Jewish tradition places him at the extreme right wing of the Conservative movement. Time and again he cautions his more liberal colleagues not to tamper with the Halakhah in order to accommodate popular pressures. With commendable frankness he concedes that many standard practices of Conservative congregations, such as mixed seating or riding to services on the Sabbath, cannot be condoned by Jewish law.

Yet one cannot help wonder whether Professor Cohen's love for Jewish tradition is not blind to the implications of his own theological position. It must be love that makes him blind to the fact that "the arguments which the historical interpretation of Judaism advances for submitting to the law and the commandments are less cogent and persuasive than the reasoning of Orthodoxy". Any impartial observer should be quick to recognize that the very foundation of all religious observance is bound to be

corroded by the basic tenets of "Historic-Traditional" Judaism.
From a logical point of view it hardly makes sense to expect a
modern Jew to abide by ancient rules and regulations that were
supposedly developed in response to the needs of a by-gone era.
If, as the historical school contends, the development of the Oral
Law represents merely a certain stage in the long evolutionary
process of a Judaism that finds itself in a state of perpetual flux,
there is no reason why we should acknowledge the authority of
talmudic law. If the talmudic sages were entitled to change the
Written Law to keep abreast of the requirements of their age,
why should our generation feel constrained to uphold the im-
mutability of the principles formulated by Talmudic Judaism?
Does not Professor Gordis have logic on his side when he charges
this specimen of historic Judaism with the creation of a dichotomy
between "the creative past and the degenerate present?"

Professor Cohen's position becomes intelligible only in the light
of the powerful influence exerted by the "logic of the heart"
which so often triumphs over human reason. Marshall Sklare, the
astute analyst of the Conservative movement, has called attention
to the striking ambivalence in the attitudes of many Conservative
scholars. Intellectually, they wholeheartedly embrace the "scientific," "positive-historical" approach. Emotionally, they cannot
cut the umbilical cord which ties them to the practices of Orthodox Judaism.

Torn asunder by this inner conflict, Conservative scholars not
only recoil from drawing those logical inferences from their
premises that would undermine religious observance, but they are
even impelled to make statements which are totally incompatible
with their point of view. Thus Professor Cohen urges his colleagues "to cope with the problem of Jewish law in the spirit of
. . . Rabbi Isaac Elchanan," in spite of the fact that the latter
is one of the leading lights of a movement which in another
chapter is accused of seeking to "freeze Judaism in a mold two
centuries old." Conceivably, students of depth psychology may
be able to unravel the mystery of how one can recommend that
scholars, who are engaged in the "creative reinterpretation" of
Judaism in the tradition of a Frankel, Geiger, and Schechter,

should pattern themselves after an old-fashioned rabbi exemplifying a school of thought that allegedly "has bogged down in a morass of stubborn literalism and dogmatism."

Be that as it may, there is no doubt that Professor Cohen goes overboard in compensating for whatever Orthodox leanings might be ascribed to him. In the darkest colors imaginable, he portrays Orthodoxy as a hotbed of reaction, a victim of "smug complacency and spiritual inflation."

Since, by the author's definition, Orthodoxy is a petrified fossil that is out of touch with life, it follows by a remarkable specimen of circular reasoning that the neo-Orthodox rabbis flout the tenets of pristine Orthodoxy when they pursue secular studies or preach in English. That these self-same practices belie the stereotyped image of Orthodoxy as a stagnant, inflexible relic of the past is something that simply does not occur to one who feels constrained to equate Orthodoxy with "the form in which Judaism was crystallized during the eighteenth century."

Professor Cohen's ambivalence towards Orthodoxy is matched by his ambiguity in the exposition of his own views. There is no way of gleaning from his writings whether he subscribes to the rabbinic doctrine that the words of the Pentateuch were "literally" inspired. Although committed to "the divine origin of the Law," the author leaves us in considerable doubt whether he is prepared to regard Moses as anything more than an "inspired Lawgiver."

Even more puzzling is his attitude towards the nature of the Oral Law. On the one hand, he implies that the Rabbis were cognizant of the fact that their ingenious methods of interpretation constituted an actual modification of the original law. Accordingly, they devised the hermeneutical rules and developed the Midrashic exegesis as a subterfuge, because they wanted to conceal under the guise of interpretation what, in point of fact, amounted to a deliberate modification of religious law. On the other hand, he suggests that it was only naïveté born out of unfamiliarity with history and philology that made it possible for the talmudic sages to delude themselves into thinking that their forced interpretations were not distortions but elucidations of the real intent of the biblical text.

Either of the two alternatives abounds with unsavory features.

If the Rabbis deliberately took liberties with the original law and merely pretended that their bold innovations represented legitimate interpretations, then, at the very least, they must be charged with misinterpretation. If, however, the operations of the rabbinic mind reflect sheer naïveté in matters historical or philological, it is difficult to see why sophisticated scholars should feel constrained to uphold the authority of religious leaders whose rulings were predicated upon gross ignorance of pertinent and relevant data. In either case, we would have ample grounds for disqualifying the teachers of old from serving as mentors for our age.

This painful dilemma arises, of course, not of incidental defects in Professor Cohen's exposition, but out of the pitfalls and self-contradictions inherent in the Conservative approach, which credits the talmudic sages with the *creation* of the Oral Law. Unless one is prepared to accept the traditional view which establishes an organic connection between the Written and the Oral Law, regarding the latter not as a subsequent modification but a concomitant elucidation of the former, one cannot help but impugn either the intellectual honesty or competence of the framers of the Oral Law.

It cannot be argued that these unpleasant alternatives are the necessary price we must pay for an approach to Jewish law that reckons with its dynamic, evolutionary character. Nothing would be further from the truth than the belief that the positive-historical school has a monopoly on progress and development. As a matter of fact, any data (in contradistinction to mere theories and constructions) adduced by the champions of "Historical" Judaism can easily fit into the conceptual framework of the traditionalist. The point in issue between the two schools is *not* at all whether, or to what degree, Jewish law has undergone modifications over the ages. The real issue is this: were the changes and developments that occurred during the talmudic period the result of the creation of an Oral Law that was superimposed upon biblical Judaism, or did the Rabbis, employing principles that ultimately derived from divine revelation on Mt. Sinai, interpret both the Written and the Oral Torah in the light of the historic conditions of their time? The traditionalist maintains that since "Torah has seventy faces," as the Rabbis put it, the meaning of a given

law may be affected by variations in historic realities. Developments in the law, therefore, reflect not the abrogation of "the"
original meaning but the application of divinely revealed or sanctioned processes that enable us to interpret an eternally binding
law in accordance with the specific requirements of a given generation.

This process of interpretation, insofar as the traditionalist is
concerned, is by no means, as Professor Cohen implies, merely
"a mechanical application of pre-existing rules." Long before the
advent of the Historical school, the traditionalists fully recognized that they were entrusted with a *Torat Chayyim*—a living
Law. Halakhic problems are not the kind that can be solved by
advances in the field of cybernetics. Halakhic questions call for a
creative approach; they cannot be answered by some electronic
calculator which grinds out its answers the way an electrical brain
finds the solution to a complex differential equation.

It is precisely this creative aspect of the halakhic process that
led the sages to the remarkable statement "both these and these
are the words of the living God," that at times even conflicting
halakhic opinions represent, in the final analysis, legitimate elucidations of the word of God. The Torah "is not in Heaven"; it
must be interpreted by the proper authorities of each generation.
Since no human being can completely guard himself against the
intrusion of personal value judgments in the selection, interpretation, or application of relevant texts to concrete situations, a ha-
lahkic opinion inevitably contains some subjective components.
But however tinged it may be by subjectivity, its legitimacy as a
halakhic opinion is assured as long as it has been evolved by *bona
fide* halakhic procedures.

Because the halakhic process is characterized by a continuous
interaction between subjective and objective components, it is
natural that changes in historical conditions will lead to far reaching repercussions in the realm of Halakhah. This is not at all a question of "adapting" or "adjusting" the law to meet novel conditions, but of interpreting and applying it within the frame of reference of new circumstances. When, according to the Aggadah,
R. Akiva found in the Torah meanings that had eluded Moses, he

was not creating a new Torah. What he did was something altogether different. Reading the Torah in the light of the conditions of an entirely different age, he discovered *chidushei Torah, new meanings* of the Torah. Yet, in spite of their manifest novelty, they were implicitly contained in the Torah as received by Moses on Mount Sinai. It must be borne in mind that this dynamic character of the law is an integral part of the *Massorah*, the chain of Tradition dating back to Sinai, not something that was grafted upon the Torah later on to prevent its obsolescence and decay. To employ the well known rabbinic simile, just as different sparks are emitted when a hammer breaks a rock into pieces, so does the word of God yield numerous meanings. And it is the function of the Halakhah scholar, employing creative halakhic processes, to unravel the specific meaning which the timeless message of Sinai holds for his own time.

Obviously, this view is a far cry from the historic position which dwells upon the distinction between essential and contingent aspects of the law. Thus, in the words of Professor Cohen, "Jewish law has undergone a long and eventful process of evolution without altering its original essence or nature, or modifying its pristine principles and purposes." Because Traditional Judaism is committed to the divinely revealed law in its totality, it must object to the cavalier treatment accorded to the minutiae of the law. Alterations cannot be condoned on the ground that they allegedly affect not the essence but only relatively trivial details. Traditional Judaism cannot brook any departure from the divine will. Developments in the law are legitimate only if, down to the last detail, they conform to the canons of interpretation by which the law is applied to the ever changing historic realities.

Apart from the basic weakness of the position which is set forth with so much grace and charm in *Law and Tradition in Judaism*, there are a number of other serious flaws. Thus Professor Cohen is guilty of a logical non-sequitur when, from the premise that the Rabbis knew the difference between *peshat* and *derash*, he draws the conclusion that they were conscious of changing the letter of the law when they employed the method of *derash*. This reasoning is obviously faulty, for the Rabbis always emphasized that *peshat* was only one of many approaches to the meaning of the Torah. Similarly, we may question the propriety of characterizing *asmakhta* as a "legal fiction" since the Rabbis never pretended that laws derived by this process (in contradistinction to a genuine *derashah*) possessed more than purely rabbinic sanction. One may also take exception to the categorical statement that in case of conversion the presence of the court at the immersion was not required by the Talmud, since numerous authorities interpret the relevant talmudic texts in a different fashion. "That covering the head during a religious service is merely a custom" runs counter to the talmudic law requiring *ituf* for at least some occasions of prayer.

To turn to less legalistic matters, we are struck by the author's persistent attempt to downgrade the concept of duty in Jewish thought. That conscience is to be conceived "as a moral impulse implanted in the heart rather than a sense of duty" can hardly be substantiated on the flimsy evidence that in describing conscience both Scripture and Talmud employ terms that refer to the heart. Moreover, we must bear in mind that in ancient Jewish writings the term "heart" does not possess the emotional overtones of our present day usage. In classical Jewish terminology, the heart is conceived as the seat of the intellect, whereas the kidneys (not the heart) are regarded as the source of sentiments. This being the case, references to the heart hardly warrant the conclusion that Jewish ethics is based on moral sentiment rather than a sense of duty. The author also completely disregards the famous dictum, *gadol metzuveh ve'oseh mi-mi she'eno metzuveh ve'oseh*, which implies that an act motivated by a sense of duty ranks higher than one prompted by moral sentiment.

Conceivably, this glorification of sentiment at the expense of duty is symptomatic of the entire approach of the author, whose position can be vindicated only by what since the days of Pascal is known as "the logic of the heart." Recent developments in the Conservative camp clearly show that the movement cannot be halted on the level of reverence and regard for Jewish law that still characterizes the writings of Professor Cohen. Driven by its own dynamics, the Conservative movement is gradually reaching the logical conclusions of its system, and advocates radical revisions that go far beyond the pale of the "creative interpretation" espoused by Professor Cohen. Thus, *Law and Tradition in Judaism* serves as a monument to an untenable approach to Jewish law, which is becoming obsolete because, for all its brilliance and scholarship, it contains within itself the seeds of its own destruction.

NOTES

1 *Law and Tradition in Judaism*, by Boaz Cohen (New York: The Jewish Theological Seminary of America, 1959).

EMANUEL RACKMAN

*

The Future of Jewish Law

ISRAEL has revived much. The tongue of the prophets has been resurrected there to become its official language. The study of the Bible was made universal. Even military experts profess their need of the Book of Books. Tourist guides refer to it in almost every comment. National contests involving demonstrations of its mastery attract thousands of spectators as baseball games do in the United States.

Rabbi Kook's prayer that the old shall be renewed is being fulfilled. But what of Jewish law? Will or can historic Jewish jurisprudence become the basis for the legal order of the autonomous Jewish republic of our day?

It may surprise many that this is not now the situation. However, except for family law and such cases as come before the rabbinical courts with the consent of all parties, the legal system of Israel is a composite of Ottoman, British, and French doctrines and rules. The Israeli parliament, the Knesset, has not radically altered the pattern. Partisans of the Halakhah (Jewish Law) have always urged the renaissance of the ancestral legal heritage. They had hoped that the revival of Jewish law would enhance the national revival even as the revival of Hebrew did. To their voices is now added the voice of Israel's Chief Justice—Professor Mosheh Silberg—in a small but stimulating volume entitled *Principia Talmudica* or *This Is the Way of Talmud*.[1]

The volume merits careful analysis and evaluation. The view of a Chief Justice always carry weight. Moreover, the author teaches law at the Hebrew University in Jerusalem and thus influences hundreds of students who will one day become members of Israel's bench and bar. Because he is identified with no political party his recommendations do not reflect party claims or advantages and are, therefore, respected by Israel's intelligentsia. Unlike a colleague of his on the same bench, he has no personal frustration that blocks him emotionally *vis-a-vis* the Halakhah and his consideration of its viability in a modern state is objective and well balanced. Thus while one may differ with Professor Silberg on one point or another, his book dare not be ignored, for it will play an important role in the emergence of Israel's legal order. Indeed, many of its most significant sections have already been translated into English and published in the *Harvard Law Review*. That is why more than the usual book review is warranted and this essay purports to be a rejoinder in what hopefully may become a continuing dialogue among those who love Jewish law and crave its renaissance at the same time that they are realistic with regard to the present situation of that law and the milieu in which its revival is projected.

I

The heart of Professor Silberg's argument is that Jewish law has a character all its own. It is religio-centered, or, as the author of this essay has in his own writing described it, it is theocentric rather than power-centered. In Jewish law there is no separation of divine law from positive law. Occasionally, there may be a different legal rule applicable to matters sacred or ritualistic but the legal system is monistic. Doctrines, principles, rules, precedents—all are integral parts of the same Halakhah, and talmudic dialectic cites, challenges, and differentiates, recognizing no dichotomy between what is God's and what is Caesar's. Talmudic discourse has a basic unity—civil and religious law are one.

Since the source of the law is a bilateral covenant between God and Israel, and this covenant is so deeply entrenched as the root norm of the entire legal system, even God is a legal "person," bound by the very law He promulgated. His role in its very interpretation is prescribed by the rules explicitly or implicitly contained in the covenant. From this seed or beginning all that is unique about Jewish law flowers. And Professor Silberg writes feelingly of this uniqueness.

The author's approach is to be commended. He helps all students of the law to appreciate that the Halakhah is a very rich legal system. It can excite the intellect and quicken the ethic of any jurist. It has legal concepts analagous to those of the most advanced jurisprudence and its methodology as well as its concepts can be analyzed and communicated in terms familiar to all lawyers in the Western world. To many moderns all of this comes as a welcome surprise, inducing national or ethnic pride.

However, precisely because the book has so many virtues, its conclusion comes as a crushing disappointment. Silberg wants the revival of Jewish law but without its focus on God or religion. Judges and legislators are themselves to choose what rules of the Halakhah they shall retain and what they shall discard. God is dethroned—nay, removed as a covenantor, and man becomes the sole arbiter of justice.

Now, if the role of God in the legal heritage was an important factor in the achievement of a blessed uniqueness, can one retain the blessing without His continuing participation? And if His role was only a legal fiction and the good came rather from the monistic character of the law—the interdependence of divine and positive law (both of which in fact had their real source in man)—then can one hope to keep such a fiction alive in a secular state, hell-bent on relegating religion to the individual conscience instead of recognizing it as part of the legal order?

Jewish ethics describe obligations involving man's relationship with his fellow-man. In the folios of Talmud these relationships are integrated in almost every morsel of the dialectic. Eliminate the former and what is left that is different from positive law or that can produce the uniqueness which Professor Silberg reveres as the hallmark of Jewish law?!

II

To pose this question to Professor Silberg, however, is not to relieve the burden of those who champion the cause of the Halakhah for the modern state. Those who want to retain the traditional theocentricity must explain how they will legislate to make Jewish law viable today, since only a few will deny the need for legislation in the present. They must also explain how they will *amend* and *annul*, since amendment and annulment are as necessary as legislation. Legislation, amendment, and annulment, there always were. However, the guardians of the Halakhah enjoyed both the confidence and authority of Jews. In modern Israel they enjoy neither. Certainly the state is not prepared to recruit its judges and legislators from their ranks. Will they, therefore, withdraw into a closed community in which they enjoy the confidence and authority of a few and await the Messianic age, or will they help to revive and develop Jewish law even though secularists are its guardians? This they could do, if they chose. They could in their continuing encounter with God—the other party to the covenant—explore and articulate the insights of Jewish law for the present; they could provide the juridic insights and draft statutes even for secular judges and legislators. They could be creative even as Professor Silberg was in many chapters of his volume and perhaps they would cause their theocentric outlook to have an impact on the legal order—on both legislative enactment and judicial interpretation. Especially in family law—where they do still have jurisdiction—they could demonstrate the viability of the Halakhah by the legislative power which the Halakhah vouchsafes unto them.

Perhaps an institute for Jewish law could be established comparable to the various committees that coined new Hebrew words in the last half-century in order that the Hebrew tongue may be reborn. The institute would comprise scholars of all orientations. The goal would be the continuance of Jewish law. Insofar as the development can be contained within the total frame of the Halakhah it should be encouraged so that there shall be no needless divisiveness in the Israeli Jewish community. If there is no alternative to Professor Silberg's proposal, then in vain does he sing the praises of a law which even for him can no longer be what it once was, because its heart has ceased to beat,—its soul, its God, no longer throbs in the circle responsible for legal development. Man will have assumed complete control over it and it will no longer differ from other systems of positive law. The ancient Jewish sources will be of historical interest as will Roman sources, and Turkish sources. But the thread with the past—the denominator which gave uniqueness—God—will be no part of it.

I I I

However, even as a paean to Jewish law, Professor Silberg's book warrants critical evaluation. His exuberance is often greater than his argument. Let one assume with him that the time has come for Israeli jurists to draw upon Jewish precedents instead of British precedents for such lacunae as exist in the law. Is it the mere fact that they are *Jewish* precedents that makes them *ipso facto* preferable? In the very case (in the closing chapter) in which he and his colleagues urged the use of Jewish precedents he did not undertake to demonstrate their superiority over related rules of other legal systems. Even a fervent Jewish nationalist should regard the value of justice as a higher value than historical continuity. And in the final analysis this is the criterion that will win the hearts of those who must decide the future character of Israeli jurisprudence.

Thus in his chapter on Law and Equity, Professor Silberg classifies and summarizes the principles of Jewish equity jurisprudence. The classification and the summary are comprehensive. One is convinced that as equity always was a corrective of strict law in England, so Jewish law is blessed with the same remedial potential. Moreover, his claim that most concepts of British equity jurisprudence are to be found in Jewish law is also valid. But the uniqueness of the Jewish system of equity receives only a parenthetical reference. And there is virtually no argument that this uniqueness can make for a juster judicial system than was enjoyed by the Romans who also had equity law as well as strict law, or the British and Americans who share a rich legal heritage comprising the common law of the king's courts and the more flexible rules of the king's conscience which was exercised by his chancery.

A more impressive discussion of the same theme is to be found in Dr. K. Kagan's volume [2] on Roman, English, and Jewish law. Dr. Kagan proved the thesis that in the Roman and English systems there was a separation of equity law from strict or common law—the different judicial powers actually resided in different persons, while in Jewish law, law and equity were one. Equity was an integral part of the law. The same judges exercised both powers in their articulation and enforcement of the law. Professor

Silberg makes casual references to this point but neither he nor Professor Kagan spell out the advantages of a unified approach. Perhaps they both assumed—and not improperly—that lawyers will recognize the advantages immediately. Nevertheless lawyers also know that the unification can be, and is being, achieved in modern legal systems by legislation. In the final analysis, then, Jewish law can only be regarded as superior because it has the potential to yield such a unity: the duty of each and every judge to mete out justice in the fullest sense of the term by balancing the law's predictability as based on adherence to precedents with what is "good and righteous in the eyes of God." Every judge in the Jewish system is thus not a servant of the state. He is rather God's agent, serving Him, above all else. His accountability to God is the rationale for his broad judicial power. Theocentricity lies at the heart of this superior quality which Jewish law has. Yet can one discard that theocentricity and hope to retain the advantage?

I V

Professor Silberg's most original insight, and one of his most significant, is contained in the sixth chapter of the book. He maintains that unlike most other legal systems Jewish law is duty-oriented rather than right-oriented. The focus of attention is always on the obligation of the obligor rather than the claim of the claimant. Thus debts must be paid not so much because the lender has a right to the money he advanced to the borrower but rather because the borrower has a duty to fulfill a *Mitzvah*—a mandate of God or social ethics.

Perhaps one day historians will pass judgment on our generation and its mores and record that one important cause of our economic, political and social malaise is the denigration of duty and the enthronement of right and privilege. We glory in our bills of rights. We have rights against the state, seldom duties to it. Everyone knows of his right to social security and unemployment insurance; few are equally impassioned about the duty to vote or serve on juries. Employees know of their right to strike, their right to organize, their right to vacations; few are as alert with regard to their duty to give their employers an honest day's work. Even children know their rights against their parents; few are as keen about the measure of their obligation under the fifth commandment of the Decalogue.

It is, therefore, refreshing to ponder a legal system whose key word is obligation rather than privilege. Needless to say, right and duty are correlatives. Whenever anyone is under a duty, someone else has a right to the performance of the duty, and vice versa. However, the question is, where do we place the emphasis? In Jewish law, the emphasis is on the duty, and a social order that stresses duty rather than right will inevitably—by the very nature of duty—cause people to be less self-centered and more mindful of the "thou's" in society than of the "I."

Yet in authentic, historic Judaism this result was achieved because Jewish jurisprudence was God-centered. Indeed one can hardly visualize the result being achieved in any other way. To goad one to the affirmation of one's rights and privileges, the self is adequate. After all, it is in the interest of self to do so. However, to goad one to the performance of duty there must be something that transcends the self. If obedience to duty is only the fulfillment of a mandate of the self, it cannot enjoy more status, and command more respect, than insistence on one's rights.

Whether Kant's position on the moral autonomy of the self can be reconciled with Judaism is the theme of a recent study by Professor Emil Fackenheim.[3] But Professor Fackenheim himself in earlier studies [4] demonstrated that the very aggrandizement of the self in a humanistic ethic—in which the self is the final arbiter of right and wrong—destroys humility and the sense of creatureliness that are basic in Judaism's order for man. A commitment to duty can hardly thrive in any other setting. Either state, society, mankind—anything other than self—can provide the basis on which we posit obedience to duty as the higher good. Yet it was the unique characteristic of Jewish law that it did not deify state, society or mankind. States can be tyrannical; majorities of men can give sanction to Hitlerism. In Judaism what was right was "the will of God," as Carl Friedrich expressed it. One's duty to do the right transcended not only one's self-interest but also the mandates of multitudes with superior power. However, once duty is man-made, in a completely secularized jurisprudence, Jewish law will have forfeited its special genius and its claim to be resurrected since it can no longer yield what once made it a boon.

V

Yet even if the renaissance of Jewish law were to be accomplished, as Professor Silberg earnestly wishes it to be, he realizes how numerous are the halakhic views on almost every issue. One can find authorities for almost every conceivable alternative with respect to every question. The legal literature is vast and it comes from almost every part of the globe. According to Professor Silberg, it would be necessary for a democratically elected parliament to adopt codes, and select the rules it prefers. The parliament would not be bound by those canons for decision heretofore prevailing in the Halakhah. It would be the sense of justice of the legislators that would constitute the final authority. One cannot argue with Professor Silberg on this point. He is realistic. He knows Israel and he fully appreciates how impossible it would be to arrive at codification on any basis other than the sense of justice of the legislators. Some legislators might ask themselves, "What is the will of God in the instant situation?" The majority, however, are secular humanists. Yet, why should the latter, proceeding from their purely secular premises, not prefer to start *de novo*, and instead of choosing from among the precedents of Jewish law, make the legal systems of the entire world their hunting ground and choose, from the infinite variety of rules available, that rule which their sense of justice deems best? Indeed, there are Israelis who feel just this way about it. To counter this argument one appeals to Jewish nationalistic sentiments. However, it would be most unjust to permit such sentiments to block the adoption of the rule regarded as most just, even if its source is non-Jewish.

And here again, one must look to Judaism as a religion for the ultimate validity of any claim that Israel ought use the Halakhah for her basic jurisprudence. It is because God willed this law for His people that we adhere to it. Because He willed that we develop its insights and perfect its justice, we have never failed to study it. Jews have differed among themselves—the precedents and their differences are legion. But all authorities were motivated by the divine mandate—to heed His will. Eliminate theocentricity and all appeals for the revival of Jewish law must be without heart.

VI

Perhaps Professor Silberg's readiness to eliminate theocentricity is due to something more than a realistic awareness of the impossibility of winning acceptance for it in our day. Perhaps he is not really convinced that it is precisely theocentricity that is the most important cause for any special greatness that the Halakhah enjoys. True, the integration of divine and positive law in talmudic literature is achieved. But does the divine law give the positive law that which it would not otherwise have? Does Judaism as a religion make the ethics and the equity of Jewish civil and criminal law superior? This question is addressed particularly to the sixth and seventh chapters of his book.

For example, he develops at great length the contrast between Jewish law and Anglo-American common law with regard to the unenforceability of illegal promises. Anglo-American law usually leaves the parties where it finds them, and the courts will offer no relief whatever. Thus it might sometimes be that the wrongdoer will even enjoy the fruits of his illegal act because he is in possession of the fruit. Jewish law, on the other hand, will occasionally help the disadvantaged to retrieve a loss. The debtor who paid usury may be able to recover what was unlawfully exacted from him.

However, his generalizations are faulty. Even in the case of usury, not all types are recoverable by the debtor. Furthermore, in the case of overcharging by a vendor, Jewish law imputes a waiver or forfeiture when the overcharging is less than a sixth, even though the seller deliberately contrived to keep the overcharge within that limitation in order that he might profit by the forfeiture. And if *Chazakah* (the right of the defendant to hold on to what he has until the plaintiff demonstrates a superior right) is the principal rule in Anglo-American cases involving illegal contracts, it certainly plays no less central a role in Jewish law.

However, one of the greatest characteristics of the Halakhah is its emphasis on substantive justice rather than procedural regularity. This is why equity and strict law were never isolated from each other in separate courts or separate systems. This is also why very few talmudic folios deal with forms of action, pleadings, judgments or executions. And since it is procedure or adjective law that usually deters judges from dealing with a cause as a *gestalt* and hampers the generally just adjudication of an entire controversy, Jewish judges were the better able to get to the essence of the parties' rights and duties and do what justice required. Yet, to delegate such broad power to the judges one must be certain of their integrity and commitment to justice. Unlike the guardians in Plato's *Republic* they are not to rely upon mystical illumination alone. They are bound by precedents and rules. Veer they must between the recorded heritage of their forbears and their own overpowering sense of justice. Judges were expected to be both saints and scholars. Their awareness of God and their continuing encounter with Him in the judicial process was the glory of Jewish law. But their training was more than the training of scholars. It was a religious calling involving the fulfillment of a role delegated by Him. All of this must, of necessity, vanish when judges are men whose sole guide is the concept of justice prevalent in their society with no link with the Infinite and His will with respect to the issue or cause at hand. The values implicit in social studies become the ultimate.

One knows that Professor Silberg personally does not share this view. Why then should he not be impolitic—if to be impolitic is necessary—and argue without equivocation for that theocentricity without which the flower that we do have must wither and become only a relic of a glorious past!

VII

To continue the dialogue between Professor Silberg and those who are in agreement with him, this reviewer must also discuss several specific items as well as the general thesis.

1. Professor Silberg argues that Jewish law in many instances fixes rigid standards. Perhaps as he suggests, Jewish law was meant principally to be a guide for the layman who must be told pre-

cisely at what point the lawful becomes unlawful. However, other legal systems are equally rigid at times, while in some situations broader and more flexible criteria are available to the judge for his decision.

According to American law, for example, a mortgage is in default the day after payment is due, no matter what excuse the mortgagor can offer for his failure to pay. This is also true of the period of grace allowed for the remitting of premiums on insurance policies. Similarly, the day for reaching one's majority is fixed. Biological, emotional, and intellectual maturity at an earlier or later date is immaterial.

Yet standards of care in bailments are very variable—according to the views of judges and jurors. And this is also true of Jewish law. Local customs and mores always affect the terms of contracts in all systems of law, Jewish law not excluded. Therefore, one wonders whether Professor Silberg is not generalizing too much from too few particulars when he posits uniqueness in Jewish law in connection with the rigidity of its standards.

2. Yet, nowhere is the Halakhah's rigidity more apparent than in connection with its rule of proximate cause in tort. Consequently the Halakhah modified its own original position, and its strict rules with regard to *Gerama* became more viable with the more liberal rules of *Garmi*. To fathom the distinction still baffles analysts of Halakhah, but whatever the distinction, the resultant liberalization of the rules is apparent.

But there the rigid standard was for judges—not laymen. Thus there was a rigidity which Professor Silberg cannot explain by reference to the Halakhah's orientation toward laymen. Similarly there was rigidity in connection with the impeachment of witnesses which was exclusively a phase of the judicial process and again not lay-oriented.

3. In Chapter 2 of his book he also argues that the talmudic dialectic frequently results in what is virtually a re-writing of the rules contained in the Mishnah and sometimes the result is even the opposite of that which is the obvious meaning of the text under discussion. This may be true but his illustration is not a happy one. It would appear that several of the paragraphs of the first chapter of the Mishnah known as Bava Kamma (on the

second of which Professor Silberg bases his discussion) were only mnemonics for fuller versions in the *Tosefta*. This is especially true of the paragraph following the one cited by Professor Silberg. Therefore, it would appear that the second Misnah which he cites may represent only subject-headings incorporating by reference the full texts of the relevant paragraphs in the *Tosefta* and not a contradiction of them as Professor Silberg suggests.

4. The Talmud does use extreme and sometimes seemingly farfetched illustrations to vivify and verify its analysis of a rule as Professor Silberg suggests. However, one of its glories is that the legal analysis in terms of such applications often permits the emergence of a moral value or ethical insight. One such illustration is to be found in *Kiddushin* (7a). The Talmud poses this hypothetical question: "What if a man, using the correct form in every other respect, should nonetheless say that he weds only half of a woman?" If the law of sales is applicable, one can acquire half ownership of a thing. If, however, the law of consecrated things applies, then if one consecrates half of an object, the whole of it becomes holy and is subject to all the relevant prohibitions. And which rule shall be employed in the case of the betrothal of part of a woman? The initial impulse of any modern would be to say that in the interest of womanly dignity one should avoid the concept of sale wherever possible and resort to the other more refined analogy of consecration. Our sages, however, ruled otherwise—and precisely out of respect for the ethical value of consent. Their decision was that the rules of sale would apply. Precisely because they respected the rights of women, they said that when the woman has consented to only partial betrothal, one dare not—without her express will—impute any more than that to her. Her consent must be real, not constructive. Therefore, having consented to only half marriage, we cannot automatically regard her as wholly wedded. However, since there can be no partial sale of a thing which cannot be shared by partners, and we know that two men cannot share the same woman, there can therefore be no partial betrothal at all and the whole act of the husband is null. Thus by the mundane-sounding law of sale, rather than the lofty-sounding law of consecrated things, a further safeguard was built around the woman's unequivocal consent.

Thus the use of palpably far-fetched illustrations may also be for didactic purposes rather than only for clarification of the legal concept or its practical application.

5. The Halakhah countenances its own subversion—argues Professor Silberg. His third chapter is a fascinating account of the instances available. However, all of them involve the subversion of one halakhic norm to a superior halakhic norm. One may subvert the law of heave-offerings in order to feed the hungry in a famine. And one may subvert the law of the second tithe since, as the Talmud itself suggests, there is neither gain nor loss to anyone by the subversion. In the final analysis it is the owner of the produce who retains everything. However, by granting him some leniency in the observance of the law he may be encouraged to observe its more important aspects and take the proceeds of the redeemed tithe to Jerusalem. As this writer elsewhere [5] described it, this was the Torah's earliest promotion of tourism and pilgrimages to the holy city.

6. Alas, Hillel's subversion of the law which cancelled debts in the Sabbatical year continues to be misunderstood. Hillel's ordaining of *Pruzbul* was not to subvert the law. The Sanhedrin had the power to suspend the law altogether by the exercise of their prerogative of *Hefker Beit-Din Hefker*. They could do this even if the law was biblical and not only rabbinic. However, they wanted to avoid the suspension of the biblical law in the hope that one day Jews would once again observe it. They hoped that creditors would one day be more generous. Therefore, they created a form which kept alive the memory of the biblical rule. This was the function of the *Pruzbul*, not subversion but commemoration.

7. Professor Silberg recognizes that God too is subject to the Halakhah, and especially His assets in the sanctuary—consecrated things. Yet from many rules of tort and contract they are excepted. The rationale of the exceptions he does not consider. This is a serious omission. If there is no rationale, and the exceptions are dogmatic as based on biblical verses or traditions, then secular humanists will not respect a system of law which uses reason and experience to validate legal rules applicable to humans and dogmatism *vis-a-vis* consecrated things. If, however, there is a rationale to the exceptions, it should be set forth in a book which starts

with a panegyric on the universal application of the rules to God and man.

VIII

All lovers of Jewish law are in Professor Silberg's debt. He has at least written—with heart and mind—a stimulating volume. Perhaps more lovers of Halakhah will emulate him and write for the greater glory of Torah and Israel. Perhaps too a special journal will yet emerge for the articulation and development of halakhic norms for the enrichment and edification of world thought. Such a journal was already projected by an editor of TRADITION a few years ago. Rabbi Joseph B. Soloveitchik also proposed that a series of such studies be undertaken jointly by the Rabbinical Council of America and Yeshiva University. The time may be ripe for the venture. Professors of Hebrew University and Yeshiva University should join hands across the sea and in Hebrew and English—with halakhic and universally accepted juridic terms—make the world take note of a legal heritage which is perhaps its greatest.

NOTES

1 Jerusalem, Student Union of Hebrew University, 1961.
2 *Three Great Systems of Jurisprudence*, (London: Stevens & Sons 1955).
3 "Kant and Judaism", *Commentary*, Dec. 1963, (pp. 160–7).
4 See, e.g., "Self-realization and the Search for God", *Judaism*, Vol. 1, No. 4, (1952), pp. 291–306).
5 *The Rabbinical Council of America Sermon Manual* (New York: R.C.A. Press), 1961, pp. 172–5.

Contributors

ELIEZER BERKOVITS occupied rabbinic posts on three continents and is now professor and Chairman of the Department of Jewish Philosophy at the Hebrew Theological College in Skokie, Illinois. His numerous books include *Judaism: Fossil or Ferment* and *God, Man and History*.

ALEXANDER CARLEBACH, who received his LL.D. from the University of Strasbourg and was until recently Rabbi of Belfast Hebrew Congregation and of the Jewish Community of Northern Ireland, now resides in Israel. His most recent book is *Adass Jeshurun of Cologne*.

EMANUEL FELDMAN, rabbi of Congregation Beth Jacob, Atlanta, Georgia, is associate editor of *Jewish Horizon* and editor of *Tradition's* book review department.

SIMEON L. GUTERMAN, formerly Dean of Yeshiva College, is professor of history at the Ferkauf Graduate School of Humanities and Social Sciences of Yeshiva University. He received his Ph.D. from Harvard University and is the author of *Religious Toleration and Persecution in Ancient Rome*.

SIDNEY B. HOENIG, professor of Jewish history at Yeshiva University and Director of the Department of Adult Education of its Community Service Division, is the author of *The Great Sanhedrin, Guide to the Prophets, Saadia and his Life*, etc., and of articles on these subjects in the *Encyclopedia Britannica*.

IMMANUEL JAKOBOVITS, Chief Rabbi of the British Commonwealth, was until recently rabbi of the Fifth Avenue Synagogue, New York. He received his Ph.D. from the University of London and is the author of *Jewish Medical Ethics, Jewish Law Faces Modern Problems,* and *Journal of a Rabbi*. His "Survey of Halakhic Periodic Literature" is a regular feature of *Tradition*.

NORMAN LAMM, associate rabbi of The Jewish Center, New York, is the founder of *Tradition* and was its first editor. He received his Ph.D. from Yeshiva University where he is associate professor, occupying the Jakob and Erna Michael chair in Jewish Philosophy.

HOWARD I. LEVINE received his Semikhah in Israel and his Ph.D. from Yeshiva University. He is Associate Professor of Jewish Studies at Stern College.

EMANUEL RACKMAN, rabbi of Congregation Shaarei Tefilla in Far Rockaway, New York, is Assistant to the President and associate professor of political philosophy and jurisprudence at Yeshiva University. A former President of the Rabbinical Council of America and of the New York Board of Rabbis, Dr. Rackman was recently appointed to the executive of the Jewish Agency for Israel. He is the author of *Israel's Emerging Constitution* and an Associate Editor of *Tradition*.

DAVID S. SHAPIRO, rabbi of Congregation Anshe Sfard in Milwaukee, Wisconsin, teaches History of Jewish Civilization and Hebrew Literature at the University of Wisconsin. He is Associate Editor of *Hadarom* and author of scholarly volumes, the most recent of which was *Torath Mosheh Ve-haneviim*.

JOSEPH B. SOLOVEITCHIK, world renowned halakhic authority, rabbinic leader, and religious philosopher, is professor of Talmud and Jewish philosophy at Yeshiva University. Widely acclaimed as "the Rav," he is Chairman of the Halakhah Commission of the Rabbinical Council of America.

SHUBERT SPERO, rabbi of Young Israel of Cleveland, is lecturer in philosophy at Western Reserve University and the Cleveland Institute of Art.

LEON D. STITSKIN, professor of Jewish philosophy, Bernard Revel Graduate School, and Director of Community Relations and Special Publications at Yeshiva University, is the editor of Yeshiva University's "Studies in Torah Judaism" and "Studies in Judaica," and Associate Editor of *Tradition*, where he contributes the department "From the Pages Of Tradition." He is the author of *Judaism as a Philosophy* and *Judaism as a Religion*.

ISADORE TWERSKY, Chairman of the Department of Near Eastern

Languages and Literatures and Nathan Littauer Professor of Hebrew
Literature and Philosophy, Harvard University, received his Ph.D.
from Harvard University and his Semikhah from the Rabbi Isaac
Elchanan Theological Seminary. He is the author of *Rabad of Pos-
quieres* and of a forthcoming volume, *A Study of Maimonides*.

WALTER S. WURZBURGER, rabbi of Shaarei Shomayim Congregation
in Toronto and former President of the Rabbinical Council of Canada,
received his Ph.D. from Harvard University and has been editor of
Tradition since 1961.

ZVI ZINGER is the Director of the Press Bureau of the Jewish Agency's
Department of Information. He contributes regularly to the *Jerusalem
Post* and to leading Israeli reviews.

SOURCES